Possession and Ownership

EXPLORATIONS IN LINGUISTIC TYPOLOGY

GENERAL EDITORS: Alexandra Y. Aikhenvald and R. M. W. Dixon
Language and Culture Research Centre, James Cook University

This series focuses on aspects of language that are of current theoretical interest and for which there has not previously or recently been any full-scale cross-linguistic study. Its books are for typologists, fieldworkers, and theory developers, and designed for use in advanced seminars and courses.

PUBLISHED

1 Adjective Classes
edited by
R. M. W. Dixon and Alexandra Y. Aikhenvald

2 Serial Verb Constructions
edited by
Alexandra Y. Aikhenvald and R. M. W. Dixon

3 Complementation
edited by
R. M. W. Dixon and Alexandra Y. Aikhenvald

4 Grammars in Contact
edited by
Alexandra Y. Aikhenvald and R. M. W. Dixon

5 The Semantics of Clause Linking
edited by
R. M. W. Dixon and Alexandra Y. Aikhenvald

8 Possession and Ownership
edited by
Alexandra Y. Aikhenvald and R. M. W. Dixon

9 The Grammar of Knowledge
edited by
Alexandra Y. Aikhenvald and R. M. W. Dixon

PUBLISHED IN ASSOCIATION WITH THE SERIES

Areal Diffusion and Genetic Inheritance
Problems in Comparative Linguistics
edited by
Alexandra Y. Aikhenvald and R. M. W. Dixon

Possession and Ownership

A Cross-Linguistic Typology

Edited by
ALEXANDRA Y. AIKHENVALD and
R. M. W. DIXON

Language and Culture Research Centre
James Cook University

OXFORD
UNIVERSITY PRESS

OXFORD
UNIVERSITY PRESS

Great Clarendon Street, Oxford, OX2 6DP,
United Kingdom

Oxford University Press is a department of the University of Oxford.
It furthers the University's objective of excellence in research, scholarship,
and education by publishing worldwide. Oxford is a registered trade mark of
Oxford University Press in the UK and in certain other countries

First published 2013
First published in paperback 2015

Published in the United States of America by Oxford University Press
198 Madison Avenue, New York, NY 10016, United States of America

British Library Cataloguing in Publication Data
Data available

Library of Congress Cataloging in Publication Data
Data available

ISBN 978–0–19–966022–3 (Hbk.)
ISBN 978–0–19–872300–4 (Pbk.)

Contents

Preface

Every language has a way of expressing possessive relationships. The marking and the conceptualization of these vary across languages and cultures. This volume aims at investigating the varied facets of possession and associated notions.

The volume starts with a typological introduction outlining the marking, and the meaning, of possession within a noun phrase, a clause, and a sentence, focusing on correlations between possessive structures, and cultural and social aspects of its conceptualization by speakers. It is followed by revised versions of thirteen of the fifteen presentations from the International Workshop 'Possession and Ownership', held at the Language and Culture Research Group, the Cairns Institute, James Cook University, 27 September–2 October 2010. An earlier version of Chapter 1 had been circulated to the contributors, with a list of points to be addressed, so as to ensure that their detailed studies of individual languages were cast in terms of a common set of typological parameters.

The week of the Workshop was an intellectually stimulating and exciting time, full of discussions and cross-fertilization of ideas. The authors have all undertaken intensive fieldwork, in addition to having experience of working on linguistic typology, historical comparative issues, and problems of areal diffusion. The analysis is cast in terms of basic linguistic theory—the cumulative typological functional framework in terms of which almost all descriptive grammars are cast—and avoids formalisms (which provide reinterpretations rather than explanations, and come and go with such frequency that any statement made in terms of them is likely to soon become inaccessible).

It is our hope that this volume will provide a consolidated conceptual and analytic framework covering the major parameters of variation in the expression of possession across the world, and how it correlates with cultural parameters.

We are grateful to all the participants in the Workshop who took part in the discussion and provided feedback on presentations at various stages—Ton Otto, Chia-jung Pan, Dineke Schokkin, Borut Telban, Daniela Vavrová, and Sihong Zhang. We owe a special debt of gratitude to Brigitta Flick and Elena Rhind, for helping us organize the Workshop in a most efficient manner. Brigitta Flick's editorial assistance was, as always, invaluable.

The Workshop was made possible through a grant from the International Science Linkages—Humanities and Creative Arts Programme (ISL–HCA), awarded to Aikhenvald by the Australian Academy of the Humanities. We also gratefully acknowledge financial assistance from the Faculty of Arts and Social Sciences and from the Cairns Institute at James Cook University.

As with previous volumes emanating from our International Workshops (also published in the series *Explorations in Linguistic Typology*), we owe a considerable debt to John Davey, our editor at Oxford University Press. His indomitable support makes volume editors, and their book, feel wanted.

Notes on the contributors

ALEXANDRA Y. AIKHENVALD is Distinguished Professor, Australian Laureate Fellow, and Director of the Language and Culture Research Centre in the Cairns Institute and the College of Arts, Society and Education of James Cook University. She has worked on descriptive and historical aspects of Berber languages and has published, in Russian, a grammar of Modern Hebrew (1990). She is a major authority on languages of the Arawak family, from northern Amazonia, and has written grammars of Bare (1995, based on work with the last speaker who has since died) and Warekena (1998), plus *A grammar of Tariana, from northwest Amazonia* (Cambridge University Press, 2003; paperback 2007), in addition to essays on various typological and areal features of South American languages. Her lengthy grammar, *The Manambu language from East Sepik, Papua New Guinea*, was published by Oxford University Press in 2008 (paperback 2010). Other monographs with OUP are *Classifiers: a typology of noun categorization devices* (2000, paperback 2003), *Language contact in Amazonia* (2002, paperback 2010), *Evidentiality* (2004, paperback 2006), *Imperatives and commands* (2010, paperback 2012) and *Languages of the Amazon* (2012). *Address*: The Cairns Institute, James Cook University, PO Box 6811, Cairns, NQld 4780, Australia; *e-mail*: Alexandra.Aikhenvald@jcu.edu.au.

FELIX K. AMEKA teaches African Linguistics at Leiden University, and is a Visiting Researcher of the Language and Cognition Group, Max Planck Institute for Psycholinguistics, Nijmegen, the Netherlands. His interests are in language description/documentation, typology, semantics, pragmatics, contact, areal and anthropological linguistics, ethnography of communication, and West African languages. He has numerous publications on these topics. He has also (co-)edited volumes on grammar-writing, locative predication, tense–aspect-modality, Ghanaian linguistics, and interjections. Currently, he is documenting Likpe language and culture (Ghana) and preparing a pan-dialectal grammar of Ewe (with James Essegbey). He is Editor-in-Chief of the *Journal of African Languages and Linguistics*. *Address*: Department of African Languages and Cultures, LUCL, Faculty of the Humanities, University of Leiden, P.N. van Eyckhof 3, 2311 BV, Leiden; The Netherlands; *e-mail*: F.K.Ameka@hum.leidenuniv.nl.

ISABELLE BRIL is Senior researcher at CNRS-LACITO (Laboratoire des Langues et Civilisations à Tradition orale) in Paris. Her research interests centre on the syntax, semantics, and typology of Oceanic and Austronesian languages. She has done fieldwork on Kanak languages in New Caledonia. Her main publications are a dictionary *Dictionnaire nêlêmwa-nixumwak-français-anglais* (Peeters 2000) and a grammar of Nêlêmwa *Le nêlêmwa (Nouvelle-Calédonie): Analyse syntaxique et sémantique* (Peeters, 2002). She is the editor with Ozanne-Rivierre of a volume on *Complex predicates in Oceanic languages: studies in the dynamics of binding and boundedness* (Mouton de Gruyter, 2004) and editor of a volume on *Clause-linking and clause hierarchy: syntax and pragmatics.* (SLC 121, Benjamins, 2010). *Address*: CNRS-Lacito, 7 rue Guy Môquet, 94800 – Villejuif, France; *e-mail*: ibril@vjf.cnrs.fr.

Alan Dench is Professor of Linguistics and Dean of the Graduate Research School at the University of Western Australia. His principal area of expertise lies in the documentation and grammatical description of Australian Aboriginal languages, especially those of Western Australia. He has written grammars of three languages of the Pilbara—Panyjima, Martuthunira, and Yingkarta—and is working towards a description of Nyamal. In addition to primary grammatical description he has made contributions to the historical and comparative analysis of Australian languages, and has written in the general area of ethno-linguistics. His work also includes contributions to studies of language contact. *Address*: Linguistics M258, University of Western Australia, Crawley, WA 6009, Australia; *e-mail*: Alan.Dench@uwa.edu.au.

R. M. W. Dixon is Adjunct Professor and Deputy Director of the Language and Culture Research Centre in The Cairns Institute and School of Arts and Social Sciences of James Cook University. He has published grammars of a number of Australian languages (including Dyirbal and Yidiñ), in addition to *A grammar of Boumaa Fijian* (University of Chicago Press, 1988), *The Jarawara language of southern Amazonia* (Oxford University Press, 2004, paperback 2011) and *A semantic approach to English grammar* (Oxford University Press, 2005). His works on typological theory include *Where have all the adjectives gone? and other essays in semantics and syntax* (Mouton, 1982) and *Ergativity* (Cambridge University Press, 1994). *The rise and fall of languages* (Cambridge University Press, 1997) expounded a punctuated equilibrium model for language development; this is the basis for his detailed case study *Australian languages: their nature and development* (Cambridge University Press, 2002). He is also the author of the three volume work *Basic linguistic theory* (Oxford University Press, 2010–12) and of an academic autobiography *I am a linguist* (Brill, 2011). *Address*: The Cairns Institute, James Cook University, PO Box 6811, Cairns, NQld 4780, Australia; *e-mail*: Robert.Dixon@jcu.edu.au.

Zygmunt Frajzyngier is Professor of Linguistics at the University of Colorado in Boulder. His research interests include: discovery and proofs of meaning; cross-linguistic study of syntax; grammaticalization; discoveries of forms and functions of hitherto undescribed languages; typological and comparative Afroasiatic and Chadic linguistics. His recent books include: *Grammar of Wandala* (2012), *Grammar of Gidar* (2008); *Grammar of Mina* (with Eric Johnston and Adrian Edwards, 2005); *Grammatical and semantic relations in Hausa: 'point of view' 'goal' and 'affected object*' (with Mohammed Munkaila, 2004), *Explaining language structure through systems interaction* (with Erin Shay, 2003). Honors and recognition: Humboldt Research Award; Visiting Professor, University of Nice; Visiting Scholar, Max Plank Institute for Evolutionary Anthropology; Research Associate, CNRS, Nice, and in 2009 he was appointed to Pays de la Loire chaire régionale de chercheur étranger. *Address*: Department of Linguistics, 295 UCB, Boulder, CO 80309-0295, USA; *e-mail*: Zygmunt.Frajzyngier@colorado.edu.

GLORIA GRAVELLE has worked in Mexico, Colombia, and Indonesia totalling more than twenty-five years of linguistic field experience. As a research linguist in New Guinea, she has done extensive study of the Meyah and Moskona languages in the Bird's Head, producing linguistic, literacy, and other reading materials. She received a Ph.D. in linguistics from Vrije Universiteit, Amsterdam and has served as a linguistic consultant, translator, and instructor in numerous linguistic courses for SIL. She is currently working in Zambia. *Address*: 25418 Palmer PL, Black Diamond, WA 98010, USA; *e-mail*: gj_gravelle@tsco.org.

ROSITA HENRY is Professor of Anthropology at James Cook University, Australia and a Research Fellow of the Cairns Institute. She has been employed at James Cook University since 1992, and is currently serving as Head of Discipline of Anthropology. Rosita is currently the President Elect of the Australian Anthropological Society and will serve as President in 2011–12. Her research concerns the poetic politics of relationships between people, places, and the nation-state in Australia and the Pacific. She is co-editor of *The Challenge of Indigenous Peoples: Spectacle or Politics?* (2011) and author of numerous articles on the political anthropology of place and performance. Her monograph, *Performing Place, Practising Memories. Aboriginal Australians, Hippies and the State*, is due to be published in 2012, by Berghahn Books (Oxford). *Address*: School of Arts and Social Sciences, James Cook University, Townsville, Qld, 4811, Australia; *e-mail*: Rosita.Henry@jcu.edu.au.

YONGXIAN LUO, Ph.D. in linguistics (1996), Australian National University, has worked extensively on Tai-Kadai languages in south China and surrounding regions. His publications include *The Subgroup Structure of the Tai Languages* (1997), *A Dictionary of Dehong, Southwest China* (1999), *The Tai-Kadai Languages* (co-edited with Diller and Edmondson, 2008), *The Buyang Language of South China* (with Li Jinfang, 2010), and *A Reference Grammar of Yanqi, a Zhuang dialect of Wuming* (with Wei Jingyun and He Shuang, 2011), along with several dozen articles and book reviews. *Address*: Melbourne Institute of Asian Languages and Societies, University of Melbourne, Parkville, Vic 3010, Australia; *e-mail*: yongxian.luo@gmail.com.

LEV MICHAEL is an Assistant Professor at the University of California, Berkeley. He received his Ph.D. from the University of Texas at Austin in 2008, writing his dissertation on the social and interactional functions of evidentiality in Nanti society. He has also carried out fieldwork on Iquito (Zaparoan), Omagua (Tupí-Guaraní-based contact language), Maijuna (Tucanoan), Matsigenka (Arawak), Muniche (Isolate), Vacacocha (Isolate), and Záparo (Zaparoan). His research publications include work on phonology, prosody, the typology of reality status, and aspects of the language/culture nexus. He is currently preparing a descriptive grammar of Matsigenka. *Address*: Department of Linguistics, University of California, Berkeley, CA 94720, USA; *e-mail*: levmichael@berkeley.edu.

Mark W. Post is Lecturer in Linguistics at the School of Behavioural, Cognitive, and Social Sciences, University of New England, Australia. He specializes in the typology and diachrony of the languages of Greater Mainland South-East Asia, especially Tibeto-Burman and Tai, and is Secretary of the North East Indian Linguistics Society. *Address*: School of Behavioural, Cognitive, and Social Sciences, UNE, Armidale, NSW 2351, Australia; *e-mail*: markwpost@gmail.com.

Anne Storch is Professor of African Languages and Linguistics at the University of Cologne. Her principal research has been on the Jukun languages of Nigeria, on the Atlantic language family, on Western Nilotic, and on African speech registers. Her publications include *Das Hone und seine Stellung im Zentral-Jukunoid* (Cologne, 1999), *The Noun Morphology of Western Nilotic* (Cologne, 2005) and several edited volumes. Her book *Secret Manipulations* (dealing with secret languages and speech registers in Africa) was published in 2011 (OUP, New York). She is currently finishing a grammar of Luwo (Sudan). *Address*: Institut für Afrikanistik, Universität zu Köln, Meister-Ekkehard Str. -7, D-50923 Cologne, Germany; *e-mail*: anne.storch@uni-koeln.de.

Michael Wood is a Senior Lecturer in Anthropology at the Cairns Campus of James Cook University. For a long time he has worked with Kamula speakers in PNG. He is currently working on three PNG based projects that concern HIV/AIDS related issues. He also works with Rosita Henry on a project concerning the history of artefacts collected in the 'Wet Tropics' that surround Cairns. He is also interested in issues to do with climate change and the recent development of carbon credit schemes in PNG. *Address*: School of Arts and Social Sciences, James Cook University, PO Box 6811, Cairns, NQld 4780, Australia; *e-mail*: Michael.Wood@jcu.edu.au.

Abbreviations

1	1st person
2	2nd person
3	3rd person
A	transitive subject
ABL	ablative
ACC	accusative
ACT.FOC	action focus
ADD	additive
AGR	agreement, agreement marker
AGT.NOMZ	agentive nominalizer
ALIEN	alienator
ALL	allative
ALN.POSS	alienable possession
ALTR	alterphoric
ANAPH	anaphoric
ANIM	animate
ANTR	anterior
APP	appositive
APPL	applicative
APPLIC	applicative
APROX	addressee-proximate
AR	Arabic
ART	article
ASP	aspect
ASP:PERF	aspect perfective
ASS	assertive
ASSC	associative
ASSERT	assertedly
ASSOC	associative
ATR	Advanced Tongue Root

ATTRIB	attributive
AUG	augmentative
BEN	benefactive
C	construct marker
C.FOC	contrastive focus
CAUS	causative
CC	copula complement
CL	classifier
CM	class marker
CM.PL	class marker plural
CN	connector
CNGNT	congruent discursive stance
COLL	collective
COM	comment marker
COMIT	comitative
COMP	complementizer
COMPL	completive
COMPT	complementary
COND	conditional
CONJ	conjunction
CONS	consequence
CONT	contrastive
CONTR	contrast
COP	copula
COS	change-of-state
CQ	content question
CS	copula subject
CTEMP	contemporaneous
DAT	dative
DEC	declarative
DEF	definite
DEM	demonstrative
DEM.DIST	distal demonstrative

DEM.PROX	proximal demonstrative
DEP	dependent
DET	determiner
DIR	direct
DISJ	disjunctive marker
DS	different subject
du, DU	dual
DUB	dubitative
DUR	durative
E	extension to core
EFF	effector
EMPH	emphatic marker
ENUM	enumerative complex
EP	epenthetic
EPC	epenthetic consonant
EPV	epenthetic vowel
ERG	ergative
EV	event
EX	existential
exc	exclusive
EXCL	exclusive
EXIST	existential
F	Fula (Fulfulde)
FEM, fem, F, f	feminine
FOC	focus
FRUST	frustrative
FUT	future
FUT.CONTR.DYN	contrastive dynamic future
GEN	genitive
GENL	general
GENP	genitive phrase
GIV	'given/known information'
GO	goal

H	Hausa
H, h	human
HAB	habitual
HL	human locative
HORT	hortative
HYP	hypothetical
HYPOTH	hypothetical
HYPTH	hypothetically
ID	identifying
IDEO	ideophone
IMMED	immediate
IMP	imperative
IMPERV	imperfective
IN	inner space
INAN	inanimate
inc	inclusive
INCH	inchoative
INCL	inclusive
INCP	incipient
IND	individuator
INDIC	indicative
INST	instrumental
INTENS	intensifier
INTER	interrogative
INTERJ	interjection
INTR	intransitive
IRR	irrealis
IRR.I	irrealis, i-class verb
ITER	iterative
JUS	jussive
K	Kanuri
L.A.	locative anaphora
LIG	ligature

LINK	linker
LOC	locative
LOCP	locative phrase
MASC, masc, M, m	masculine
MATRI	matriline
MED	mediative
MIR	mirative
N	noun
NAGNT	non-agentive
NAT	natural object
NCL	noun class
NEG	negation, negative
NEUT, N, n	neuter
NF	non-final
NOM	nominative
NOMIN	nominal marking
NOML	nominal
NOMZ	nominalizer
NP	noun phrase
NPAST	non-past
nsg, NSG	non-singular
NSU	non-subject core (O or E)
NUM	numeral
NUM.CL	numeral classifier
NUMB	number
NVIS	non-visual
O	transitive object
OBJ	object
OBL	oblique
ODIR	other-directed
ON	extension 'on'
OPT	optative

PAN	Proto-Austronesian
PART	particle
PASS	passive
PATRI	patriline
PB	phrasal boundary
PBC	Proto-Benue-Congo
Pe	possessee
PER	perfect
PEPRO	possessive pronoun
PERT	pertensive
PERV	perfective
pl, PL	plural
PN	possessed noun
PNM	proper noun marker
POc	Proto-Oceanic
POL	polite
POSS	possessive
POT	potential
PPN	Proto-Polynesian
PQ	polar question
PQI	polar question intonation
Pr	possessor
PRel	possessive relation
PRED	predicative
PREP	preposition
PRES	present
PRES/PROG	present progressive
PRHD	pre-head determiner
PRIV	privative
PROG	progressive
PROHIB	prohibitive
PROP	proprietive
PROXTOP	proximal topic
PRSUFF	possessor suffix
PRT	partitive

PSHD	post-head determiner/postposition
PSYCH	psych-inchoative
PUNC	punctual
PURP	purposive
QUAL	qualifying expression
QUOT	quotative
REAL	realis
REAL.A	realis, a-class verb
REAL.I	realis, i-class verb
RECIP	reciprocal
REDUP	reduplicated
REFL	reflexive
REL	relative
RELC	relative clause
RELN	relator noun
REM	remote
REM.PAST	remote past
REV	reversative
S	intransitive subject
S_a	'active' S, marked like A
S_o	'stative' S, marked like O
SAP	speech act participants
SCR	subject cross-reference
SDIR	self-directed
SEMB	semblative
SEP	separative
sg, SG	singular
SG/INDEF	singular indefinite
SIM	simultaneous
SLEV	same topographical level
SPROX	speaker-proximate
SS	same subject
STAT	stative

SU	subject
SUBJ	subjunctive
SUF	suffix (verb derivational suffix)
T	target extension
TAM	tense–aspect–mood
THM	thematic
TMP	temporal
TOG	together extension
TOP	topic
TR	transitive
UFP	utterance final particle
UNPOSS	unpossessed
UNREAL	unrealized
V	verb
VASSIM	vowel assimilation
VCC	verbless clause complement
VCS	verbless clause subject
VEN	venitive
VENT	ventive
VIA	viative
YK	you know

1

Possession and ownership: a cross linguistic perspective

ALEXANDRA Y. AIKHENVALD

1 Preamble

Every language has a mechanism for expressing possession, within a noun phrase and within a clause. Some languages have a dedicated, possessive, construction. Others express possessive meanings through a more general, 'associative', noun phrase. The nature of the Possessor (Pr), of the Possessee (Pe), and of the Relationship between them (PRel) underlies the gamut of cross-linguistic variation. These are intertwined. The meanings, and the forms, of possessive noun phrases are addressed in §2.

Possessive relations can be expressed beyond a noun phrase, within a predicative structure. Predicative possession appears to be more specialized in its expression than possessive relations within a noun phrase. Within a clause, Possessive relationships can be expressed through manipulating argument structure, and beyond clause boundaries. This is the topic of §3.

Possessive marking may have other functions in a language, including the expression of subject and object, benefactives, locatives, and so on. We look at the recurrent patterns, and their possible motivation, in §4.

Some linguistic categories show more obvious correlations with cultural values, social hierarchies, and their conceptualization than others. Genders, noun classes, and classifiers tend to mirror social and cultural stereotypes and patterns of human perception. Geographical features of a terrain—such as a hilly, or a riverine environment—are often reflected in demonstrative systems. Along similar lines, underlying social institutions, concepts, and attitudes may correlate with the expression of possession. As a consequence, language and culture contact tends to affect the linguistic treatment of possessive relations, and the categorization of the Possessor and the Possessee. This is the topic of §5.

Just as every language has a way of expressing possession and similar relations, every society has a way of conceptualizing ownership, and concomitant relations of association and identification. The linguistic expression of possession and ownership often has overtones of power, and control. This is the topic of §6. A brief summary in §7 is followed by an overview of this volume.[1]

2 Meanings and forms in possessive noun phrases

Like many linguistic terms, 'possession' is somewhat ambiguous. As Lyons (1977: 722) put it, 'in everyday usage the term "possession" is more or less equivalent to "ownership" (though jurists may draw sharp distinction between the two terms): whatever X is said to possess may be described as his property. In traditional grammatical usage "possession" and "possessive" are construed much more broadly. Indeed, it can be argued that they are highly misleading: it is only a minority of what are traditionally called possessive constructions that have anything to do with property or possession'.

The linguistic expression of 'possession' within a noun phrase can be viewed as one of the realizations of a broader concept of association or relationship between two nouns (see Chapter 2, on Nêlêmwa, Chapter 7 on Galo, Chapter 8 on Mandarin, Chapter 10 on Likpe, §4 of Chapter 13 on Temboka, and Chapter 11 on Wandala). Or there may be one or more dedicated possessive noun phrase types which cover the core meanings associated with Possessive relationship (see Chapter 3 on Moskona,

[1] This chapter outlines the concepts, and parameters of variation, in the expression of possession in its many guises. As in all my previous work, the statements here are based on careful investigation of about five hundred grammars of languages from different parts of the world, on which reliable information could be found. To keep this chapter to a reasonable size, I could not cite all the examples of a particular phenomenon. If a certain phenomenon was found in more than half the languages under consideration, I call it 'relatively frequent'. Note, however, that what appears rare to us at the present stage of language documentation may turn out to be much more frequent when we start learning more about languages, and areas, so far poorly described. This is one reason why I avoid any statistical counts at this stage. Until the majority of human languages have been thoroughly analysed and documented, it seems most judicious to follow a qualitative approach, leaving quantitative analysis until such time in the future when more data is available and can be assessed.

It is hard if not altogether impossible to give even partial justice to the existing literature on possession. The must-reads on possession include Chapter 16 of Dixon (2010b), Seiler (1983), and especially Heine (1997a, b), with particular attention to cognitive schemata in possessive structures. Chappell and MacGregor (1996) is a compendium on body-part and other 'inalienable' possessive structures. Mithun (1999: 249–59) is an in-depth account of possession patterns in North American Indian languages. Blust (2009) and Lynch, Ross, and Crowley (2002) address the main issues of possession in the Oceanic domain. Stolz et al. (2008) addresses the distribution of possessive constructions in the languages of Europe as a putative linguistic area based on a limited corpus. Additional contributions are in McGregor (2009). External possession as a cross-linguistic phenomenon is discussed in Payne and Barshi (1999). Baron, Herslund, and Sørensen (2001) contains useful materials on possessive constructions across the world. An exhaustive overview of referent and relationship classification in possessive constructions is in Chapter 5 of Aikhenvald (2003a).

4 on Manambu, Chapter 5 on Martuthunira, Chapter 6 on Nanti, and Chapter 9 on Hone). Grammatical tests may help disambiguate various possessive and non-possessive meanings of what seems to be the same construction.

We start with the recurrent 'core' meanings realized through possessive constructions, and then turn to further meanings associated with these, and to their expression and disambiguation in §2.1–3. The semantic nature of Pr, Pe, and Possessive relationships are discussed in §2.4. Classifiers in possessive constructions are the topic of §2.5.

2.1 *The core types*

What grammarians describe as 'possessive constructions' may cover a wide range of meanings (see §2.2). We distinguish the following central, or 'core', meanings for possessive noun phrases which recur across languages:

(A) ownership (of property);
(B) whole–part relations, including body parts and plant parts (also see individual studies in Chappell and McGregor 1996);
(C) kinship relations, covering (C1) blood or consanguineal relations, such as 'mother' or 'father' and (C2) affinal relations, such as 'spouse'.

In many languages, a possessive noun phrase is typically used to express whole–part relationships (*John's head*), kinship (*John's father*), property, and association in general. *John's house* may refer to the house John owns, or the house he lives in (but does not own), or the house he is associated with (for example, designed, or built, or drew a picture of).

That is, essentially the same construction is used for all three kinds, in English and many Indo-European languages. All types of combinations of A, B, and C are found across the world's languages.

Kinship and whole–part—including body-part—relationships can be expressed in one way, and other types of ownership in another way. In Mussau-Emira, an Oceanic language, body parts and kinship terms are possessed 'directly'—that is, a possessive suffix attaches directly to the noun, for example *tama-ghi* 'my father', *nima-m* 'your arm'. Possession of other referents involves an additional marker whose choice is dictated by the way in which the item is to be handled, and its semantic group: 'my chicken' translates as *kie-ghi paolo ateva* (POSS:DOMESTIC.ANIMAL-my chicken sg)—literally, 'my domestic animal chicken' (Brownie and Brownie 2007, and §1 of Chapter 2, for an Oceanic perspective).

Whole–part and body part relationships may be expressed differently from ownership and kinship. In Puluwat, a Micronesian language, body part terms take possessive markers directly, as in *páy-iy* (hand-1sgPOSS) 'my hand' (Elbert 1974: 35, 55, 58–9). Kinship terms and other items require an additional element which takes the possessive suffix and whose choice depends on the meaning of the Possessee:

(1) náy-iy át
child-1sg son
my son (*lit.* my-child son)

(2) wá-áy citosa
vehicle-1sg car
my car (my-vehicle car)

Whole–part relationship (B) is marked differently from (A) and (C) in Manambu (Chapter 4). Or kinship 'possession' can stand apart from ownership and body part constructions. In Mandarin Chinese, an 'associative phrase' involving the linking particle *-de* 'genitive' is used for possessive constructions involving body parts and Possessees of other sorts. The constructions with kinship terms stand apart from the rest in that the marker can be omitted (see §2.3.1 of Chapter 8). Also see Chapter 3, on the special marking of kinship terms in Moskona, and a more complex system in Nêlêmwa, in Chapter 2.

Kinship possession and whole–part relationship (often encompassing body parts) reflect a closer link between the Possessor and the Possessee than conventional ownership constructions. A kin relation, or a body part, is always seen with respect to a 'Possessor', thus reflecting what Ameka refers to as a 'bio-cultural' relationship in Likpe (in Chapter 10). This intrinsic, intimate, and obligatory relationship has been termed 'inalienable' possession.

Culturally important objects—'name', 'house', or 'canoe' in river-dwelling or maritime cultures—may also fall within the realm of inalienably, or obligatorily, possessed items. And the composition of obligatorily possessed class may change in the language's history, for instance, as a result of a grammaticalization of body part terms as spatial relators—see Chapter 2 on Nêlêmwa; Chapter 6 on Nanti; Chapter 3 on Moskona; Chapter 4 on Manambu; Chapter 10 on Likpe; and Chapter 11 on Wandala.[2]

2.2 *'One construction fits all'*

In many languages (including approximately half of those addressed in this volume), one type of noun phrase has a broad range of meaning, covering association, modification, and also subsuming the three core types associated with possession (A, B, and C in §2.1).

[2] As a result of known, and unknown, historical developments, the distinction between alienable and inalienable possession in many individual languages is far from being cut and dry: one often finds it hard to explain exceptions. The alienable class typically includes A, and the inalienable almost always includes B, while C may sometimes be split between alienable and inalienable. Pace Nichols (1992), these occasional problems does not make the distinction any less valid (just like opaque gender assignment in languages such as German does not invalidate the fact that gender has at least some semantic basis). See §2.4.

In addition to the core types, broad 'association' noun phrases tend to subsume

(i) association in general (*Paul's dentist*),
(ii) orientation and location based on extension of a whole–part relation or reinterpretation of a body part (*top of the mountain, bottom of the pile*), and
(iii) attribution and properties in general (*the man's temperament*) (see Dixon 2010b: 262–3, and further examples there).

Associative or attributive *de-* constructions in Mandarin Chinese discussed in Chapter 8 cover all these meanings. A similar range of meanings are described for Galo (Chapter 7), Likpe (Chapter 10), and Wandala (Chapter 11).

The same construction as the one employed for possession and ownership may cover spatial relations, time, and quantification. This is the case in Nêlêmwa (Chapter 2), Likpe (Chapter 10), and Wandala (Chapter 11). Expressions of quantity in English are superficially possessive-like, cf. English *a kilo of sugar*. Similar constructions refer to material, for example *house of stone*, and even to a characteristics of a person or an object, for example *a bear of a man, a slip of a girl*, or *a man of honour*. This is the case in many other languages, such as Portuguese *amor de pessoa* (love of person) 'lovely person', or French *ce diable de fille* 'this devil of a girl'.[3]

In Ewe a construction with a linker *ɸé* may code any kind of alienable relationship, or semantic link, between the Possessor and the Possessee. *Ama ɸé tɔmedeze* (Ama POSS pot), 'Ama's pot', 'could be the one Ama made or bought or had been using' (Ameka 1996: 791). The same construction is used for propensities of people and animals, such as bravery or stupidity.

Different types of relationships between nouns can be expressed differently. In Likpe, a classificatory, or 'kind of', relation is expressed through a noun phrase with the linker *(e)to*—similarly to ownership, possession, association, and so on. The neighbouring Ewe uses compounds for this purpose, setting classification relations apart from other types of association (§3.1 of Chapter 10). Classification, and some of the whole–part relations, can be expressed through classifiers. This is the case in Nanti (§5 of Chapter 6) and in many languages with classifiers, including those from Amazonia (Aikhenvald 2003a: 271–304, 2012).

A number of language-internal tests may help distinguish between those meanings which relate to possession and those which do not (also see Dixon 2010b: 261–5). These include:

(i) Can the construction be rephrased with predicative possession (e.g. 'have' or 'belong')?
(ii) Can the construction be rephrased using a possessive pronoun?

[3] See Nikiforidou (1991) on possessive constructions in Greek and Müller (2001) on Spanish.

(iii) If there is an alternative possessive marker, can it be applied to the construction (e.g. English marks possession with *of* and with *'s*; Hebrew marks possession with *šel* 'of' or with the construct state)?
(iv) Can the construction be rephrased as a content interrogative on Possessor ('whose', 'of which, what')?

A quantification construction with *of* in English fails all these tests. *A kilo of sugar* cannot be rephrased as either **sugar has a kilo* or **a kilo belongs to sugar*. A possessive pronoun cannot be used (???*its kilo*). An *'s* construction **sugar's kilo* is not a viable alternative to *a kilo of sugar*. And it does not make sense to ask *whose kilo?* expecting the answer 'of sugar'.

Paraphrases with predicative possessive constructions help identify truly possessive meanings of noun phrases in Likpe (Chapter 10) and in Wandala (Chapter 11). So does a paraphrase with a content interrogative. That such tests are applicable shows that in these languages possession is an independent grammatical concept, and not just a semantic corollary of a general concept of 'association'. This also raises the question of a 'mismatch' in possessive meanings within a noun phrase and a predication—we return to this in §3.1.5.

Grammatical relations in deverbal nominalizations often employ the same marking as that of possession. In *John's arrival*, *John* is the subject of 'arrive' which looks like the Possessor, and *arrival* looks like the Possessee (further references and typological background are in Dixon 2010b: 263–7; Aikhenvald 2011; Lichtenberk 1985 discusses this phenomenon in Oceanic languages). However, this similarity is only superficial.

A nominalization such as *John's arrival* can be rephrased as *the arrival of John*, or as *John arrived* but not as **John had an arrival* or **an arrival belonged to John*. That is, it cannot be rephrased with a predicative possessive construction. Also see §4, for further examples of the overlap between marking Possessor, Possessee, and expression of grammatical relations.

2.3 *How to mark possession*

2.3.1 *The gamut of marking devices* Formal marking within a possessive NP may involve the following.

A. Order of words within an NP constituent Marking possession involves simple juxtaposition. Possessor can precede the Possessee, as in (3), from Tucano:

(3) Yɨ'ɨ̂ pa-ko
I parent-FEM
my mother

Or it can follow, as in (4), from Kam, a Tai-Kadai language (Yang and Edmondson 2008: 521; numbers indicate tones):

(4)	səm^{31}	jau^{11}
	room	I
	my room	

The order of components may correlate with the types of Possessees. In Maybrat, a non-Austronesian language spoken on the Bird's Head Peninsula in the Papua province of Indonesia, possessive constructions involving body parts, kinship terms, and spatial nouns (many of which are the same as body parts) require the order Possessor–Possessee. The Possessee takes a prefix which agrees with the Possessor in person, gender, and number (Dol 2007: 85). Possession of all other referents requires order Possessee–Possessor.

B. Marking on possessor This is typically achieved with the so called 'genitive' case, as in German (also see Martuthunira, Chapter 5; Galo, Chapter 7; and Temboka, Chapter 13):

(5)	das	Buch	[meines	Vaters]
	ART.NEUTER.SG	book	my.GEN.SG.MASC	father-GEN.SG
	my father's book			

C. Marking on possessee This can be achieved with the 'pertensive' marker, as in Nêlêmwa (Chapter 2), Martuthunira (Chapter 5), and Wandala (Chapter 11).[4] The following example is from the Lolovoli dialect of North-east Ambae, an Oceanic language (Hyslop 2001: 167):

(6)	gamali-ni	Robert
	club.house-PERTENSIVE	Robert
	Robert's club house	

Another option involves pronominal cross-referencing, for example Mussau-Emira *natu-na ateva Kealo* (child-3SG.POSSESSOR Kealo) 'Kealo's child' (*lit.* 'his one child Kealo') (also see Moskona, §4.2 of Chapter 3, with a different order).

D. Marking on both, as in (7), from Turkish (Lewis 2000: 41):

(7)	ev-in	sahib-i
	house-PERTENSIVE	owner/master-his
	the house's owner	

[4] The term 'pertensive' was coined by Dixon (2010b). It is based on the Latin verb *pertinēre* 'belong' and straightforwardly relates to the function of the marker: it shows that the referent 'belongs' to something or someone. Alternative terms include 'construct state' in the Semitic and also, more recently, in the Oceanic linguistic tradition (see Chapter 2). In Turkic and Iranian, the same phenomenon is known as 'izafet'.

E. Using an independent marker, as in Mandarin Chinese (Chapter 8), Likpe (Chapter 10), and (8), from Ewe (Ameka 1996: 791):

(8) kofí ɸé awu
Kofi POSS garment
Kofi's garment

The choice of marking may correlate with kinds of Possessees. In Ewe, possession of body parts, kin terms, and some socio-cultural relational terms, is marked by juxtaposition:

(9) [ɖeví-á-wó tɔ́gbé] dze dɔ
child-DEF-pl grandfather fall sickness
The grandfather of the children has fallen sick.

That is, the closer the relationship the less marking is involved, following the iconicity principle—see the following section.

2.3.2 *Iconic motivation* Whole–part and kinship relations involve a closer link between referents than does ownership. A part can hardly be conceived without the whole. A body part has to be conceptualized with respect to the whole body or the body's owner. A kinship relationship involves two participants, one defined with respect to the other. These are usually subsumed under 'inalienable' possession (or 'obligatory' possession), as distinct from alienable possession for items which can occur on their own independently of a 'whole'.

Following the principle of iconic motivation in grammar (Haiman 1983: 793–5, 1985: 130–6), we expect an 'inalienable' relationship to involve less formal marking than an alienable one. This is typically the case.

A construction with alienable possession can be the same as or similar to one with inalienable possession, with an additional grammatical marker. In Warekena, an Arawak language of Northern Brazil, inalienable possession is expressed by prefixes to the Possessee, for example *pi-yuʃana* (2sg-voice) 'your voice, language, word'. Alienable possession involves a pronominal prefix and a special possessive suffix to the Possessee, for example *pi-murupa-re* 'your canoe'. This pattern is recurrent in all Arawak languages (see Nanti, §3.1–2 of Chapter 6, and Aikhenvald 1999; a general view of Amazonian languages is in Aikhenvald 2012: 162–9).

The choice of an additional grammatical marker within an alienable possession construction can depend on the properties of the Possessee, and the nature of the relationship within the construction. This is the essence of classifiers in possessive constructions (see §2.5, and §1.3.1 of Chapter 2).

In Yuman languages, inalienable possession is indicated by a prefix on the Possessee, or a prefix on the Possessee plus a pronoun. Possession of alienably possessed nouns is expressed either by a noun followed by a classifier with affixes indicating possession, or by a noun with possessive suffixes attached to it. There are two classifiers, one for 'pets and domestic animals', and the other a general one. A possessive classifier for 'pet' in Yavapai is exemplified with (10) (Carlson and Payne 1989; also see Aikhenvald 2003a: 127–8):

(10) qoleyaw ʔ-ñ-hat
chicken 1sg-GENITIVE-CL:PET
my chicken (chicken-my pet)

The marking for alienable possession can be segmentally longer than that for inalienable possession. In Hatam, a Papuan language from the Bird's Head Peninsula, inalienable possession includes body parts, parts of plants, and kinship. It is expressed via juxtaposition of Possessor and Possessee marked with a pronominal prefix: *biei ni-mmeng* (tree 3sg-leaf) 'tree leaves'. Alienable possession is expressed by juxtaposing Possessor, possessive prefix to the possessive linker *de* and the Possessee, as in *di-cig ni-de micim* (1sg-father 3sg-POSSESSIVE spear) 'my father's spear' (Reesink 1999: 49–50).

Alienable possession may involve analytic structures, with inalienable possession employing synthetic structures. This is the case in Moskona, also from the Bird's Head Peninsula (see §4.1 and §4.2 of Chapter 3), in Mekeo, an Austronesian language from the Gulf Province of Papua New Guinea (Haiman 1985: 131), and in Nêlêmwa (§2 of Chapter 2). Further examples are in Dixon (2010b: 286–8).

The marker of possession or association can be optional in constructions involving kin and body parts. In Likpe (§3.5.1 of Chapter 10) kinship terms referring to close relatives do not require the linker *(e)to*. Along similar lines, whole–part relationships in Martuthunira are coded through simple apposition (§3 of Chapter 5), unlike other relations between nouns.

That is, the iconicity principle predicts that a construction with inalienable possession will never be more analytic, or require more formal marking than alienable possession.

This principle is reflected in the Oceanic linguistic terminology. Inalienable possession involves attaching possessive markers directly to the noun, for example North-east Ambae *karu-ku* 'my leg'. This is known as 'direct possession'. Alienable possession involves attaching possessive markers to an additional grammatical word—a relational classifier, creating 'indirect possession' (see Lynch et al. 2002; Lichtenberk 1983a, 1985). 'My sugarcane' in North-east Ambae is *me-ku tovu* (REL.CL:DRINKABLE-1sg sugarcane', literally 'my sugarcane to drink (suck)' (Hyslop 2001: 183–4) (see §2.5.1, and §1 of Chapter 2). The same principle applies in Moskona—see §4.1–2 of Chapter 3.

If classifiers are used in constructions with inalienable possession, they will also occur in those with alienable possession, but not the other way round. This is the case in 'Dongo-ko (Pasch 1985, 1986), Hmong, and many languages of north-western Amazonia (see §2.5.2, and Aikhenvald 2012: 290–2).

2.3.3 *Iconicity and individuation* Proximity in surface realization reflects a stronger conceptual link between the components which form one whole. But if one of them is individuated, a more analytic structure is used. This aspect of the iconicity principle is rarely taken into account in typological studies.

Toqabaqita distinguishes synthetic, or direct, and analytic possession. As befits an Oceanic language, inalienably possessed nouns (including body parts, items such as 'name', and kinship terms) occur in synthetic constructions with direct possession. Nouns of other semantic groups do not take possessive suffixes directly. An inalienably possessed noun can be used in an analytic possessive construction, with a subtle difference in meaning. A body part term accompanied with a possessive suffix is not individuated: *maa-ku* (eye-1sg) refers to 'my eye' or 'my eyes'. But if an 'eye' is to be individuated, an analytic construction is employed, as in *maa nau maqi* (eye 1sg this) 'this eye of mine' (Lichtenberk 2008: 398–401, 2005). An individuated Possessee stands on its own. And this is reflected in its surface realization, as an independent noun.

The possessive linker *ɸé* can be used with kinship terms in Ewe, if the closeness of the Possessive relationship is 'de-emphasized', so as to 'draw the attention to the distinct character' of either the Possessor or the Possessee (Ameka 1996: 800). A similar principle applies in Nêlêmwa (§3.1, and §3.2.1 of Chapter 2), Martuthunira (§3, and especially examples (51a) and (51b) in Chapter 5), Galo (§2.2.13 of Chapter 7), and Hone (§2.2 of Chapter 9).

When a body part gets grammaticalized as a spatial orientation term, its meaning becomes more generic. It thus comes as no surprise that the most grammaticalized spatial terms in Likpe do not require a linker unlike those which are less grammaticalized (see §3.5.2 and Table 2 of Chapter 10).

2.3.4 *Possession and person: the special status of 'me' and 'you'* Correlations between possessive marking and the person of the Possessor reflect a rather different aspect of iconic motivation. In a number of languages, if the Possessor is the speaker or a Speech Act Participant, the possessive construction is more 'closely knit'. In possessive constructions which require a linker in Tinrin (an Oceanic language from New Caledonia), the linker can be omitted if the Possessor is first person singular (Osumi 1996: 444). Suppletive possessed forms are employed in 'Dongo-ko, a Mba language from Uganda, for a number of salient kinship terms with first and second person singular Possessor, for example *ámà* 'my mother', *nyá* 'your mother' (Pasch 1986: 240–1).

In Ewe (Ameka 1996: 792, 801–2), if the pronominal Possessor is first or second person, the possessive linker *ɸé* is omitted and the link between the Possessor and the Possessee is indicated by a high tone only.

Kinship possession by first person is expressed in a special way in Martuthunira (§2 and example (39) of Chapter 5), and in Nanti (§3.6 of Chapter 6) (also see §4.3 of Chapter 11, for specific forms of first person 'intimate' possession in Wandala).

Following a similar principle, Speech Act Participants ('I' and 'you') as Possessors in Moskona can be marked synthetically (§4.3.2 of Chapter 3). The omission of the possessive marker with the first person singular Possessor in Mandarin Chinese (§5.5 of Chapter 8) has a different effect: it emphasizes the speaker's authority.

What belongs to 'you' and 'me' as the Speech Act Participants can be envisaged as more close and more intimate, bearing a closer relationship to what Bally (1996: 33) referred to as the 'personal domain'. Conceptual proximity goes together with proximity in surface realization. This 'egocentric' aspect of possessive marking provides further evidence for the special status of speech act participants. We now turn to further aspects of the semantic nature of Pr, Pe, and the Possessive relationship.

2.4 *Possessors, possession classes, and Possessive relationships*

Possessive constructions vary depending on the meanings of (i) the Possessor (Pr), (ii) the Possessee (Pe), and (iii) the Possessive relationship.

2.4.1 *Possessors* Generally speaking, a Possessor tends to be animate, or human (also see §2.3.1 of Chapter 7, on Galo). A content interrogative often refers just to an animate Possessor. This is the case in Martuthunira (§5 of Chapter 5) and in numerous other languages.[5] The Possessor is often expressed with a personal pronoun or a proper name. It typically occupies a relatively high position on the Nominal Hierarchy (Dixon 1994: 85). The Nominal Hierarchy reflects the likelihood for participants of different semantic types to occur in A (transitive subject) or in O (transitive object); this ranges from 1st and 2nd person pronouns, demonstratives and 3rd person pronouns, proper names, human, animate, and to inanimate common nouns (see §3.2.4). The gamut of possible Possessors is much more restricted than that of Possessees.

A pronominal Possessor is often expressed differently from the Possessor of other grammatical classes. Indo-European languages have special sets of possessive pronouns. Tupí-Guaraní languages use personal prefixes for pronominal Possessors, and juxtaposition for Possessors of other types (Jensen 1999: 152–3) (also see §3 of Chapter 10, on Likpe). Reflexive possession—whereby the Possessor is coreferential with the subject, or another argument—may acquire special marking, as is the case in

[5] See Dixon (2012); my pilot results based on the examination of grammars of *c.* five hundred languages confirm this.

Slavic languages (Ivanov 1989), and Mangghuer, a Mongolic language from China (Slater 2003: 176).

The type of possessive construction may depend on whether the Possessor is human or animate (also see the discussion in §3 of Chapter 2 on Nêlêmwa). In Mussau-Emira, an Oceanic language, 'direct' possession is used for body parts of humans. Body parts of animals and plant parts require an associative construction, 'with', rather than a possessive structure (Brownie and Brownie 2007: 75). One says *natu-na ateva Kealo* (child-3sgPOSSESSOR Kealo) 'Kealo's child', but *laa ng-ai* (branch ASSOC-tree) 'branch of a tree' (Brownie and Brownie 2007: 76; 84).

In Awa Pit, a Barbacoan language from Ecuador, a human or a referential Possessor is marked with the genitive enclitic *=pa/=wa*, for example *Santos=pa pimpul* 'Santos's leg' (Curnow 1997: 123). For non-human Possessors, the construction involves simple apposition: *kwizha pimpul* 'dog's leg'. Human and non-human Possessors are marked differently in Moskona (A in §4.2 of Chapter 3). In Nanti, a generic human Possessor requires different marking from a generic non-human one (§3.4 of Chapter 6). Constructions with non-human or inanimate Possessors in Hone express location or association. If Possessors are animate, the relationship is that of ownership (§2.1 of Chapter 9).

2.4.2 *Possessees and possession classes* In many languages, nouns divide into broad categories roughly termed 'alienably possessed' and 'inalienably possessed'.[6] The latter typically subsume those referents which are conceptualized as closely related to the Possessor. They tend to cover whole–part relations (including body parts, plant parts, and spatial terms, many of which are based on grammaticalized body part terms), and some, or all, kinship relations. Culturally significant items may also belong here. The former are often an 'all else' category.

The grammatical division into two possession classes tends to occur in indigenous languages spoken by small communities (see further discussion in Dixon 2010b: 278). However, many languages have a way of distinguishing a whole–part relationship (including body part possession) from relationships of other kinds, within a clause, if not within a noun phrase. We return to this in §3.2–3.

The exact semantic content of the 'inalienable' set varies (see §1.3.1 of Chapter 2, on partial predictability of possession classes in Nêlêmwa). All kinship terms, and all body parts are inalienably possessed in Tariana, an Arawak language, with the exception of 'hair'. In Mussau-Emira, directly possessed nouns include kinship terms, human body parts, 'name', and a number of terms intimately associated with the person—'knife', 'house', and 'canoe'.

[6] Terminology used for these notions varies. Some grammarians employ the term 'obligatory possessed' for 'inalienable' possession, and 'optionally possessed' for alienable. Another alternative is 'inseparable' versus 'separable': see Boas (1911) for Tsimshian.

Different kinds of kinship can be split across possession classes: for instance in Lango, a Nilotic language, affinal relations ('wife') are treated as alienably possessed, and blood relations as inalienably possessed, on a par with body parts (Noonan 1992); also see Ameka's (1996: 881) discussion of 'alienable' morphology of body parts in Ewe. Or kinship possession can be different from any other sort (see Dixon 2010b: 284, especially on Jarawara). Moskona (§4.3.2 of Chapter 3) and Martuthunira (Chapter 5) distinguish different possession patterns for close and less close kin. All kin terms in Nanti (§3.6 of Chapter 6) are obligatorily possessed. The further the kin from the ego, the more morphologically complex the construction. Affinal kin relationship is expressed through alienable possession constructions (involving prefixes and suffixes). Consanguineal kin relationship involves inalienable marking (just prefixes).

Terms for consanguineal female kin always occur with possessive suffixes in Hone. Kinship terms referring to other relatives do not have to be 'possessed'. Storch hypothesizes that this principle reflects a vestige of the erstwhile matrilineal kinship system among the Hone, now all but gone (§2.1.1 of Chapter 9).

Inalienably possessed nouns may be divided into further subclasses depending on their 'separability'. In Koyukon, an Athabaskan language, most terms for body parts and kinship have to be possessed (Thompson 1996: 655–61). But terms for some body products which can be in a sense separate from the body—such as 'blood', 'excrement', 'urine', 'tears', and 'milk'—are alienably possessed. So are 'abnormal' parts of the body, for example 'wart', 'boil', 'scab'. (And also see §3.6 of Chapter 6, for the discussion of canonical and non-canonical body parts in Nanti.)

Tinrin employs a bound noun construction if 'the referent is something inherent/inseparable'. In contrast, the 'link' noun construction is used when the referent is something already separated from the possessor. The noun *wii* as bound noun refers to 'soul, shade, picture', for example *wii-nrî* (soul-3sg) 'his soul', and as a link noun to fibres already removed from what they were part of, for example. *wii-nrâ-nrî* (fibre-LINK-3sg) 'his fibre' (Osumi 1996: 454).

There may also be unexplainable 'irregularities' within an individual subclass (see, for instance, the discussion in §2.5 of Chapter 2, on Nêlêmwa). In 'Dongo-ko, possessive constructions with kinship nouns do not include classifiers (see §2.4). The only exception is 'sister-in-law': this term occurs with a classifier referring to people, animals, and various inanimate objects (Pasch 1986: 240ff; 1985: 75). Along similar lines, the term for 'brother' in Paumarí is the only term for a blood relative to be alienably possessed. Alienably possessed body parts in Paumarí are *joho* 'breast' and *afo'afo* 'lungs'; all the rest are inalienably possessed (Chapman and Derbyshire 1991: 256–7). In Moskona, 'child' is not treated as a kin term in terms of its possession class (§4.3.1 of Chapter 3).

This cross-linguistic variability does not invalidate the concept of 'close' or 'inalienable' possession. It does highlight the necessity for a fine-grained semantic analysis of each group, and also for possible historical motivations in some 'exceptions' (as in §2.5 of Chapter 2).

The semantic difference between 'inalienable' possession, on the one hand, and 'alienable' possession on the other can help to distinguish the meanings of polysemous nouns. This shows how important, and how tangible, this distinction may be.

In Koyukon, the stem *tl'enh* can mean 'bone' or 'leg'. As 'leg', it is alienably possessed. As 'bone' it is not (Thompson 1996: 661). In Puluwat, a Micronesian language, a directly possessed noun *sasing-iy* 'my photograph' refers to a picture of me. The same noun in an alienable possessive construction *ná-á-y sasing* (CL:SMALL.FOREIGN.OBJECTS-my photograph) refers to my camera, or a picture taken by me or belonging to me. The directly possessed noun *pwóóŕ-oy* means 'my coffin', and if alienably possessed *yá-áy pwóóŕ* (GENERAL.POSS.CL-1sg box) 'my box' (Elbert 1974: 61–2). Similar distinctions occur in Nêlêmwa (§3.6.2 of Chapter 2).

Along similar lines, in Tariana an alienably possessed form *kale* means 'wind'; if inalienably possessed, *-kale* means 'breath, heart'. This is a bound form and cannot occur without a personal possessive prefix. A similar example from Galo is in §2.2.2 of Chapter 7.

In the Lolovoli dialect of North-east Ambae, body parts are inalienably ('directly') possessed, for example *karu-ku* 'my leg'. But a body part of an animal which one intends to eat can be alienably possessed, e.g. *ga-ku karu-gi* (classifier-food-1sg leg-ALIENABLE) 'my leg to eat (e.g. of chicken)' (Hyslop 2001: 183–4).

In Wandala (§4.4 of Chapter 11), changing possession classes for the 'older brother' and for 'father' implies a change in meaning: both mean 'boss' if used within an alienable possession construction. This may reflect a social hierarchy conceptualized through kinship relations.

Changing the way in which a noun can be possessed—from inalienable to alienable—involves recategorizing the referent, in terms of its individuation. We saw, in §2.3.3, that in Toqabaqita, an Oceanic language, body part terms and a few 'inalienably possessed' nouns can occur in analytic possessive constructions if individuated. This adds a further dimension to the semantic and pragmatic motivation behind possession classes. The choice of a possession class may correlate with the meanings of a referent. We return to this in §2.4.6.

2.4.3 *'Unpossessed' forms* Inalienably possessed nouns cannot occur on their own. They are, in a sense, 'obligatorily' possessed and can be considered 'bound'. A number of languages have a special way of creating free nouns out of such bound forms. To be able to occur without a Possessor, an obligatorily possessed noun in Hixkaryana, a Carib language from Brazil (Derbyshire 1985: 203), takes the suffix *-nano* 'depossession' which replaces possessive prefixes and suffixes, e.g. *r-aho-nɨ* (1sg-stool-POSS) 'my stool', *aho-nano* (stool-UNPOSS) 'stool(s)'.

In Koyukon (Thompson 1996: 666–7), non-possessed forms of body parts are marked with the prefix *k'e-*. For instance, *nelaane* 'flesh' appears with an obligatory Possessor if it refers to Possessor's own flesh. In its 'depossessed' form marked with *k'e-*, it refers to flesh which is no longer part of a living being:

(11) be-nelaane'
3sg-meat/flesh
his/her (own) flesh

(12) se-k'e-nelaane'
1sg-NONPOSSESSED-meat/flesh
my (animal's) meat (to be eaten)

The majority of Arawak languages of South America have such a 'non-possessed' suffix, **-tʃi* or *-hVi* (Aikhenvald 1999: 82[7]), for example Bare *nu-nene* 'my tongue', *nene-hei* 'tongue in general, someone's tongue', Pareci *no-tiho* 'my face', *tiho-ti* 'someone's face'. This often occurs just with body part terms, as in Pareci. In other Arawak languages this suffix can also occur with nouns of other groups, such as Warekena *nu-deka* 'my possession', *deka-ʃi* 'possessions in general'. In Nanti this suffix is used with just a few body part terms and terms for personal inalienable possession (§3.4 of Chapter 6). Many Arawak languages tend to lose this suffix (see the discussion of its fate in Tariana and other North Arawak languages in Aikhenvald 2003a: 129).

In many languages of the Arawak family, this same suffix is also used to form deverbal nominalizations, for example Warekena *-yanata-* 'write', *nu-yanata-ʃi* 'my writing'. The suffix which makes a bound noun into a free form has a similar function in verbs: a verbal root typically accompanied by suffixes and clitics can occur on its own once it takes the 'non-possessed' nominalizer. Along similar lines, inalienably possessed nouns can occur without a Possessor in Moskona only if prefixed by the nominalizer *m-* (C of §4.2 of Chapter 3).

2.4.4 *What cannot be 'possessed'* Some cultures have a world-view in terms of which certain things can never be owned. In Macushi (Abbott 1991: 86), names of plants, such as *pattia* 'watermelon', natural phenomena, for example *meren mere'* 'rainbow', and some species of animals, for example. *waikin* 'deer', in addition to address forms of kinship terms never occur in possessive constructions. 'Obligatorily unpossessed' items in Hixkaryana—another Carib language—include *xerye* 'manioc', *tuna* 'water', and *koso* 'deer'. In Moskona, nouns 'denoting natural phenomena and uncontrollable events or entities, such as disease' cannot be possessed: they are conceptualized as non-volitional entities affecting a person (§4.1.2 of Chapter 3).

[7] This marker is sometimes also referred to as 'absolute' suffix. Lev Michael (Chapter 6) calls it 'alienator'. Also see Aikhenvald (2012: 170–2), for an overview of this technique in Amazonian languages.

Stars, deities, natural elements, and general terms for humans cannot be possessed in Nêlêmwa (§7 of Chapter 2).

In Waurá, an Arawak language of the Xingu region in Brazil, non-possessable items include natural phenomena, such as *kamá* 'sun', *a'napi* 'rainbow', and *kaa'lũti* 'star', and some artefacts, such as *e'pi* 'axe' (this can be used in possessive constructions, but with a different suppletive stem, *ni'-gãwa* 'my axe') (Richards 1973; also see Aikhenvald 2012: 169–70). Similarly, in Nanti (§3.6 of Chapter 6) 'features of the natural world which exist without human intervention', including 'sun', 'forest', and 'water', are not used in possessive constructions.

Along similar lines, in Dakota, a Siouan language, 'natural objects like land, water, animals including the dog but excepting the horse cannot take the possessive pronoun, because under aboriginal conditions they could not be exclusive property of anyone' (Boas and Deloria 1941: 128). Since, 'according to Dakota concepts certain objects, particularly natural objects and food, cannot be personal property', reflexive verbal forms are used to express possession (Boas and Deloria 1941: 90, 103). That is, instead of saying 'I slaughtered my buffalo', a speaker would say 'I slaughtered buffalo for myself' (Mithun 2001: 307–8).

In many languages, kinship terms distinguish address forms, or vocative forms, and reference terms. Address terms typically cannot be possessed, as in Nanti (§3.6 of Chapter 6), Tariana (also Arawak), and many East Tucanoan languages. Arguably, address terms have a built-in first person reference (interestingly, the form *ina* in Nanti functions as the vocative 'mother!' and as the first person referential possessive form, 'my mother': see §2.3.4). In Hone (§2.1.2 of Chapter 9) personal names cannot occur in possessive constructions. Address forms in Nêlêmwa are alienably possessed free nouns. Most reference terms are directly (that is, 'inalienably') possessed (§2.5 of Chapter 2). Three reference terms come from erstwhile address terms, and are exceptions to this rule: they are alienably possessed.

'Unpossessability' of items can be viewed as a matter of common sense within a particular culture (as it appears to be the case in Galo: see §2.2.2 of Chapter 7). The late Marcília Fontes, my first teacher of Hohôdene Baniwa, said to me once, explaining that the term for cockroach cannot be possessed 'Who would want to own a cockroach?'

However, the fact that in Baniwa—as in Dakota—land, water, sun, and so on cannot be used in possessive constructions alerts us to the fact that the 'unpossessability' is a grammatical rule, rather than a semantic oddity. Why would different languages and cultures have different limits on 'possessability' of terms? The whole idea of not being able to 'possess' something may reflect traditional attitudes to ownership. Or it may be rooted in cultural and religious practices. Words referring to male body effluvia and sexual organs are taboo in Hone (§2.1.2 of Chapter 9): their existence is supposed to be secret. These terms never occur with a possessive suffix.

2.4.5 *Further parameters in Possessive relationships* We have seen that Possessive relationships can be 'close'—or 'inalienable'—or less 'close'—or 'alienable'. A Possessive relationship may extend to the present, or be confined to the past. It can be permanent, or temporary. The relationship between Possessor and Possessee can be conceived as 'proximate' or 'remote'. And it may, or may not, involve Possessor's control.

A. Possessive relationships and time. Most North Carib languages distinguish past and non-past possession: what I had before and what I have now. This applies to both alienably and inalienably possessed nouns, e.g. Macushi (Abbott 1991: 86–7):

(13) u-ye —inalienably possessed item, present possession
1sg-tooth
my tooth

(14) u-ye-rî'pi —inalienably possessed item, former possession
1sg-tooth-FORMER.POSSESSION
my former tooth

(15) u-wa'ka-ri —alienably possessed item, present possession
1sg-axe-POSS
my axe

(16) u-wa'ka-ri-rî'pi —alienably possessed item, former possession
1sg-axe-POSS-FORMER.POSSESSION
my former axe[8]

Possessive constructions in West Greenlandic (Fortescue 1984: 172) can combine with markers of past and future, to express what one used to have, and what one is to have. There is an additional suffix *-taaq* 'newly acquired'.

B. Temporary and permanent possession. A number of languages distinguish items owned by someone on a temporary basis—for instance, borrowed—from those owned permanently. The nominal suffix *-ut(i)* in West Greenlandic (Fortescue 1984: 172–3) marks personal possession considered 'alienable or temporary'. The suffix 'usually refers to something acquired and/or disposable... Dogs, kayaks, sleds and other single essential pieces of equipment do not take this affix—unless temporarily borrowed'. A form *niqaa* (3+meat) refers to animal's flesh, while *niqiu-taa* (3sg+meat+TEMPORARY.POSSESSION) refers to meat 'caught/stored by or assigned

[8] In these and other examples from Carib languages (see Derbyshire 1999 and Aikhenvald 2012: 162–3, for an overview) the scope of tense distinction on nouns is possession, not the referent itself. Also see Dixon (2004: 297), for future marking on an NP as relating to future possession, not the future state of the referent. Nordlinger and Sadler (2004) mistakenly confused this with nominal tense widespread in other South American languages.

TABLE 1.1. **Possessor's control or lack thereof: an example from Tongan**

Functions	'Subjective' possessive marker	'Objective' possessive marker
With action nominalizations: distinguishes subject and object	ˈeku taki POSS:SUBJ leading 'my leading, my leadership' (I am the leader)	hoku taki POSS:OBJ leading 'my being led'
With other nouns: associated with control of the Possessor	ˈeku pale POSS:SUBJ prize 'prize awarded by me'	hoku pale POSS:OBJ prize 'prize awarded to me'
	ˈeku tuˈi POSS:SUBJ king 'king whom I appoint'	hoku tuˈi POSS:OBJ king 'king whose subject I am'

to him (the hunter)'. And *savia* 'his knife' is 'an inalienable piece of a hunter's equipment, *saviutaa* is 'the knife he (now) owns' (see §6). Also see Dixon (2010b: 275; 1972: 105–10) for an analysis of temporary possession in Dyirbal, and §§1.2–3, Chapter 5, on Martuthunira.

C. Possession and control. Polynesian possessive constructions distinguish relationships initiated with or without a Possessor's control (Wilson 1982: 123–30). Consider Tongan (Churchward 1953: 78–87). Table 1.1 illustrates what Churchward calls 'objective' and 'subjective' possessives. In nominalizations, the 'subjective' possessive corresponds to the verb's subject, and the 'objective' possessive to its object. Using *ˈeku* for 'my' 'implies that I am active, influential, or formative', 'towards the thing mentioned', while 'the use of *hoku* for '"my" implies that the thing mentioned is active, influential, or formative' towards me (Churchward 1953: 81).

Things which require 'subjective' possession include goods, money, tools, utensils, etc. which I own or use, as well as animals and birds I own or use, things that I drink or eat, make, mend, or carry, and also persons in my employment and under my control. 'Objective' possession covers 'things which are provided for me', 'persons or things which surround, support, control, or affect me, or on which I depend'.[9]

Controlled possession is coded through pertensive and the 'source genitive' in Martuthunira (§1.1 and §1.4 of Chapter 5). The omission of the possessive marker with the first person singular Possessor in Mandarin Chinese (§5.5 of Chapter 8) emphasizes personal authority of a high-ranking individual (see §6 below).

[9] See a more detailed discussion of Fijian in Dixon (1988), (2010b: 307–10); and further analysis in Wilson (1982) and Harrison (1988).

D. Proximity of relationship. In the Hohôdene dialect of Baniwa, alienably possessed nouns with animate reference can take either suffix *-ni* or suffix *-te*. In (17), a dog has a fairly intimate relationship with the Possessor; it takes the *-ni* suffix (Aikhenvald 2003a: 143).

(17) nu-tʃinu-ni
1sg-dog-poss.PROXIMATE
my dog (the one I brought up)

In (18), the dog is less closely associated with the Possessor, and it takes the *-te* suffix.

(18) nu-tʃinu-te
1sg-dog-poss.NONPROXIMATE
my dog (the one I found)

Cognate possessive markers in Warekena of Xié, also North Arawak, refer to the physical distance between Pr and Pe: the suffix *-ne* is used if the Pe is close to the speaker, and *-te* implies that the Pe is at a distance from the speaker and is closer to the addressee (Aikhenvald 1998: 293–7, own fieldwork):

(19) nu-mukawa-ne
1sg-rifle-POSS.CLOSE
my rifle (right here)

(20) nu-mukawa-te
1sg-rifle-POSS.DISTAL
my rifle (over here)

Cognate suffixes in other Arawak languages are assigned depending on the meaning of the noun (see Aikhenvald 1999, 2012: 167–9), and also its phonological make-up, as in Nanti (see §3.2 of Chapter 6).

Possessive relations can be further classified in terms of how the Possessee can be 'manipulated', or 'owned' (depending on its nature as well as that of the relationship: §2.5.1).

2.4.6 *Possessive marking and discourse* Possessive constructions can vary along a further set of parameters, to do with discourse prominence and focality of Possessor, Possessee, or the relationship between them.

In Awa Pit (Curnow 1997: 123) the genitive *=pa/=wa* is used to mark a human Possessor with a specific referent (§2.4.1).

(21) awa=wa pit
person=POSS language/tongue
the person's tongue

If a human Possessor has generic reference, as in (22), the genitive marker is not used:

(22) awa pit
person language/tongue
the language of the people (the Awa Pit)

Focusing on the Possessor in Warembori (Donohue 1999: 27) involves using free pronouns as well as the possessive prefix used in non-focused constructions, for example *e-me-ro* (1sg-house-INDICATIVE) 'my house', *iwi e-me-ro* (I 1sg-house-INDICATIVE) '(it's) my house'. In Nanti, if the Possessor is in contrastive focus, it precedes the Possessee (§3.1 of Chapter 6). Alternatively, contrastive Possessor focus can be expressed with a free possessive pronoun (see the discussion of the two techniques in other Arawak languages in Aikhenvald 1995).

We saw, in §2.3.3, how analytic structures can become a means of individuating the Possessee within a possessive construction. Possession often correlates with definiteness and referentiality of the Possessee (see §4, and Jespersen 1924: 110). Following a similar principle, an analytic construction with a possessive marker is preferred to synthetic constructions in Manambu (§3.4 of Chapter 4) if the Pr or the Pe is in focus.

If a language has several possessive constructions, the conditioning factors for their use may involve specificity and discourse status of the components. Possession in English can be marked with *'s* on the Pr preceding the Pe or by preposition *of* before Pr following the Pe. Dixon (2010b: 295–6) shows that the *'s* alternative is preferred if Pr is human, specific, and singular; or if Pe is specific and singular, or if Pr is 'familiar information' and/or expressed with a shortish NP.

2.5 *Classifiers in possessive constructions*

Treating one noun as 'closely', or 'inalienably' possessed, and another one as 'loosely', or 'alienably possessed' involves categorizing the relationship between the Pr and the Pe. Further subclassification of Possessive relations in constructions with alienable possession involves relational classifiers—§2.5.1. A further option is categorizing the Possessee in terms of its inherent properties—§2.5.2. Relational classifiers categorize the relationship between the two nouns. Possessive classifiers categorize the Possessee.

2.5.1 *Relational classifiers* Relational classifiers specify the nature of an alienable relationship between the Pr and the Pe. They are an almost exclusive property of the Oceanic subgroup of Austronesian languages (see Chapter 2 for an overview of Oceanic languages and the discussion of Nêlêmwa). A minimal system involves having a relational classifier for 'alimentary' possession (food) and one for general possession (everything else), as in Manam and Kaliai-Kove (also see Lichtenberk 1983a, b, Dixon 2010b: 276–7).

Relational classifiers stand apart from any other classifier types (Aikhenvald 2003a: 144–6 offers a general typological perspective). Unlike other types of classifiers—be they numeral, verbal, or deictic—their choice is determined by the kind of relationship between Pr and Pe, and occasionally, some properties of Pe. One can only drink what is drinkable, and eat what is edible. This is similar to selectional restrictions on verbal objects—such as 'eat' and 'drink' (which, in Oceanic languages, have given rise to relational classifiers).

This is how it works. North-east Ambae has four possessive classifiers: *ga-* 'food possession', *me-* 'drink possession', *bula-* 'natural or valued object possession' and *no-* 'general possession'. 'Our food' will be referred to as *ga-da hinaga* (CL:FOOD-1sgINCL.POSS food), and medicine, considered drinkable, as *me-mu panadol* (CL:DRINK-2sgPOSS panadol) 'your panadol'. The classifier *bula-* covers ownership of animals and crops, natural items, European goods, and objects of adornment. The classifier *na-* is used with the rest of the nouns (Hyslop 2001: 177–80).

Polysemous nouns can be differentiated with classifiers. *Matui* 'coconut' refers to mature coconut for eating if used with *ga-*, to juice from mature coconut for drinking if used with *me-*, to coconut tree or plantation if used with *bula-*, or to coconut tree or fruit to be used for a specific purpose (e.g. selling, trunk used in building) and particularly copra. Nêlêmwa has a rich set of relational classifiers (examples are in C of §1.3.1 of Chapter 2).

More extensive systems of relational classifiers offer further possibilities of categorizing the Pe. We can recall that Mussau-Emira (Brownie and Brownie 2007: 71–86) distinguishes direct and indirect possessive constructions. Directly possessed nouns include kinship terms, human body parts, 'name', and a number of terms intimately associated with the person—including 'knife', 'house', and 'canoe'. The indirect possessive construction is formed by adding a possessive suffix to a possessive classifier placed before the Possessee. The possessive classifier refers to the way in which the item is to be handled, or type of relationship, or to the class to which the item belongs. The full list of classifiers is in Table 1.2.

Note that 'knife' is an inalienably possessed noun. The same form gave rise to a classifier for cutting instruments. This is a typical path of grammaticalization for obligatorily possessed forms, from a noun to a classifier (see Aikhenvald 2003a).

Just as in most Oceanic languages, classifiers highlight different uses for the same object. A chicken can be viewed as a domestic animal, as in (23).

(23)	kie-ghi	paolo	ateva
	POSS.CL:DOMESTIC.ANIMAL-1sg	chicken	sg.I
	my chicken (domestic animal)		

TABLE 1.2. **Possessive classifiers in Mussau-Emira**

Classifier	Meaning	Origin
ai-	trees, e.g. *ai* 'tree', *paea* 'pawpaw', *aranna* 'pandanus sp'	'tree, wood' (noun)
ale-	building, e.g. *ale* 'house', *ale manga* 'temple' (holy house)	'house' (noun)
ane-	food, e.g. *ghila* 'bird', *kauu* 'sweet potato', *uri* 'banana'	?
gholu-	juicy foods, e.g. *asi* 'taro', *paea* 'pawpaw', *makere* 'sago'	'eat something juicy' (verb)
iema-	cutting instruments, e.g. *kaputu* 'adze', *kulum* 'axe'	'knife' (noun)
ilimo-	water craft, e.g. *anua* 'ship', *paanaka* 'boat'	'canoe' (noun)
kalu-	abstract personal items, e.g. *kiukiu* 'story', *dinao* 'debt', *ni-aikaaia* 'faith', *saavoto* 'evil', *sessa* 'sickness'	?
kapu-	personal relationships, e.g. *taumattuu* 'person' (helper, employee), *tau ng-ai-ppoa* 'spokesman' (*lit.* person who speaks', *kingi* 'king', *god* 'god'	'friend, sibling' (noun)
kie-	domestic animals, e.g. *pato* 'duck', *paua* 'dog', *paolo* 'chicken'	?
kura-	things giving light, e.g. *sulu* 'dry coconut leaf torch', *lama* 'lamp'	'fire' (noun)
ropi-	things to drink, e.g. *manu* 'water', *niu* 'coconut'	'drink'(verb)
uma-	pieces of land, gardens, e.g. *asi* 'taro garden', *kauu* 'sweet potato garden', *utana* 'garden'	?
usu-	things to suck juice from, e.g. *aranna* 'pandanus sp.', *tou* 'sugarcane'	'suck juice from' (verb)
une-	general things, e.g. *laka* 'basket', *ai-kuu-kuuvati* 'shotgun' (*lit.* instrument for shooting), *kou ng-uru* 'hat' (head-covering)	?

Or as food (24):

(24) ane-ghi paolo ateva
POSS.CL:FOOD-1sg chicken sg.I
my chicken (to eat)

A coconut can be owned as a tree (25). Or the contents of it can be drunk (26):

(25) ai-ghi niu eteae
POSS.CL:TREE-1sg coconut sg.II
my coconut tree

(26) ropi-ghi niu eteae
POSS.CL:DRINK-1sg coconut sg.II
my coconut (to drink)

Relational classifiers in Oceanic languages reflect culture-specific ways of handling the Possessee. Fijian dialects of Eastern Viti Levu have a classifier for an object which the Possessor contributes 'as a customary obligation—a mat or pig for presentation at a feast, a house being built for a chief, or a spade to be used in a communal garden project' (Geraghty 2000: 246). This same marker (*loga-/laga-*) is also used as a relational classifier for totems in part of northeast Viti Levu. A classifier system may contain a form for possessing valuable objects, as in Raga (Lichtenberk 1983a: 154). We return to this in §6.

Relational classifiers in Pohnpeian, a Micronesian language (Keating 1997, 1998), reflect the social status of the Pr, and also the Possessive relationship and the nature of the Pe. The language distinguishes 22 classifiers in common register, unmarked for politeness. The Honorific, or 'exaltive' register also has 22, 14 of which are the same as in the common register. The rest are different. The general classifier *ah* and also *nah* 'general; dominance of Possessor' correspond to one honorific classifier *sapwellime*. Two 'common register' classifiers *kene* 'edible' and *nime* 'drinkable' correspond to three in the honorific speech: *koanoat* 'possession of food/drink by paramount chief', *pwenieu* 'possession of food/drink by paramount chieftainess', and *sahk* 'possession of food/drink by secondary chief'. In contrast, the humiliative register (used to address socially inferior people) has just one classifier, *ah tungoal*. The forms and meanings are illustrated in Table 1.3 (based on Keating 1997: 252–3, 255, 258).

In the humiliative register there is just one kind of possessive classifier, a combination of general classifier *ah* and a specific humiliative classifier *tungoal* (*lit.* 'food'); all the semantic distinctions present in honorific and common style classifiers are neutralized. The same noun can be used with different classifiers, depending on the status of the Pr:

(27) nah pwutak
POSSESSION.MARKER.UNMARKED boy
her/his boy (unmarked for status)

If talking about someone of a high status possessing something, (28) will be appropriate:

(28) sapwellime N pwutak
POSSESSION.MARKER.HIGH.STATUS Title boy
highly respected N's boy (N is a chief)

And if the Pr is low in status, (29) is the one to use:

(29) ah tungoal pwutak
POSSESSION.MARKER LOW.STATUS boy
his/her (a humble person's) boy

TABLE 1.3. **Possessed classifiers and speech styles in Pohnpeian**

Common	Semantics	Honorific	Semantics	Humiliative
ah	general classifier			
nah	general, dominance of possessor	*sapwellime*	general classifier	
kene	edible	*koanoat*	possession of food/drink	
nime	drinkable	*pwenieu* *sahk*	by paramount chief idem by paramount chieftess idem by secondary chief	
sapwe	land	*nillime*	land	
imwe	buildings	*tehnpese*	buildings	
were	vehicles	*tehnwere*	vehicles	
kie	sleeping padsv	*moatoare*	things to sleep on	
ipe	sleeping covers			
ulunge	pillows			
rie	siblings			*ah tungoal*
kiseh	relatives			
ullepe	maternal uncles			
wahwah	nieces, nephews			
sawi	clan members	same as in common speech		
pelie	peers			
seike	catch			
pwekidah	share of feast food			
mware	name, title, garland			
ede	names			
tie	earrings			
dewe	location			

Pohnpeian provides a paramount example of how attitudes to possession and the societal structure can be understood through possessive marking—the topic of §6.

2.5.2 *Classifying the Possessee* A possessive noun phrase may contain a classifier for a Possessee, without necessarily categorizing the way in which the Pr is using or possessing the Pe. This is the essence of possessive classifiers (distinct from relational classifiers).

GENERIC CLASSIFIERS can categorize the Possessee in possessive constructions. An example, from Yavapai, a Yuman language, was given in (10). Generic classifiers are always restricted to alienable possession. Languages vary as to how many generic

TABLE 1.4. **Possessive classifiers in Palikur**

-pig	'pet'; used with domesticated animals	*gi-pig pewru* (3m-pet dog) 'his dog'; *gi-pig mutom* 'his sheep'
-mana	'food'; used with fruit and vegetables	*pi-mana uwas* (2sg-food orange) 'your orange'
-mutra	'plant'	*n-amutra pilatno* (1sg-plant banana) 'my plant-banana' (the one I planted)
-win	'catch; animal caught to eat'	*nu-win arudiki* (1sg-catch tapir) 'my catch-tapir' (the tapir I caught)
-kamkayh	'child'	*nu-kamkayh awayg* (1sg-child boy) 'my son', *nu-kamkayh tino* (1sg-child daughter) 'my daughter'

nouns can be used as possessive classifiers. Apalaí (Koehn 1994) appears to have a large set of generic possessive classifiers for nouns denoting fruit, animals, and food stuff that cannot directly take possessive markers. (Also see Abbott 1991, for Macushi; Aikhenvald 2012: 290–2).

Or just a subset of generic nouns can be used as classifiers. In Palikur, a North Arawak language spoken in northern Brazil and French Guiana, only five of the many generics can be used as classifiers (Aikhenvald and Green 1998)—see Table 1.4.[10]

The number of generic classifiers can be more restricted. In Yuman languages inalienable possession is indicated by a prefix on the Possessee, or a prefix on the Possessee plus a pronoun. Possession of alienably possessed nouns is expressed either by a noun followed by a classifier with affixes indicating possession, or by a noun with possessive suffixes attached to it. There are two classifiers, one for 'pets and domestic animals', and the other a general one (Hualapai, Maricopa *-hat* 'pet'; Hualapai *-wi:nych*, Maricopa *nywish* 'general possession').

To indicate alienable possession in Uto-Aztecan languages, a possessive prefix is attached to the classifier. Languages typically have two or three classifiers, which distinguish animacy and humanness. Papago and Northern Tepehuan have animate and inanimate classifiers. Papago classifier *soi-* with an animate noun is illustrated in (30) (Saxton 1982: 186–7).

(30) has-ču ṣoi-g-ǰ g Huan
what-thing CL:ANIMATE-ALIENABLE-GENITIVE ART Juan
What kind of animal does Juan have? (*lit.* what kind of animal of Juan?)

[10] This is a feature of a few Tupí-Guaraní, a number of Jê languages (see Rodrigues 1999a, b), and Kipeá-Kariri (Macro-Jê) (Ribeiro 2002b: 77, 86; Rodrigues 1997: 72-4).

Classifiers in possessive constructions can categorize the Pe in TERMS OF ITS INHERENT PROPERTIES. If classifiers are used exclusively in possessive constructions, they tend to occur with alienably possessed nouns. This is the case in Nêlêmwa (C of §1.3.1, Chapter 2; further examples are in Aikhenvald 2003a).

Classifiers which occur in possessive constructions and in other contexts—for instance, as numeral, verbal, or noun classifiers—occur with inalienably, and with alienably possessed nouns. Body parts in Tariana are inalienably possessed and have to take possessive prefixes, e.g. *nu-whi-da* (1sg-head-CL:ROUND) 'my head'. Alienably possessed nouns, such as *iri-da* (rubber-CL:ROUND) 'rubber ball', cannot take prefixes. Classifiers in Tariana are also used with verbs, demonstratives, and numerals, and on the nouns themselves.

Both types of nouns can be used in possessive noun phrases with classifiers (see Aikhenvald 2007a, on a similar system in Baniwa, a related language):

(31) nu-ya-da nu-whi-da
1sg-POSS-CL:ROUND 1sg-head-CL:ROUND
my head

(32) nu-ya-da iri-da
1sg-POSS-CL:ROUND rubber-CL:ROUND
my rubber ball

In Hmong, a Miao-Yao language (Bisang 1993: 29–30), classifiers can also be used with inalienably, and with alienably possessed nouns (also see Pacioni 1997, on Cantonese).

(33) nws tus txiv ntxawn tus ntxhais
he CL:LIVING.BEING uncle CL:LIVING.BEING daughter
the daughter of his uncle

(34) nws rab riam ntaj
he CL:ARTEFACT sword
his sword

There is just one difference in classifier use with alienable and inalienable items: a classifier can be omitted if the item is inalienably possessed, but not if it is alienably possessed. *Paj caj poj niam* (Paj Caj's wife) or *koj npe* (you name) 'your name' do not have to have a classifier. This agrees with the iconic principles of possessive marking: the closer the possessive relationship, the closer the items are in surface structure. The same set of classifiers is used with numerals, for example *ib tus tsov* (one CL:LIVING.BEING tiger) 'one tiger' and as noun classifiers express definiteness, for example *tus tsov* (CL:LIVING.BEING tiger) 'the tiger'.

Possessive classifiers can reflect cultural stereotypes and the ways of mapping linguistic categories into language—inasmuch as classifier systems do so in general.

Relational classifiers stand apart from other classifier types in that they more easily reflect social relations, status, and values, as we will see in §6.

Further cross-linguistically important issues for investigating possession within a noun phrase include the problem of what is the head of a possessive noun phrase (see the discussion of Manambu in Chapter 4, and Nanti in §3.5 of Chapter 6). In Martuthunira (§3, example (52) of Chapter 5), the 'whole' rather than the part is the head of a part–whole construction. In a number of languages, such as Kamaiurá (Tupí-Guaraní, Brazil: Seki 2000) and Jarawara (Arawá, Brazil), the Possessor is the syntactic head of phrases with inalienable possession. This is intuitively plausible—inalienable possession, such as whole–part, is 'about' the Possessor, the whole being more important than the part. In alienably possessed constructions, the Possessee is the head (see Dixon 2010b: 296–8, and Dixon 2000 on various tests for identifying a head in a noun phrase). This is taken up in §2 of Chapter 14.

Another issue is how to mark the lack of something, or 'not having' something. Australian languages typically have a privative suffix to express this meaning (see §1.6 of Chapter 5, and §1 of Chapter 14), as do some Amazonian languages. Balto-Finnic languages use the abessive case. A full investigation of the gamut of options lies outside our purview in this chapter.

3 Beyond a noun phrase: possession within a clause

A Possessive relationship can be established within a clause, in the form of a predicative possession—§3.1. Possessive Relationships can also be reflected in the manipulation of grammatical relations, including incorporation—§3.2. Or they can be realized through special topicalization or relativization patterns—§3.3.

3.1 *Predicative possession*

Marking predicative possession may involve a verb of ownership 'have', or 'belong'. Or a language may employ an existential construction or a locational construction with a copula verb. The choice of a predicative possessive construction may depend on the possessive relation, the semantics of the Possessee or the Possessor, and further parameters including their definiteness, animacy, and focus.[11]

A verbless clause whose major meaning is identification between two referents can encode permanent possession and inclusion. A special derivational affix to a Possessee is a further alternative.

[11] Such division of labour of predicative possessive constructions is termed 'split possession' by Stolz et al. (2008). Also see Isachenko (1974), Heine (1997a), and especially Dixon (2010b: 299–305). Perniss and Zeshan (2008) is a study of possession, and correlations between possessive and existential structures in Sign Languages. The approach to predicative possession by Stassen (2009) differs from ours, in its predominant focus on cogntive and historical dimensions. Some of the data of languages quoted there are incorrect.

We saw, throughout §2, that in many languages core possessive meanings are covered by a 'catch-all' associative, attributive, or modificational noun phrase. In most of these languages, there are dedicated ways of expressing predicative possession (this is what licenses its use as a disambiguating test for the various meanings of a more general attributive noun phrase: see §2.2, and examples from Wandala (Chapter 11) and Likpe (Chapter 10)). In other words, while there is often a generic noun phrase, there is hardly ever a generic predicative construction which subsumes possession as one of its overtones.

3.1.1 *Verbs of ownership* A verb of ownership, 'have', is typically a transitive verb, with Pr as the subject (A) and Pe as the object (O). While in some languages it is a regular verb (cf. Dixon 2010b: 299; and Heine 1997a: 20–1, 48–9), in others it is morphologically deficient. In English, it cannot form a passive (except in idiomatic meanings). In Tariana, the verb 'have' cannot combine with any morphological derivations—causative, reciprocal, or passive. And in Tamambo, an Oceanic language from Vanuatu, *-noha* 'have' is the only transitive verb which cannot occur with any tense or aspect markers. Verbs of possession—and copula verbs—often do not allow imperative formation, as in Harar Oromo, Amharic, and Tariana (also see §4.1 of Chapter 4, on irregularities of 'have' in Manambu).

Not infrequently, a verb 'have' is the product of reinterpretation and grammaticalization of a verb meaning 'hold, grab, take, carry, obtain, acquire', for example Spanish and Portuguese *tener* 'have', originating in Latin *tĕnēre* 'hold, retain, maintain' (see Corominas 1961: 548, and Heine 1997a: 48–9). Tariana *-de* 'have' is cognate to Baniwa of Içana *-de:* 'hold, take'. In Korean Sign language, the sign glossed as 'have in hand' is 'clearly based on the physical action of grabbing but has grammaticalized and can now be used in a wide variety of possessive contexts' (Perniss and Zeshan 2008b: 19–20).[12] Possessive verbs in Martuthunira (§4 of Chapter 5) include 'grab, catch' and 'hold, keep', and in Galo 'hold, have (with oneself)' and 'carry, wear' (§3.4 of Chapter 7) denote temporary possession. This corresponds to Heine's 'Action Pattern' of possessive marking.

A verb 'have' can come from other sources. In Manambu, it also functions as a copula 'be' and 'become', and a positional verb 'stand'. A possessive verb *nu-cáapica* 'have, hold in one's hand' in Piapoco is a derivation from *-cáapi* 'hand' (Klumpp 1995: 62–3). A further possessive verb *-a:θu-* 'have, belong' (Reinoso Galindo 2002: 198–9) is derived from a nominal possessive marker of the same form.

English, and many other languages, have several further, fully regular, verbs with a meaning similar to 'have' or 'come to have': *own*, *possess*, *acquire*, *obtain*, or a corresponding negative verb such as *lack*. Each has its own semantic properties, and

[12] Also see Gamkrelidze and Ivanov, Vol. 1 (1984: 225, 289) for a link between 'have' and 'hold' across Indo-European languages (including Baltic and Slavic); also see Isachenko (1974: 42).

domain of usage (also see §3 of Chapter 14). For instance, one can be 'possessed' by a spirit, and 'own' an argument. Mandarin Chinese (§4.1 of Chapter 8) is especially rich in verbs of possession and ownership whose choice depends on the degree of control, and on what one owns. These meanings are relevant for a general understanding of how the notions of possession and ownership are conceptualized and embedded in linguistic usage.

The Pr is the subject of a 'have' verb, and the Pe is the object—this is what Heine (1997a) and Heine and Kuteva (2002) refer to as H-possession. Reversing the grammatical relations results in *belong*-verbs—B-possession. A 'have' construction is 'about' the Possessor, while a 'belong'-construction is about the Possessee (see Heine 1997a: 29–31; Seiler 1983: 61). That is, the distinction is pragmatically-based. In *belong*-constructions, the subject Pe is typically definite, while the Pr may be indefinite. In *have*-constructions, the Pr is usually definite, and the Pe may be indefinite.

In many Indo-European languages *have*- and *belong*-constructions involve verbs. In Estonian, Colloquial Welsh, and a number of Slavic and Baltic languages, the equivalent of a 'have' construction is a copula clause. The reverse, 'belong to', can be expressed with a verb. The following examples are from Estonian (Viitso 2007: 94). Manambu (§4 of Chapter 4) would use a verb in (35), and a verbless clause in (36).

(35) Jaanil on auto
Jaan+ADESSIVE is car
Jaan has a car. (*lit.* To Jaan is a car)

(36) [See auto]$_S$ kuulub Jaanile
this car belong.3sgPRES Jaan+ALLATIVE
This car belongs to Jaan.[13]

This alerts us to a recurrent distinction made within possessive predication (but not usually within possessive noun phrases): that of definiteness of the Pr and the Pe, or focality of either of these. A similar distinction is made through verbless clauses in Moskona (§5 of Chapter 3). The terms H(ave) and B(elong) possession are thus treacherous—just like any English-centric terminology. The underlying concepts are better described using relevant parameters. In Moskona, if the Possessor is not the focus, the Possessee can be definite or indefinite, and different techniques are then used. A Topic clause is employed for the definite Possessee, and a verb 'bear, carry' for an indefinite one (§5.1 of Chapter 3). If the Possessee is focused, possession is expressed through the use of existential classificatory verb 'lie'.

3.1.2 *Copula constructions and verbless clauses* Possessive Relationships can be expressed with copula constructions. Either the Pr or the Pe can be copula subject

[13] There is a copula clause alternative for (ii): *see auto on Jaani oma*, and a verbal (rarely used) alternative for (i): *Jaan omab autot.*

(CS), or copula complement (CC). Importantly, different copula constructions may reflect different overtones of possession.

The copula complement can be marked as a locational as in Estonian (35) (cf. Heine 1997a: 50–2 on various ways of marking what he calls 'Location schema').[14] Or it can be marked as 'accompaniment' (Heine 1997a: 53–4), as in Yimas (Foley 1991: 305):

(37) yampaŋ kantk-n amayak
head.CLASS.VI.sg with-1sg COP.1sg
I have a head. (*lit.* I am with head)

This is reminiscent of 'associative' marking of predicative possession of any sort in Wandala (§7 of Chapter 11). In Manambu (example (21), §4.2 of Chapter 4) 'accompaniment' (being 'with' something) reflects temporary possession.

A further alternative is 'goal' marking, typically by dative case, as in Hungarian (also see Heine 1997a: 59–61, on Goal schema):

(38) nek-em van macskám
DAT-1sgPOSS exists cat+1sgPOSS
I have (my) cat.

An intransitive verb 'exist' can also be used to express possession. A possessive NP is then its only argument. In Jarawara both the copula *ama-* 'be' and the intransitive verb *-wata-* 'exist' can be used this way (Dixon 2004: 381; described by Heine 1997a: 58–9 as 'Genitive schema'):

(39) a. okoto ama-ke
1sg.POSS+daughter be-DEC.fem
I have a daughter. (*lit.* my daughter is)

(39) b. okoto wata-ke
1sg.POSS+daughter exist-DEC.fem
I have a daughter. (*lit.* my daughter exists)

We find similar examples in Nêlêmwa (Chapter 2), Moskona (Chapter 3), Nanti (Chapter 6), Galo (Chapter 7), Hone (Chapter 9), Likpe (Chapter 10), and Wandala (Chapter 11). The choice between an existential/possessive structure and a structure of another type depends on the Possessee in Nanti, on the kind of possession in Hone, and on the focus relationships and definiteness of the Possessee in Moskona. The same form can cover locational, existential, and possessive meanings: however, as Ameka points out in §4 of Chapter 10, conditions of use depending on the Possessee and the contexts are subtly different.

[14] The link between existence, possession, and location was originally captured by Clarke (1978).

Alternatively, a possessive existential clause consists of the Possessor marked as the topic, with the Possessee as the S and the only obligatory argument of the existential verb (Heine's 1997a: 61–2 'Topic schema'). This is one of the options for a possessive clause in Cahuilla, a Uto-Aztecan language (Seiler 1983: 58):

(40) néʔ né-pas ø-híw-qal
I 1POSSESSOR-older.brother 3sg-live-DUR
I have a brother. (*lit.* I, my brother lives)

A verbless clause with an extraposed and topicalized Possessor is used in North-east Ambae, if the Possessor has to be expressed with a free pronoun or noun phrase—following the principle of the 'Topic schema' in possessive existential clauses (Hyslop 2001: 369). The Possessor of 'house' is also expressed as a suffixed 'bound' pronoun:

(41) [Ngie,]$_{TOP}$ vale-na gai-rue
3sg house-3sgPOSSESSOR NUM.CL-two
S/he has two houses. (*lit.* S/he, her/his houses two)

The Topicalization strategy for predicative possession is used if the Possessee is definite (as in Moskona, §5.1.2 of Chapter 3), and also if the Possessor is what the clause is about (see examples (23–26) in Chapter 4). The topicalization strategy tends to be just one of the strategies for expressing predicative possession in the languages I surveyed.

A copula clause or a verbless clause with the meaning of identification may be a further alternative. In Manambu (§§4–5 of Chapter 4), a verbless identification clause expresses permanent association with an item which is intrinsically connected with a clan. Here, a possessive construction reflects a cultural concept. This is reminiscent of how identification with a clan is expressed through juxtaposition in Dyirbal (§2.2 of Chapter 14). We return to this in §6.

The choice between different ways of marking predicative possession depends on Possessor, Possessee, and especially the type of relationship: whether permanent or temporary, and inchoative ('acquisition') or static ('having in one's possession'). We turn to this in §3.1.4.

3.1.3 *Possessive derivations* Possession can be expressed with derivational affixes. West Greenlandic has a derivational suffix *-qar-* 'have' and *-qi-* 'have as' (Fortescue 1984: 171–2), added to the Pe. The Possessor is expressed with a bound pronoun:

(42) aningassa-ati-qar-punga
money-ALIENABLE-HAVE-1sgPOSSESSOR:INDICATIVE
I have (some) money.

One of the most stable features of Arawak languages is the prefix *ka-* whose major function is to derive possessive adjectives and predicates, e.g. Bare *ka-witi-w hiñatʃati*

(POSS/ATTRIB-eye-fem.sg woman) 'a woman has (good) eyes'. Its negative counterpart is *ma-*, as in Bare *ma-witi-w hiñatʃati* (POSS/ATTRIB.NEG-eye-fem.sg woman) 'a woman has no eyes, is eyeless, is blind' (see the summary in Aikhenvald 2002: App. 2). In Tariana, the *ka-* derivation is used for predicative kinship possession: (43) is the only way of saying 'X has a wife (or is married)':

(43) Juse ka-sa-do-pidaka
José POSS/ATTRIB-spouse-FEM-RECENT.PAST.REPORTED
José has a wife. (is married)

This can be compared to English expressions like *I am monied now.* The difference lies in the obligatory character of such derivations in Arawak languages: (43) is the only way of saying 'have a wife'. This technique is restricted to obligatorily possessed nouns. Its negative counterpart involves the prefix *ma-* and has the same restriction.

Just as in a possessive noun phrase, different predicative constructions within one language may reflect different types of Possessee, Possessive relationships, and Possessors. This takes us to the next section.

3.1.4 *Referents and relationships in predicative possession* The distinctions made within possessive noun phrases reflect the nature of Possessor, Possessee, and that of the Possessive relationship. Along similar lines, predicative possession may be marked differently depending on the properties of the (i) Possessee, (ii) Possessive relationship, and (iii) the Possessor (also see Heine 1997a: 20–1). However, the distinctions made are not the same.

(I) EXPRESSION OF PREDICATIVE POSSESSION DEPENDS ON THE POSSESSEE Predicative possessive constructions may have further semantic distinctions absent from possessive noun phrases. West Greenlandic (Fortescue 1984: 171–2) has a number of derivational suffixes for expressing predicative possession. Their choice depends on the Possessee's properties, for example *-gig-* 'have a good (something)', *-lug-/-lup-* 'have a bad (something)', *-kit-* 'have a small', and *-tu-* 'have much/a big':

(44) uummati-lup-puq
heart-have.bad-3sg.INDIC
He has a bad heart.

Awa Pit has two verbs 'have': *waj* 'have (a body part)' and *míj* 'have (everything else)' (Curnow 1997: 100–1). This distinction is not made in noun phrases.

Or different possessive constructions can be employed, reflecting the same categorization of nouns as in Possessive NPs. In Koyukon (Thompson 1996: 668–9), the verb *-t'aanh* 'have' is used with alienably possessed nouns:

(45) leek es-Ø-t'aanh
dog. 1sg:SU-CL-have
I have (own) a dog.

With kinship nouns, which are inalienably possessed, possession is indicated with the verb 'be' marked with an 'areal' prefix:

(46) S-ode hoo-Ø-laanh
1sg-older.sister. AREA-CL-be
I have an older sister. (*lit.* My older sister is)

The general principle behind such distribution appears to be as follows. If there is an alternative construction to possession marked with a verb—for example an existential or a copula clause—the 'have' verb will tend to be used for alienable possession involving ownership, or for less time-stable relationships, and the other construction for whole–part and kinship, and for permanent possessions.

Along similar lines, in Jarawara the verb *-kiha* 'have' can only be used with alienably possessed nouns, for example 'I have two dogs'. Kinship possession is expressed with a copula or an existential clause (see (39a–b), 'My daughter is'/'My daughter exists' meaning 'I have a daughter'). Along similar lines, 'he has big feet' is rendered as 'his big feet are' (Dixon 2004: 381). In Paraguayan Guaraní, verbless clauses are employed for predicative possession of inalienably possessed nouns, and the 'have' constructions are used for alienably possessed nouns (Velazquez-Castillo 1996: 69–83).

Nanti (§4.1, and Table 6.4 of Chapter 6), has two possessive verbs 'have' expressing ownership of inalienable items: one is used if the Possessee is definite, and the other one if it is indefinite. Two existential verbs—one for animate, and one for inanimate possessees—are used with obligatorily possessed kinship terms and body parts.

Why so? Verbless clauses, and copula clauses are essentially used for time-stable relationships. Thus, they are expected to cover whole–part and kinship relations. Verbal clauses may correlate with the agency of the 'owner', and allow variation in terms of time-stability and temporality of possession. The intrinsic semantics of clause types is what underlies a cross-linguistic tendency to use 'have' with less intimate, less stable, and more alienable possession.

(II) EXPRESSION OF PREDICATIVE POSSESSION DEPENDS ON THE POSSESSIVE RELATIONSHIP We can recall that a typical feature of Oceanic languages is relational classifiers which categorize the relationship between the Pr and the Pe, jointly with properties of Possessee. The same distinctions can be reflected in possessive verbs.

In Pohnpeian, only two of numerous relational classifiers (see Table 1.3), the honorific *sapwellime* and the humiliative *tungoal*, can form verbs: *sapwellimaniki* (to have:EXALTIVE) refers to possessions owned by someone of higher status than the speaker, and *tungoaleniki* refers to ownership by someone of a lower status.

In Puluwat, a language with thirty-five relational classifiers, a possessive verb can be derived *from* each classifier, to refer to 'having' the Possessee (Elbert 1974: 58–9). A reduplicated derivative indicates provisional or temporary ownership and a form with suffix *-ni* (or one of its allomorphs) indicates full or permanent ownership. Consider:

(47) *náy-iy kolaak* (CL:ANIMALS-1sg dog), 'my dog', *lit.* 'my child dog'
nawú-nawú kolaak 'to have or raise a dog' (temporarily)
-nawú-ni kolaak 'to own or keep a dog' (permanently)

(48) *yá-áy rawsis* (CL:GENERAL-1sg trousers) 'my (general) trousers'
yá-á-yá rawsis 'to borrow, wear temporarily, or use trousers'
yá-ni rawsis 'to keep or own trousers'

(49) *wá-áy citosa* (CL:VEHICLE car) 'my car', *lit.* 'my vehicle car'
waa-wa citosa 'to drive or use a car'
waa-ni citosa 'to keep or own a car'

We can see that predicative possessive constructions express distinctions additional to the corresponding noun phrases. Besides having a predicative counterpart for each of the thirty-five options for relational classifiers, predicative possession distinguishes temporary and permanent 'ownership'. Similar distinctions have been described for Manambu (Chapter 4), and Galo (Chapter 7). Hone has two predicative possessive constructions (§3.1 of Chapter 9). One expresses possession as a continuous state. The other one refers to acquiring something.

This comes as no surprise. Predicative expressions tend to reflect time, completion, continuity, and further aspectual features. Time-stability is considered a feature of nouns. This could be the reason for a relative scarcity of examples of permanent versus temporary possession for noun phrases (see §2.4.5).

(III) MARKING PREDICATIVE POSSESSION DEPENDS ON THE POSSESSOR As mentioned in §2.4.1, Possessors are more semantically restricted than Possessees: they tend to be animate or human. In Trio, the temporary possession construction only allows animate Possessors (Carlin 2004: 459–62). In Boumaa Fijian, a Possessor in 'a true possessive construction' has to be human. The same applies to predicative possession. When Dixon 'tried to describe a dog dressed in a coat' saying 'this dog *has* a garment', this was 'firmly corrected' to a construction with the verb 'wear', ' this dog is *wearing* a garment' (Dixon 1988: 129). Dyirbal has two alternative verbless clause constructions for predicative possession. In positive clauses, a human possessor is stated (in possessive form) as a verbless clause subject with the possessee in the function of a verbless clause complement. An inanimate possessor is stated in plain form as a verbless clause subject, while the possessee marked with comitative suffix constitutes the verbless clause complement—see §1 of Chapter 14.

The choice of possessive construction in North-east Ambae (Hyslop 2001: 368–9) depends on the expression of Possessor in a different way: verbless clauses are employed unless the Possessor is expressed with a noun phrase or a free pronoun, 's/he', as in (41): then a Topicalization strategy is used.

3.1.5 *To conclude: semantics and form in possessive predication* Predicative possessive constructions cannot be considered 'poor relatives' of NP possessive structures. On the contrary: some features—such as permanent versus temporary possession—appear to be more salient with predicative than with NP-level possession. This is a corollary of the concept of time-stability generally associated with predication.

Many languages have more than one way of expressing possession within a clause. The following generalizations can be made (based on examinations of numerous grammars, original fieldwork, and also chapters in this volume).

I. If a language has a verb of possession and another construction for predicative possession, the verb is likely to be used with alienably rather than inalienably possessed items. The other construction (that is, a copula or a verbless clause) will be used with other Possessees.
II. A Topicalization strategy is typically restricted to definite Possessee, or topical Possessor.
III. Predicative possessive constructions are sensitive to definiteness and focality of Possessee and Possessor, and to temporality of possession (temporal versus permanent distinction).
IV. Predicative possessive constructions may have additional aspectual distinctions, such as 'owning' something and 'coming into possession', or 'acquiring' (something).
V. If a language has classificatory existential verbs (see Aikhenvald 2003a: 158–9, and §4.1 of Chapter 13), the functionally unmarked verb is likely to be used in a possessive-cum-existential predication. This is the case in Moskona and in Manambu (Chapters 3 and 4). Any of the four classificatory existential verbs can be used in possessive predications in Temboka (examples (13)–(17) in §4.1 of Chapter 13). This points towards the absence of markedness relationships in this language.

The cognitive and cultural grounding for these generalizations is yet to be explored. In §6, we briefly discuss some cultural motivations for the ways in which possession is expressed within noun phrases and in predications.

A word on 'negative possession', or absence of possession. Some languages have inherently negative verbs of 'not having', such as English *lack* or Koyukon *kkelaa* 'gone, missing' used for Possessees of all sorts, both alienable and inalienable. Along similar lines, all predicative possessive constructions in Manambu are negated in the same way. This is also the case in Nêlêmwa (see §6.3 of Chapter 2) and in Nanti (see §4.1 of Chapter 6). The privative derivation is a common way of expressing negative possession in Martuthunira and other Australian languages (§1.6 of Chapter 5). In Arawak languages, such derivation is restricted to obligatorily possessed nouns (§3.1.3). We leave this for a separate investigation.

3.2 *Clausal arguments, and possession*

In numerous languages, the Possessor may be coded as a core grammatical relation—for instance, the direct object or the addressee of the verb. It then gets 'split off' from the Possessee; the two now form two different constituents.

This can be achieved through a variety of means. One involves 'promoting' the Possessor into a core function and 'demoting' the Possessee which is marked as an oblique. This is commonly referred to as 'external possession'—see §3.2.1. Alternatively, the Possessee may be incorporated into the verb, and the Possessor becomes the direct object or the intransitive subject—see §3.2.2. Or a special verbal derivation may signal 'promotion' of the Possessor into a core slot. What do these techniques have in common, and why is the Possessor treated differently from a Possessee? This is the topic of §3.2.4.

3.2.1 *'External' possession* Some languages have a construction whereby the Possessor is treated as a core argument (direct object or the subject) and the Possessee as an oblique. This usually happens if the Possessor and the Possessee are in a whole-part, or kinship relationship, or if there is a close link between them. The possessive noun phrase is closely knit semantically. For the components to be individuated, or foregrounded, the possessive noun phrase has to be 'split'. This technique has come to be called 'external' possession.[15] An alternative term could be 'Possessor separation'.

Consider English. In (50), a possessive NP 'my hand' is in the object slot. In (51), the Possessor, 'me', is the object. 'The hand' is marked as an oblique. The pragmatic effect of the change in marking grammatical relations—from Pr in an NP to the object—is to do with affectedness. 'I' is presented as more affected in (51):

(50) He hit my hand.

(51) He hit me on the hand.

[15] Also known as 'Possessor ascension', 'raising', or 'promotion'. This term is problematic since it implies that Possessor acquires a higher status (see Mithun 2001, for some criticism). A comprehensive study of external possession is in Payne and Barshi (1999). An external possession construction in French is exemplified at the beginning of §6.4 in Chapter 2.

In English, as in many other languages, alternations like the one in (50) and (51) are not available for nouns other than body parts. *He hit my dog* cannot be rephrased as **He hit me on the dog* no matter how much I cherish my dog. Propensity predicates in Galo (§3.7 of Chapter 7) and external Possessor constructions with body parts as Possessees in Likpe (§4.2 of Chapter 10) also set body-part 'possession' apart from relationships of other sorts.

External possession can include close possession—such as, for instance, the clothing one is wearing. (52), from French, is only acceptable if 'she' is wearing the clothing with the sleeve:

(52) Il la tire par la manche
he her:ACC pulls by the sleeve
He pulls her by the sleeve. (her sleeve)

'External possession' may be obligatory, as in Haya, a Bantu language of Eastern Tanzania (also see Heine and Reh 1984: 54–5):

(53) ŋ-ka-hénd' ómwáan'$_O$ ómukôno$_O$
I-PAST-break child arm
I broke the child's arm.

In Hyman's (1977: 101) words, 'failure to promote the Possessor invariably implies that the body part has been previously severed from the whole', as in (54):

(54) ŋ-ka-hénd' ómukôno gw' ómwáan'
I-PAST-break arm of child
I broke the (detached) arm of the child.

Grammaticalized external possession is a further means of setting body parts and whole–part relationships apart from other types of relationships. In Romance and Germanic languages, and in Haya, this is the only place in the grammar where 'inalienability' matters.

External possession constructions occur when the Possessor has to be treated as a separate entity. They imply that the Possessor has been significantly affected. Epps (2008: 229) remarks, that in Hup, 'this external possession strategy appears to be limited strictly to body parts, through which the animate Possessor is directly affected and is thus more relevant or salient than the actual possessed body part itself', as in (55):

(55) ʔám-ăn ʔãh yɔmɔy yók tán-áh
2sg-OBJ 1sg anus stab FUT.CONTR-DYN
I'll stab you in the anus! (*lit.* 'I will anus-stab (to) you)

This can be contrasted with a more conventional strategy in Hup involving an NP as a single constituent, 'where the action of setting fire to the house can only indirectly affect the Possessor, Vulture'.

(56) tɨnɨ̆h mɔ̆y tɨh tuj-d'ak-yaẽ-ay-áh
3sg.POSS house 3sg set.alight-stick.against-FRUST-INCH-DEC
He (Bone-Son) set his (Vulture's) house on fire (in vain).

Focusing on the affectedness of the Pr—or the 'whole' in a whole–part relationship—may be independent from the alienable and inalienable possession classes in NPs. Human body parts are alienably possessed in Hup. Rearrangement of grammatical relations on the clause level is a means of 'breaking up' a close relation between a whole and its part, giving discourse prominence to one of these, and marking its affectedness (also see §3, in Chapter 5). In Manambu (§3.6 of Chapter 4), if the 'Possessor' of a body part or of a kin is particularly affected, the Possessor (and not the body part or the kin term) is cross-referenced on the verb. This agrees with the correlations between type of construction and individuation of the referent outlined in §2.3.3.

3.2.2 *Noun incorporation and possession* In languages with noun incorporation, incorporating the Pe into the verb has an effect similar to that of 'external' possession. This process also typically applies to body parts and whole–part relationships. In Mithun's (2001: 291) words, the construction with incorporation 'is used when the individual translated as the Possessor is considered the most significantly affected participant in an event or state'.

Just like 'external possession', this is a way of splitting the close connection between the Pr and the Pe.[16] In Nadëb, from the same family as Hup, the Pe can be incorporated, and then the Pr acquires a more prominent status (Weir 1990: 323ff). In (57), the Pr is not given any particular prominence:

(57) tʉg ɨ̃ɨ da-tés
tooth 1sgPOSS THEME-hurt
My tooth hurts.

And in (58), the Pr is prominent and affected:

(58) ɨ̃ɨh tʉg=da-tés
I tooth=THEME-hurt
I have a toothache. (*lit.* I tooth hurt)

[16] Possessive incorporation typically applies to possessive noun phrases in the function of a direct object or intransitive subject, in agreement with the general principles of incorporation (Aikhenvald and Dixon 2011). In terms of the typology of noun incorporation, this type of incorporation is known as 'manipulation of case' (Mithun 1984). In most South American languages, only obligatorily possessed nouns can be incorporated. Michael (§4.2.1 of Chapter 6) mentions that only inalienably possessed nouns can be incorporated in Nanti. See the discussion of incorporability of nouns and the function of 'Possessors' in Aikhenvald (2007b, 2012: 132–8).

Rearranging grammatical relations in Pe incorporation and external possession constructions is indicative of a relationship type (typically whole–part and other relations characterized in terms of their proximity between Pr and Pe), rather than of possession classes. Noun incorporation is typically limited to inalienably possessed nouns and especially body part terms. See extensive discussion of body part incorporation, Possessor ascension, and the manipulation of grammatical relations in Nanti in §4.2.1 of Chapter 6, and the discussion of 'grooming' constructions in Nêlêmwa in §6.4 of Chapter 2.

3.2.3 *Verbal derivations and possession* A few languages of the world have a special verbal derivation which encodes a whole–part or another core Possessive relationship. The reversative denominal derivation in Nanti (§4.2.2 of Chapter 6) encodes a whole–part relationship between an argument of the verb and a nominal element within the verb stem. Nanti also has a separative applicative derivation (§4.2.3 of Chapter 6) which indicates that the object introduced by the applicative is the Possessor of the 'demoted' object, and the subject of the verb is involved in the process of 'deprivation' (hence the name 'separative').

Another rare option are possessive applicatives. These are a valency-rearranging device, whereby the verb takes an affix indicating that the Possessor has acquired the status of an object (called 'applied object'). The effect of a possessive applicative is very similar to that of 'Possessor promotion' to a core argument (see §3.2.2, on how this happens in noun incorporation). The marker *-ta-* in Bilua (Obata 2003: 173–6) signals that the Possessor has been particularly affected by the action, and has acquired the status of the direct object. The Pe is backgrounded and acquires the status of an oblique. The derivation applies to possessive constructions which express whole–part relations, and intimate possessions. Possessive applicatives are also a feature of Salish languages (see Gerdts and Kiyosawa 2005, 2007; Mattina 1995; also see Dixon 2012: ch. 25).

3.2.4 *Addressing the imbalance: Possessor and Possessee as clausal arguments* The three techniques which result in rearranging grammatical relations of the Possessor and the Possessee have three features in common.

1 First, they tend to be used if there is a close link between the Pr and the Pe, that is, there may be a need for individuating these two.
2 Secondly, the effect of each of the three techniques is 'splitting' the close relationship between the Pr and the Pe. These no longer form one noun phrase.
3 Thirdly, the Pr becomes a core argument, and the Pe is either 'demoted' to an oblique position, or gets incorporated into the verb. The effect is very similar: the Pr gets individuated, and assigned special prominence, that is foregrounded. The Pe gets backgrounded.

This latter pattern is recurrent across the world's languages. There are no instances of Possessor incorporation, and Possessee's 'promotion' to a core argument. In many languages one can rephrase *I slit the monkey's throat* as *I slit the monkey on the throat* ('external possession') or as *I throat-slit the monkey* (incorporation). But one can never say the equivalent of **I monkey-slit the throat*, nor **I slit throat on the monkey*. Why so?

The likely reason lies in the semantic nature of Possessor. A Possessor tends to occupy a relatively high position on the Nominal hierarchy: a prototypical Possessor is animate, or human, and expressed with a personal pronoun or a proper name (see §2.4.1). It is thus more prone to be higher on the Nominal hierarchy than the Possessee, and thus more likely to be foregrounded and individuated. This is especially the case with body part and whole–part relationships: the whole, and the 'owner' of a body part (Possessor) is likelier to be more prominent than the part itself, which can only exist with respect to the whole.

Discourse backgrounding is a major function of noun incorporation (see Mithun 1984). The Pe is likelier to be backgrounded, and the Pr to be foregrounded—there is thus no need for Pr incorporation, nor for Pe 'promotion' in external possession. The 'ban' on Pr incorporation in the world's languages is reminiscent of the lack of A/Sa incorporation, thus forming a further link between Prs and 'agentive' subjects (see §4).

3.3 *Possessive relationships beyond a clause*

A further means of clausal marking for whole–part relationships typically involves body parts and kinship terms. What is known as the 'double subject' construction in Mandarin Chinese and perhaps many other East Asian languages (Chappell 1996, and §4.2.1 of Chapter 8) essentially involves topicalization of a Possessor. Such a construction would consist of two juxtaposed noun phrases in clause-initial position where 'both have a subject-like role with respect to the verb' (Chappell 1996: 466). The verb is typically stative or intransitive. The first NP typically refers to the whole, and the second to its part. The two may form one intonation unit if the first one is a pronoun.

The construction delineates what Chappell (1996) calls the 'personal domain', covering body part possession and whole–part relationships on the clausal level in Mandarin Chinese (see further discussion in Chappell 1996: 476). This is another way of explicit marking for body part and whole–part relations in a language where this is not expressed at the NP level.

Whole–part or close possession can be expressed in yet another way, by means of RELATIVIZATION on the Possessor. In Manambu, a Possessor can appear as a common argument (CA) in a relative clause only if it is closely associated with the Possessee. This covers kinship relations, body parts, and physical states. That is, 'men whose wives died' is literally 'wife they-died men', 'man whose hand you shook' is 'hand you-shook man', and 'girl whose asthma goes up' is 'asthma it-goes up girl' (see §3.6 in Chapter 4). A similar phenomenon is described for Moskona (§6 of Chapter 3). A similar principle appears to apply in a number of East Asian languages, where Possessor can be relativized on (e.g. Sun and Lin 2009). This requires further study, especially in connection with the problem of prominence of the common argument in relativization (also see §4.3.2 of Chapter 8, on Mandarin Chinese).

External possession, noun incorporation, verbal derivations, 'double subject' constructions, and relativization are deployed in expressing whole–part possession and close possession in general. These are independent of whether alienable and inalienable possession is distinguished anywhere else in the grammar. The existence of such constructions confirms the cross-linguistic validity of the idea of close, or tightly bound, Possessive relationship within the 'personal domain' as opposed to relationships of other sorts.

4 Possessive marking in its further uses

Possessive markers may have additional meanings and extensions, not directly related to possession, nor to ownership (also see Dixon 2010b: 292–3).

A. Possession, purpose, and benefaction are often expressed in a similar way. In a number of Oceanic languages, relational classifiers can be used to express beneficiaries and purpose. Future possession in Macushi, a Carib language, involves the benefactive postposition *ton* e.g. *u-yewî ton* (1sg-house BEN) 'my future house; house for me' (Abbott 1991: 87, and §2.4.5).

In (59), from Kusaiean, an Oceanic language, the generic classifier *la* is first used as a relational classifier, just to mark possession ('Sepe's fish'). It is subsequently used as a marker of beneficiary, 'for' (Lee 1975: 262):[17]

(59) Sohn el mole-lah ik la-l
John 2sgSU buy-ASPECT fish GENL.POSS.CL-3sg.POSS
Sepe ah la-l Sru
Sepe DET GENL.POSS.CL-3sg.POSS Sru
John has bought Sepe's fish for Sru.

In many languages of the world, genitive—the case typically marking Possessor in a possessive construction—and dative—the case marking purpose and beneficiary—share the form. This type of case syncretism is found in many Australian languages (see Dixon 2002: 167). The marker *-gu* covers dative/purposive and also genitive in

[17] Song (1997, 2005) offers a historical scenario of development from classifiers to markers of 'benefaction' in Micronesian languages.

Walmatjarri, Mangarayi, and in Bunuba (see further discussion in Dixon 2010b: 291). In the Western Desert language, the same marker covers purposive and genitive (dative case is expressed differently). The same pronominal forms are used in Berber languages as possessive suffixes on nouns and dative and beneficiary markers on verbs.

The genitive marker in Galo (§2.4.3 of Chapter 7) also marks oblique noun phrases with the meanings of mediative ('means') and viative ('path/way') (also see §4 of Chapter 13 on the polysemy of the genitive in Temboka). The ablative in Galo appears to stem from a combination of the erstwhile locative plus genitive (§2.4.4 of Chapter 7).

B. Possession and the marking of a clausal function. A genitive may have the same form as an oblique case, as in many Indo-European languages, with their 'almost general syncretism between the ablative and the genitive' (Kuryłowicz 1964: 194).

In a number of ergative languages, the genitive marker has the same form as the ergative case (expressing A, transitive subject, a function within a clause). These include Eskimo, Adyghe (a North-west Caucasian language), many Formosan languages (Chia-jung Pan, p.c.) and Ladakhi, a Tibeto-Burman language from India (Koshal 1979: 64-76). Genitive case can mark objects of transitive verbs, in some Indo-European and Balto-Finnic languages, e.g. Estonian. And in Koyukon, the same marker expresses possession and the O and indirect object on the verb (also see Boeder 1968).

Genitive case marks non-canonical subjects (which occur with verbs of perception, volition, and mental processes) in numerous Indo-Aryan, some Dravidian languages and also in Finnish.[18]

Pronominal possessive affixes can mark a variety of clausal functions. In Moskona (§4.2 of Chapter 3) Possessor prefixes mark the subject on verbs. Modifying pronouns which mark possession in Wandala can also express the point of view of the subject if used on verbs (example (3) in §3.2 of Chapter 11). Subject, object, and possessive pronouns have the same form in Kamula (Routamaa 1994: 45, and §3 of Chapter 12). The same set of prefixes marks Possessor on the noun and also the transitive subject (A) and the intransitive active subject (S_a) which is marked the same way as the A throughout Arawak and Arawá languages of South America (see Aikhenvald 2012: 176). The A/S_a markers also mark Possessors across Mayan languages.

In Carib, Tupí-Guaraní, many Tupí and Jê languages, also of South America, the same set of prefixes expresses Possessor on noun, the O and the S_o (the subject of a

[18] See Sands and Campbell (2001: 269–77) on Finnish, Kachru (1990) on Hindi, Arora and Subbarao (2004) on Dakkhini and Konkani.

stative verb) on the verb (see, e.g., Seki 2000: 137–9). A similar pattern is found in Lakota (Allen 1964).

A marker of inalienable possession can double as an exponent of one clausal function, and a marker of alienable possession as an exponent of another one. In Creek and other Muskogean languages the marker of alienable possession has a meaning of 'dative', and the marker of inalienable possession expresses O and S_o (Martin 1993).

Correlations between the type of possessive marking and their clausal functions appear to be language- or family-specific. Just a handful of cases offer a meaningful explanation for a particular pattern.

In Mohawk, an Iroquoian language, the Possessor of inalienably possessed nouns—mostly body parts—has the same form as the subject of active intransitive verbs (S_a), what Mithun (1996) calls 'agent possessor'. The Possessor of alienably possessed nouns has the same form as the object of the verb—'patient possessor'. In Mithun's (1996: 646) words, 'noun roots requiring agent possessors refer to body parts that are identified with their owners', and 'those requiring patient possessors are classified as discrete possessions'. That is, a focus on Possessor of body parts warrants the same marking as the 'agent'. And the focus on the possessed item itself warrants the 'patient' marking.

Nankina, from the Yupna family in New Guinea, has a variety of possessive constructions, whose meanings depend on whether the Possessive relationship is permanent or temporary, whether the possession or the Possessee is in focus, and whether volition of an animate Possessor is involved (Spaulding and Spaulding 1994: 124–8). Active possession emphasizes that 'the possession is due to an act of will of the possessor'. Its marking is the same as that of an agentive and volitional subject in a transitive clause, and that of a 'source' ('from') (Spaulding and Spaulding 1994: 29–33). The semantic link between 'active' Possessor and the 'agent' is straightforward.

It is possible that further work may reveal hitherto unknown principles of semantic motivation for the numerous clausal functions of possessive markers.

C. Possessive marking can express grammatical relations in nominalizations and in subordinate clauses. As we saw in §2.2, the genitive marker in English expresses the subject and the object of nominalizations. (However, the resulting construction is only superficially similar to a possessive noun phrase, since it fails the tests outlined in §2.2.) Within the present volume, the same marking is used in possessive noun phrases and to express arguments of a nominalization in Nêlêmwa (§4 of Chapter 2), Mandarin Chinese (§2.2 of Chapter 8), and also in Likpe (§3.1 of Chapter 10). Genitive case in Galo marks the subject of subordinate clauses of a variety of types (see §2.4.1 of Chapter 7, and Sands and Campbell 2001: 277–9 on genitive subjects in subordinate clauses in Finnish in the context of non-canonically marked arguments).

D. Possessive marking may be associated with definiteness. As Jespersen (1924: 110) puts it, 'an adjunct consisting of a genitive or a possessive pronoun always restricts, though not always to the same extent as the definite article. *My father* and *John's head* are as definite and individualized as possible, because a man can only have one father and one head'. However, in most instances, expressions like *my brother* and *John's hat* 'will be understood as perfectly definite'. A possessive marker within a noun phrase may develop connotations of a marker of definiteness, via extended anaphoric use, as is the case in Yucatec Maya, Permic languages (Komi and Udmurt), and Turkish (Fraurud 2001). Also see Chapters 8 and 9 on the expression of definiteness within possessive constructions in Mandarin Chinese.

E. Possessive marking as exponent of relative clauses. We saw, in §2.2, that possessive-like constructions often cover any type of modification. French *ce diable de fille* 'this devil of a girl' and English *a book of red colour* have the surface appearance of possessive constructions. In many Sinitic languages, the possessive marker *de* appears with a wide variety of modifiers—see §2 of Chapter 8, on Mandarin Chinese. Similarly, in Galo (§2.3.5 of Chapter 7), the genitive marker is used in a variety of associative functions.

The attributive prefix *ka-* in Arawak languages is widely used in possessive derivations (see §3.1.3, and example (38)). The same prefix also denotes a property in general, and is used for deriving agent nominals. In Tariana, *ka-sa-niri* (REL/ATTRIB-spouse-MASC) means 'have a husband', and *ka-inu* (REL/ATTRIB-kill/hunt) means 'hunter, the one who hunts'. This is also a relativization strategy.

The semantics of possessive pronouns in Hone is unusual (see §2.1.3 of Chapter 9): they express reflexive, reciprocal, and mirative meanings. The possessive marker in Chinese (§5.4 of Chapter 8) has developed into a marker of 'previous' aspect, similar to English *have.*

Each of the not-quite-possessive uses of the possessive markers may provide a foundation for reinterpreting a possessive morpheme as an exponent of another category. The erstwhile marker of association can extend to cover possession of all types. The possessive marker *ni* in Taba, an Austronesian language of the South Halmahera area, is used in a wide range of associative meanings, subsuming possession. In other Austronesian languages, such as Fijian, *ni* marks association which is different from possession per se (Bowden 2001: 235; Dixon 1988: 124).[19]

[19] Pathways of grammaticalization of possessive markers are discussed in Heine and Kuteva (2002), Heine (1997a). In a number of Sinitic languages, a classifier (originally accompanying a deictic and a noun) becomes reanalysed as a marker of modification and then as a possessive marker (Tianqiao Lu, p.c.; Pacioni 1997).

5 Possession and language contact

The meanings and the marking of possessive constructions are frequently affected by language contact. In Tariana, the only Arawak language spoken within the multilingual area of the Vaupés River Basin, alienable possession is expressed via juxtaposition of the Pr and the Pe, following the pattern in the genetically unrelated East-Tucanoan languages, spoken in the same area. Retuarã, a Tucanoan language, has developed possessive prefixes, adapting to its Arawak neighbour, Yucuna (Aikhenvald 2002: 80–3).

Possessive constructions in some dialects of Hlai, a Tai-Kadai language spoken in China, have been influenced by Mandarin Chinese. The original Hlai possessive construction consisted of a Possessee followed by the Possessor (60). Under the influence of Chinese, a new possessive construction emerged: the Possessor is followed by the possessive marker *di* (borrowed from Chinese *de*) followed by the Possessee (Ostapirat 2008: 646):

(60) vəŋ^{4} kə^{5} —an original Hlai construction
clothes I
my clothes

(61) kə^{5} di^{2} vəŋ^{4} —an innovative construction influenced by Chinese
I POSS.MARKER clothes
my clothes

According to Klamer, Reesink, and van Staden (2008: 123), the order Pr–Pe has spread from non-Austronesian to Austronesian languages of the East Nusantara area of the Moluccas.[20]

The composition of a possession class can be affected by the dominant language. The expansion of analytic marking of kinship possession in Moskona (compared to related languages) may be attributed to contact with Malay traders (§7 of Chapter 3). Juxtaposition as a strategy for marking kinship possession in Likpe may have been influenced by Ewe, a dominant language (§5 of Chapter 10).

Many speakers of Modern Lakota (Ullrich 2008: 776) converse in English most of the time. Following the English pattern, speakers are using analytic possessive constructions—traditionally used for alienable possession—to also include inalienably possessed items, such as body part and kinship terms. Along similar lines, at the

[20] The history of possessive marking in Austronesian languages is a matter of some dispute (see Blust 2009). A distinction between alienable and inalienable possession is believed to have developed in Proto-Eastern-Malayo-Polynesian as a result of non-Austronesian substratum (van den Berg 2009). The order in possessive constructions is an areal feature in the Caucasian Sprachbund (Chirikba 2008: 41).

Patterns absent from most languages in a contact situation tend to become obsolete. The unpossessed forms of nouns and possessive nominal suffixes are a feature of most Arawak languages, but not of Tucanoan. They are almost completely gone from Tariana (see Aikhenvald 2003b: 128).

time of Schmidt's fieldwork (Schmidt 1985: 60–1), younger members of the Dyirbal-speaking community were using the construction with alienable possession for items which had traditionally been treated as inalienably possessed. In the late 1980s, Bessy Jerry and Andy Denham, erstwhile speakers of traditional Dyirbal, had no one but the younger generation to speak the language to. They 'modified their grammar towards that in general use among younger members of the community', expanding the use of the construction with alienable possession (Dixon 1991: 199–200).

If one language in a family has classifiers in possessive constructions, and others do not, language contact may be the reason for this. A number of nouns in Palikur require a generic classifier (see Table 1.4). This principle, alien to most Arawak languages, is prominent in Carib languages, with whom the Palikur used to be in contact. Possessive classifiers in Tariana noun phrases mirror the patterns in East-Tucanoan languages (Aikhenvald 2002: 81). Possessive classifiers in Sinitic languages are restricted to Cantonese and other Yue dialects. Their similarities to possessive classifiers in Hmong and other Miao-Yao languages suggest a Miao-Yao influence (Matthews 2007: 231).

Possession within a clause can be equally affected by contact (see Heine 1997a). The Tariana verb *-de* 'have' follows the same patterns of use as the verb 'have' *kió*, in the neighbouring Tucano.[21] Transitive uses of *káa-* 'be (there), have' in Galo (§3.3 of Chapter 7) could be a relatively new development, under the influence of neighbouring Indo-European languages. Copula constructions and a positional verb in possessive clauses in Hone bears an impact of the now dominant and unrelated Hausa (§3.1 of Chapter 9). The verb 'see' in Likpe may have acquired a possessive meaning 'come to have something' as a result of Ewe influence (§5 of Chapter 10).

Possession is so susceptible to the impact of language—and culture—contact for the following reason. The expression of possession often reflects cultural conventions and relationships within a society (in the spirit of Aikhenvald 2006). Once societies and their languages come into contact, the most relevant possessive relationships have to adjust to the new cultural environment. This takes us to the next section.

6 Possession in grammar and society

Some linguistic features are plainly more susceptible to reflecting societal structures and practices than others. Language planning, political correctness, and societal changes play a role in shaping up gender and classifier systems (see Aikhenvald 2003a and references there). Imperatives and commands reflect social hierarchies.

[21] See Heine and Kuteva (2005), on shared grammaticalization patterns in possessive structures worldwide, and Heine and Kuteva (2006) on shared possessive structures in the languages of Europe as a linguistic area. Patterns of 'split possession' in the languages of Europe are remarkably similar (Stolz et al. 2008).

Meanings encoded within possessive structures often reflect the relationships within a society, and change if the society changes.

The wealth of possessive constructions and their many meanings in Moskona coincide with 'both the values and activities integral to a strong sense of private ownership and focus on possession' in the Moskona society (§8 of Chapter 3). Galo society is very different: the concept of ownership is much less robust (§4 of Chapter 7). And the Galo language has special structures for possessive predications, but no dedicated possessive noun phrase. The wealth of possessive verbs in Mandarin Chinese (Chapter 8) reflects the varied ways in which objects can be owned. This highlights the importance of ownership in the Mandarin society.

Not every language displays such striking correlations between cultural patterns and their linguistic expression. But their existence highlights the importance of a cultural anthropological vantage point in linguistic analysis.

6.1 *How possessive structures can reflect relationships, values, and concepts*

Classificatory kinship relationship is the backbone of many traditional societies. This is reflected in special kinship possession. Puluwat has a set of possessive classifiers for classificatory siblings and for parents.[22] The on-going changes in the kinship system are reflected in the classifier use (Elbert 1974: 61–3). Particularly close kinship relationships ('dear kin') acquire special encoding in Martuthunira (§5 of Chapter 5).

Relational classifiers in Pohnpeian transparently reflect power relationships and social positions within the society (Keating 1997, 1998). These classifiers distinguish three registers. The common register is unmarked for social status, while the exaltive register reflects the special high status of the Possessor. The humiliative register reflects the opposite: that the Possessor is of a low status (see Table 1.3). In order to use and understand the system correctly, one has to have a good grasp of how the Pohnpeian society is organized. In other words, a linguist has to be somewhat of an anthropologist.

The conceptual link between possession and social status may be manifested through a shift from common speech to honorific register. In Pohnpeian ideology, the spiritual power *manaman* resides in high-status persons and is transferred to their possessions (Keating 1998: 100–15). Similarly, in Javanese, intimate possessions of high-status individuals are marked in the honorific language, just like the individuals themselves (Errington 1988: 165–6). Possession and ownership are directly linked to power and dominance.

The omission of a possessive marker with the first person singular Possessor in Mandarin Chinese (§5.5 of Chapter 8) is a way of emphasizing the personal authority

[22] In many small societies, there is an algorithm for determining how each person is related to everyone else in the community, e.g. mother's sister's children and father's brother's children are classified in the same way as true siblings.

of a high-ranking individual. Once again, the expression of possession reflects one's position in the society.

The connection between ownership and power may be reflected in the etymology of verbs of ownership. In Slavic and Baltic languages, 'to own' has the same origin as a verb meaning 'to master, to dominate' (Vasmer 1976: 218; Gamkrelidze and Ivanov 1984: 752, 938).

The Modern English usage of the verb 'own' points in a similar direction. According to the *Oxford English Dictionary* (2010 edition), this verb implies 'control over or direction of (a person or thing)'. The 'owner of the debate' is the one who directs it, and the 'owner of the fight' is its initiator. That 'possession' is associated with an all-encompassing control is reflected in notions such as 'spirit possession' (see Behrend and Luig 1999): a spirit or some other external presence inhabiting, controlling, and 'owning' the body and the mind of the 'possessed'.[23]

An association between kinship relations, ownership, and control is reflected in additional overtones of kinship terms. The same word can mean 'father' and 'owner', as in Tariana *yarusi haniri* (goods father), Tucano *apeká paki* (goods father) 'rich man, literally father of goods' and Tok Pisin *papa bilong graun* (father of land) 'owner of the land'. This term has been recently introduced into Kamula as *taena y'a* (literally 'the land's father'), to translate the new concept of 'landowner' (see §5 of Chapter 12). This is reminiscent of how in Wandala (§4.4 of Chapter 11) the terms for 'older brother' and for 'father' can mean 'boss' if they occur within a pertensive possession construction (and not within a relational modification construction typical for kinship terms). This may reflect a social hierarchy conceptualized through kinship relations.

The semantic composition of possession classes often reflects cultural conceptualization of individual objects, and the value attached to them. Important items—such as 'house', 'canoe', 'name'—are often treated as inalienably possessed, that is, intrinsically linked to the Possessor (see §2.1). Numerous Oceanic languages have a special relational classifier for 'valuable' possessions. Some Fijian dialects have a classifier for an object to be contributed as a customary obligation, and others a classifier for totems (§2.5.1). A cross-linguistic study of classifiers of different types has shown that 'value' is a primary semantic feature only of relational classifiers (Aikhenvald 2003a: 294). Genders and other kinds of classification can have value as an extension, but hardly ever as a primary meaning.

In Trio (Carlin 2004: 476), a possessive construction cannot be used in the meaning of 'having an illness'. This is to do with the conceptualization of an all-encompassing disease which has greater powers than a Possessor would: a malaria

[23] This connection is reminiscent of the link between possession and location, as suggested by Lyons (1977: 473). In Keating's (1998: 101) words, 'a linkage between possessive constructions and location points again to the spatial domain as a salient site for constructing social asymmetry'.

'takes/grabs' someone, 'after which that person is "inside" the illness which surrounds him or her'. The same applies to Moskona where illnesses are considered as non-volitional entities which uncontrollably affect people (see §4.1.2 of Chapter 3).

The 'identification' construction in Manambu is employed in talking about totemic 'possession' of items and names owned by each subclan. They are frequent in name debates which restate the subclan's rights to 'name ownership' (§5 of Chapter 4). Such usage reflects the underlying conceptualization of oneself, one's clan, one's totems, and the corresponding names as being one entity. This is an example of an almost perfect correspondence between the cultural conceptualization of a relationship and its linguistic expression.

6.2 *How possessive constructions can reflect cultural changes*

Newly acquired cultural practices may affect the composition of possession classes. In Dakota (Boas and Deloria 1941: 128), 'animals including the dog but excepting the horse' used to belong to the class of 'unpossessable' nouns: they could not take possessive prefixes. But 'at present the cattle on large ranches are considered as property and not as food. Therefore they are expressed as separable property by the prefix *t'a*.' A newly introduced practice of having cattle on a ranch as property has affected possessive marking in the language.

In West Greenlandic, the scope of the temporary possession marker *-ut(i)* 'appears to have been extended in use in recent years to include the notion of legal ownership (or other forms of formally or tacitly recognized possession). These new forms of ownership are said to cover houses and girlfriends (Fortescue 1984: 172). The newly introduced concepts of land ownership in the Temboka society may, in the future, acquire special linguistic expression (Chapter 13). This is already happening among the Kamula (Chapter 12).

The possessive classifier for 'canoe' in Puluwat now subsumes a car and a scooter. The classifier *na-* (from the noun 'child') was traditionally used for junior persons and small objects. This is now extended to a great many small foreign objects (money, pencils, knives, and shoes). Such extension of classifiers in Puluwat is accompanied by 'leveling of distinctions in the form of increasing use' of general classifiers, to replace specific ones (Elbert 1974: 62).

6.3 *Essential possessions and their linguistic correlates*

Some possessable items, and some Possessive relationships, are more salient than others. The 'unmarked' Possessee is the one which is most obvious, and most essential to one's livelihood. Ullrich (2008: 505) remarks that in Lakota, 'when talking about horses speakers often used only the possessive pronoun'. In Tariana, *nu-yarupe* 'my thing' is immediately understood as referring to 'my language', and has to be specified further if it refers to something else. In the linguistic area of the Vaupés

River Basin where Tariana is spoken, language is the most important badge of people's identity, and also the basis for marriage patterns. No wonder that 'language' turns out to be the most obvious possession.[24]

Possessive markers and status in possession may relate to some of the 'typical' possessions. The humiliative general classifier *tungoal* in Pohnpeian is transparently related to low-status food and low-status eating. This reflects a recurrent connection between low-status possession and consumption—food or eating (Keating 1997: 261–2); people of low status are being construed as analogous to food.

In contrast, the honorific classifier *sapwellime* consists of *sahpw* 'land' and the honorific form *lime* 'hand/arm'. That is, 'most possessions of chiefs or chieftesses are categorized through this classifier as having some of the same attributes as "land" and "hand"' (Keating 1997: 263)—reflecting the importance of land tenure for chiefs and chieftesses. Land is conceived of as the source of nourishment. And if high status is associated with 'generativity' (Keating's term) in terms of food production, then low status is associated with food itself and its consumption. In Keating's words, 'the two constructed domains of low- and high-status possession, *sapwellime* and *tungoal*, can also be seen in terms of a model of distribution vs. consumption, with the chief as the archetypical agent (or energy source, i.e. land) and the lower-status people as the archetypical patient (consuming or receiving energy)' (1997: 265).

This is the essence of a metaphorical connection between the expression of possession, and especially relational classifiers, and the conceptualization of environment—that is, possession and ownership of food and of land.

We can recall that in the traditional Dakota, natural objects—including land—could not be used in a possessive construction (§2.4.4). This reflects a traditional hunter-and-gatherer lifestyle of the nomadic Siouan peoples for whom planting would be considered an insult to the mother-earth (David Rood, p.c.).

Traditionally, land was not considered 'ownable' among the Nanti (similarly to the Baniwa of Içana, also Arawak). As a result of encounter with Western concepts of land ownership through contact with the Matsigenka, who are much more exposed to Western influence, the Nanti started talking about land ownership. The word for 'land' is now used in a possessive construction (§6 of Chapter 6).

The notion of possession—including that of land—in the Western tradition is linked to control and power. The *Oxford English Dictionary* defines possession as 'the action or fact of holding something (material or immaterial) as one's own or in one's control', and 'the state or condition of being so held'. In legal language, possession involves 'visible power or control as distinct from lawful ownership', and specifically,

[24] A similar principle appears to apply to Tucano, from the same multilingual area of the Vaupés River Basin (Ramirez 1997: 284). Further issues to investigate involve connections between possession and taboo. In Tariana *duite* 'hers (animate)' is a conventional way of referring to a woman's vagina (so as to avoid the tabooed lexical item).

'exclusive control of land'. The patterns of land ownership among the Temboka appear to be integrated into their discourse (Chapter 13). The property claims among the Kamula have been extended beyond land to further 'new valuables' (logs, oil, winds, pollution, and carbon), through identification with unseen spirits, the powerful owners of new riches (Chapter 12). Further discussion of what possession, and ownership, may imply, is in §3 of Chapter 14.

The relationship between land, peoples, and languages among many Aboriginal groups in Central and Northern Australia is defined differently. In Rumsey's (1993: 200, 204) words,

> Languages, or even mixtures of them, are directly placed in the landscape by the founding acts of Dreamtime heroes. From that point on, the relation between language and territory is a necessary rather than a contingent one. People too, or their immortal souls, are similarly grounded in the landscape, in the form of spirit children (or 'conception spirits') associated with specific sites, and via links through their parents to more extensive regions. But the languages were already placed in those regions before any people came on the scene. The links between people and languages are secondary links, established through the grounding of both in the landscape.

Language 'ownership' is part of the same package: 'Jawoyn people are Jawoyn not because they speak Jawoyn, but because they are linked to places to which Jawoyn is also linked'. This is rather unlike the Western association between territory and language as 'a contingent one, subject to change as one people conquers or assimilates another'.

As Walsh (2002: 233) put it, the distinctive features of language ownership are, for indigenous Australian groups, 'birthright; rule-governed; permanent; non-voluntary; linkage between a language and its territory; the lack of necessity for language knowledge'. That is, in one current view of Aboriginal language ownership, one does not have to be a 'language user' to maintain their status as 'language owner'. However, this aspect is undoubtedly an artefact of the rampant language loss in colonial times. Many Aboriginal groups have lost the knowledge of their languages, and are now in the process of redefining themselves and their concepts to justify this gap.

This attitude to language is markedly different from that among the groups of the multilingual Vaupés River Basin area where languages are still vibrant. One's father's language is a badge of one's identity. But unless one speaks it, and speaks it perfectly, one is destitute; to be a proper language owner one also has to be its competent user. Just like in Aboriginal Australia, not all users are owners: it is inappropriate to refer to a language other than that of one's father as one's own language. One can never be an authority on the language which is not one's own, no matter how well one speaks it. Each language is intrinsically linked to the land where one's ancestors had dwelt or moved through. This is a permanent, non-controllable link, obtained by birthright.

But once you lose competence in your father's language, you have lost it all (see Aikhenvald 2002, on identity issues for those who in fact had lost their father's languages; similar attitude is found among some Australian groups).[25]

The focus is on belonging and ultimate identification with land, and subsequently with language, rather than with a 'controllable' possession. This is similar to totemic 'ownership' of various areas and parts of the world and the universe by Manambu clan groups. The clan group whose totemic areas extend to the east, and include the east wind, counts Australia within its totemic 'boundaries' (expressed with identification construction: §5 in Chapter 4). But this is not controlled ownership—rather, a spiritual association and identification (reminiscent of the ownership of wind, logs, oil, and other new valuables by the Kamula and their spirits, in Chapter 12). In §3.1 of Chapter 14, Dixon addresses the ways in which Western concepts of possession, ownership, and control of language, and of land, override the indigenous notions, resulting in a culture clash and the deterioration of original concepts.

7 Possession and ownership: what can we conclude?

Every language has a way for expressing possession within a noun phrase. This can be expressed by apposing Pr and Pe, attaching a marker to the Pr, or to the Pe, or to both. The core meanings of possessive constructions include ownership, whole–part, and kinship relationships. Each of these can be marked differently, creating the basis for distinct possession classes. There may be a dedicated possessive noun phrase, or a more general phrase expressing modification and a plethora of further meanings, including association, material, quantification, and more. Possessive and non-possessive meanings can often be disambiguated through paraphrases with possessive predications.

Possessive constructions vary depending on the nature of the Possessor (Pr), the Possessee (Pe), and the Possessive relationship. Not uncommonly, those constructions which involve a close link between Pe and their Pr (typically, whole–part relations and body parts) are marked differently from others. This distinction is known as that of inalienable versus alienable possession. The marking of two kinds of Possessive relationship tends to follow the principle of iconicity in linguistic expression. Possession by Speech Act Participants ('me' or 'you and me') may be expressed through special, fused forms.

In some languages, inalienably possessed nouns have to take a special set of affixes, in order to be used without a Possessor. The semantic content of alienable and

[25] R. M. W. Dixon, p.c.; Rumsey (2010: 137–8) mistakenly analyses this identification with father's language among the Indians of the Vaupés area as 'language ownership'. Further issues of language as identity badge in the Vaupés area are discussed by Aikhenvald (2002), based on first-hand fieldwork.

inalienable possession varies. The same noun can be used in different constructions, as a way of highlighting its different aspects without multiplying vocabulary.

POSSESSION CLASSES can be viewed as a means of categorizing nouns. Further such means involve RELATIONAL CLASSIFIERS, often, but not always, restricted to constructions with alienable possession. They categorize the relationship between the Pr and the Pe, and also the ways in which the Pe can be manipulated by the Pr (e.g. 'eaten', 'drunk', 'worn', 'valued'). POSSESSIVE CLASSIFIERS categorize the Pe, either in terms of its generic nature, or in terms of its animacy, shape, and other inherent properties.

POSSESSIVE RELATIONSHIPS can be further categorized in terms of their controllability, permanency (or time-stability), and time of possession (present, past, or future). The marking in possessive constructions can also depend on the focus on its three components—Pe, Pr, and the relationship itself.

While there is often a generic noun phrase subsuming possession, there is hardly ever a generic predicative construction which subsumes possession as one of its aspects.

Expressing possession WITHIN A CLAUSE involves establishing a Possessive relationship, that is, a possessive predication—shown in verbs of ownership, copula constructions, and verbless clauses, and possessive derivations. In those languages where several predicative possessive constructions are available, verbs of ownership tend to express less permanent and less close relationships than copula and verbless clauses. Verbless clauses tend to express relationships of identification and inclusion between Pr and Pe. Other parameters relevant for predicative possession include definiteness and topicality of Possessor and Possessee, and inchoative and stative aspects.

Possessive relationships can also be expressed by MANIPULATING CLAUSAL ARGUMENTS, 'splitting' the possessive noun phrase. Then, the Pr within a noun phrase becomes the core argument (the object) of the verb (this is often referred to as 'Possessor raising' or 'promotion'), and the Pe becomes an oblique. The typical effect is that of individuating and foregrounding the Pr.

Another way of achieving a similar effect on the Pr is by incorporating the Pe into the verb. In most languages, manipulating possessive constructions as clausal arguments is only available for close Possessive relationships—normally including body parts, other whole–part and kinship possession, as a way of individuating and foregrounding the Pr and backgrounding the Pe. The reason why the Pr tends to be foregrounded and the Pe tends to be backgrounded lies in the cross-linguistic tendencies in Pr's semantics: Pr tends to be animate or human, or otherwise high-ranking on the Nominal Hierarchy. Just a few languages have verbal derivations (e.g. possessive applicatives) operating on a similar principle.

External possession, possessive incorporation, possessive applicatives, topicalization ('double subject') constructions, and constraints on relativization on the

Pr apply to close Possessive relationships (often just whole–part). These reflect universal semantic features.

Possessive markers may have ADDITIONAL FUNCTIONS in the grammar. Possessors and beneficiaries are often marked in the same way. In some languages, possessive markers also express the A (transitive subject), in others they are the same as the O (object marker). In just a few cases, a semantic motivation can be provided: volitional Possessors in Nankina, from Papua New Guinea, are marked in the same way as subjects, and non-volitional Possessors are not (see B in §4).

Possessive meanings, and possessive structures are highly DIFFUSIBLE in language contact situations. One reason for this lies in a strong correlation between possessive concepts and societal and cultural concepts and conventions. Possessive patterns may reflect people's lifestyles. Culturally important items—such as 'house', 'knife', 'canoe' in a society of river-dwellers or sea-farers—are treated as closely, or 'inalienably' possessed. Relational classifiers often reflect kinship relationships, and societal structure and values.

Power relationships and status can be marked in relational classifier constructions, as is the case in Pohnpei. Using different possessive constructions may reflect different, culturally anchored, types of ownership, with distinct structures used for talking about totemic and symbolic ownership and ownership of something concrete.

Possession and ownership is often identified with POWER, CONTROL, and AUTHORITY. As the society changes, new, formerly 'unownable', objects become a matter of property. Land ownership in Nanti is a case in point. The composition of possession classes changes, following new societal conventions.

8 About this volume

This volume aims at a cross-linguistic account of the gamut of possessive structures (covering noun phrase, predication, and going beyond the clause) in terms of the parameters and issues outlined in the present chapter.

We start, in Chapter 2, with Isabelle Bril's analysis of a highly complex system of expressing ownership, possession, kinship, and whole–part relations (including the use of possessive classifiers) in Nêlêmwa, an Oceanic language from New Caledonia. Chapters 3 and 4 address patterns of marking possession in two languages spoken on the island of New Guinea. Gloria Gravelle describes Moskona, from East Bird's Head in Indonesian Papua, with its intricate array of synthetic and analytic possession depending on the meanings of the possessee, and unusual distinctions in possessive predications. Manambu, a Ndu language from the Sepik area of the former German New Guinea, described by Alexandra Aikhenvald, has numerous possessive constructions. There are special ways of expressing culturally important non-material possessions—such as names. Possession in Martuthunira, from the Pilbara region of Western Australia, is discussed by Alan Dench (Chapter 5). This language, now extinct, has a wealth of possessive structures. They reflect the importance of kinship relationships, the backbone of the Martuthunira society.

We then turn to other parts of the world. Possession in Nanti, one of the least known Arawak languages from a remote part of Peru, is discussed by Lev Michael (Chapter 6), in the context of other Arawak languages, and the cultural changes the formerly isolated Nanti are now facing. In Chapter 7, 'Possession and association in Galo language and culture', Mark Post analyses the expression of possession and its cultural counterparts in this Tibeto-Burman language.

Chapter 8, by Yongxian Luo, focuses on possession in Mandarin Chinese. A noun phrase with the enclitic *de* expresses a variety of meanings, including possession, association, attributes, time, location, and orientation. Its omission correlates with the meanings of the noun phrase. Mandarin Chinese has a wide range of possessive verbs. Possessive relationships are also realized through manipulation of clausal arguments.

We then turn to the African continent. In Chapter 9, Anne Storch addresses possession in Hone, a Jukunoid language from Nigeria. Here, possession in the noun phrase reflects the erstwhile matrilineal society (now almost gone). Possessive predication is different in meanings, and in form, from that within a noun phrase. Possession in Likpe, a Kwa language from Ghana, is discussed by Felix Ameka (Chapter 10). Just like its many relatives, the language has a general associative noun phrase also employed for possession. Within a predication, possession, location, and existence overlap in their marking. This is similar to the patterns disclosed by Zygmunt Frajzyngier (Chapter 11) in Wandala, a Chadic language from Cameroon and Nigeria.

It is important to investigate correlations between linguistic expression of possessive structures of all sorts and the conceptualization of ownership, alongside the impact of societal changes on the ways in which possession is expressed. Each of Chapters 2–11 address the ways in which linguistic form may reflect the cultural patterns, the attitudes to possession, and the impact of change. Chapters 12 and 13 stand apart from the rest: they focus on indigenous conceptualization of ownership and the ways in which this understanding evolves in the modern world. Both are written by eminent anthropologists, and provide an additional perspective on ownership.

Chapter 12 by Michael Wood, 'Spirits of the forest, the wind, and the new wealth: defining some of the possibilities, and limits, of Kamula possession', offers a snapshot of Melanesian understanding of what can be possessed, and by whom. He then discusses the ownership of land, spirits, and newly introduced valuables—oil, logs, carbon, and winds—in connection with the 'imaginative possibilities of spirits', many of them unseen. The fusion of the spirits with the commodified natural resources defines the current Kamula discourse about what they do, and what they do not, possess. In contrast to other Melanesian groups (including the Manambu of the

Sepik), the Kamula property claims go beyond social relationships construed as those of identification. They are defined by exclusionary relations with powerful Others—including the spirits. The concept of alienation and Otherness in possession opens a yet unexplored avenue for rethinking the issues of close and alienable possession. The concepts of new wealth and the new ways for talking about these hold a clue for our understanding of how possession and culture correlate, and how they are being talked about.

Temboka speakers live in the Western Highlands of Papua New Guinea. Chapter 13, by Rosita Henry, 'Being and belonging: exchange, value, and land ownership in the Western Highlands of Papua New Guinea', offers a case study of newly developing issues to do with state-based legal concepts of land ownership and customary law concerning land among a group of Temboka speakers. The traditional attitude to the land as an 'ultimate gift' and its conceptualization as inalienable and inclusive property remains, and survives. Through the absorption of new laws and new transactions, land value is now transformed into 'the value of place as a form of sociality, imbued with social relations'. This further reinforces the links between possession and societal values (see §6). Even more importantly, it highlights the importance of a notion of inalienability in the Temboka conceptualization of possessions. (The language itself does not have a grammatically marked alienability distinction.)

In the final chapter, R. M. W. Dixon offers further remarks on two issues not covered in this chapter. He addresses comitative and privative used for predicative possession, with a special focus on Australian languages, especially Dyirbal. He then goes on to discuss the problem of what can be the head in an appositional construction with inalienable possession. Dyirbal and Jarawara (an Arawá language from southern Amazonia)—whose data are based on Dixon's extensive fieldwork—are prime examples of how the Possessor can be the head of such a construction, and what tests can be employed to demonstrate this. What can be possessed, and owned in different cultures, Western and non-Western? This is the topic of §3 of Chapter 14; Dixon explores the nature of connection and association with 'name', 'language', and 'land' pervasive among indigenous people, and distorted by their forced integration into the realm of Western values, and Western goods. Expression of possession becomes a matter of politics, and policies. Social and linguistic issues become intertwined.

For a typological collection, this volume is unusual. We go beyond addressing purely linguistic structures, in our attempt to marry linguistic concepts with ideas embedded in anthropological research. In Ameka's words (§1 of Chapter 10), this is crucial 'for the exploration of the reflexive relation between language, culture, and modes of thinking and in particular of the ways in which culture and cognition are encoded in grammar'. May this be a fruitful start for an evolving partnership!

References

Abbott, M. 1991. 'Macushi', pp. 23–160 of *Handbook of Amazonian languages*, Vol 3, edited by D. C. Derbyshire and G. K. Pullum. Berlin: Mouton de Gruyter.

Aikhenvald, Alexandra Y. 1995. 'Person-marking and discourse in North-Arawak languages', *Studia Linguistica* 49: 152–95.

——. 1998. 'Warekena', pp. 215–439 of *Handbook of Amazonian languages*, Vol. 4, edited by Desmond C. Derbyshire and Geoffrey K. Pullum. Berlin: Mouton de Gruyter.

——. 1999. 'The Arawak language family', pp. 65–105 of *The Amazonian languages*, edited by R. M. W. Dixon and Alexandra Y. Aikhenvald. Cambridge: Cambridge University Press.

——. 2002. *Language contact in Amazonia*. Oxford: Oxford University Press.

——. 2003a. *Classifiers: A typology of noun categorization devices*. Oxford: Oxford University Press.

——. 2003b. *A grammar of Tariana, from northwest Amazonia*. Cambridge: Cambridge University Press.

——. 2006. 'Grammars in contact: A cross-linguistic perspective', pp. 1–66 of *Grammars in contact: A cross-linguistic typology*, edited by A. Y. Aikhenvald and R. M. W. Dixon. Oxford: Oxford University Press.

——. 2007a. 'Classifiers in multiple environments: Baniwa of Içana/Kurripako: A North Arawak perspective', *International Journal of American Linguistics* 27: 475–500.

——. 2007b. 'Typological dimensions in word formation', pp. 1–65 of *Language typology and syntactic description*, Vol. 3, edited by T. Shopen. Cambridge: Cambridge University Press.

——. 2011. 'Word-class changing derivations in typological perspective', pp. 221–89 of *Language at large. Essays in semantics and syntax*, by Alexandra Y. Aikhenvald and R. M. W. Dixon. Leiden: Brill.

——. 2012. *Languages of the Amazon*. Oxford: Oxford University Press.

—— and R. M. W. Dixon. 2011. 'Explaining associations between intransitive subject (S) and transitive object (O)', pp. 143–69 of *Language at large. Essays in semantics and syntax*, by Alexandra Y. Aikhenvald and R. M. W. Dixon. Leiden: Brill.

—— and Diana Green. 1998. 'Palikur and the typology of classifiers', *Anthropological Linguistics*, 40: 429–80.

Allen, W. Sidney. 1964. 'Transitivity and possession', *Language* 40: 337–43.

Ameka, Felix. 1996. 'Body parts in Ewe grammar', pp. 783–840 of Chappell and McGregor (eds).

Arora, Harbir Kaur and Karumuri Venkata Subbarao. 2004. 'Syntactic change and convergence', pp. 25–47 of Bhaskarao and Subbarao (eds), Vol. 1.

Bally, Charles. 1996. 'The expression of concepts of the personal domain and indivisibiliy in Indo-European languages', pp. 31–61 of Chappell and McGregor (eds).

Baron, Irene, Michael Herslund, and Finn Sørensen (eds.). 2001. *Dimensions of possession*. Amsterdam: John Benjamins.

Behrend, Heike and Ute Luig. 1999. 'Introduction', pp. xiii–xxii of *Spirit possession. Modernity and power in Africa*, edited by Heike Behrend and Ute Luig. Oxford: James Currey.

Bhaskarao, Peri and Karumuri Venkata Subbarao. 2004. *Non-nominative subjects*, Vols 1 and 2. Amsterdam: John Benjamins.

Bisang, W. 1993. 'Classifiers, quantifiers and class nouns in Hmong', *Studies in Language* 17: 1–51.

Blust, Robert. 2009. *The Austronesian languages.* Canberra: Pacific Linguistics.

Boas, Franz. 1911. 'Tsimshian', pp. 283–422 of *Handbook of American Indian languages,* Part 1. (Smithsonian Institution, Bureau of American Ethnology, Bulletin 40). Washington, DC: Government Printing Office.

—— and Ella Deloria. 1941. *Dakota grammar.* Washington, DC: US Government Printing Office.

Boeder, Winfried. 1968. 'Transitivität und Possessivität', pp. 179–209 of *Festschrift Wilhelm Giese. Beiträge zur Romanistik und allgemeinen Sprachwissenschaft.* Hamburg.

Bowden, John. 2001. *Taba: Description of a South Halmahera language.* Canberra: Pacific Linguistics.

Brownie, John and Marjo Brownie. 2007. *Mussau Grammar essentials.* Ukarumpa: SIL-PNG Academic Publications.

Carlin, Eithne B. 2004. *A grammar of Trio, a Cariban language of Suriname.* Frankfurt am Main: Peter Lang.

Carlson, R. and D. Payne. 1989. 'Genitive classifiers', pp. 89–119 of *Proceedings of the 4th Annual Pacific Linguistics Conference.* Eugene: University of Oregon.

Chapman, S. and D. Derbyshire. 1991. 'Paumari', pp. 161–354 of *Handbook of Amazonian languages,* Vol. 3, edited by Desmond C. Derbyshire and Geoffrey K. Pullum. Berlin: Mouton de Gruyter.

Chappell, Hilary. 1996. 'Inalienability and the personal domain in Mandarin Chinese discourse', pp. 465–527 of Chappell and McGregor (eds).

—— and William McGregor (eds). 1996. *The Grammar of Inalienability. A typological perspective on body part terms and the whole-part relation.* Berlin: Mouton de Gruyter.

Chirikba, Viacheslav A. 2008. 'The problem of the Caucasian Sprachbund', pp. 25–93 of *From linguistic areas to areal linguistics,* edited by Pieter Muysken. Amsterdam: John Benjamins.

Churchward, C. M. 1953. *Tongan grammar.* London: Oxford University Press.

Clarke, Eve. 1978. 'Locationals: Existential, locative, and possessive constructions', pp. 85–126 of *Universals of human language,* Vol. 4, edited by Joseph H. Greenberg, Charles A. Ferguson, and Edith A. Moravcsik. Stanford: Stanford University Press.

Corominas, Joan. 1961. *Breve diccionario etimologico de la lengua castellana.* Madrid: Editorial Gredos.

Curnow, Timothy Jowan. 1997. 'A grammar of Awa Pit (Cuaiquier): An indigenous language of South-western Colombia'. Ph.D. dissertation, Australian National University.

Derbyshire, D. C. 1985. *Hixkaryana and linguistic typology.* Texas: Summer Institute of Linguistics and the University of Texas at Arlington.

——. 1999. 'Carib', pp. 23–64 of Dixon and Aikhenvald (eds).

Dixon, R. M. W. 1972. *The Dyirbal language of North Queensland.* Cambridge: Cambridge University Press.

——. 1988. *A grammar of Boumaa Fijian.* Chicago: University of Chicago Press.

——. 1991. 'A changing language situation: The decline of Dyirbal, 1963–1989', *Language in Society* 20: 183–200.

——. 1994. *Ergativity*. Cambridge: Cambridge University Press.
——. 2000. 'Categories of the noun phrase in Jarawara', *Journal of Linguistics* 36: 487–510.
——. 2002. *Australian languages: Their nature and development*. Cambridge: Cambridge University Press.
——. 2004. *The Jarawara language of southern Amazonia*. Oxford: Oxford University Press.
——. 2010a. *Basic linguistic theory*, Vol. 1, *Methodology*. Oxford: Oxford University Press.
——. 2010b. *Basic linguistic theory*, Vol. 2, *Grammatical topics*. Oxford: Oxford University Press.
——. 2012. *Basic linguistic theory*, Vol. 3, *Grammatical topics*. Oxford: Oxford University Press.
——. and Alexandra Y. Aikhenvald (eds). 1999. *The Amazonian languages*. Cambridge: Cambridge University Press.
Dol, Philomena. 2007. *A grammar of Maybrat, a language of the Bird's Head Peninsula, Papua Province, Indonesia*. Canberra: Pacific Linguistics.
Donohue, Mark. 1999. *Warembori*. Munich: Lincom Europa.
Elbert, S. H. 1974. *Puluwat grammar*. Canberra: Pacific Linguistics.
Epps, Patience. 2005. 'A grammar of Hup'. Ph.D. dissertation, University of Virginia.
——. 2008. *A grammar of Hup*. Berlin: Mouton de Gruyter.
Errington, J. Joseph. 1988. *Structure and style in Javanese. A semiotic view of linguistic etiquette*. Philadelphia: University of Pennsylvania Press.
Foley, William A. 1991. *The Yimas language of New Guinea*. Stanford: Stanford University Press.
Fortescue, Michael. 1984. *West Greenlandic*. London: Croom Helm.
Fraurud, Kari. 2001. 'Possessives with extensive use: A source of definite articles', pp. 243–67 of *Dimensions of possession*, edited by Irène Baron, Michael Herslund, and Finn Sørensen. Amsterdam: John Benjamins.
Gamkrelidze, T. V. and Vyach. Vs. Ivanov. 1984. *The Indo-European language and the Indoeuropeans* (Indoevropejskij jazyk i indoevropejcy). Tbilisi: Izdateljstvo Tbilisskogo Universiteta.
Geraghty, Paul. 2000. 'Possession in the Fijian languages', *Sprachtypologie und Universalienforschung* 53 (3/4): 243–50.
Gerdts, Donna and Kaoru Kiyosawa. 2005. 'The function of Salish applicatives', *Proceedings of the 10th Workshop on the Structure and Constituency of Languages of the Americas*, UBCWPL 17: 84–94.
—— and ——. 2007. 'Combinatorial properties of Salish applicatives', *Papers for the 42nd International Conference on Salish and Neighbouring Languages*, UBCWPL 20: 176–219.
Haiman, John. 1983. 'Iconic and economic motivation', *Language* 59: 781–819.
——. 1985. *Natural syntax. Iconicity and erosion*. Cambridge: Cambridge University Press.
Harrison, S. P. 1988. 'A plausible history for Micronesian possessive classifiers', *Oceanic Linguistics* 27: 63–78.
Heine, Bernd. 1997a. *Possession. Cognitive sources, forces and grammaticalization*. Cambridge: Cambridge University Press.
——. 1997b. *Cognitive foundations of grammar*. New York: Oxford University Press.
—— and Tania Kuteva. 2002. *World lexicon of grammaticalization*. Cambridge: Cambridge University Press.

Heine, Bernd and Tania Kuteva. 2005. *Language contact and grammatical change*. Cambridge: Cambridge University Press.

—— and ——. 2006. *The changing languages of Europe*. Cambridge: Cambridge University Press.

—— and Mechthild Reh. 1984. *Grammaticalization and reanalysis in African languages*. Hamburg: Helmut Buske.

Hyman, Larry. 1977. 'The syntax of body parts', pp. 99–118 of *Haya grammatical structure. Southern California Occasional Papers in Linguistics* 6, edited by E. R. Byarushengo, A. Duranti, and L. M. Hyman. Los Angeles, CA: GSIL Publications.

Hyslop, Catriona. 2001. *The Lolovoli dialect of the North-east Ambae language, Vanuatu*. Canberra: Pacific Linguistics.

Isachenko, Alexander V. 1974. 'On "have" and "be" languages', pp. 43–77 of *The Slavic forum. Essays in linguistics and literature*, edited by Michael S. Flier. The Hague: Mouton.

Ivanov, Vjach. Vs. (ed.) 1989. *Kategorija possessivnosti v slavjanskikh i balkanskikh jazykakh*. Moscow: Nauka.

Jensen, Cheryl. 1999. 'Tupí-Guaraní', pp. 125–64 of Dixon and Aikhenvald (eds).

Jespersen, Otto. 1924. *The philosophy of grammar*. London: George Allen and Unwin Ltd.

Kachru, Yamuna. 1990. 'Experiencer and other oblique subjects in Hindi', pp. 59–76 of *Experiencer subjects in South Asian languages*, edited by Manindra K. Verma and K. P. Mohanan. Stanford: CSLI.

Keating, Elizabeth. 1997. 'Honorific possession: Power and language in Pohnpei, Micronesia', *Language in Society* 26: 247–68.

——. 1998. *Power sharing: Language, rank, gender and social space in Pohnpei, Micronesia*. New York: Oxford University Press.

Klamer, Marian, Ger Reesink, and Miriam van Staden. 2008. 'East Nusantara as a linguistic area', pp. 95–150 of *From linguistic areas to areal linguistics*, edited by Pieter Muysken. Amsterdam: John Benjamins.

Klumpp, D. 1990. *Piapoco grammar*. Colombia: SIL.

——. 1995. *Vocabulario Piapoco-Español*. Santafé de Bogotá: Asociación Instituto Lingüístico de Verano.

Koehn, Sally. 1994. 'The use of generic terms in Apalaí genitive constructions', *Revista Latinoamericana de estudios etnolingüisticos* VIII: 39–48.

Koshal, Sanyukta. 1979. *Ladakhi grammar*. Delhi: Motilal Banarsidass.

Kuryłowicz, J. 1964. *The inflectional categories of Indo-European*. Heidelberg: Carl Winter Universitätsverlag.

Langacker, R.W. 1977. *Studies in Uto-Aztecan grammar*, Vol. 1, *An overview of Uto-Aztecan grammar*. Dallas: Summer Institute of Linguistics and the University of Texas at Arlington.

Lee, K.-D. 1975. *Kusaiean reference grammar*. Honolulu: University Press of Hawaii.

Lewis, Geoffrey. 2000. *Turkish grammar*. 2nd edn. Oxford: Oxford University Press.

Lichtenberk, Frantisek. 1983a. 'Relational classifiers', *Lingua* 60: 147–76.

——. 1983b. *A grammar of Manam*. Honolulu: University of Hawaii Press.

——. 1985. 'Possessive constructions in Oceanic languages and in Proto-Oceanic', pp. 93–140 of A. P. Pawley and L. Carrington (eds), *Austronesian linguistics at the 15th Pacific Science Congress*. Canberra: Pacific Linguistics.

——. 2005. 'Inalienability and possessum individuation', pp. 339–62 of *Linguistic diversity and language theories*, edited by Zygmunt Frajzyngier, Adam Hodges, and David S. Rood. Amsterdam: John Benjamins.

——. 2008. *A grammar of Toqabaqita*, Vol. 1, Berlin: Mouton de Gruyter.

Lynch, John, Malcolm Ross, and Terry Crowley. 2002. *The Oceanic languages*. London: Routledge.

Lyons, John. 1977. *Semantics*, Vol. 2, Cambridge: Cambridge University Press.

McGregor, William. 2009. *The expression of possession*. Berlin: Mouton de Gruyter.

Martin, Jack. 1993. '"Inalienable possession" in Creek (and its possible origin)', *International Journal of American Linguistics* 59: 442–52.

Matthews, Stephen. 2007. 'Cantonese grammar in areal perspective', pp. 220–36 of *Grammars in contact: A cross-linguistic typology*, edited by Alexandra Y. Aikhenvald and R. M. W. Dixon. Oxford: Oxford University Press.

Mattina, Nancy. 1995. 'Some lexical properties of Colville-Okanagan ditransitives', *International Conference on Salishan and Neighboring Languages* 28: 265–84.

Merlan, Francesca and Alan Rumsey. 1991. *Ku Waru. Language and segmentary politics in the western Nebilyer Valley, Papua New Guinea*. Cambridge: Cambridge University Press.

Mithun, Marianne. 1984. 'The evolution of noun incorporation', *Language* 60: 847–94.

——. 1996. 'Multiple reflections of inalienability in Mohawk', pp. 633–49 of Chappell and McGregor.

——. 1999. *The languages of native North America*. Cambridge: Cambridge University Press.

——. 2001. 'The difference a category makes in the expression of possession and inalienability', pp. 285–310 of Baron, Herslund and Sørensen (eds).

Müller, Henrik Høeg. 2001. 'Spanish *N de N* structures from a cognitive perspective', pp. 169–86 of Irene Baron, Michael Herslund, and Finn Sørensen (eds.).

Nichols, Johanna. 1992. *Linguistic diversity in space and time*. Chicago: University of Chicago Press.

Nikiforidou, Kiki. 1991. 'The meanings of the genitive: A case study in semantic structure and semantic change', *Cognitive Linguistics* 2: 149–205.

Noonan, Michael. 1992. *A grammar of Lango*. Berlin: Mouton de Gruyter.

Nordlinger, R. and L. Sadler. 2004. 'Nominal tense in cross-linguistic perspective', *Language* 80: 776–806.

Obata, Kazuko. 2003. *A grammar of Bilua, a Papuan language of the Solomon Islands*. Canberra: Pacific Linguistics.

Ostapirat, Weera. 2008. 'The Hlai language', pp. 623–52 of *The Tai-Kadai languages*, edited by Anthony V. N. Diller, Jerold A. Edmondson, and Yongxian Luo. London: Routledge.

Osumi, Midori. 1996. 'Body parts in Tinrin', pp. 433–62 of Chappell and McGregor (eds).

Pacioni, P. 1997. 'Possessive constructions, classifiers and plurality in Cantonese and some other Chinese dialects', pp. 199–222 of *A report of the joint research project. Analysis and description of individual languages and linguistic typology*, edited by T. Hayasi and P. Bhaskararao. Tokyo: Institute for the Study of Languages and Cultures of Asia and Africa.

Pasch, H. 1985. 'Possession and possessive classifiers in 'Dongo-ko', *Afrika und Übersee* 68: 69–85.

——. 1986. *Die Mba-Sprachen. Die Nominalklassensysteme und die genetische Gliederung einer Gruppe von Ubangi Sprachen*. Hamburg: Helmut Buske Verlag.

Payne, Doris L. and Immanuel Barshi (eds). 1999. *External possession*. Amsterdam: John Benjamins.

—— and Thomas E. Payne. 1990. 'Yagua', pp. 249–474 of *Handbook of Amazonian languages*, Vol. 2, edited by Desmond C. Derbyshire and Geoffrey K. Pullum. Berlin: Mouton de Gruyter.

Perniss, Pamela and Ulrike Zeshan (eds). 2008a. *Possessive and existential constructions in sign languages*. Nijmegen: Ishara Press.

—— and ——. 2008b. 'Possessive and existential constructions: Introduction and overview', pp. 1–31 of Perniss and Zeshan (eds).

Ramirez, Henri. 1997. *A fala Tukano dos Yepâ-masa. Tomo I. Gramática. Tomo II. Dicionário. Tomo III. Método de aprendizagem*. Manaus: Inspetoria Salesiana Misionária da Amazônia CEDEM.

Reesink, Ger. 1999. *A grammar of Hatam, Bird's Head Peninsula, Irian Jaya*. Canberra: Pacific Linguistics.

Reinoso Galindo, Andrés Eduardo. 2002. *Elementos para una gramática de la lengua piapoco*. Bogotá: Ministério de cultura.

Ribeiro, Eduardo. 2002a. 'O marcador de posse alienável em Kariri: um morfema Macro-Jê revisitado', *LIAMES* 2: 31–48.

——. 2002b. 'The prefix *u-* in Karirí (with some Macro-Jê notes)', pp. 75–88 of *Santa Barbara Papers in Linguistics 13: Proceedings from the 5th Workshop on American Indigenous Languages (WAIL 2002)*, edited by Jeanie Castillo. Santa Barbara: Department of Linguistics, University of California.

Richards, Joan. 1973. 'Dificuldades na análise de possessão nominal na língua Waurá', *Série Lingüistica* 1: 11–29.

Rodrigues, Aryon D. 1997. 'Nominal classification in Kariri', *Opción* 13: 65–79.

——. 1999a. 'Macro-Jê', pp. 165–206 of Dixon and Aikhenvald (eds).

——. 1999b. 'Tupí', pp. 107–24 of Dixon and Aikhenvald (eds).

Routamaa, Judy. 1994. *Kamula grammar essentials*. Ukarumpa: Summer Institute of Linguistics.

Rumsey, Alan. 1993. 'Language and territoriality in Aboriginal Australia', pp. 191–206 of *Language and culture in Aboriginal Australia*, edited by Michael Walsh and Colin Yallop. Canberra: Aboriginal Studies Press.

——. 2000. 'Agency, personhood and the "I" of discourse in the Pacific and beyond', *Journal of the Royal Anthropological Institute (NS)* 6: 101–15.

——. 2010. 'Lingual and cultural wholes and fields', pp. 127–49 of *Experiments in holism. Theory and practice in contemporary anthropology*, edited by Ton Otto and Nils Bubandt. Chichester: Wiley-Blackwell.

Sands, Kristina and Lyle Campbell. 2001. 'Non-canonical subjects and objects in Finnish', pp. 251–305 of *Non-canonical marking of subjects and objects*, edited by Alexandra Y. Aikhenvald, R. M. W. Dixon, and Masayuki Onishi. Amsterdam: John Benjamins.

Saxton, D. 1982. 'Papago', pp. 93–266 of *Studies in Uto-Aztecan grammar 3: Uto-Aztecan grammatical sketches*, edited by R. W. Langacker. Dallas: Summer Institute of Linguistics and the University of Texas at Arlington.

Schmidt, Annette. 1985. *Young people's Dyirbal: An example of language death from Australia.* Cambridge: Cambridge University Press.

Seiler, Hansjakob. 1983. *Possession as an operational dimension of language.* Tübingen: Gunter Narr.

Seki, L. 2000. *Gramática da língua Kamaiurá.* Campinas: Editora da Unicamp.

Slater, Keith W. 2003. *A grammar of Mangghuer, a Mongolic language of China's Qinghai-Gansu Sprachbund.* London: Routledge.

Song, Jae Jung. 1997. 'The history of Micronesian possessive classifiers and benefactive marking in Oceanic languages', Oceanic Linguistics 36: 29–64.

——. 1998. 'Benefactive marking in Oceanic languages: From possessive classifiers to benefactive markers', pp. 247–75 of *Case, typology, and grammar*, edited by A. Siewierska and J. J. Song. Amsterdam and Philadelphia: John Benjamins.

——. 2005. 'Grammaticalization and structural scope increase: Possessive-classifier-based benefactive marking in Oceanic languages', *Linguistics* 43: 795–838.

Spaulding, Craig and Pat Spaulding. 1994. *Phonology and grammar of Nankina.* Colombia: SIL.

Stassen, Leon. 2009. *Predicative possession.* Oxford: Oxford University Press.

Stolz, Thomas, Sonja Kettler, Cornelia Stroh, and Aina Urdze. 2008. *Split possession. An areal-linguistic study of the alienability correlation and related phenomena in the languages of Europe.* Amsterdam: John Benjamins.

Sun, Jackson T.-S. and Yon-Jing Lin. 2009. 'Constraints on relativization in rGyalrong: a cross-dialect comparison.' Paper presented at 4th International Conference on Sino-Tibetan Languages and Cultures, November 2–4, 2009. Payap University, Chiang Mai, Thailand.

Thompson, Chad. 1996. 'On the grammar of body parts in Koyukon Athabaskan', pp. 651–77 of Chappell and McGregor (eds).

Ullrich, Charles. 2008. *New Lakota dictionary.* Bloomington: Lakota Language Consortium.

van den Berg, René. 2009. 'Possession in South Halmahera—West New Guinea: Typology and reconstruction', pp. 327–58 of *Austronesian linguistics and culture history. A festschrift for Robert Blust*, edited by Alexander Adelaar and Andrew P. Pawley. Canberra: Pacific Linguistics.

Vasmer, Max. 1976. *Russisches etymologisches Wörterbuch. Erster Band: A–K.* Heidelberg: Carl Winter Universitätsverlag.

Velazquez-Castillo, Maura. 1996. *The grammar of possession. Inalienability, incorporation and possessor ascension in Guaraní.* Amsterdam: John Benjamins.

Viitso, T.-R. 2007. 'Structure of the Estonian language', pp. 9–129 of *Estonian language*, edited by Mati Erelt. Tallinn: Estonian Academy Publishers.

Walsh, M. 2002. 'Language ownership: A key issue for native title', pp. 231–44 of *Language in native title*, edited by John Henderson and David Nash. Canberra: AIATSIS.

Weir, E. M. Helen. 1990. 'Incorporation in Nadëb', pp. 321–63 of *Amazonian linguistics: Studies in Lowland South American Indian languages*, edited by Doris L. Payne. Austin: University of Texas Press.

Wilson, William H. 1982. *Proto-Polynesian possessive marking*. Canberra: Pacific Linguistics.

Yang, Tongyin and Jerold A. Edmondson. 2008. 'Kam', pp. 509–84 of *The Tai-Kadai languages*, edited by Anthrony V. N. Diller, Jerold A. Edmondson, and Yongxian Luo. London: Routledge.

2

Ownership, part–whole, and other possessive–associative relations in Nêlêmwa (New Caledonia)

ISABELLE BRIL

'Possessive constructions' is a general term referring to an extensive and complex grammatical system of Noun–Noun determination or modification in Nêlêmwa, used in functions and contexts which are not restricted to the expression of possession or ownership *per se*, but are used in broader semantic contexts including kinship, body parts, part–whole relations, attributes, as well as quantification or partitive relations conceived as a subtype of part–whole relations, also including various associative relations (Dixon 2010: 262ff.).[1] Possessive constructions also correlate with distinct noun categories, bound vs. free nouns, themselves selecting distinct constructions types: direct constructions (for all bound nouns and free nouns 1 and 2) or indirect constructions (for free nouns 3) which express semantic contrasts between close-inherent relations vs. more distant-contingent-transient relations. Two further parameters are at play, the animacy and definiteness of the determiner: definite human determiners correlate with ownership/possession or kinship relations, while non-human determiners, inanimates especially, select other types of relations.

'Possessive' constructions subdivide into core possessive relations and non-core associative or attributive relations (see Chapter 1).

- The core semantics are ownership (x possesses y in some inherent or contingent way), kinship (x is a kin of y), body parts, and part–whole relationship (x is a part of y), including part–whole quantification (§5).

[1] I wish to thank Alexandra Aikhenvald and Bob Dixon for comments on this chapter, which has also greatly benefitted from the discussions and comments from the workshop's participants.

- The non-core semantics of 'possessive' constructions refer to inherent properties (x is an attribute/property of y), as in *bubuxa ciic* 'the green of this tree' or *ni mobwa mwa* 'in the decayed house' (*lit.* in the decay of the house), to class inclusion or hyponyms such as 'pig's food' (hyponym of 'food') (§§3.2; 3.5), the location or orientation of entities, conceived as the semantic and functional extension of part–whole relations, like *ni hâlû taap* 'under the table' (*lit.* in the shade of the table), time relation as in example (7), and associative relations (x is associated/pertains to y) as in causal, purposive, comitative, benefactive relations (see §3.6.3).

Section 1 presents some general features of nominal possessive constructions in Nêlêmwa; §2 analyses possession by animates; §3 deals with part–whole relationship; §4 focuses on the possessive determination of deverbal nouns; §5 deals with the determination of quantifiers; §6 centres on predicative possession; and §7 offers some conclusions.

1 General characteristics of Nêlêmwa

1.1 *Argument structure and constituent order*

Nêlêmwa is a verb first language. Nominal arguments are post-verbal [VOA], but subject pronouns stand before the verb in [sVo] order. It has a mixed accusative–ergative system: it is accusative with subject/object pronouns, but post-verbal nominal arguments are marked as absolutive and ergative with [verb ABS.patient ERG. agent] order. Single nominal arguments of intransitive verbs are absolutive (with VS order). Absolutive is marked ø, ergative markers are *ea-* (+ genitive animate NP) and *ru* (for inanimates) (Bril 2002: 134–42).

1.2 *Structure and characteristic features of possessive determination*

Direct and indirect possessive constructions are a hallmark of Oceanic languages. In Nêlêmwa, as in other Kanak and Oceanic languages, these constructions correlate with distinct noun classes (bound/relational nouns and free nouns). In languages lacking noun classes, direct and indirect constructions express semantic distinctions. In Manam for instance, direct constructions such as *baligo-gu* 'my grass skirt' (that I'm wearing) refer to an active or close relation, while indirect ones express a non-active or abstract relation with the possessed entity as in *baligo ne-gu* 'my grass skirt' (when I'm not wearing it) (Lichtenberk 1985a: 109).

Nêlêmwa has a head-dependent (possessee–possessor) structure. Direct possession is marked either by a postposed possessor NP (as in *mwa agu hleny* 'this person's house' (*lit.* house person this)) or by a possessive pronoun suffixed to the possessee (*mwa-ny* 'my house') (Table 2.1). Indirect possession is marked by a linker, as in *bu i na* 'my hook' (*lit.* hook of me). Pronouns marking indirect possession are formally

TABLE 2.1. **Direct and indirect possessive pronouns**

	1sg	2sg	3sg	1du.incl.	1du.excl.	1pl.incl.	1pl.excl.	2du	2pl	3du	3pl
Possessive suffixes (direct possession	*-ny*	*-m*	*-n*	*-(h)î*	*-man*	*-hâ*	*-va*	*-mon*	*-wa*	*-(h)li*	*-(h)la*
Indirect possession	*i na*	*i yo*	*i ye*	*i (h)î*	*i man*	*i hâ*	*i va*	*i mon*	*i wa*	*i (h)li*	*i(h)la*

similar to the oblique objects pronouns of verbs. Possessive pronouns only refer to animates, inanimates are ø-marked.

1.3 *Morphosyntactic and semantic features of possessive constructions*

1.3.1 *Noun classes and possessive constructions* There are two main noun classes: bound/relational nouns and free nouns (see Table 2.2). A few lexical items belong to both categories with semantic differences (*mwa* 'house', *mwa-t* 'container'), (§3.6.1). Free nouns further subdivide into the following three classes on morphosyntactic grounds: free nouns 1 have direct (juxtaposed or affixed) determination, free nouns 2 have direct determination with some root modification, free nouns 3 have indirect determination (marked by linkers *i*, *o*).

TABLE 2.2. **Noun classes**

		Root form with				
Type of determination	Noun Types	animate determ.	non-human determ.	Meaning	Possessed form	
direct	Bound nouns	*kua-n*	*kua-t*	foot	*kua-ny* *kua-t taap*	'my foot' 'the table leg'
	Classifiers	*khoo-n*	*khoo-t*	meat food	*khoo-ny nok* *khoo-t puaka*	'my fish to eat' 'pig's food'
	Free nouns 1	*mwa*		house	*mwa-ny*	'my house'
direct with root modif.	Free nouns 2	*wany*		boat	*waja-ny*	'my boat'
Indirect	Free nouns 3	*bu*		hook	*bu i na*	'my hook'

The distribution of lexical items within these noun classes is only predictable for broad semantic fields: direct constructions express inherent, close relationships (including most kinship terms, body parts, etc.), while indirect constructions express transient, contingent, or remote relationships. But there are limits to semantic predictability in Nêlêmwa: for instance, *ka* 'year', *hmwaluk* 'moon, month', *taan* 'day', and *bwan* 'night' belong to different noun classes. This relative unpredictability results in part from mechanisms of language change.

(1) BOUND NOUNS Bound nouns have specific features: their citation form has an obligatory relational suffix varying with the category of the possessor: *-n*[2] (for humans), *-t* (for inanimates or non-specific humans), as in *kua-n* 'his/her foot' (+human), *kua-t* 'its foot' (of a table).

The *-t* suffix is the trace of a construct[3]/pertensive morpheme, that is of a relational marker on the possessee (on the term 'pertensive', see Chapter 1 this volume and Dixon 2010). This morpheme cliticizes to the root as suffix *-t*, which marks these nouns as relational. It also allows inherently relational nouns to occur independently (like the de-relational marker in Tolai, Mosel 1984: 40–3); *-t* also occurs on some deverbal nouns (see §4.2). It is 'probably a reflex of a former non-personal possessive relator' (Ozanne-Rivierre 1991: 327–30). It corresponds to *-t/-r* in neighbouring Nyelâyu, and could be related to the non-personal connector (rV) in Paici and to the form *tè-* (from *dè-n* 'his property') in Cèmuhî.

Bound nouns express inherently relational entities including objects in controlled and close relations. They include:

(i) all relational and possessive classifiers;
(ii) kinship reference terms (but address terms are link nouns);
(iii) body parts, some of which also serve as locative markers (§3.6.3);
(iv) nouns expressing causal, consecutive, purposive/benefactive or malefactive, comitative relations (§3.6.3);
(v) notions such as: *boo-t/-n* 'smell', *yaara-t/-n* 'name', *hâlûû-t/-n* 'shadow, image', *uye-t/-n* 'image, portrait', *kagu-t/-n* 'spirit', *faxe- /-n* 'taboo', *maada-t/-n* 'memory', *dera-t/-n* 'fear', *kaxaaxa-t/-n* 'support, certainty, trust';
(vi) abstract notions, *hâmwa-t/-n* 'replacement', *shala-t/-n* 'reserved object', *hâlee-t/-n* 'desired object', *bwaavaxe-t/-n* 'result, value, worth', *bwaga-t/-n* 'appendix, residue, left-over space';

[2] *-n* might also be the trace of a cliticized construct suffix. In Drehu (Loyalty Islands), the obligatory determiner of bound nouns is *-n* (Moyse-Faurie 1983: 168) which might be cognate with the non-personal genitive relator *ni? (Ozanne-Rivierre 1991: 332).

[3] Construct morpheme is the traditional label used to refer to such forms in Oceanic or in African languages (Creissels 2009), it is similar to the label pertensive used in this volume.

(vii) inherent properties and qualities *hnye-t/-n* 'size', *thala-t/-n* 'width', *ura-t/-n* 'length', *avi-t/-n* 'side, flank', *âda-t/-n* 'slowliness, delay', *wada-t/-n* 'speed', *mobwa-t* 'decay';
(viii) modal nouns, *jaxa-t/-n* 'measure, ability, power, possibility', *awa-t/-n* 'will, heart, desire', *fha-t* 'charge, duty', *hnabwa-t* 'charge, duty';
(ix) time nouns *yeewa-t/-n* 'time'; locative, spatial nouns, *ni wooxa-t/-n* 'in the middle, among', *nanamwa-t* 'in the middle' (of a surface, an item), *na-t* 'interior', *fera-t* 'beneath';
(x) almost all quantifiers expressing partition from mass or count nouns (§5.2);
(xi) interjections: *mee-m!* 'listen!', *pwâ uta-m!* 'serves you well!', *habwaa-hla!* 'how nice they are!'.

Some are mostly used as predicates, with a possessive determiner expressing a core argument: *awa-ny nok* 'I want fish' (*lit.* will-my fish).

(1) kaxaaxa-ny aug hleny
support-POSS: lsg person this
I count on this person. (*lit.* will-my support)

(2) co â me hâmwa-ny
2sg go CONJ replacement-POSS:1sg
You're going to replace me. (*lit.* to be my substitute)

(3) na holaee-n
1sg leave-POSS:3sg
I say good-bye to him. (*lit.* I take his leave)

(II) FREE NOUNS Free form nouns have bare citation forms, like *mwa* 'house', *bulaivi* 'club'. Free nouns 1 have direct determination like *mwa-m* 'your house'. Free nouns 2 display some root modification prior to direct determination (like *wany* 'boat' > *waja-m* 'your boat'). Free nouns 3 are link nouns indirectly possessed, like *bulaivi i yo* 'your club'.

(III) POSSESSIVE AND RELATIONAL CLASSIFIERS A last noun class requires classifiers for possessive constructions. These classifiers are bound nouns themselves. Some of them are relational classifiers specifying a type of relation, function, or use of the possessee (Lichtenberk 1983; Aikhenvald 2003). Most are intermediate between possessive and relational classifiers and specify some inherent property or feature of the possessee, as well as a type of relation to it. The classifier is the head of the construction. It takes a possessive suffix and is followed by an adjunct possessee.

(4) caa-**ny** kuvic
starch.food-POSS:1sg yam
my yam (to eat)

Classifiers in New Caledonian languages generally pertain to specific domains, such as food, drinks, plants, baskets, animals, and weapons.[4] They express inherent properties of food types (flesh, starch, vegetable or leaves, crabs, etc.), types of ingestion (*kêâ-n nu* 'his coconut' (to drink)), or types of food processing (*maa*- chewed food):

Nêlêmwa classifiers:

khoo-	'meat or fish food'	*caa-*	'starch food' (poc *ka-, *kani 'eat')
kûû-	'vegetable food'	*khora-*	for sugar-cane, coconut flesh
maa-	'chewed food'	*kêâ-*	'drinks'
ââ-	'plant tubers/seedlings'	*thiiva-*	'flower seedlings'
aadaxi-	'weapons'	*pwaxi-*	for pets, or cattle (*lit.* child)

Keet 'basket' is also used as a possessive classifier: *kee-ny keala* 'my fishing basket' (*lit.* basket-my fishing basket) (Bril 2002: 367).

The classifier *aadaxi-* originally referred to stone weapons, like *aadaxi-ny tale* 'my sling-stones' (*lit.* CL-my sling). It now extends to all types of weapons or cutting objects, such as *aadaxi-n jixet* 'his gun', *aadaxi kaava* 'the cutting fin of the Naso unicornis' (unicorn fish) tail'.

As expected with relational classifiers, some nouns may occur with various classifiers, depending on the semantics of the relationship:

caa-ny manyoong	'my cassava' (*caa-* classifier for starch food)
ââ-ny manyoong	'my cassava' (*ââ-* classifier for seedlings and plantations)
khoo-ny nok	'my fish' (*khoo-* food classifier for meat or fish)
fha-ny nok	'my fish' (*fha-* classifier for carried objects, brought from fishing)

(5)	xam	aa	kia-a	mwa	fha-n	nok
	ASS	ITER	there.is.no-least	ASS	load-POSS:3sg	fish

He has again not brought back anything from fishing.

2 Possessive constructions with animates

The types of constructions (direct, semi-direct, or indirect) are constrained by noun classes.

[4] Xârâcùù and Iaai also have a general classifier for possessed goods. In Iaai (Loyalty Islands), the classifier may be a repeater, as in *nuu-k nu* 'my coconut tree' (CL-my coconut tree) (Ozanne-Rivierre 1976: 191).

2.1 *Direct construction of bound nouns and free nouns 1*

Bound nouns and free nouns 1 are directly marked by a possessive suffix or a juxtaposed noun, and express an inherent ownership or association.

(I) BOUND NOUNS Bound nouns have an obligatory construct *-t/-n* suffix on their citation form. The suffix *-t* occurs with inanimate or non-specific human determiners. Compare: *kua-t* 'its foot' (+inanimate), *kua-t taap* 'the leg(s) of the table'; *kua-n* 'his/her foot' (animate), *kua Pwayili* 'Pwayili's foot'; the suffix *-n* cannot co-occur with a nominal possessor.

Apart from bound nouns, the *-t* suffix also occurs in constructions expressing part–whole relationships between inanimates, or with the relational forms of free nouns 2 and on nouns suffixed by the construct suffix *-a* (see §§3.3; 3.4.2). It also occurs on some nominalizations (§§4.1.2; 4.2).

(II) FREE NOUNS 1: DIRECT INHERENT DETERMINATION Free nouns 1 have direct inherent possessive marking, like bound nouns. Nouns belonging to this category are for instance: *mwa* 'house', *do* 'assagai', *du* 'bone', *she* 'head-support', *igu* 'duty, work', *awôlô* 'dwelling', *duba* 'percussion instrument', *mwa-ny* 'my house', *mwa Pwayili* 'Pwayili's house'.

2.2 *Root modification of free nouns 2*

The possessive construction of free nouns 2 displays some root modification which is often the trace of an older Proto-Oceanic form (Bril 2002: 35–8, 358).

ka	'year'	*ka**u**-n*	'his age'	POc * taq**un**
nâxâât	'day'	*nâxââl**i**-n*	'his day'	PAN *daqa**Ni**
hma	'left'	*hma**u**-n*	'his left side'	POc * m**au**Ri
wany	'boat'	*waj**a**-ny*	'my boat'	POc *waŋka
pôn	'hair'	*pole-n*	'his/her hair'	POc *pulu
kic	'belly'	*kiya-n*	'his/her belly'	POc * **tia**ni
hâbwan	'clothes'	*hâbwali-ny*	'my clothes'	
dep	'mat'	*dewo-m*	'your mat'	
wadat	'sling'	*wadali-ny*	'my sling'	

(6) ku wa-giik kau-ny hmwiny
PERV CL-one year-POSS:1SG here
I have been here for a year. (*lit.* it is one my year here)

These root modifications only occur with possessive or relational constructions; deictic or anaphoric determiners only trigger intervocalic sandhi on nouns ending with a stop (Table 2.3).

2.3 *Indirect construction of link nouns (free nouns 3)*

Link nouns require a linker (*i* + for humans, a possible reflex of POc *qi), and *o* + for collective/non-specific human or inanimate determiners (see §3.5). They express more distant, alienable, transient possession, loan words, nominalized stative or intransitive verbs. Cardinal numerals also belong to this type (see §§4.1; 5.1).

Some are used as predicative nouns:

(7) ku hule i yo hna-mu hmwiny?
PERV long.time LINK 2sg NMZ-stay here
Have you been staying here long? (*lit.* long time of you staying here?)

(8) kâyaa i hla hagi shâlaga
habit LINK 3pl fish crab
They are used to fishing crabs. (*lit.* habit of theirs fishing crab)

While the linker *i* is specific to indirect possessive determination, *o* also occurs in hyponymic relations with inanimate determiners.

Noun classes and their constructions are summarized in Table 2.4.

2.4 *Mixed possessive and qualifying constructions*

When bound or free nouns have both a possessive and a qualifying determiner, the two types may not be stacked, and the noun is repeated:

(9) waja-ny wany hnap (*waja-ny hnap)
boat-POSS:1sg boat sail
my sail-boat

(10) ââdaxi-m ââdaxi naat (from ââdak 'stone')
stone-poss:2sg stone oven
your oven stones

Compare with:

(11) ââdaxi naara-m
stone oven-POSS:2sg
the stones of your oven

TABLE 2.3. **Demonstrative vs. possessive determination**

Root	Demonstrative determination	Possessive determination
wany	*wany eli* 'that boat'	*waja-m* 'your boat'
ka	*ni ka eli* 'that year'	*pwadu kau-n* 'he is two years old' (*lit.* two year-his)
cet	*cer-eli* 'that cooking-pot'	*cela-ny* 'my cooking-pot'

TABLE 2.4. **Possessive constructions and noun classes in Nêlêmwa**

Nominal categories	Determination	Morphosyntactic devices	Type of possessor or determiner	**Semantic correlates**	
Bound nouns	Direct	possessive suffix	humans	Inherent **ownership**	
		nominal apposition	specific animates		**inherent relations (part–whole, hyponym)**
	construct suffix	suffix *-t* + nominal apposition	non-specific animates; inanimates		**inherent relations (part–whole, hyponym)**
Free nouns 1	direct	possessive suffix	humans	Inherent **ownership**	
		nominal apposition	animates		
Free nouns 2	semi-direct	phonic change (type (C)V) before possessive determination	humans	Inherent **ownership**	
			animates; inanimates		inherent relations
Free nouns 3	indirect linker	linker ***i***	specific humans	Alienable, transient **ownership**	
		linker ***o***	non-specific animates; inanimates		contingent, transient relation
All free nouns	**construct** suffix	suffix *-**a***	mostly inanimates		inherent relations (part–whole, hyponym)
All noun types	**construct** marker	nasalization	inanimates		part–whole, associative, hyponym

2.5 *Kinship*

The main distinction for kinship terms is between address and reference terms, not between kins and in-laws. Address terms are free, indirect nouns, while reference terms are bound nouns with direct possession. There are three main exceptions, *hua* 'grandfather', *gee* 'grandmother', and *âlô* 'father's sister', which are indirectly possessed with *i*. These former address terms have come to be used as reference terms. The reference term *kibuu-n* 'grandfather' is now only used in ceremonial speeches.

(I) DYADIC KINSHIP An interesting aspect of kinship in Nêlêmwa is dyadic kinship terms[5] referring to couples or groups, such as grandmother/-father and grandson/-daughter, mother's brother/sister and nephew/niece, step-father and step-son, co-spouses, brother and sister relation, etc. (Bril 2002: 367–8). Dyadic kinship terms are marked by a circumflex *â-* ~ *am-*. . . *-n*.[6] The kin term used is the one that refers to the lower pole of the age and social hierarchy (i.e. children and women; elder people, elder men particularly, are held in high respect). Thus the dyadic term *â-vabuu-n*[7] 'grandfather and grandson/daughter' is based on *pabuu-n* 'grandson/-daughter', as in *hliibai â-vabuu-n* 'the (2) grandfather and grandson/ -daughter' (*lit.* those 2 grandfather and grandson/daughter). Similarly, the dyadic term referring to a married couple, *â-maawa-n* 'the couple', is based on *maawa-* 'spouse'.

3 Part–whole and other relations with inanimate determiners

Part–whole and other associative constructions also subdivide into direct, semi-direct or indirect constructions, with a similar distinction between inherent vs. contingent relationship. However, they are morpho-phonologically more complex than ownership, and involve various construct/pertensive suffixes. Those applying to inanimate determiners display the greatest variety of constructions.

3.1 *Compound nouns vs. part–whole relationship*

In contrast with possessive part–whole constructions, compound nouns are juxtaposed without any morpho-phonological modification, but in a different order.[8] Compare the compound *wany hnap* 'sail boat' (*lit.* boat sail) with the part–whole relationship *hnawu wany* 'the boat's sail' (*lit.* sail of boat).[9]

[5] Also attested in other Oceanic and Kanak languages (La Fontinelle 1976; Ozanne-Rivierre 1991).

[6] *am-* before < *th, kh* > and *â-* before all other consonants. The suffix *-n* is another relic trace of the 'construct' marker.

[7] Intervocalic sandhi: [p] > [v].

[8] In Manam (Lichtenberk 1985b) measure terms 'a string of fish', 'a bag of coprah' are juxtaposed compounds, like qualifying compounds 'sweet potato'.

[9] Other examples of qualifying N–N compounds refer to properties, *âlô thaamwa* 'young girl' (*lit.* child-woman), *daan pânâât* 'stony-path' (*lit.* path stone), species (*duu paan* 'pandanus leaf').

3.2 *Part–whole constructions with* BOUND NOUNS: *the construct suffix* -t

The construct suffix *-t* occurs with inanimate determiners or with non-specific animate determiners.

3.2.1 *Possession vs. creation of hyponyms* Compare constructions with an animate, specific possessor in (12a–13a), with constructions in (12b–13b) where the suffix *-t* co-occurs with non-specific animates: *puaka* and *aayo* refer to the whole class, as specifiers of a kind of food, and express class-inclusion—by defining a hyponym of food—rather than ownership:

(12)	a.	khoo	puaka	mwexi	b.	khoo-**t**	puaka
		food	pig	there		food-*t*	pig
		(It's) the food of the pigs over there.				(It's) pig's food. (reference to kind)	

(13)	a.	khoo	aayo-â	b.	[khoo-**t**	aayo]	nok
		food	chief-poss:1pl.inc		food-*t*	chief	fish
		(It's) our chief's food-share.			Fish is chief's food. (reference to kind)		

3.2.2 *Concrete vs. abstract body parts for non-human animates* If the body–part relationship is inalienable with a definite possessor as in (14a), the construction is direct without *-t*. If it refers to a severed body part as in (14b), *-t* remains and the relation tends towards typing. The scope of the demonstrative is on the whole hyponym *shi-t shâlâga* 'crab claw' in (14b).

(14)	a.	hâk	[shi	[shâlâga	ena]]	b.	hâk	[[shi-**t**	shâlâga]	hleny]
		big	claw	crab	that		big	claw-*t*	crab	this
		The claw(s) of that crab is/are big.					This crab claw is big.			
		(possession, body part)					(relational, severed body part)			

In Tolai, 'the de-relationalised form of the body part is used if it refers to a body part that has been separated from its body' (Mosel 1984: 43, 214). In Longgu (Solomon Islands, Hill 1994) and in Tigak (New Ireland, Beaumont 1979: 62) determination is indirect with split part–whole relationship.

3.2.3 *Part–whole relationship for inanimates* The construct suffix *-t* also appears in part–whole relationships of inanimate entities as in (15a), while body–part relations with definite human possessors are juxtaposed (15b).

(15)	a.	kua-**t**	taap	hleny	b.	kua	âlô	hleny
		foot-*t*	table	this		foot	child	this
		the legs of this table				this child's feet		

Part–whole relationships of inanimate entities and human body parts are thus treated differently, as also noted in Tolai by Mosel:

Nouns denoting body-parts are *only inalienably* possessed if they refer to the *body-parts of human beings or animals*, but not if they denote parts of plants or objects. In that case, they enter N1-*na*-N2 relational constructions. (Mosel 1984: 42)

3.2.4 *Concrete part–whole vs. abstract spatial relationship* The suffix *-t* occurs in part–whole relationships of inanimates when the part is a concrete, distinct entity, as in *kua-t taap* 'the legs of the table'. It does not occur in more abstract, spatial relations such as *boda wany* 'the stern of the boat', *boda ara-xua-ny* (*lit.* hind surface-foot-my) 'my heel', *boda-(f)wamwa* (*lit.* hind country) 'the north of the country', *maa-(f) wamwa i Uvea* 'in the south of Ouvea' (*maa-t/-n* 'face, front'), *bwa ara-maa mwa* 'at the front of the house'.

3.3 *Part–whole and other associative relations with free nouns 2*

Determination of free nouns 2 is semi-direct with some root modifications, which are often an etymological trace that is retained in the determined form, but is lost in the bare form of the word.

daap	'ashes'	*daaw**vu**- fagau-n*	'the ashes from his body'	POc *dapu
daan	'path'	*dââ**lâ** malep*	'the path of life'	POc *nsalan
bwan	'night, date'	*bwa**li** perui eli*	'the day of the meeting'	POc *boŋi
nâxâât	'day'	*nâxââ**li** hôdam*	'a day of fast'	PAN *daqaNi
hnap	'sail'	*hnawu wany*	'the sail of the boat'	
pum	'smoke'	*pubu yaavic*	'the smoke of the fire'	

The semantics include part–whole, body secretions and excretions, container–content relationships, inherent properties, specific uses, etc.

The genitive construction of some of these free nouns 2 is inalienable: *hnawu wany* 'the sail of the boat', *hnawu-t* 'its sail'; *naat* 'earth oven', *naara-ny* 'my oven', *naara wan* 'an oven of (containing) turtles'.

3.4 *Construct markers for part–whole relations with inanimate determiners*

Two other construct/pertensive markers, one involving the nasalization of the possessee's final vowel and the other the suffix *-a*, result from the incorporation of former linkers.

3.4.1 *Nasalization: all noun types with inanimate determiners* The nasalisation of the final vowel of the possessee occurs with all noun classes, but only with inanimate determiners. It marks a part–whole relationship (secretions, product, ingredient, container–contained), as well as the specification of material, destination, etc.

Nasalization results from the cliticization, then loss of a former genitive *NV linker or construct suffix *-N, with regressive nasalization of the final vowel. This linker or construct suffix may reflect the POc associative linker *ni (Lichtenberk 1985a; Lynch 1996) which is still attested as *-n* in other New Caledonian languages[10] (Ozanne-Rivierre 1991: 332–3). Compare Nêlêmwa *cîî ciic* 'the bark of the tree' (*cii-t* 'skin, bark'), with Nemi *cii-n*[11] *ceec* 'the bark of the tree'. In Iaai, the linker *-en* expresses destination or relation, while qualification is juxtaposed (as in Nêlêmwa).

Iaai (Loyalty Islands, Ozanne-Rivierre 1976: 186-187)

		inanimate determiner	qualification
umwa	'house'	*umw-**en** galu* 'shelter for boats'	*uma weto* 'stone house'
taŋ	'basket'	*taŋ-**en** owic* 'basket for bananas'	*taŋ owic* 'a basket of bananas'

In Manam, two of the three markers of inalienable possession are the general classifier *ne-* which also marks a part–whole relationship, kinship, edible relation, psychological states and the suffix *-ŋa* used for collective meaning ('taro crumbs, pubic hair') (Lichtenberk 1985b: 295).

Nasalization in Nêlêmwa occurs on all noun types as shown below:

Bound nouns (see Bril 2002: 31–33)

pwa-t	'fruit'	*pwâ nu* 'coconut' (*lit.* fruit.of coconut)	POC *pua(q) 'fruit
		pwâ-xîlûû *waja-ny* fruit.of-anchor boat-my 'the anchor of my boat'	
cii-t	'skin, bark'	*cîî vagau-ny*[12] 'my skin'	POC *kulit 'skin'
waa-t	'root'	*wââ pat* 'the root of the fern'	POC *wakaR 'root'
kuu-t	'seedling'	*kûû kuk* 'seedling of sugar-cane'	POC *qulu 'head, top'

Free nouns 1

fwa	'hole, opening'	*fwâ-jahoot* 'the mouth of the river'	
keet	'basket'	*kêê-puyiu* 'basket for valuables';	PPN *kete

Compare with *kee-ny* 'my basket' and with the compound: *ke-paan* 'pandanus basket'.

[10] Drehu's non-personal genitive linker *n(e)* (*waaca ne gutu* 'chicken leg'), might be cognate with *ni.

[11] The construct suffix is often homonymous with the 3rd person singular pronominal suffix, but they are morphologically distinct.

[12] Direct possession **cii-ny* is ungrammatical.

Free nouns 2

kha	'liana, rope'	*khâ-kîlû* 'the chain of the anchor' (*kîlû* 'anchor');	
	compare with:	*khau-ny* 'my rope'	POC *taqun
pôn	'hair, feather'	*pôô nua-n* (*lit.* hair mouth-his) 'his beard'	
	compare with:	*pôle-n* 'his/her hair'	POC *pulu

Free nouns requiring classifiers:

wi	'water'	*wîî-ciic* 'sap of the tree', *wîî-nu* 'coconut water'	
		wîî thii-n 'mother's milk' (*lit.* liquid breast-her)	POC *waiR

Compare with *kêâ-ny wi* 'my(drinking) water' (CL.drink-my water) and with a compound: *wii naam* 'drinking water' (*naam* 'sweet, tasteless') (Bril 2002: 33).

Free nouns 3

muuc 'flower' *mûû-ciic* 'tree-blossom'; compare: *muuy-i na* 'my flower'

Other concomitant morphological changes include the loss of final -C#:

fot	'sparks'	*fô yaavic*	'fire sparks'	
yhoot	'shoot'	*yhôô-bolaa*	'shoot of banana tree'	
dexet	'rust, sap'	*dexê-ciic*	'sap of tree'	
kiit	'bundle'	*kîî-ciic*	'bundle of firewood'	
ciic	'tree, wood'	*cîî mwa*	'main rafts of the house'	POC *kai

They also include the drop of the last syllable (Bril 2002: 33–4; 366), as in *shâget* 'content', whose reduced form *shâ-* expresses container–contained configuration applying to some body parts like *shâ-idaamaa-ny* 'the pupil of my eye', *shâ-kiya-ny* 'my bowels' and to other part–whole relations like *shâ-wany* 'the crew of the boat'; *shâ-vhaa* 'the meaning of the words'.

3.4.2 *Construct suffix* -a: *inherent relationship with non-human determiners* The suffix *-a* could be the trace of POc *ka, a marker of subordinate, uncontrolled possessive relation. Manam has a reflex *-ʔa* for inalienable constructions in which the determiner is an immediate source of the possessee, or a part of the possessee (as in 'my shadow, fire-smoke, eye-mucus, mango-juice') (Lichtenberk 1985b: 295).

(I) DETERMINATION OF FREE NOUNS In Nêlêmwa, relational constructions with *-a* occur with non-human, mostly inanimate determiners and express inherent relationship (part–whole, properties, by-product, excretions) (Bril 2002: 360–1). They occur with all free noun classes, ± directly possessed, including loan words. Once turned into inherently relational forms by *-a*, these nouns may then host the suffix *-t* (like bound nouns) if the determiner is inanimate, as in *hiing* 'husk-fibre', *hiiga nu* 'coconut husk-fibre', *hiiga-**t*** 'its husk-fibre'.

shôlôk 'marrow'	*shôlôxa du* 'bone marrow'	
böök ~ *bööt* 'seed'	*bööxa wâric* 'seed of *Semecarpus atra*'	
maagoop 'beam'	*maagoova mwa* 'the main beam of the hut'	
kabaeep 'lintel'	*kabaeeva mwa* 'the lintel of the house'	
nigut 'central post'	*nigula mwâ* 'the main post of the hut'	
pot 'noise, din'	*pora bira* 'the noise of the waves'	*pora-**t*** 'its noise'
hmwaluk 'moon'	*hmwaluxa tilu* 'the month of harvesting',	*hmwaluxa-**t*** 'month of'
mwêêp 'wake'	*mwêêva nok* 'wake of the fish'	*mwêêva-**t*** 'its wake'

Free noun 2	relational determination	possession
wat 'link, cord, vein'	*war-a bwaa-n* 'his head-band' band-C head-his	*wale-ny* 'my belt'

Loan words	relational determination	possession
baek 'bag'	baex*a* *shuka* 'a bag of sugar'	*baex-i na* 'my bag'
miit 'meat'	*miira puaxa* 'pork meat'	***khoo-ny*** *miit* 'my meat'

(II) DETERMINATION OF PROPERTY NOUNS WITH *-a* Determination of property or state nominals, nominalizations, and ordinals are also marked by the construct suffix *-a* (§§4.1.2; 4.2; 5.1), as in *khûûk* 'roar' > *khûûx **a** loto* 'the roar of the car'; *dâlâk* 'deep' > *dâlâx **a** fwâ-wi* 'the depth of the water'; *pwaaluk* 'heavy (or) heaviness' > *pwaalux **a** -t* 'its weight'; *hulak* 'old' > *hulax **a** kavebu* 'the aged men of the clan' (Bril 2002: 362).

(16) nôôlî bubux-**a** ciic hleny
look:TR green-C tree this
Look at the green of this tree!

(17) pwââdagax-**a**[13] jowo ena
NOMZ-be.beautiful-C door-frame that
the beauty of this door-frame

(III) SUMMARY OF PART–WHOLE AND ASSOCIATIVE RELATIONSHIPS Part–whole and associative relationships are the most diverse in Nêlêmwa and other New Caledonian languages. In Cèmuhî, bound nouns are directly owned, but link nouns are marked by no fewer than five linkers which have different semantics and may all carry possessive suffixes (Rivierre 1980: 152–7): *tè-* (probably from *dè-n* 'property') marks alienable relationship; the other three linkers *ko-*, *hê-*, *nè-* mark a part–whole relationship and inclusion (*ko-* is also a locative, indirect object marker), *hê-* (marks

[13] Compare with *pwââdagax-i ak hleny* (*lit.* beautiful-LINK man this) 'the handsomeness of this man'.

part–whole or body–part relationship), *nè-* only marks relationships between inanimate nouns and occurs in verbo-nominal determination.

3.5 *Determination of free nouns 3 with inanimate or non-specific human determiners*

Indirect determination by inanimate or by non-specific human entities, is marked by *o* (also a locative preposition) and expresses contingent, accessory, or subjective relationship (in contrast with the construct suffix *-a*). It often defines types or hyponyms as in (18a); compared with possessive determination in (18b):

(18) a. hân xe shaya o ak
hunting TOP work LINK man
Hunting is men's work. (hyponym of work)

(18) b. shaya i thaamwa eli
work LINK woman that:ANAPH
(It's) the work of that woman.

The functions of *o* in Nêlêmwa are reminiscent of *ko-* in Cemuhî or *xo-* in Nemi (which are also locative markers meaning 'on': *wâ xo hiu-ng* 'the vein on my hand'), with one important difference: *ko-* and *xo-* have possessive suffixes (Cemuhî *cinu ko-n* 'his illness'; Nemi *daama xo-ng* 'my chief': Ozanne-Rivierre 1991: 337). They mark nominal determination as well as indirect objects of verbs.

3.6 *Categorial and construction variations*

A few nouns occur both as bound and free nouns with different meanings.

3.6.1 *Variation with animacy and specificity* These variations are conditioned by the two main factors: animacy and specificity of the determiner (Bril 2002: 370–2). The bound form with the suffix *-t*, occurs with inanimate or with non-specific animate determiners and expresses part–whole relationships; while the free form occurs with specific animate possessors (Table 2.5).[14]

Compare *doo-t pa* 'the sting of the stingray' (generic/kind), with body–part relation *doo pa* 'the stingray's sting' with a specific animate determiner. The forms *mwa* 'house' ~ *mwa-t* 'container' show similar variations (Table 2.6).

The two words, *da* and *daa-t* (from POc *daRaq 'blood'), have drifted further apart: *da* 'blood' is a link noun with a human possessor (*da i na* 'my blood'[15]) and a

[14] Ozanne-Rivierre (1991: 324) points out that body parts in Drehu are usually free nouns, while part–whole relationship of inanimates are bound nouns occurring with the non-personal genitive marker *-n(e)*: *im* 'arm' > *ime-n* 'sleeve'.

[15] In other Kanak languages, 'blood' is inalienable; in Nêlêmwa, *daa-ny* 'my blood' is only accepted as meaning 'my kin'. A more common expression is *wîî-agu* 'blood' '*lit.* the liquid of people'.

TABLE 2.5. **Categorial variation**

Bound noun (+ inanimate or non-specific animate Det^{er})	Free noun 1–3 (+ human Det^{er})	Free noun 3 (+human Det^{er})
doo-t 'sting, thorn'	*do* 'spear, assagai'	
daa-t 'sap, secretion'		*da* 'blood'
mwa-t 'container'	*mwa* 'house'	
	hulak 'ancestor'	*hulak* 'husband'

TABLE 2.6. **Categorial variation of *mwa* ~ *mwa-t***

Bound noun: *mwa-t* 'container' Relational determination with *-t*	Free noun: *mwa* 'house' Direct possession
inanimate determiners ***mwa-t*** *wi* 'water-pot' ***mwa-t*** *hele* 'knife-sheath'	
non-specific animate determiners ***mwa-t*** *agu Pum* 'the dwellings of people in Poum' *mwa-**r**-âlô* 'placenta' (container of child) (lenition *t* > *r*)	possession with **specific animates** *mwa agu mahleena* 'these people's houses' *mwa âlô hleny* 'this child's house' *mwa-ny* 'my house'

bound noun *daa-t* 'fluid, sap' with a non-human determiner (*daa-t ciic* 'the sap of the tree'). Compare with the juxtaposed compound *daa ciic* 'tree sap'.

3.6.2 *Contingent or inherent relations: choice of constructions* Very few nouns allow varying constructions correlating with inherent or contingent relations, rather than ownership. One of them is *fwâhuk* 'tale, story':

(19) *fwâhuxa-**ny*** 'my story' (of what I am) (direct contruction)
*fwâhuux-**i** na* 'my story' (that I know) (indirect contruction)
*fwâhuk **nai** na* 'my story' (one about me) (locative contruction)
story LOC 1sg
*fwâhuk **na** **shi-ny*** 'my story' (told from my viewpoint)
story LOC side-POSS:1sg

3.6.3 *Categorial change and grammaticalization* The last type of categorial change correlates with the grammaticalization of bound nouns referring to body-part or part–whole relationships into adpositions.

(I) LOCATIVE ADPOSITIONS Body parts are common sources of adpositional markers: *shi-t/-n* 'hand, side' is thus used as a locative, beneficiary adposition 'to, at', *ara-maa-t/-n* 'face, front' as a locative adposition 'before', like *duaxi-t/-n* 'back, behind', etc.

Bwaa-t/-n 'head, top' grammaticalizes as *bwa* 'on' with contact, and as *bwaat* without contact: consider the body part *bwaa Kaavo* 'Kaavo's head', the part–whole relation *bwaa hoogo* 'the top of the mountain', the locative preposition *bwa hoogo* 'on the mountain'. Without contact or adjacence, the bound form *bwaa-t* grammaticalizes as a locative adposition with indirect determination under the form *bwaar-o* (+ inanimate), *bwaar-i* 'above'.

(20) je bwaa-r-**i** ye
LOC.PRED top-*t*-LINK 3sg
It is above him/her.

In Longgu (Hill 1994: 9, 15), locative nouns mostly express part–whole relationships; disconnected, non-adjacent relations are also marked by indirect constructions, which may vary with other parametres such as visibility.

Other morpho-phonological changes occur in Nêlêmwa; for instance *bwa thala mwa* 'to the side of the house' marks a part–whole relationship (*thala-t* 'side'), while the adposition *thara wi-yaak* 'by the sea-side' marks a spatial boundary, not a part–whole relation.

(II) CAUSAL OR BENEFACTIVE NOMINAL ADPOSITIONS Bound nouns like *puxe-t* 'stump, base' (POC *puqun) or *paxi-t* 'tuber, reason' also function as nominal causal adpositions (Bril 2002: 129–30). *Puxe-t* has two different constructions:

1 One involves the construct device of nasalization and refers to a part–whole or close relationship, as in *puxê/pwê nu* 'coconut (tree) stump', *puxê mwa* 'the wall of the house', *puxê agu* 'the origin of people', and to causal relations such as (21):

(21) puxê u-perui i hla
origin NOMZ-meet LINK 3pl
(It's) the reason of their meeting.

2 The bound form also grammaticalizes as a causal (detrimental or benefactive) adposition as in (22), with indirect determination *puxer-i* if the determiner is human (23); compare with *bwaar-i ye* 'above him' (20).

(22) kio i mago-yo xe puxe-**t** duk
NEG 3sg sleep-good TOP origin-*t* noise
(If) he did not sleep well, it's because of the noise.

(23) kio i kaaluk xe puxe-**r-i** na
NEG 3sg fall TOP origin-*t*-LINK 1sg
(If) he did not fall, it's thanks to me (benefactive).

(III) COMITATIVE, BENEFICIARY, MALEFACTIVE NOMINAL ADPOSITIONS Among other adpositional bound nouns are those marking comitative (*mudi-n* 'company, with') and malefactive cause (*âlââ-t* 'ailment'):

(24)	a. co	â	mudi	thaamwa	ena	b. co	â	mudi-n
	2sg	go	company	woman	that	2sg	go	company-POSS:3sg
	Go with that woman.					Go with her/in her company.		

(25)	thân	noo-n	âlââ	khon	bai
	block	throat-POSS:3sg	ailment	cough	ANAPH
	His throat is hoarse from coughing. (*lit.* ailing from cough)				

4 Possessive determination of nominalizations

Genitive constructions of nominalizations vary with verb types, but follow the mentioned strategies with the linkers *i*, *o*, and the construct suffix *-a* (Bril 2002: 372–8).

4.1 *Nominalized stative and intransitive verbs*

Possession of nominalized stative and intransitive verbs is marked by *i*, *o*, and by *-a* if some inherent relation is involved.

(26)	u-haxaxa	i	na
	NOMZ-fear	LINK	1sg
	my fear		

An *o*-marked inanimate determiner is marked resumptively by *le* (27) (Bril 2002: 375):

(27)	u-taabwa	**o**	mwa	khere	>	u-taabwa **le** 'its shape'
	NOMZ-sit	LINK	house	holy		
	the shape of the temple					

4.1.2 *Contingent* o *vs. inherent* -a The three possessive constructions of nominalized stative verbs appear in (28): *i* (+animate), *o* and *-a* for inanimates; *o* marks contingent, subjective property, while the construct suffix *-a* expresses inherent, objective property.

(28)	a. u-pwââdagax-**i**	ye
	NOMZ-be.handsome-LINK	3sg
	his handsomeness (contingent, +animate determiner)	

(28)	b. u-pwââdagax-**o**	jowo	ena	> *u-pwâââdagak* **le** 'its beauty'
	NOMZ-be.beautiful-LINK	door-frame	that	
	the beauty of this door-frame (contingent on the speaker, +inanimate determiner)			

(28)	c. u-pwââdagax-**a**	jowo	ena	> *u-pwâââdagax-**a**-t* 'its beauty'
	NOMZ-be.beautiful-C	door-frame	that	
	the beauty of this door-frame (inherent, objective, +inanimate determiner)			

4.2 *Nominalized transitive verbs with the construct suffix* -a

Nominalized transitive verbs usually have the patient as their prime determiner, marked by *-a*, and indicating an inherent part–whole relationship (29).

(29) shi aa-hobwaxe-**a** mwa eli
at AGT.NOMZ-keep:TR-C house ANAPH
at (the place of) the ward of that house

This inherently relational form may then host the suffix *-t* (as in §3.4.2 above) when the determiner is inanimate. The agent (when mentioned) appears as the indirect possessive determiner of the nominalization as in (30).

(30) u-diya-**a-r-i** na (intervocalic sandhi : *-t* > *-r*)
NOMZ-do-C-*t*-LINK 1sg
(It's) my way of doing it. (*lit.* the doing of it of me) (**u-diya-**a** i na*)

To sum up, inanimate patient determiners are marked like inherent part–whole relationships, while agent determiners are indirect. To promote the agent as the prime possessive (indirect) determiner, the nominalized verb must be detransitivized (Bril 2002: 376–7).

5 Relational determination of quantifiers

Ordinals, cardinals, and various quantifiers display similar determination by *i*, *o*, *-a*.

5.1 *Ordinal and cardinal numbers*

Ordinals are suffixed by the construct suffix *-a* (which may host the *-t* suffix), indicating an inherent relationship between the entity and its rank (Bril 2002: 385–6).

(31) *wa-du* 'two' (*lit.* CL-2; *wa-* classifier of long objects)
*wa-du-**a** wany* 'the second boat'; *wa-du-**a-t*** 'the second'

Cardinal numbers are marked indirectly by *i* (+human), *o* (+inanimate or non-specific animate):

(32) aa-xi-ax-**i** ak
CL-one-man-LINK man
They are/there are twenty men. (*aa-xi-ak* 'twenty' is literally 'one man')

5.2 *Measure nouns, part–whole quantification*

The quantification domain of various other nominal quantifiers is expressed by ±direct genitive determiners, varying with the nominal class of the quantifier (Bril 2002: 403–5). Many quantifying expressions (*khooba-t* 'number') and partitioning quantifiers are bound, inherently relational nouns with direct genitive determiners referring to part–whole relation, *hmava-t* 'part', *khola-t* 'piece, part, nephew', *hava-t* 'portion' (widthwise), *neya-t* 'part, piece, middle' (lengthwise), *ava-t* 'amount, some', *bale-t* 'pair, companion, the other' (of a pair), (Bril 2002: 393–6):

(33)	hli	uya	aa-ru	ava-hla[16]
	3du	arrive	CL-two	amount-POSS:3pl

Two of them have arrived. (*lit.* 'two of their amount')

(34)	i	fhe	bale-va	aa-xiik
	3sg	take	companion-POSS:1pl.exc	CL-one

He took one of us.

Others refer to quantifying operations: *mwêêloo-t* 'remnant/remain' (after substraction), *haxaa-t* 'lack' (before completeness), *au-n* 'n-times' (Bril 2002: 383–5, 390–2):

(35)	êna	xe	ku	haxaa-wa
	now	TOP	PERV	lack-POSS:2pl

Now there's (only) you missing. (also meaning 'now it's your turn')

(36)	[ku	***au***-xan	***au-n***]	hna-oot
	PERV	times-three	times-POSS:3sg	LOC.NMZ-sing

He's sung three times. (*lit.* three times his times of singing)

6 Possession within a clause: possessive predication

By contrast with the complex system of nominal possession, possessive predication is straightforward. There are no copula and no possessive verbs expressing 'have' or 'belong'. Possessive predication is marked either by non-verbal possessive predicates, or by existential predication.

6.1 *Non-verbal possessive predication*

The non-verbal predicate is the possessed entity, as in *pwaxi-ny hoona* (*lit.* child-my that) 'that one is my child'.

(37)	yada-ny	foliix-ena
	goods-POSS:1sg	thing-that

This thing belongs to me.

[16] Compare a construction with a numeral: *aaru i hla* (two LINK 3pl) 'they are two'.

6.2 *Existential predication with* fo *or* je

Existential possessive predication is marked by *fo* or *je* 'there is', as in *fo pwaxi-n* 'she has a child/children'; its negative counterpart is *kia* 'there is not': *kia pwaxi-n* 'she is childless / has no child'.

(38)

sho	o	fo	awôlô-hli
good	if	there.is	house-POSS:3du

They should have a house. (*lit.* it is good if there is home-their)

The locative predicate *je* refers to a permanent property, while *fo* only predicates its existence.

(39)

je	hnabwa-t	bwa	kua-ny
be.LOC	trace	on	foot-POSS:1sg

I have a scar on the/my foot.

(40)

fo	hnawo	bwa	kua-n
there.is	wound	on	foot-POSS:3sg

He has a wound on his foot.

Fo also occurs in various possessive expressions referring to effects or abstract concepts, such as *fo yeewa-ny* 'I have the time' (*yeewa-t/-n* 'time'), *fo jaxa-m* 'you have the ability' (*jaxa-t/-n* 'measure, size'), *fo dera-n* 'he's afraid' (*dera-t/-n* 'fear, respect') (Bril 2002: 100–2). The possessive determiner is the sentient entity as in *fo awa-hla* 'they're brave' (*lit.* 'there is heart-their'). When mentioned, the cause of the effect ('mother' in (41)) appears as the prime genitive determiner and the sentient entity is peripheral:

(41)

fo	maada	axomoo-hla	na	shi
there.is	nostalgia	mother-POSS:3pl	LOC	side
hlaabai	pwaxi-n			
those:ANAPH	child-POSS:3sg			

The children long for their mother. (*lit.* there is nostalgia of their mother on the side of the children)

Compare with *na maax-i maada-m* (*lit.* I die-of absence-your) 'I feel nostalgic about you'.

6.3 *Negative and privative possessive predication with* kia *'there is not'*

Both negative and privative possessive predication are expressed by *kia* 'there is not'.

(42)

kia	khoo-n	nok
there.is.no	CL.flesh-POSS:3sg	fish

He did not have his (share of) fish.

(43) i oome na kia jitua i ye
3sg come CONTR there.is.no bow LINK 3sg
He came without his bow.

6.4 *Incorporation of body part: grooming*

There are no external possession constructions, such as 'je *me* lave *les* mains' 'I wash my hands' (*lit.* I me wash hands) in French. Incorporation of body parts is restricted to expressions referring to grooming (44). When possible, an intransitive verb is preferred (45):

(44) hla shaxa pôô-nu
3pl shave:INTR hair-face
They shave. (they beard shave)

(45) na khet vs. **na** khiri pôô-bwaa-**ny**
1sg comb:INTR 1sg comb:TR hair-head-POSS:1sg
I comb. I comb my hair.

An affected body part or a disease appears as the verb's argument:

(46) khîlû bwaa-ny
hurt head-POSS:1sg
I have a headache. (*lit.* my head hurts)

7 To conclude

Possessive constructions in Nêlêmwa are fundamentally constrained by noun classes, with very few cases of overlap. This is not a general feature of Oceanic languages; in Tolai or Manam, for instance, ± direct possessive constructions express semantic differences (inherent vs. contingent) independently from noun classes. The second pervasive and basic feature is that the system of N–N relational determination, with ± direct constructions, has distinct semantics, contrasting inherent–inclusive relations and contingent–accessory relations. Ownership is a subdomain of the core semantics of possessive constructions which express a broader relational system (see Table 2.4). Ownership correlates with animate and specific possessive determiners; if not, the relations expressed apply to other relational types (part–whole, partitioning, association, or hyponyms). Table 2.4 shows that bound nouns have this whole semantic range: the same grammatical construction expresses ownership (*caa-hla* 'their starch food'), kinship (*kââma-hla* 'their father'), body part (*bwaa-hla* 'their head'), partitioning and quantification (*ava-hla* 'some of them'), and association *mudi-hla* '(in) their company'.

The greatest morphological complexity in Nêlêmwa occurs with part–whole or other relational types, involving construct/pertensive markers such as suffix *-t*, nasalization, or suffix *-a*, which are traces of various construct morphemes, also found in other Kanak and Oceanic languages. Their distribution also varies with similar distinctive features of determiners (± animate and ± specific) and the same (inherent vs. contingent) relational semantics. The smaller noun class which requires possessive/relational classifiers provides further evidence that possession/ownership is a subpart of a wider relational system. Finally, not all entities are possessible; for instance, stars, deities, elements (wind, rain), and nouns with generic reference (*ak* 'man', *thaamwa* 'woman', *agu* 'person') are not.

References

Aikhenvald, Alexandra Y. 2003. *Classifiers: A typology of noun categorization devices.* Oxford: Oxford University Press.

——. 2007. 'Typological dimensions in word formation', pp. 1–65 of *Language typology and syntactic description*, Vol. 3, *Grammatical categories and the lexicon*, edited by Timothy Shopen. Cambridge: Cambridge University Press.

Beaumont, C.H. 1979. *The Tigak language of New Ireland.* Canberra: Pacific Linguistics (B-58).

Bril, Isabelle. 2000. *Dictionnaire nêlêmwa-nixumwak-français-anglais.* LCP 14. Paris: Peeters.

——. 2002. *Le nêlêmwa (Nouvelle-Calédonie): Analyse syntaxique et sémantique*, LCP 16. Paris: Peeters.

Creissels, Denis. 2009. Construct forms of nouns in African languages, pp. 73–82 of *Proceedings of Conference on Language Documentation and Linguistic Theory* 2, edited by Peter K. Austin, Oliver Bond, Monik Charette, David Nathan, and Peter Sells. London: SOAS.

Dixon, R. M. W. 1988. *A grammar of Boumaa Fijian.* Chicago: Chicago University Press.

——. 2010. *Basic linguistic theory.* Vol. 2. *Grammatical topics.* Oxford: Oxford University Press.

Hill, Deborah. 1994. 'Spatial configurations and evidential propositions', Working paper no. 25, Cognitive Anthropology Research Group, Max Planck Institute for Psycholinguistics, Nijmegen.

Hooper, Robin. 1985. 'Proto-Oceanic *QI', pp. 141–67 of *Austronesian linguistics of the 15th Pacific Science Congress*, edited by Andrew Pawley and Lois Carrington. Canberra: Pacific Linguistics (C-88).

La Fontinelle (de), Jacqueline. 1976. *La langue de Houaïlou.* Paris: SELAF (TO 17).

Lichtenberk, Frantisek. 1983. 'Relational classifiers', *Lingua* 60: 147–76.

——. 1985a. 'Possessive constructions in Oceanic languages and in Proto-Oceanic', pp. 93–140 of *Austronesian linguistics at the 15th Pacific Science Congress*, edited by Andrew Pawley and Lois Carrington. Canberra: Pacific Linguistics (C-88).

——. 1985b. *A grammar of Manam.* Oceanic Linguistics Special Publication no. 18. Honolulu: University of Hawaii Press.

Lynch, John. 1996. 'Proto-Oceanic possessive-marking', pp. 93–110 of *Oceanic studies: Proceedings of the first international conference on Oceanic Linguistics*, edited by J. Lynch and Fa'afo Pat. Canberra: Pacific Linguistics (C-133).

Mosel, Ulrike. 1984. *Tolai syntax and its historical development*. Canberra: Pacific Linguistics (B-92).

Moyse-Faurie, Claire. 1983. *Le drehu, langue de Lifou (Iles Loyauté)*, LCP 3. Paris: SELAF.

Ozanne-Rivierre, Françoise. 1976. *Le iaai, langue d'Ouvéa (Nouvelle-Calédonie)*. Paris: SELAF (TO 20).

——. 1991. 'Incorporation of genitive relators in the languages of New Caledonia and the Loyalty Islands', pp. 321–38 of *Currents in Pacific linguistics. Papers in Austronesian languages and ethnolinguistics in honour of G. W. Grace*, edited by Robert Blust. Canberra: Pacific Linguistics (C-117).

Pawley, Andrew. 1973. 'Some problems in Proto-Oceanic grammar', *Oceanic Linguistics* 12: 103–188.

Rivierre, Jean-Claude. 1980. *La langue de Touho. Phonologie et grammaire du cèmuhî*. Paris: SELAF (TO 30).

Ross, Malcolm. 1998. 'Possessive-like attribute constructions in the Oceanic languages of Northwest Melanesia'. *Oceanic Linguistics*, 37(2): 234–76.

——. 2001. 'Proto Oceanic **i,*qi* and **-ki*', pp. 259–78 of *Issues in Austronesian Morphology: a focusschrift for Byron W. Bender*, edited by Joel Bradshaw and Kenneth L. Rehg. Canberra: Pacific Linguistics 519.

3

Possession in Moskona, an East Bird's Head language

GLORIA J. GRAVELLE

1 Possession in Moskona

This chapter discusses the constructions which are used in Moskona possession phrases and expressions of predicative possession. In Moskona there are two marking strategies found in possession phrases which reflect the three types of relationships between possessors and possessees. There are four predicative possession constructions where the parameters of focus and definiteness play a defining role, but do not reflect the three types of relationships found in possession phrases.

2 The Moskona language

The Moskona language, a member of the East Bird's Head family, is spoken in the eastern half of the Bird's Head on the island of New Guinea, in the province of West Papua, Indonesia (Gloria Gravelle 2010). Speakers of the language number between 5,000 and 7,000.

Moskona has a rigid AVO/SV constituent order and a topic position which precedes the clause core. Six types of serial verb constructions have been observed in Moskona, as well as distinctive constructions which utilize body parts to express emotional states. Non-core arguments are marked with a preposition. A minimal verbal clause may consist of a single predicate, as the subject is obligatorily expressed as a prefix on the verb. All negation is clause level with the negator occurring clause-finally. Phrases are left-headed. Modifiers of the noun head typically number no more than one qualifier and a quantifier in an NP, although more are possible.

The major lexical categories are nouns and verbs with adjectives as a subclass of intransitive verbs. Minor categories include adverbs, prepositions, deictics, numerals, and various classifiers.

There are seven categories of affixation marked on the verb, which include an obligatory subject prefix, optional prefixes for irrealis, aspect, causation, a verbalizer, a circumfix denoting reciprocal object, and (reduplicated) suffixes indicating aspect.

There are three systems which classify nouns, two utilizing classifiers and one utilizing classificatory verbs. In addition, nouns (excluding proper names) may be grouped as those which denote types of humans and are definite as to number and those which do not denote humans and are indefinite as to number. Nouns which are indefinite as to number are either alienable or inalienable nouns and are defined morphophonologically. Alienable nouns, with the exception of recent loans, have the fused segment /m/ in root-initial position (e.g. *mow* 'land' or *mod* 'house'). This segment may possibly be a fossilized alienable noun class marker or the nominalizing prefix *m-* 'NOMZ', but forms without the fused segment have not been observed. Inalienable nouns have a non-high vowel in root-initial position (e.g. *osum* 'nose' or *egak* 'leg'). Nouns which denote humans are subdivided into generic nouns denoting types of humans (e.g. *orna* 'man' or *eferiok* 'small child') and nouns denoting a kinship relationship (e.g. *-okera* 'older sibling same sex' or *-edina* 'grandparent').[1]

3 Core types of possessive relationships

This section will discuss the three core types of possessive relationships found in Moskona: part–whole, possession, and kinship, as well as ownership and association which are also included under possession. Each of these core types is distinguished in a possessive noun phrase through the type of possession strategy employed.

Part–whole relationships are expressed directly through synthetic marking of the possessee. General possession, ownership, and association are expressed through analytic marking. Kinship relationships may be marked synthetically or analytically, and in some cases utilize both simultaneously, but analytic marking predominates. These types of possessive relationships are not distinguished in predicative possession constructions, but the parameters of focus and definiteness play a role instead.

4 Possession in noun phrases

The possessive noun phrase has the fixed order Possessor–Possessee, that is its structure is [Pr NP]. The possessor may be a noun phrase or a pronoun. The possessed noun is accompanied by either a possessive pronoun (pr) or a possessive prefix (pr-) denoting the possessor preceding the possessed noun. As possession is marked on the possessee, the nominal possessor is typically omitted if retrievable from context.

[1] Symbolization used in examples follows the established orthographic conventions, utilizing <j> for /ʤ/, <c> for /ʧ/, <f> for /ɸ/, <h> for /x/, <r> for /ɾ/ and <y> for /j/.

4.1 *Indirect posssession, and unpossessable nouns*

The nature of the possessee determines the type of construction which the possession phrase forms. The nature of the possessor affects the choice of prefix on a possessed inalienable noun only, but does not affect marking on alienable nouns.

4.1.1 *Indirect possession* Those entities which are not considered inherently possessed or inextricably linked to a possessor have ownership which may be transferred and are marked as alienable nouns. These alienable nouns comprise items which occur in nature (e.g. *merga* 'tree/wood' or *mow* 'land') but may also include items made by humans (e.g. *meru* 'handle' or *mosom* 'ax'). Possession of an alienable noun is marked analytically by a possessive pronoun (pr), such as *ofon* 'his/her' in (1) and (2) or *mifmin* 'our.pl' in (3), preceding the possessed noun (Pe). This structure [Pr pr-Pe] is also reflected in the definite predicative possessive 'have' construction (§5.1.1), and contrasts with the predicative possessive non-verbal 'belong' construction (§5.2.2) which has the structure [Pe Pr pr].

(1) ø-ejena ofon mamga
3sg-woman his/her pestle
the woman's pestle

(2) ø-orna nomi ofon mar ø-okowa
3sg-man that:GIV his/her thing 3sg-debt
the man's indebtedness

(3) mif mifmin mow ed-em
we.pl our.pl land NCL:2-CONTR
our (pl) other land (meaning: our other property)

There are nine possessive pronouns in Moskona, shown in Table 3.1, which distinguish three persons and three degrees of number.

TABLE 3.1. **Possessive pronouns**

sg	1	*dadin*
	2	*buwun*
	3	*ofon*
du	1	*yefyen*
	2	*yogyen*
	3	*ergen*
pl	1	*mifmin*
	2	*yuyun*
	3	*erin*

The possessive pronouns appear to have been originally a construction composed of a personal pronoun (e.g. *mif* 'we.pl') and a pronominal/possessive prefix (e.g. *mi-* '1pl') attached to a possession marker (such as **en* 'POSS'). For example, the possessive pronoun *mifmin* 'our.pl' may be analysed as composed of the morphemes *mif-mi-en* (we.pl-1pl-POSS) or the possessive pronoun *yuyun* 'your.pl' as *yua-yi-en* (you.pl-2pl-POSS). In *yuyun* the final /a/ of the pronoun *yua* has been elided and the vowels of the prefix and possessive marker **en* have coalesced. A similar construction with a possessive marker *–en* 'POSS' is found in Sougb, a related language, in the construction *me-en* (3sg-POSS) 'his/her' (Reesink 2002: 218). In Moskona there is no longer a functional possession marker, such as **en* 'POSS'. The present forms have become highly fused, most containing only fragments of the original components, so that the vowels are not easily explained. This proposed origin construction suggests that at one time possessees in extant indirect possession phrases (i.e. alienable nouns) were marked by a possessive prefix, the same possessive prefixes which mark inalienable nouns, plus a possession marker. The addition of a marker for possession of alienable nouns has been discussed in §2.3 of Chapter 1.

4.1.2 *Unpossessable nouns* Nouns which are unpossessable include those denoting natural phenomena and uncontrollable events or entities, such as disease. These are viewed as a type of non-volitional entity affecting a person. The affecting entity, such as *mekek* 'fungus' in (4) or *misirna* 'sickness' in (5), occurs as the agent in a transitive clause, utilizing the verb *en* 'do', with the experiencer as object.

(4) mekek ø-en eri
fungus 3sg-do they.pl
They have a fungal infection.

(5) misirna ø-en ofa
sickness 3sg-do s/he
S/he has a sickness.

4.2 *Direct possession*

Inalienable nouns, which refer to entities which are considered inextricably linked to the whole, are marked for possession synthetically as a direct possession phrase. The structure of a direct possession phrase is [Pr pr-Pe], in which a possessive prefix, such as *y-* 'du' in (6), *di-* '1sg' in (7) or ø- '3sg' in (8), which indexes the person and number of the possessor, attaches to the possessed inalienable noun, forming a single phonological word. In (8) the NP *mesogun nomi* (papaya that: GIV) 'the papaya' is the non-human possessor of the inalienable noun *eferu* 'segment'. The inalienable noun *eferu* is marked with ø- '3sg' which indexes all non-human possessors (see below

TABLE 3.2. **Possessive prefixes**

	Singular	dual	plural
1	*di-*		*mi-*
2	*bi-*	*y-*	*Yi-*
3	*ø-*		*i-*

(I) POSSESSORS IN DIRECT POSSESSION PHRASES Iconically, the prefix on the possessee indicates a direct or permanent relationship. The possessive prefixes are given in Table 3.2.

(6) ergog y-oduy
they.du du-front
their front(s)

(7) di-egak
1sg-leg
my leg

(8) mesogun nomi ø-eferu
papaya that:GIV 3sg-segment
a slice of the papaya (*lit.* the papaya its segment)

These prefixes have three other functions in the language: (1) They index the subject on verbs in both transitive and intransitive clauses, including derived intransitives in which the subject is patient/experiencer. (2) They occur on verbal modifiers in a noun phrase, indicating agreement with the person and number of the noun modified. (These verbal modifiers may be verbal adjectives, quantifiers, or verbal specifiers.) (3) They occur on nouns denoting types of humans to indicate the person and number of the referent.

(II) POSSESSORS IN DIRECT POSSESSION PHRASES In addition to the type of possessee affecting the choice of possessive construction, the type of possessor affects the choice of possessive prefix attached to an inalienable noun. Possessors are divided into two types, human and non-human. If the possessor is human, the possessive prefix on the inalienable possessee will indicate the person and number of the possessor, such as *i-* '3pl' attached to *ebirorha* 'skull' in (9). If the possessor is non-human, regardless of animateness, the prefix on the inalienable possessee will be the third person singular prefix ø- '3sg', the same prefix which indicates third-person singular for human possessors (see Table 3.2). This may be observed in the prefix ø- '3sg' attached to *ebrosurs* 'crown of head' in (10) and *owoka* 'name' in (11), with the broader context of (11) indicating there are two dogs. This coincides with the indefiniteness of number feature for all nouns which do not refer to humans.

(9) i-osnok i-ebirorha
3pl-person 3pl-skull
people's skulls

(10) memega ø-ebrosurs
mountain 3sg-crown.of head
mountain peak

(11) mes ø-owoka Masur dokun Masik
dog 3sg-name sandfly and mosquito
The dogs' names were Sandfly and Mosquito.

For dual human possessors, only *y-* 'du' is used, as all dual person markers have undergone neutralization of person (see Table 3.2). To distinguish person for dual possessors, a possessive pronoun, such as *ergen* 'their.du' in (12), is required.

(12) ergen y-ejmeg
their.du du-spine
their backs

(III) POSSESSEES IN DIRECT POSSESSION PHRASES Possessees in part–whole relationships extend beyond parts of humans, animals, and plants to numerous inanimate objects in nature, and are reflected in the grammar as inalienable nouns, such as *okun* 'side' in (13).

(13) memega ø-okun
mountain 3sg-side
(the) mountain's side

A number of intangible things which are closely associated with a person's identity are also included, such as *ofoms* 'effort/energy', *owas* 'strength', *efena* 'spirit/image/character', *owoka* 'name', *oga* 'speech', and *okowosos* 'footprint'. But all items which are human-constructed are expressed as alienable nouns. Thus, most concrete cultural items, such as *mosom* 'ax', *mesina* 'stringbag', and *marog* 'arrow', are not included in expressions of part–whole relationships.

(IV) NONPOSSESSED INALIENABLE NOUNS Inalienable nouns are rarely expressed as non-possessed forms and only a few have been observed. In these non-possessed forms, the root of the inalienable noun is prefixed by *m-* 'NOMZ', a generic nominalizer, as in *m-ofuga* (NOMZ-blood) 'bloodiness', *m-oga* (NOMZ-speech) 'personal affairs', *m-efer* (NOMZ-sore) 'woundedness', and *m-owj* (NOMZ-lip) 'edge of cliff'. If reference must be made to a human body part independent of its possessor, the third-person plural prefix *i-* '3pl', as the non-referential or impersonal form, is attached (e.g. *i-oforna* (3pl-bone) 'the bones').

(v) LOCATION ASSOCIATION There is a construction which denotes location or orientation association, quite likely based on an extension of the part–whole relationship. The juxtaposition of the anchor noun (that is, the noun referring to the whole) and the 'part' noun in the construction is structurally similar to that of inalienable possession but has a meaning which is similar to that of prepositions. There are 15 inalienable nouns functioning as spatial relator nouns used in location constructions. The location construction is always preceded by a preposition, which may be generic or specific with regards to location, such as *jig* 'LOC' preceding the location construction *merga ø-eferu ø-ewekesa* (wood 3sg-segment 3sg-midst) in (14) or *had* 'toward' preceding *mod ø-ejmeg* (house 3sg-spine) in (15).

(14) jig merga ø-eferu ø-ewekesa
LOC wood 3sg-segment 3sg-midst
between the boards

(15) had mod ø-ejmeg
toward house 3sg-spine
toward the back of the house / behind the house

For many of these location expressions, no preposition exists which parallels the location expression (e.g. there is no preposition with the meaning 'behind'). This is not a true possession construction, as the construction loses its location meaning if rephrased as a predicative possession construction, with a possessive pronoun or with a content interrogative.

4.3 *Possession on nouns which denote humans*

Nouns which denote humans fall into two general groups: generic nouns denoting types of humans and kinship nouns. Generic nouns denoting types of humans are always marked for possession analytically. Kinship nouns may be marked either analytically or synthetically.

4.3.1 *Generic nouns which denote types of humans* When the possessee is a generic noun denoting a type of human, the possessor is always indicated by a possessive pronoun (pr), such as *ofon* 'his/her' in (16) and (17) and *mifmin* 'our.pl' in (18). The possessive phrase structure is [Pr pr-Pe], the same structure found in the possessive phrase for indirectly possessed nouns (see §4.1). The generic nouns denoting types of humans include general nouns, such as *orna* 'man', *ejena* 'woman', *efer* 'child', and age associated nouns, such as *ej=efer* 'young woman' and *orenekena* 'elderly man', as in (17). Prefixes on generic nouns denoting types of humans indicate the person and number of the possessee in a possession phrase, not the possessor, thus *i-osnok* (3pl-person) in (16) means 'people', not 'their person'.

(16) misi ofon i-osnok
bandicoot his/her 3pl-person
the bandicoot's people (anthropomorphically meaning: the clansmen of the bandicoot)

(17) ofon i-orenekena
his/her 3pl-elderly.man
his old men (meaning: elder tribesmen)

(18) mifmin i-ejena
our.pl 3pl-woman
our (pl) women

The noun meaning 'child' is not treated grammatically as a kinship noun in Moskona, but as a generic noun referring to a type of human requiring a possessive pronoun to signal possessor, such as *ofon* 'his/her' in (19). This is in contrast to the other languages of the East Bird's Head Family which treat 'child' as a kinship noun and mark it synthetically for all possessors.

(19) Orocomna ofon y-efer=es y-erg-ak
Orocomna his/her du-child=male du-NCL:1-two
Orocomna's two sons

There are two other nouns denoting types of humans, *meesa* 'enemy' and *mosta* 'victim', which are indefinite as to number and phonologically similar to alienable nouns, as they have an /m/ segment root-initially. For these possession is expressed with a possessive pronoun preceding the possessee, as in *ofon meesa* (his/her enemy) 'his/her enemy'.

4.3.2 *Kinship nouns* The possessive prefixes on kinship nouns are not the same as those which indicate possessor on inalienable nouns, but have phonological similarity to them in that they may have similar consonants in common, but are not the same structurally.

Expression of possessors for kinship nouns is split across possession strategies. Kinship possession is marked both analytically and synthetically, as some kinship nouns are marked with a mixture of prefixes and possessive pronouns, depending upon the person and number of the possessor. This mixed strategy contrasts with the other two languages of the East Bird's Head Family, Meyah and Sougb, in which all possessors of kinship nouns are marked synthetically (Reesink 2002: 219, Gilles Gravelle 2010: 106). These limited possessive prefixes for kinship nouns appear to be the remnants of an earlier synthetic system in which a complete set of possessive prefixes distinguished all possessors on kinship nouns.

First- and second-person possessors, as speech participants, are frequently distinguished from other possessors. That is, for Moskona kinship nouns only first-person singular possessor and in a few instances second-person possessors are marked synthetically, such that the possession phrase has the structure [pr-Pe]. For example, *ed-ew-era* (1sg.kin-sibling.op.sex-older) 'my older sibling of the opposite sex' and *eb-edina* (2sg.kin-grandparent) 'your grandparent' are marked synthetically. This same phenomenon is mentioned by Lev Michael (Chapter 6) and in Chapter 1, this volume. The perceived conceptual closeness of first and second person coincides with proximity in surface realization. No grammatical distinction is made between consanguineal and affinal relationships in marking possession.

(I) KINSHIP NOUNS MARKED ONLY ANALYTICALLY Kinship nouns *mosu* 'mother' and *mekew* 'father' are marked analytically with a possessive pronoun indicating possessor, such as *ofon* 'his/her' in (20), preceding the possessed noun. This same structure [Pr pr-Pe] is also found in the possession phrases for alienable nouns. Likewise, the noun *efer* 'child' (as well as *efer=ej* 'daughter' and *efer=es* 'son'), a generic noun used to denote a type of human but used with a kinship meaning, requires a possessive pronoun to index possessor, for example *dadin efer=ej* (my child=female) 'my daughter'.

(20) Eriefiosga ofon mosu
Eriefiosga his/her mother
Eriefiosga's mother

Nominal expressions for siblings of parents are phrasal and are marked analytically, as in *dadin mosu ø-ejena* (my mother 3sg-woman) 'father's older sister'. Nouns *-ahina* 'husband' and *-ohena* 'wife', prefixed with *m-* 'NOMZ', are marked analytically when used referentially, as in (21). Only when used vocatively is the possessor marked synthetically, as the possessive prefix *ed-* '1sg.kin' is applied, as in *ed-ahina* (1sg.kin-husband) '(my) Husband'.

(21) Iwari ofon m-ohena
Iwari his/her NOMZ-wife
Iwari's wife

The kinship noun *-edina* 'grandparent/grandchild' is a reciprocal (polar) term and is marked primarily analytically. The exception is second-person singular, which is distinguished morphologically with the prefix *eb-* '2sg.kin', as in *eb-(e)dina* (2sg.kin-grandparent) 'your grandparent'. This structure [pr-Pe] does not have a nominal possessor as the possessor is a speech participant. All other persons are marked with *m-* 'NOMZ' and require a possessive pronoun to indicate possessor, such as *dadin* 'my' in (22).

(22) dadin m-edina
my NOMZ-grandparent
my grandparent

Nouns denoting brother-in-law or sister-in-law use the reciprocal term *-efina* 'sibling.in.law'. The prefix *m-* 'NOMZ' occurs on the root for all but first-person singular, which is marked for possessor with *ed-* '1sg.kin', as in (23). Possessor is analytically marked for all other possessors, such as *ergen m-efina* (their.du NOMZ-sibling.in.law) 'their brother/sister-in-law'.

(23) ed-efina
1sg.kin-sibling.in.law
my brother/sister-in-law

(II) KINSHIP NOUNS MARKED ANALYTICALLY AND SYNTHETICALLY For nouns which refer to siblings, possession is mostly marked synthetically, but in addition some must also be marked analytically. The possessive prefixes for same sex siblings are *ed-* 'sg.kin', *y-* 'du', *mi-* '1pl', *yi-* '2pl', and *i-* '3pl'. The dual prefix *y-* and the plural prefixes are identical to the prefixes marking the possessor on inalienable nouns. Person distinctions are neutralized in the singular kinship markers so that the first-person singular prefix *ed-* '1sg.kin' is used for all singular persons, thus both singular and dual possessors require a possessive pronoun to signal person. For example, the singular prefix *ed-* '1sg.kin' and the possessive pronoun *dadin* 'my' are required in (24).

(24) dadin ed-ok-era
my 1sg.kin-sibling.same.sex-older
my older sibling of the same sex

The possessive prefixes marking the possessor on siblings of the opposite sex have similarities to those used for siblings of the same sex. First-person singular possessor is marked with *ed-* '1sg.kin', but person distinctions are neutralized for second person singular and dual possession markers, so that *ey-* 'du.kin' marks second person singular and dual. The prefix *ey-* 'du.kin' and the possessive prefix *y-* 'du' used to mark the possessor on inalienable nouns have the phoneme /y/ as a similarity. All other person and number distinctions have been neutralized, so that the prefix *mi-* '1pl.kin' marks the possessor on siblings of the opposite sex. Thus, with the exception of the first-person singular possessor, a possessive pronoun, such as *mifmin* 'our.pl' in (25) or *buwun* 'your.sg' in (26) is required to distinguish person and number.

(25) mifmin mi-ew-era
our.pl 1pl.kin-sibling.op.sex-older
our older sibling of the opposite sex

(26) buwun ey-ew-esa
your.sg du.kin-op.sex-sg
your younger sibling of the opposite sex

These prefixes which distinguish first- and second-person possessor may reflect a more closely knit possessive expression, as the possessor is a participant in the speech act with a closer association than that of a non-participant. The non-participant possessors are lumped together under a single prefix.

5 Possession expressed by a clause

Moskona has four predicative possession constructions. The two constructions which focus on the possessor are 'have' constructions, and the two constructions which focus on the possessee are 'belong' constructions. The 'have' predicative possession constructions may have either a definite or indefinite possessee. The 'belong' predicative possession constructions must have a definite possessee, as predicated in Chapter 1, this volume.

5.1 *'Have' constructions*

In 'have' predicative possession constructions, the choice of construction type does not depend upon the possessor or the type of relationship, but on the type of possessee, whether it is definite or indefinite, a type of distinction not made in the possessive noun phrase constructions. Predicative possession constructions meaning 'have' can express the possession relationships associated with general possession and ownership, kinship, and part–whole relationships. Thus, those constructions which express the meaning 'have' may also mean 'own' or 'possess' if the possessee is non-human (e.g. pigs, dogs, or houses).

5.1.1 *Definite 'have' constructions* As definiteness requires a unique reference, the definite 'have' construction always indicates a definite possessee, in that it refers to a specific person, even though in other languages it may be expressed as indefinite, such as the English free translation 'a child' in (28). Those 'have' constructions which are definite have two possible structures: the first is a topic–comment construction, the second a topicalized possessor construction.

In the topic–comment structure, the possessor as topic/subject (TOP) and possessee as comment are juxtaposed, with the structure [(as for) Pr, Pe (exists)], suggesting the reading 'as for you, your dogs exist', meaning 'you own the dogs' as in (27) or 'as for me and my husband, our child exists', meaning 'I and my husband have a child' in (28). More accurately, the structure is [Pr pr-Pe], the same structure found in the possessive noun phrase when possession of an alienable noun is expressed (see §4.1).

These predicative possessive 'have' constructions correspond to Heine's Topic Schema (1997: 61).

(27) [yua]$_{TOP}$ yuyun mes
you.pl your.pl dog
You (pl) have/own the dogs. (*lit.* you, your dogs)

(28) [dif dokun dadin mahina]$_{TOP}$ yefyen ø-efer.
I and my husband our.du 3sg-child
I and my husband have a child. (*lit.* I and my husband, our child)

In definite 'have' constructions with an extraposed or topicalized possessor the structure is [Pr Pe Pred]. The possessor is expressed as a topic and the possessee as subject of the clause. The predicate may be non-verbal, such as the numeral construction *ibah ciyja* in (29) or verbal, such as the adjectival verb *eseter* in (30).

(29) [efer orna miyahta nomi,]$_{TOP}$ ofon mohena ibah ciyja
child man rich that:GIV his/her wife NUM:human five
The rich guy has five wives. (*lit.* the rich guy, his wives are five) (child = guy)

(30) [mer owokca]$_{TOP}$ ofon merah ø-ofog ø-eseter
room subunit his/her fire 3sg-cloud 3sg-be.much
The side room had lots of smoke. (*lit.* the side room, its smoke was a lot)

When the possessed is an inalienable noun, such as *owos* 'skin' in (31) or *ebrot* 'horn' in (32), in addition to the possessive prefix (pr-), a possessive pronoun, such as *ofon* 'his/her', is also required in the subject portion of the construction. This construction has the structure [Pr pr pr-Pe Pred].

(31) [ejen(a)-ekena]$_{TOP}$ ofon ø-owos ø-orur-ur.
woman-be.red his/her 3sg-skin 3sg-be.wrinkled-REDUP
The old woman has very wrinkled skin. (*lit.* old woman, her skin is wrinkled)

(32) [mekrus]$_{TOP}$ ofon ø-ebrot ø-etkebra
deer his/her 3sg-horn 3sg-be.short
The deer has short horns. (*lit.* the deer, his horns are short)

A 'have' construction with a topicalized possessor is negated with the negative adverb *éra* 'NEG' and if verbal, the verb is marked for irrealis with *em-* 'IRR', as is *edegejga* in (33) and *edeses* in (34), as are all negated verbs.

(33) [Dif]$_{TOP}$ dadin miyefen ø-em-edegejga éra.
I my money 3sg-IRR-match.up NEG
I don't have enough money. (*lit.* I, my money doesn't match up (to the need))

(34) [i-osnok noga i-ofojok erá,]$_{TOP}$ erin marotot
3pl-person REL 3pl-poor THM their.pl possessions
ø-em-edeses éra
3sg-IRR-be.many NEG
People who are poor don't have many possessions. (*lit.* people who are poor, their possessions are not many)

In a topic–comment 'have' construction, the predicate is non-verbal, as in (35) and (36), and is negated with the addition of *éra* 'NEG' clause-finally. When a definite (and referential) possessee has been negated, meaning the asserted nominal is denied, the contrastive specifier *ergem*, which may mean 'one (of many)' or 'any/some' is added.

(35) [bua]$_{TOP}$ buwun mofun dokun ember ø-erg-em éra.
you.sg your.sg vine and bucket 3sg-NCL:1-CONTR NEG
You don't have a/any rope and bucket. (*lit.* you, one of your rope and bucket are not)

(36) [dif]$_{TOP}$ dadin pensil ø-erg-em éra.
I my pencil 3sg-NCL:1-CONTR NEG
I don't have a/any pencil. (*lit.* I, one of my pencils is not)

5.1.2 *Indefinite 'have' construction* The indefinite 'have' construction, with the structure [Pr have Pe], utilizes the transitive verb *ok* 'bear' or 'carry on shoulder' to carry the meaning 'have'. The lexical content of the verb has semantically bleached from physically having in possession to a generalized non-referential possession. The possessor is encoded as the clausal subject and the possessee is encoded as clausal object, such as possessor *mow* 'land' and possessee *mesren* 'coarse grass' in (37), possessor *mem* 'bird' and possessee *efej* 'hair' in (38) and possessor *mem ofok* 'cassowary' and possessee *efeycua* 'cartilage' in (39). The possessor is not restricted, but the possessee is always indefinite, that is, has no specific referent. The third-person singular prefix ø- '3sg' marks the subject on the verb *ok* for all non-human referents. This type of construction corresponds to what Heine calls an Action Schema (Heine 1997: 47).

(37) mow noki erá ø-ok mesren ø-ekena gijga
land this:GIV THM 3sg-bear coarse.grass 3sg-be.red only
This place just has brown coarse grass.

(38) mem romreg ø-ok ø-efej
bird all 3sg-bear 3sg-hair
All birds have feathers.

(39)

mem	ofok	nomi	ø-ok	ø-efeycua
bird	lowland	that:GIV	3sg-bear	3sg-cartilage

The cassowary has cartilage (for a breast bone).

Indefinite 'have' constructions are negated with the negator *éra* 'NEG' which occurs clause-finally. The verb *ok* 'bear' is marked for irrealis with the prefix *em-* 'IRR', as in (40) and (41).

(40)

mos	nomi	ø-em-ok	ø-ewes	éra
fish	that:GIV	3sg-IRR-bear	3sg-fat	NEG

Those fish don't have fat.

(41)

mekrus	erá,	ofa	ø-em-ok	ø-ewek	éra
deer	THM	s/he	3sg-IRR-bear	3sg-gallbladder	NEG

Deer, they don't have gallbladders (meaning: they don't reason)

5.2 *'Belong' constructions*

The 'belong' constructions are limited in possessive relationship to signifying ownership or general possession. The possessee is always definite. There are two types of 'belong' constructions, one verbal and one non-verbal.

5.2.1 *Verbal 'belong' construction* In the verbal 'belong' construction, the structure is [Pe exists to Pr], as the possessee, such as *mar* 'thing' in (42), fills the subject position and the possessor appears in a dative adjunct phrase. The construction uses the existential classificatory verb *ah* 'lie' to mean 'be' or 'exist', along with the preposition *gug* 'to (someone)' to mark indirect object, such as *bua* 'you.sg' in (43). The pronominal prefix ø- '3sg' on the verb indexes the person and number of the subject, the non-human possessee. This type of 'belong' construction corresponds to Heine's Goal Schema (1997: 47, 59–61).

(42)

mar	nomi	ø-ah	gug	y-erg(og)-aha
thing	that:GIV	3sg-lie	to	du-they.du-REFL

The thing belongs to the two of them alone. (*lit.* the thing lies to themselves)

(43)

mow	nomi	ø-ah	gug	bua	ros
land	that:GIV	3sg-lie	to	you.sg	still

The land still belonged to you. (*lit.* the land lies to you still)

In a unique variation of the verbal 'belong' construction, no preposition marks the possessor as adjunct, as the possessor is expressed as an affix on the verb. The reciprocal pronominals can take the positions of the core argument's object and indirect object. Core arguments in Moskona are marked by position alone. Thus, neither the reciprocal object or indirect object is marked by a preposition. The bound reciprocal form is the circumfix *em- -ima* '(to) each other'. Thus, the verbal 'belong' construction may be a single verb word with *ah* 'lie' as the root, as in (44).

(44) y-em-em-ah-ima
du-IRR-RECIP-lie-RECIP
They would belong to each other. (meaning: be married)

Verbal 'belong' constructions may be negated with the negator *éra* 'NEG', which occurs clause-finally. The verb *ah* 'lie' is marked for irrealis with *em-* 'IRR', as in (45) and (46).

(45)

mar	ø-oskur	ø-em-ah	gug	yua	éra
thing	3sg-bad	3sg-IRR-lie	to	you.pl	NEG

(The) bad things don't belong to you. (meaning: its not your fault)

(46)

mar	mosorna	ø-erg-em	ø-em-ah	gug	eri	éra
thing	hunger	3sg-NCL:1-CONTR	3sg-IRR-lie	to	they.pl	NEG

None of the food belongs to them.

5.2.2 *Nonverbal 'belong' construction* The non-verbal 'belong' construction with the structure [Pe (is) Pr pr] is equative with an identification function, corresponding to Heine's Equation Schema (1997: 65–6). It is somewhat similar to the English Equation predication construction 'the thing is ours' / 'the thing belongs to us'. It exists alongside the verbal 'belong' construction and serves as an additional means to express a 'belong' predicative possession construction in which the possessee is the copular subject (COPS), such as *mar nomi* in (47) and (49) and *mod nomi* in (48).

(47)

[mar	nomi]$_{\text{COPS}}$	ergog	ergen
thing	that:GIV	they.du	their.du

The things belong to them. / The things are theirs.

(48)

[mod	nomi]$_{\text{COPS}}$	erá	ø-ekok	ofon
house	that:GIV	THM	3sg-father	his/her

The house belonged to his father. / The house was his father's.

(49)

[mar	nomi]$_{\text{COPS}}$	erá	mifmin
thing	that:GIV	THM	our.pl

The things belong to us. / The things are ours.

No examples of a negated non-verbal 'belong' construction have been observed, although negation of this construction may be possible.

6 External possession

In a possessive NP, possessors and possessees are never separated syntactically, except for relativization of possessees. In the case of external possession, the possessor may receive the focus by becoming an argument of the verb. This is achieved through separation of the possessor and possessee through relativization of the possessor. In the clause in (50), the topicalized possessor *eri* (they.pl) in the definite 'have' construction *eri erin i-oduy oyf-omof* (they.pl their.pl 3pl-front be.good-REDUP) 'they have good fronts' has been relativized and *eri* 'they.pl' has become a core argument, the object of the verb *ohojoh* 'destroy'. Similarly in (51), the possessor *eri* (they.pl) has been relativized and become the object of the verb. The possessees *erin i-oduy* (their.pl 3pl-front) in (50) and *erin eteyj-ah* (their.pl eye-be.alive) in (51) do not occur in an oblique phrase as in many instances of external possession, but as the subject of the relative clause.

(50)	Ofa	ø-ohojoh	eri	[noga	erin	i-oduy	oyf-omof]
	s/he	3sg-destroy	they.pl	REL	their.pl	3pl-front	be.good-REDUP
	nomisi						
	that.former:GIV						

S/he ruined them who had good fronts. (front of torso = seat of emotion)
(meaning: s/he hurt their feelings or destroyed their happiness)

(51)	Ofa	ø-ohojoh	eri	[noga	erin	eteyj(a)-(eb)ah
	s/he	3sg-destroy	they.pl	REL	their.pl	eye-be.alive
	[noga	oyf-amof]]				
	REL	good-REDUP				

S/he ruined them whose lives were good. (alive eye = life)
(meaning: s/he ruined their lives)

The possessor and possessee must be in a part–whole relationship, that is the possessee must be an inalienable noun, thus external possession is restricted to those possessees which are directly possessed.

7 Possession and language contact

The Moskona had contact with Malay-speaking people as early as 1663 primarily through trade and specifically through the slave trade. Slave trading ships, authorized by the raja of Rumbati, were observed in Bintuni Bay around this time and were mentioned in reports by Europeans working in the area (Haenen 1998: 236). Slave trading was practised extensively on the south coast of the Bird's Head with the export of slaves lasting until the end of the 1800s. This prolonged contact with speakers of an Austronesian language may have led to the change of possession strategy for marking possessor on kinship nouns in Moskona, possibly being the driving influence behind the transition from synthetic kinship possession marking to the predominantly analytic one currently employed in the language. This analytic marking strategy, discussed in §4.3.2, distinguishes Moskona from Meyah and Sougb, the two other languages of the East Bird's Head Family which exclusively employ a synthetic strategy for marking kinship nouns. Meyah and Sougb may not have had the extensive contact with Malay that Moskona had, or if so incorporated other features which did not involve their kinship possession strategy.

8 Possession in society

Such an abundance of constructions in possessive expressions (both nominal and predicative) suggests that the society has a strong focus on possession and ownership and a strong sense of private possession as a value central to the culture. This strong sense of private possession is reflected socially in the extensive reciprocity system within the culture, both in material possessions given and services rendered, such as intangible indebtedness accrued toward themselves which can later be repaid with tangible things. The sense of private ownership (and required reciprocity) is so strong that nothing is given without an expected repayment, and there are numerous expressions for repayment or for recouping goods owed. Thus the numerous possession constructions in the grammar of the language coincide with both the values and activities integral to a strong sense of private ownership and a focus on possession.

References

Givón, Talmy. 1984. *Syntax. A functional-typological introduction.* Vol. 1. Philadelphia: John Benjamins.

Gravelle, Gilles. 2010. *Meyah: A language of West Papua, Indonesia.* Canberra: Pacific Linguistics.

Gravelle, Gloria. 2010. 'Moskona: An East Bird's Head language of West Papua, Indonesia'. Ph.D. dissertation, Vrije Universiteit, Amsterdam.

Haenen, Paul. 1998. 'History, exchange and myth in the southeastern Bird's Head', pp. 235–56 of *Perspectives on the Bird's Head of Irian Jaya, Indonesia,* edited by Jelle Miedema, Cecilia Odé and Rien A. C. Dam. Amsterdam: Rodopi.

Heine, Bernd. 1997. *Possession. Cognitive sources, forces, and grammaticalization.* Cambridge: Cambridge University Press.

Reesink, Ger. P. 2002. 'A grammar sketch of Sougb', pp. 181–275 of *Languages of the Eastern Bird's Head,* edited by Ger P. Reesink. Canberra: Pacific Linguistics.

4

Possession and ownership in Manambu, a Ndu language from the Sepik area, Papua New Guinea

ALEXANDRA Y. AIKHENVALD

1 The Manambu and their possessions

A salient feature of the Manambu of the Middle Sepik River Basin, and of the neighbouring and related Iatmul, is a focus on clan ownership of ancestral names and totems, inherited through one's father. Within the Manambu tradition, the world is divided into totemic areas belonging to different subclans, indentified through ownership of names. This totemic ownership only partly determines rights to the land. And it is distinct from how one possesses other, more material, objects. My major concern in this chapter is how these concepts are reflected in the linguistic practices of the Manambu, and the Manambu grammar.[1]

Manambu is a member of Ndu language family—the largest in the Sepik area in terms of numbers of speakers. The language is spoken by about 2,500 people in several major villages (Avatip, Malu, Yawabak, Apa:n, and Yambon in East Sepik Province, Ambunti district),[2] and by smallish expatriate communities in major cities of Papua New Guinea.

[1] Similar principles have been described for a number of other Sepik groups, especially the Iatmul, neighbours, relatives, and major rivals of the Manambu, and also the Murik, the Mountain Arapesh, the Abelam, and the Kwoma. Cf. Gregory Bateson's (1958: 228) statement about the closely related Iatmul as a people for whom personal names form 'a theoretical image of the whole culture'.

[2] See Aikhenvald (2004) and (2008: ch. 22) on the position of the Ndu family in the Sepik River Basin, and of Manambu within it. I am indebted to my Manambu family, especially Yuamali Jacklyn Benji Ala, Pauline Agnes Yuaneng Luma Laki, Gemaj, Jenni Kudapa:kw, John Sepaywus, and many others, for helping me in my attempts to learn their fascinating language. I am grateful to R. M. W. Dixon for providing feedback.

2 The Manambu language: a typological snapshot

Manambu is one of the most morphologically complex languages of the Ndu family. In all likelihood, this complexity is due to intensive contact with known and unknown peoples in the Sepik area, as a result of tribal wars and the Manambu expansion (see Aikhenvald 2009a).

Manambu is nominative-accusative, predominantly suffixing with just two productive prefixes, synthetic, and agglutinating with some fusion.[3] Nouns have two covert genders (feminine and masculine, marked via agreement in the singular only) and three numbers (singular, dual, and plural) marked on modifiers and on verbs. Gender assignment for humans is sex-based; for other groups of nouns it is based on size and shape. Thus, a small location will be referred to as feminine, and a large one as masculine; a short stretch of time as feminine, and a long one as masculine (cf. (3)).

Possessive constructions with pronominal Possessor (see Table 4.1, and §3.4, type C) require agreement in gender and in number with the Possessee marked on the pronominal Possessor. The masculine singular agreement marker is *-də*, and the feminine is zero or *-l*.

(1) a-də ñən-a-də ma:m
that-masc.sg you.fem.sg-LINK-masc.sg older.sibling
that elder brother of yours

Noun phrases with modifiers require a linker on the modifier (see Aikhenvald 2008: 71–3). The linker also occurs in one type of possessive construction (B, §3.3). The linker is most frequently *-a-*, e.g. *du-a-ñan* (man-LINK-child) 'male child', *vyakat-a ta:kw* (good-LINK woman) 'good woman', *du-a-ya:b* (man-LINK-road) 'men's road'. If a noun phrase with a linker has four syllables or more, it has to form two phonological words; otherwise it forms one word.

Verbs can be intransitive, or ambitransitive (most are of S = A type; but there are some S = O).[4] There are rather few strictly transitive or ditransitive verbs. A constituent cannot be negated without negating the whole clause (this is why negative possession—or 'lacking' something—is relevant only for predicative possession).

A member of any word class can head the predicate of an intransitive main clause. Verbs then take tense-sensitive verbal cross-referencing suffixes. Depending on clause type and mood, modality and aspect, either just the subject (A or S) or the subject and an additional constituent can be cross-referenced.

Other word classes can occur in the predicate slot. Then, they take nominal cross-referencing enclitics with no tense, modality, or aspect distinctions. If tense has to be

[3] A full grammar of the language is in Aikhenvald (2008).
[4] See Dixon (2010: 124), for the basics of transitivity classes across the world's languages.

expressed in a clause without a lexical verb, a non-verb has to be used as a copula complement of the support verb *tə* which also means 'stand', 'have', and 'be, become' (when used as a copula with some copula complements). Manambu has nine further copula verbs (we return to these in §4.2).

3 Meanings and forms of possessive noun phrases

Marking possession within a noun phrase in Manambu is relatively simple. There are no possessive classifiers, nor any complex division of nouns into possession classes. We distinguish five types of possessive constructions summarized in Table 4.1. These differ in terms of (i) overt marking; (ii) order of Pr and Pe; (iii) semantics; (iv) specificity of the Pe; and (v) animacy of the Pr.

What all the constructions have in common is that the Possessee is invariably the head.

We start with the type E, whole–part construction which stands apart from the rest in terms of its word order and restrictions on the animacy of the Possessor.

3.1 *Whole–part constructions*

A whole–part construction consists of a term for a body part (referring to something other than a part of a human body) or a plant part, or a spatial term accompanied by the linker and followed by the 'whole', or the notional 'Possessor'. The 'Possessor' has to be inanimate.

TABLE 4.1. **Possessive constructions in Manambu**

Marking	Semantic overtones	Possessor
A. Juxtaposition Pr-Pe (§3.2)	any kind of ownership, including kin and body parts; Possessee non-specific	any noun or personal pronoun
B. Pr-linker Pe (§3.3)	purpose, location, attribution	any noun except for personal names; not personal pronouns
C. Pr pronominal possession marker Pe (§3.4)	any kind of ownership, including kin and body parts; Possessee specific	any noun or interrogative or personal pronoun
D. Origin (Pr-*kə* Pe) (§3.5)	origin, association	any noun or personal pronoun
E. Whole-part (Pe-LINK-Pr) (§3.1)	whole–part, spatial relationships, orientation	inanimate noun

Whole–part constructions with plant parts include *səp-a-lap* (skin-LINK-banana) 'banana skin', *tək-ə-mi* (seed-LINK-tree) 'seed of a tree, medicine'. A plant part can be used to describe a shape: *ga:l* means 'branch', and *gala-ta:b* (branch+LINK-hand) refers to a fork-like space between the fingers on one's hand.

Human body parts used in whole–part constructions refer to spatial attributes of objects, for example *yala-wi* (belly+LINK-house) 'the inside of the house', *mutam-a wi* (face-LINK-house) 'the front of a house', *tama-val* (nose+LINK-canoe) 'nose of a canoe', *mada-ñəg* (testicles+LINK-mosquito.net) 'underneath mosquito net'. Orientation terms also occur in this construction type, for example *api* 'top' in *api ñəg* 'on top of mosquito net', and *ñəd* 'middle' as in *ñəd-ə–wi* (middle-LINK-week) 'middle of the week'.

A noun referring to an animal or an insect can appear as 'Possessor' in the whole–part construction. Then, its referent is inanimate: *kui-a-bal* (meat-LINK-pig) 'meat of (dead) pig' refers to pork, and not to the flesh of the living animal.

Whole–part constructions cannot contain modifiers or multiple possessors. The Possessee (Pe) is the head of the noun phrase. In (2), the gender agreement on the demonstrative and on the modifier 'big' is with 'nose' and not with the canoe:

(2)	a-də	nəma-də	tama-val
	DEM.DIST-masc.sg	big-masc.sg	nose(masc)+LINK-canoe(fem)
	that big nose of a canoe (*nose of that big canoe)		

Body parts and plant parts can occur in possessive constructions of other types, but with a different meaning.

3.2 *Possessive constructions with juxtaposition*

Possessive constructions of the type A, marked via JUXTAPOSITION, impose no restrictions on the Possessor or on the Possessee in terms of their animacy. The meaning of the construction covers a broad semantic range, from possession proper to attribution. Possessor—which precedes the Possessee—can be a noun or a pronoun, e.g. *ta:kw ya:b* '(a) woman's road', *Yuaya:b amæy* 'Yuayab's mother', *bal ya:m* (pig smell) 'smell of a pig', *wun amæy* (I mother) 'my mother', *kwaj məl* (bat eye) 'eye of a bat', *məd kui* 'cassowary's flesh'.

These constructions always form two phonological words. Either the Possessor or the Possessee can consist of a noun phrase with a modifier, e.g. [*kə-də təp*] *wa:ñ* (DEM.PROX-masc.sg village line) 'the line of this village', *wun* [*nəma wi*] (I big+fem.sg house) 'my big house' (further examples are in Aikhenvald 2008: 170–4).

The Possessee is the head, since it determines the gender and number agreement. The feminine cross-referencing on the possessive NP (in brackets) in (3) indicates agreement with the feminine noun *wa:ñ* 'genealogical line' (the feminine gender is used here because the line is small).

(3)	alək	[[kə-də	təp]	wa:ñ]	kwasa-l
	this.is.why	DEM.PROX-masc.sg	village(masc)	line(fem)	small-3fem.sgNOM

This is why the descent line of this village is small.

Multiple possessors are posssible, e.g. *Yuakalu wi yawa:r* ([[Yuakalu [house]] [post]]) 'post of of the house belonging to Yuakalu'. The possessee is always the head in this construction type.

3.3 *Possessive constructions with a linker*

Possessive constructions of the type B marked with a linker cover a broad range of meanings typically associated with possession (see the overview in Chapter 1, this volume). The meanings include:

- purpose, e.g. *məl-a-glas* (eye-LINK-glass) 'eyeglass, spectacles', *ab-a-wapwi* (head-LINK-dress) 'headdress, hat', *ab-a-ñəg* (head-LINK-leaf) 'umbrella', *diy-a-wi* (excrement-LINK-house) 'toilet';
- location, e.g. *taba-ñə* (hand+LINK-sun) 'wrist watch' (*lit.* hand sun), *taba-yi* (hand +LINK-fire) 'hand-held torch';
- attribution and propensity, e.g. *təp-a ta:kw* (village-LINK woman) 'village women', women', *gwalugw-ə ja:p* (clans-LINK thing/valuable) 'traditional valuables, things of clans', *ap-a-sə* (bone-LINK-name) 'main name bestowed by paternal relatives' (*lit.* the name of the bone identified with patrilineal descent).

In terms of their semantic range, possessive constructions of this type are similar to noun phrases with multiple meanings (which also include possession) in Galo (Chapter 7), Mandarin Chinese (Chapter 8), and Likpe (Chapter 10).

While possessive constructions marked via juxtaposition have a purely possessive meaning, constructions with the linker do not. For instance, a juxtaposed construction *təp sə* (village name) means 'the name of a village'. In contrast, *təp-a-sə* (village-LINK-name) refers to 'village name', or a name given to a person in the village and by the villagers.

Back in the old days, Avatip, the major village where the Manambu live, used to be consistently in danger of attacks which were most likely to come from across the river. To protect women, and non-initiated men and children, two roads were in use: the one further away from the river intended for women and children, and the one closer to the river intended for men who would be prepared to brace the potential danger. The road intended for women is called *takwa-ya:b* (woman+LINK-road) 'road for women', and the road intended for men is *du-a-ya:b* 'road for men'. The danger of attack is gone, but the roads are still in use, and are referred to in this same way. Inhabitants of other Manambu villages know them as an 'Avatip' phenomenon (the river bank in Malu is too narrow to have two roads).

In contrast, a juxtaposed construction *ta:kw ya:b* (woman road) means 'a woman's road', that is, a road which belongs to a woman, for instance a road goes through a woman's garden and is her property; and *du ya:b* is 'a man's road' (that is, a road belonging to a man and his property).

A construction with a linker can form one or more phonological words depending on the number of syllables (see §2). Constructions with a linker often acquire somewhat unpredictable meanings (see 'watch' above).

3.4 *Possessive constructions with a pronominal possessive marker*

Possessive constructions with a pronominal possessive marker (type C) are similar in their meaning to possessive noun phrases marked through juxtaposition. They are used for ownership of any sort, including kin and body part. The difference between the two is that in this construction, the Possessee has to have a specific—and not a generic—referent. The Possessor can be a personal pronoun, an interrogative, or a noun (or a noun phrase of any length).

If the Possessor is a personal pronoun or the interrogative *sə* 'who', the pronoun itself serves as a possession marker. Agreement in gender and number is always marked on the pronoun. Third-person singular and dual (that is, non-plural) pronouns, and the interrogative *sə* 'who?' take the possessive marker *-kə-*, e.g.

(4) *wun-a amæy* (I-LINK+fem.sg mother) 'my mother'[5]
wun-a-də asa:y (I-LINK-masc.sg father) 'my father'
də-kə amæy (he-POSS+fem.sg mother) 'his mother'
də-kə-də asa:y (he-POSS-masc.sg father) 'his father'
sə-kə-də asa:y (who-POSS-masc.sg father) 'whose father?'

If the Possessor is a noun or a noun phrase, the non-plural Possessor is followed by a third person pronoun agreeing with the Possessor and accompanied by the suffix *-kə-* and gender and number suffix agreeing with the Possessee (also see (1)):

(5) du   də-kə-bər   ta:kw
man   he-POSS-dual   woman/wife
man's two wives

If the Possessor is plural, the possessive marker *-kə-* is not used:

(6) du   daya-di   sə
man   3pl+LINK-3pl   name
men's names

[5] Throughout this chapter, the hyphen - is used to mark morpheme boundaries. The symbol + indicates that morphemes are fused. For instance, *wun-a* is glossed as I-LINK+fem.sg reflecting the fact that the linker *-a-* is fused with the ø marker for feminine singular.

These constructions are preferred if Possessor or Possessee are in contrastive focus. They are particularly useful for disambiguating the sex and the number of Possessee and Possessor: *wun ñan* (I child) means 'my child' and can refer to a girl or a boy. But *wun-a-də ñan* (I-LINK-masc.sg child) unambiguously means 'my son', and *wun-a ñan* (I-LINK+fem.sg child) means 'my daughter' (also see (1)). Constructions with a pronominal possessive marker can contain a modifier to the Possessee (unlike constructions with the linker, and many juxtaposed constructions). The head of the construction is Possessee.

A possessive construction of this type can contain multiple possessors. (7) states the totemic ownership of 'this mountain' and of its name, by the Ñakau subclan:

(7) kə-də nəbək də-kə-də
DEM.PROX-masc.sg mountain 3masc.sg-POSS-masc.sg
sa:d Makəmawi-ad [[Ñakau dəya-di
name+3masc.sgNOM Makemawi-3masc.sgNOM Ñakau they-pl
nəbək] [dəya-də sa:d]]
mountain they-masc.sg name+3masc.sgNOM
The name of this mountain is Makemawi, (it is) the name of the mountain of the Ñakau clan.

The mountain referred to in (7) is known as Ambunti mountain, and is a highly visible landmark in the region.

A pronominal Possessor can constitute a verbless clause complement. Then, if Possessee is non-plural, the possessive *-kə-* appears on the possessive pronoun, as in (8). Note that the feminine singular allomorph here is *-l*:

(8) kə walina:gw ñən-a-kə-l-al
this:fem.sg biscuit you.fem-LINK-POSS-fem.sg-3fem.sgNOM
This biscuit is yours.

If the head noun within possessive constructions with first- and second-person Possessor is omitted, the *-kə-* marker has to be used (again with the feminine singular allomorph *-l)*:

(9) wun-a-kə-l kur-tukwa
I-LINK-POSS-fem.sg take-PROH
Don't take mine!

We now turn to a further use of the suffix *-kə*.

3.5 *The origin construction*

The origin construction (type D) consists of a place of origin ('Possessor') + suffix *-kə-* gender and number agreement marker with the Possessee, followed by the head noun. Its main meaning is the origin, similarly to the construction with the 'personalizing' marker *-nyə* in Likpe (§3.4.1 of Chapter 10):

(10) təp-a-kə-di | du-ta:kw
village-LINK-ORIGIN-pl | man-woman
village people; people from the village; villagers

If the head noun is feminine, the agreement marker is *-l*:

(11) kwarba-kə-l | ta:kw
forest+LINK-POSS-fem.sg | woman
woman belonging to the forest, forest woman

An origin construction indicates provenance from a clan or a country, for example *Valik gwalugw-ə-kə-də du* (Valik clan-LINK-POSS-masc.sg man) 'man from Valik clan', *Ostrelia-kə-l ta:kw* (Australia-POSS-fem.sg woman) 'woman from Australia' (also see (29)).

It may indicate loose association with the 'Possessor': *ab-a-kə-l* (head-LINK-POSS-fem.sg) 'the one to do with head' was used to refer to hair cream. A plate of food leftovers from the day before yesterday was referred to as *nagəs-ə-kə-də* (the.day.before.yesterday-LINK-POSS-masc.sg) 'a big one from the day before yesterday'. An 'origin' noun phrase cannot be discontinuous, or contain multiple possessors.

The head noun can be omitted. This is illustrated in (12). The second occurrence of a headless associative NP in this example appears in the predicate slot. Then, number and gender are effectively marked twice: once with gender-number suffix *-di* 'plural' agreeing with the omitted head noun of a possessive NP ('people'), and once with gender-number-person enclitic *-adi* 'third person plural nominal predicate'. Example (12) explains the association between the Gla:gw clan group and the 'ground' (contrasted to the opposite clan group, the Wulwi-ñawi who are associated with the light, sun, and moon):

(12) [dəy | [gla:gw-ə-kə-di]] | [kəp-a-kə-di-adi]$_{\text{PREDICATE.SLOT}}$
they | Gla:gw-LINK-ORIGIN-pl | ground-LINK-ORIGIN-pl-3plNOM
They (the people) from the Gla:gw clan group are those (people) of the ground.

A question arises here. Is the marker *-kə-* used in possessive constructions of type C and the marker -kə- in origin constructions the same morpheme or not? Synchronically, the two *-kə-* have different possibilities in terms of their use: the origin marker *-kə-* occurs with any pronoun used as a modifier, and the possessive *-kə-* does not. Unlike the possessive *-kə-* the origin marker *-kə-* can be used with a plural (or any other) pronoun. Its meaning is not the same. In (13), the origin marker is used to describe a line loosely associated with the men, but not belonging to them:

(13) [a-di du] dəya-kə-l wa:ñ
DEM.PL-pl man 3pl+LINK-ORIGIN-fem.sg line
anay kwa-na
DEM.DIST.ANAPH stay-ACT.FOC+3fem.sgSUBJECT
The line associated with those men is there (mentioned).

If we had been talking about a line belonging to the men, the possessive NP would have been *[a-di du] dəya-kə wa:ñ* (DEM.PL-pl man 3pl+LINK+fem.sg line) 'the line belonging to those men'. This demonstrates a further point in which the two *-kə-* morphemes differ. The feminine singular agreement marker within the origin construction is always *-l*. Within possessive constructions type C, it is zero within an NP, and *-l* only if the construction is used headlessly (as we saw in (8) and (9)).

The two morphemes *-kə-* can be analysed as synchronically different but related forms, or as a single form with different grammatical possibilities. Historically the two are related. One piece of evidence comes from mourning songs and songs about foiled marriages (see Harrison 1983; Aikhenvald 2008, 2009a, for some discussion). In the few possessive constructions in the songs, the marker *-kə-* is used in possessive constructions (with *-l* as a feminine agreement marker), e.g. *də-kə-l jukwar wun-a-kə-l ti:d* (he-POSS/ORIGIN-fem.sg sister I-LINK-POSS/ORIGIN-fem.sg co-wife) 'his sister, my co-wife'. This usage may reflect an archaic pattern. Alternatively, it may be a feature of these song styles where the relationship between the speaker and the relative being mourned or lamented is presented as less closely associated than in ordinary possession.[6]

3.6 *How body parts and kinship terms differ from other nouns*

We have seen that whole–part constructions (type E, with the 'whole' being inanimate) differ from other constructions which cover possession and related meanings. That is, nouns referring to parts of human and animal bodies and plants, and orientation terms, can be considered a special subclass of nouns in terms of their 'possessability'.

Body parts and kinship terms stand apart from nouns of other semantic groups in a further way. We can recall that in all possessive constructions in Manambu the Possessee is the head of a noun phrase: it controls agreement with the modifiers and

[6] Speakers of the Malu variety appear to extend the possessive marker *-kə-* to all third-person pronouns, and not just non-plural. This could be an innovation reflecting the levelling of the two formally similar construction types. Or it can be a retention of an older pattern. The suffix *-kə-* is also used in the formation of oblique case forms of third-person plural pronouns, as a stem marker. Whether or not this is related to the other two occurrences of *-kə-* remains an open question.

the predicate. However, if the 'owner' of a body part is particularly affected, the Possessor and not the Possessee is cross-referenced on the verb. In (14), from a tale, a turtle is complaining about those who used to eat her meat: the extent of her being affected is reflected in cross-referencing the Possessor ('I', that is the feminine turtle who is the story-teller) on the verb:

(14) [wun-a kui] kə-kwa-dana-wun
I-LINK+fem.sg meat eat-HAB-3plSUBJ-1fem.sgOBJECT
They used to eat my flesh (*lit.* they used to eat me (on) my flesh) (said the turtle).

This is somewhat similar to an 'external' possession construction: the effect of 'splitting' a possessive construction consists in focusing on the affectedness of the Possessor. This only applies to body parts and kin terms, which are in close relationship to the Possessor.

Both Possessor and Possessee can be relativized upon. If the common argument—shared by the relative clause and the main clause—is closely associated with the Possessee, the Possessee is preposed to the predicate of the relative clause followed by the common argument. That is, 'men whose wives died' is literally 'wife they-died men', 'man whose hand you shook' is 'hand you-shook man', and 'boy whose fever goes up' is 'fever he-goes up boy'. Such 'Possessees' include kinship relations, as in (15), and body parts, as in (16):

(15) [ta:kw kiya-di du] atawa gra-kwa-na-di
woman die-3plSUBJECT man thus cry-HAB-ACTION.FOCUS-3plSUBJECT
Men whose wives died (*lit.* wife they-died men) cry like that.

(16) [ta:b kur-ñəna-də du]
hand shake/get-2fem.sgSUBJ-3masc.sgOBJECT man
də-kə sə Ka:t-ad
he-POSS+fem.sg name Kat-3masc.sgNOM
The name of the man whose hand you shook (*lit.* hand you-shook man) is Kat.

A similar relative clause construction is possible whenever the connection between the Possessor and the Possessee can be conceived as close enough and culturally acceptable. That is, (16a) was judged possible:

(16) a. a:s kiya-də ñan
dog die-3masc.sgOBJECT child
a child whose dog died (*lit.* dog he-died child, or child died with respect to dog)

If the connection between Possessor and Possessee cannot be conceived as culturally acceptable, a construction like the one in (16a) is rejected. Nobody has close connections with rats, and so (16b) was rejected:

(16) b. ?wakuli kiya-də ñan
rat die-3masc.sgOBJECT child
?a child whose rat died?

The Possessor in each of these examples can be in any function in a main clause. Its function in a relative clause is the subject (S) or the object: this function is indicated by the person, number, gender, and tense markers on the predicate of the relative clause. The Possessee in the relative clause is ambiguous as to its syntactic functions: it can be considered part of the S in (15), and part of O in (16). This creates an unusual clause type, only found in relative clauses involving relativization of Possessor.

These instances—akin to external possession in Manambu—provide additional support to distinguishing body part and kinship 'possession' from those of other types.

We now turn to clausal possession which operates following different parameters and highlights the societal values of the Manambu.

4 Possession within a clause

Manambu has several ways of marking predicative possession. These involve the verb 'have' (§4.1), and a number of copula clauses and verbless clause strategies (§4.2).

4.1 *The verb 'have'*

The polyfunctional verb *tə-* 'have, be, become, stand' is frequently used for predicative possession. This is comparable to how various existential verbs are used in possessive constructions in Ku Waru (or Temboka: see §4.1 of Chapter 13), and the verb 'lie' is used in Moskona (§5.2.1 of Chapter 3).[7] When this verb means 'have', it is transitive. The verb 'have' differs from other verbs in the language in that:

(i) it cannot form an imperative (one cannot order anyone to 'have' anything: if one needs to order someone to get something, the verb *kur-* 'get' is used);
(ii) it cannot take any directional markers (which all other verbs can take);
(iii) it does not form part of aspectual and modal compounds.

The verb *tə-* in its meaning 'have' can be omitted in negative possessive constructions. If it is used as a copula 'be, become' or as a support verb, it cannot be omitted. Most nouns other than kinship and body part terms can be used as the Possessee of 'have'. In (17), the Possessee is an inanimate referent ('money'):

[7] The frequent use of 'have' in Manambu could have been influenced by Tok Pisin *gat* 'have, be'. However, I have not observed any generational differences in the use of 'have' among Manambu speakers. The verb *tə-* 'have' is cognate with the Iatmul *ti* 'stay, be' (Staalsen and Staalsen 1973). Kwoma, spoken in the same area as Manambu, but not related to it, has a possessive verb *ta* 'have' (Bowden 1997: 206).

(17)	nəma	kabak	tə-na-di
	big+fem.sg	money (*lit.* stone)	have-ACT.FOC-3plSUBJECT
	They have a lot of money.		

The verb 'have' can be used with a kinship term, but with an implication of 'coming into possession, acquiring' (this is similar to Hone, §3.1 of Chapter 9, this volume).

(18)	du-a-ñan	nak	ata	tə-bər
	man-LINK-child	one	then	have-3duSUBJECT
	Then they had one boy.			

For statements on established possession of one's kin, verbless clauses are preferred—see §4.2.

The verb 'have' is only sometimes used with body parts, to contrast possessed nouns. Example (19) comes from a tale which contrasts two birds: one has a big nose, the other one a small one. Note that the second argument of *tə-* in the meaning 'have' can be cross-referenced on the verb, just as would be the case with any other verb. This distinguishes *tə-* 'have' as a transitive verb from its other uses as a copula verb (a copula complement cannot be cross-referenced on the copula verb).

(19)	ñən	nəma-də	ta:m	tə-ñəna-d
	you.fem	big-masc.sg	nose(masc)	have-2fem.sgSUBJ-3masc.sgOBJECT
	You have a big nose (said a willy wagtail to hornbill (feminine)).			

Using 'have' with other body parts implies one's ability to use them: somebody who does listen and pay attention can be referred to as *wa:n tə-na* (ear have-ACTION.FOCUS+3fem.sgSUBJECT), literally 'has ear'. This is similar to how 'proprietive' derivations in Martuthunira are employed with body parts (§1.5 of Chapter 5).

The verb 'have' occurs with a polysemous term *mawul* 'inside, bone marrow, pith (of a tree), temper, mind'.[8] One refers to a good-hearted and even-tempered person as *vyakat-a mawul tə-na* (good-LINK 'inside' have-ACTION.FOCUS+3fem.sgSUBJECT) '(She) has a good heart and even temper'. People who agree with each other are referred to as *mawul nak tə-na-di* ('inside' one have-ACT.FOC-3plSUBJECT) 'They agree, are of the same mind'.

The verb 'have' can be negated like any other verb. In negative possessive clauses, it is frequently omitted: (20b) is a version of (20a):

(20)	a.	wun	kamna:gw	ma:	tə
		I	food	NEG	have:NEG
		I have no food, I don't have food.			

[8] *Mawul* is the major locus of emotional and mental states. See Aikhenvald (2008: 580–4). This concept appears similar to the idea of *wambung* in Karawari, a Lower Sepik group (Telban 1998: 59). *Mawul* contrasts with *kayik* 'image, ghost, carving, reflection (in water), shadow; picture, film'. *Kayik* can also be used with the verb 'have'.

(20) b. wun kamna:gw ma:
I food NEG
I have no food, I don't have food.

What we see in (20b) is a verbless clause used for negative possession. We now turn to possessive meanings expressed through verbless clauses and copula clauses.

4.2 *Possessive meanings expressed through copula clauses and verbless clauses*

Manambu has ten copula verbs (Aikhenvald 2008: 82–6) whose choice depends on the copula complement. The verb *tə-* as copula means 'exist, be, become'; then its copula complement is unmarked. If its copula complement is marked with the comitative case, it refers to temporary acquisition—or possession—of a bodily state, such as being pregnant ('having a belly, being with a belly') or acquiring breasts (about a young girl who is becoming an adult):

(21) lə bətay yala-wa tə-na
she already belly+LINK-COMITATIVE be-ACTION.FOCUS+3fem.sgSUBJECT
She is already pregnant. (*lit.* is with belly)

The copula *na-* occurs with physical states, such as *bwiyabwi na-* (hot be:states) 'be hot' (of person's skin). The copula *yasə-* occurs with physical needs and desires: *wun ka:m yasə-na* (I hunger be:desire-ACTION.FOCUS+3fem.sgSUBJECT) means 'I am hungry'. The copula *say-* 'feel' occurs with mental and physcial states: *wun wap say-na* (I shame be:feel-ACTION.FOCUS+3fem.sgSUBJECT) means 'I am ashamed, I have shame', and *wun bag say-na* ((I pins.and.needles be:feel-ACTION.FOCUS+3fem.sgSUBJECT) means 'I feel pins and needles'.

'Having' an illness such as a fever or malaria involves the copula *kwa-* 'stay' with the copula complement in dative-aversive case. Other diseases require special collocations, for example *lan* 'have a headache', or *yap war-* (breath go up) 'have asthma, have a heart attack' in (22):

(22) wun ya:p war-na
I breath go up-ACTION.FOCUS+3fem.sgSUBJECT
I have asthma or I have a heart attack (*lit.* I, breath goes up).

Example (22) is reminiscent of the 'topicalization strategy' for possession marking (see §3.1.2 of Chapter 1, this volume).[9]

Verbless clauses are preferred for statements about the 'possession' of kin and body parts. We saw in (18) that the verb 'have' with kinship terms implies 'acquiring'

[9] 'Have a wife' is phrased as *ta:kw kra-* (woman get) 'get a wife' and have a husband as *du-a-k rə-* (man-LINK-DAT sit).

a kin. If one talks about, say, how many children one has, there are two options. One involves topicalization:

(23) ñən ñanugw kas
you.fem children how.many
How many children do you have? (*lit.* You, children how many?)

This is a question about 'you'. The other option involves a verbless clause with the Possessee as the subject. This statement is about the children and how many they are:

(24) wun-a-di ñanugw mugul-adi
I-LINK-pl children three-3plNOM
My children are three.

The same principle applies to body parts. If someone has a bad eye (and is asking for glasses), they would say either (25a) (with topicalization) or (25b), with a slight pragmatic difference: (25a) highlights 'me', and (25b) is about the eye:

(25) a. wun məl kuprap-a
I+fem.sg eye bad-3fem.sgNOM
My eye is bad. (*lit.* I, eye is bad)[10]

(25) b. wun-a məl kuprap-a
I-LINK+fem.sg eye bad-3fem.sgNOM
My eye is bad.

To negate any such construction, one simply puts *ma:* 'negator' after the copula or the verbless clause complement, stripping it of any cross-referencing marking, as we saw in (20b). Verbal categories are neutralized in negative constructions in Manambu, similarly to the animate/inanimate distinction of the possessive verb in Nanti (§4.1 of Chapter 6).

In summary: verbless clauses express possession of kin and body parts. These reflect inherent and permanent ties. We now turn to a Manambu-specific use of verbless clauses for ownership beyond physical objects.

5 Intangible possessions: clans, totems, and names

5.1 *The Manambu wealth*

In traditional Manambu society, purely monetary wealth and gain is secondary to the clans' major patrimony—the names of totemic patrilineal ancestors associated with magic powers, and names of the totemic territories and of various aspects of the world around.

[10] The subject of (25a) is 'I': see arguments in Aikhenvald (2008: 531–5).

The Manambu divide into three clan groups: the Wulwi-Ñawi, associated with sun and moon, and everything bright; the Gla:gw (the 'blacks'), associated with earth and jungle, and everything dark; and the Nabul-Sablap, the in-between clan group. Clan groups are exogamous (see Harrison 1990; additions and revisions in Aikhenvald 2008, 2009a). The whole world is classified according to the clan system and their totemic attributes. In terms of territory, the world is divided into *wa:gw* 'totemic areas'. For example, the area to the east of the Sepik—including Australia—is the *wa:gw* of the Wulwi-Ñawi clan (the East wind and the eastern direction, *wali*, as owned by them). White people are adopted into this clan group (including Simon Harrison and myself, members of the Maliau clan). Sun and moon are totems of the Wulwi-Ñawi clan group. White and shiny objects, such as *sawn* 'white pelican', and also *wapwi* 'clothing', are owned by the Wulwi-Ñawi.

Every subclan has its own name(s) for important objects and natural phenomena which correspond to totemic creatures: multiple names for crocodile (general term *mu*), totemic trees, and crotons (*kwalami*), stone (*kabak*), dog (*a:s*), slit drum (*ra:b*), spirit (*apawəl*) and many more. This creates multiple synonymy, restricted just to nouns.

Totemic ownership does not necessarily imply control or physical possession of the objects. I am not aware of any members of the Maliau clan laying claims on Australia as their totemic land.

A term for a totem can also be used as address term: a person from the Gla:gw clan can be addressed as *ma-nəbi* 'bow and arrow' or *yayib* 'tree kangaroo'. The names and the address terms which relate to the person's father's clan have a different value than those bestowed by the mother's clan. I was told, by my Manambu teachers, that it is 'nicer' and 'more endearing' to address a person with names and totems of their mother's clan. Harrison (1985) suggests a different motivation. Names and address terms acquired through the maternal clan protect 'every living person' 'from the malign influence of his dead kin' and from the 'ghosts'. Patrilineal names and totems reflect inheritance and rights to ownership. Once a person dies, a patrilineal name used to be preferred (since a dead person would not require protection from ghosts: they themselves become a ghost). This is in line with the basics of the Manambu kinship system, of the Omaha type (see Harrison 1990).

Each subclan owns between 1,000 and 1,500 patrilineal names.[11] A child is given a patrilineal name *apa-sə* 'bone name', after a totemic ancestor of the subclan, when it is a few months old and is expected to live. Matrilineal names are given at bereavement of a relative. How does this relate to possession and ownership?

[11] Bateson reckons that an erudite Iatmul man 'carries in his head between ten and twenty thousand names' (Bateson 1958: 22).

5.2 *To 'own' a name*

The verb 'have' is never used with traditional names. To refer to ownership of names and belonging to clans, one employs verbless clauses stating identity between the clan and the person belonging to it. The Possessor—that is, the owner—is the subject of a non-verbal clause. The Possessee—that is, the object owned—occupies the verbless clause complement slot. In (26), a verbless clause states the ownership of the man's house called Kamajab by the Valik clan:

(26) dəy-a-də kara:b Kamajab-ad Vali:k-ad
they-LINK-masc.sg men's.house Kamajab-3masc.sgNOM Vali:k-3masc.sgNOM
Their men's house is Kamajab, it belongs to the Vali:k clan.

Similarly, in (7) the name of the Ambunti mountain (a salient landmark) is stated with a verbless clause. The second clause states 'belonging' of the mountain's name (Makemawi) to the Ñakau clan.

Belonging to a clan is also expressed through a verbless clause. The one who belongs to a clan identifies themselves with a clan's totem and an address term. Example (27) comes from a story about how the Valik clan was established by Kamkudi (originally of Gala origin), who was rescued by Sesawi, a Manambu man. Sesawi discovered Kamkudi hidden in the hollow sago tree, and asks him:

(27) mən atətawa gwalugw-adəmən
you.masc how/which clan-2masc.sgNOM
What clan do you belong to? (*lit.* you which clan you)

Sesawi replies with (28). Both brown snake and death adder are totems of the Gla:gw clan group to which the Gala are thought to belong to (since they are people of the 'bush'). Stating identity between him and these totems (also used as address terms) identifies him as the member of the same clan group as Kamkudi. Pronominal cross-referencing is clear from the context and is omitted.

(28) wun dəmakau kanukaraki
I brown.snake death.adder
'I am 'brown snake', 'death adder' (totems of the Gla:gw clan group).

A similar construction can be used to describe belonging to a place. A man from Yawabak was emphatic about him and his group belonging to Avatip, despite the fact that they live in Yawabak now:

(29) ñan Yawabak-a-kə-di-adian tasol ñan Avatəp-adian
we Yawabak-LINK-ORIGIN-pl-1plNOM but we Avatip-1plNOM
Yawabak stret ma:
Yawabak directly NEG
We are from Yawabak, but we belong to Avatip. (*lit.* we are Avatip). (We) are not really Yawabak.

Only patrilineal names can be considered a matter of lawful ownership. If one states the identity between oneself and a name, one lays claim to the whole 'descent line' and the totemic possessions associated with this. Story-tellers who consider themselves experienced orators would state their name, and then the clan the name identifies them with:

(30) Wun Səplawan wun-a-də asa:y Maliməy, wun
I Seplawan I-LINK-masc.sg father Malimey I
Sarak-adəwun-ək
Sarak-1masc.sgNOM-IMMED
I am Seplawan, my father Malimey, I am of the Sarak subclan.

A matrilineal name is not used this way. This highlights the importance of patrilineage in the Manambu culture which is reflected in predicative possession. In contrast, in Hone (§2.1.1 of Chapter 9) the possession within the noun phrase bears the vestiges of the erstwhile matrilineal society.

If members of one subclan notices one of their names being used by another subclan, they organize a name debate.[12] A name debate between the Sarak and the Wagau subclans of the Wulwi-Ñawi clan group was held on 8 October 2004, at the ceremonial house Warman (itself the property of Maliau and Nabul subclans). The object of dispute was the name *Kiginəbək*; this name and its feminine equivalent *Kiginəbəkəbər* was 'won' by the Wagau clan. The Sarak clan was awarded another name, *Kəgidəmi* and its feminine counterpart *Kəgidəminəbər* as a 'compensation'.

The debate was opened by the Councillors of Avatip. Throughout the ceremony each orator would take a bunch of crotons and, swinging himself rhythmically, would present arguments in favour of his subclan's totemic ownership of the name, starting with reciting names of ancestors, and finishing with a resounding statement of ownership for the disputed name and the descent line phrased as follows:

(31) Kiginəbək wun-adəwun
Kiginəbək I-1masc.sgNOM
I am Kiginəbək.

A claim to the totemic ownership of the Ambunti mountain was stated as follows:

(32) wun Makəmawi-adəwun
I Makemawi-1masc.sgNOM
I am Ambunti mountain.

[12] A full-scale name debate used to last for over 24 hours non-stop, and would start with song cycles connected with the subclan's origin myths. A description of a full name debate is in Harrison (1990: 159–67). Nowadays debates tend to be shorter, about 10–12 hours.

The use of the first-person pronoun here is comparable to 'segmentary' person as defined by Merlan and Rumsey (1991) and Rumsey (2000): 'I' is a cover term for a group of people (in this case, the subclan). This usage is pervasive in name debates, but not so much in stories about wars and military exploits.

A name debate is not just about a name, or the rights to use it. It is about exclusive rights to one's clan's totemic areas and history, including genealogies, and, consequently, the group's identity. A clan is equated with ritual powers, and these powers lie in the knowledge of names and totems.

Verbless clauses indicating identity between what is owned and who owns it indicate that the possessive relationship is conceived of as permanent and established. This is consistent with the general meaning of verbless clauses expressing predicative possession in Manambu.

This attitude to ownership is reflected in the modern discussions of land disputes handed to courts: ownership and control of land requires the same grammatical structures as totemic ownership and ownership of highly praised names and words. This topic requires further careful study.

6 Possession in grammar and society

Manambu has a complex system of possession marking, within a noun phrase and within a clause. Possession within a noun phrase is based on distinguishing whole–part possessive constructions (§3.2) from other types (§3.2–5). Within these, possessive constructions are marked by juxtaposition unless the Possessee is specific or definite. Then, a construction with a pronominal possessive marker is in order. A further construction type is used for relationships of purpose, location, and attribution between nouns. The 'origin' construction may be related to the construction with a pronominal possessive marker.

Body part and kinship possession stand apart from nouns of other groups in terms of their openness to external possession and relativization (§3.3). However, accessibility to relativization depends on the degree of proximity between the Possessor and the Possessee: this is where cultural conventions creep into the grammatical structure.

Possession within a clause reflects culturally entrenched values and ownership of non-material goods—the right to hereditary history through the knowledge and ownership of names and totems of one's paternal clan. This permanent belonging and possession is expressed through verbless clauses, also used for stable possession of other sorts. Constructions with the verb 'have' can be used with possessions of a transitory and less culturally significant nature.

References

Aikhenvald, Alexandra Y. 2004. 'Language endangerment in the Sepik area of Papua New Guinea', pp. 97–142 of *Lectures on endangered languages: 5—From Tokyo and Kyoto Conferences 2002*, edited by O. Sakiyama and F. Endo. Osaka: The project 'Endangered languages of the Pacific Rim'.

——. 2008. *The Manambu language from East Sepik, Papua New Guinea*. Oxford: Oxford University Press.

——. 2009a. 'Language contact along the Sepik River', *Anthropological Linguistics* 50: 1–66.

——. 2009b. 'Eating, drinking and smoking: A generic verb and its semantics in Manambu', pp. 92–108 of *The linguistics of eating and drinking*, edited by John Newman. Amsterdam: John Benjamins.

Bateson, G. 1958. *Naven* (2nd edn). Stanford: Stanford University Press.

Bowden, R. 1997. *A dictionary of Kwoma, a Papuan language of North-east New Guinea*. Canberra: Pacific Linguistics.

Dixon, R. M. W. 2010. *Basic linguistic theory*, Vol. 2, *Grammatical topics*. Oxford: Oxford University Press.

Harrison, S. J. 1983. *Laments for foiled marriages. Love songs from a Sepik River village*. Boroko: Institute of Papua New Guinea Studies.

——. 1985. 'Names, ghosts and alliance in two Sepik River societies', *Oceania* 56: 138–46.

——. 1990. *Stealing people's names. History and politics in a Sepik River cosmology*. Cambridge University Press: Cambridge.

Merlan, Francesca and Alan Rumsey. 1991. *Ku Waru. Language and segmentary politics in the western Nebilyer Valley, Papua New Guinea*. Cambridge: Cambridge University Press.

Rumsey, Alan. 2000. 'Agency, personhood and the "I" of discourse in the Pacific and beyond'. *Journal of the Royal Anthropological Institute (NS)* 6: 101–15.

Staalsen, Philip and Lori Staalsen. 1973. *Iatmul-English dictionary*. Ms. Ukarumpa.

Telban, Borut. 1998. *Dancing through time. A Sepik cosmology*. Oxford: Clarendon Press.

5

Possession in Martuthunira

ALAN DENCH

Martuthunira is an Australian language of the Pama-Nyungan family, once spoken in the Pilbara region of Western Australia. Typologically, it is strongly dependent-marking with predicate argument relations being predominantly coded by nominal suffixes. Martuthunira is unusual among Australian languages in coding arguments of verbal clauses in a consistent nominative–accusative pattern, a feature shared by a number of Pilbara languages. Other notable typological features include a productive active–passive voice contrast, patterns of switch-reference in subordinate clauses and, unlike many western Australian languages, the absence of any system of bound pronouns cross-referencing or encoding argument relations at the clause level. Martuthunira has a relatively fixed word order and shows a high degree of multiple case marking.[1]

There are three major word classes, defined by primary morphological characteristics. The class of nominals is inflected for case and number, verbs are inflected for tense aspect and modality, and a set of uninflecting particles code a range of semantic categories including negation and various propositional attitudes. The large nominal class can be further subdivided into the minor closed classes of pronoun and demonstrative alongside the open class of 'common nominals'. Proper names can be identified through their selection of particular forms of case marking morphology (some of which are shared by pronouns), which allows that common nominals can be used as proper names simply by selection of this morphology. In addition there are a number of inherently locative locational nominals and a set of special temporal nominals. There is no morphological distinction between noun and adjective, though

[1] I am indebted to †Algy Paterson, the last fluent speaker of Martuthunira for patiently teaching me what I know of Martuthunira. Algy, who passed away on 6 August 1995, was very concerned that knowledge of his mother's and mother's mother's language not disappear with his passing. I am grateful to the editors, to other contributors to this volume and to other participants at the workshop for their comments, suggestions, and criticisms. The usual disclaimers apply.

naturally enough there are differences in the distribution of particular nominals depending on their semantic content.

Nominal phrases can be defined as sequences of nominals over which some nominal suffix may be distributed. Martuthunira shows a pattern of marking in which a suffix coding a particular relation is attached to each word of the phrase, described as 'complete concord' by Dench and Evans (1988). The nominal phrase can then be described in terms of a sequence of functional slots rather than in terms of defined (parts-of-speech) classes of items. The basic pattern is: (Determiner) ^ (Quantifier) ^ (Classifier) ^ Entity ^ (Qualifier)*. The Entity slot provides the semantic head of the phrase and it is the nominal in this slot that makes the primary reference to some object or person. Nominals preceding the head restrict the reference of the head nominal by narrowing the set from which the referent is chosen. Nominals following the head have a non-restrictive modifying function (Dench 1995a: 189ff). Nominals can occur in a range of syntactic slots; head or modifier in a nominal phrase, predicate in a non-verbal ascriptive predication (primary or secondary predicate), complement in a copula clause, or as a manner second predication. While there is no formal noun/adjective distinction, nominals can be broadly classified depending on their range across these slots, with some nominals showing all five possibilities (Dench 1995a: 51ff). The syntactic flexibility of nominals is matched by that of more complex nominal expressions formed through the addition of suffixes to a nominal stem. Thus while adnominal suffixes, such as genitives and pertensives, form expressions which typically modify (as determiner or qualifier) heads, they can also occur as the sole elements in a NP. Rather than treat such constructions as NPs with a missing/ellipsed head, it is assumed here that the inflected nominal is the head (see Dench 1995a, b for discussion).

1 Meanings and forms of nominal possessive constructions

All three categories of possession identified and characterized by Aikhenvald in Chapter 1 are relevant in Martuthunira and can be distinguished in part by means of their expression.

Kin relationships are an especially important factor in social organization and in social interaction in the Martuthunira community, as in all Australian indigenous communities, and this is reflected in the structures of the language in a number of ways. There are, not surprisingly, specific constructions for coding kin relationships. These include a special form of the first person singular pronoun used in coding close kin relationships and morphemes coding particular kin relationships suffixed to pronouns (denoting the possessor). In addition, two minor suffixes ('source' and 'pertensive') most often code parent–child relations between possessor (Pr) and possessee (Pe).

Part–whole relationships are coded in nominal phrases by simple apposition and this distinguishes this type from the coding of kinship relations and ownership. General ownership possession is coded by the use of genitive-marked pronouns and nominal expressions coding the possessor. The minor 'source' genitive codes more specific controlled ownership.[2] As is very common in Australian languages, ownership possession can also be coded by the use of a pertensive comitative/proprietive suffix on the possessee. A corresponding lack of possession can be coded through the use of the privative suffix on the possessee. Although rare, the kinship pertensive 'owner' suffix, *-waya*, can also be used to mark a controlled possession. These patterns of marking ownership possession are also available, to varying extents, for coding both kinship relations and part–whole relations.

1.1 *Nominal possessive morphology*

1.1.1 *Genitive and Source* Martuthunira has two genitive suffixes to nominals coding the possessor in a nominal expression (and corresponding, sometimes irregular, pronominal forms). In the most general of terms, these suffixes have the forms:

Genitive	*-wu/-ngu*
Source	*-wura/-ngura*

The more general and most commonly occurring of these is the genitive. The source suffix is less common and has more specific semantics. This section describes the morphology of these genitive constructions—the forms of genitive-marked nominal expressions and of genitive pronouns.

Table 5.1 displays the genitive forms of a range of nominals, in comparison with the unmarked nominative stem and the accusative form. The minor genitive 'source' suffix is also shown.[3]

Genitive and accusative forms are distinct only on vowel-final 'common' nominal stems—although these are by far the most frequent forms in both the lexicon and in text. Proper names and the human interrogative/indefinite pronoun, *ngana* 'who, someone', select distinct suffix forms.

Both the genitive and accusative are reflexes of an earlier dative/genitive with the modern forms resulting from a partly functionally motivated morphemic split (see Dench 1998 for details). The syncretism rarely leads to ambiguity given that the

[2] In Dench (1995a) this suffix is glossed as 'Belonging'—nominal expressions incorporating this suffix and heading NPs denote the 'belongings' of the Pr stem. The 'source' gloss better covers the range of functions described here (and see Dench 1997).

[3] Martuthunira shares with many Australian Languages a phonological inventory comprising six series for stops and nasals, four laterals, two rhotics (trill/tap *rr* and continuant *r*), two glides (*y* and *w*), three short (*i*, *a*, *u*), and three long vowels (*ii*, *aa*, *uu*). Consonants are written as follows: bilabial, *p*, *m*, *w*; lamino-dental, *th*, *nh*, *lh*; apico-alveolar, *t*, *n*, *l*, *rr*; apico post-alveolar, *rt*, *rn*, *rl*, *r*; lamino-palatal, *j*, *ny*, *ly*, *y*; velar, *k*, *ng*, *w*. A period is used to separate a cluster of consonants where the orthography might otherwise lead to interpretation as a single segment: thus, *l.y* contrasts with *ly*, *r.t* contrasts with *rt*.

TABLE 5.1. **Selected inflected forms of Martuthunira nominals**

	Nominative	Accusative	Genitive	Source
child	*pawulu*	*pawulu-u*	*pawulu-wu*	*pawulu-wura*
daughter	*kurntal*	*kurntal-yu*	*kurntal-yu*	*kurntal-wura*
liar	*jarntany*	*jarntany-ku*	*jarntany-ku*	*jarntany-kura*
Karnuny	*karnuny*	*karnuny-ngu*	*karnuny-ngu*	*karnuny-ngura*
who, someone	*ngana*	*ngana-ngu*	*ngana-ngu*	*ngana-ngura*
	stem final segment			
Nominal	vowel	-V_i	*-wu*	*-wura*
	lateral/rhotic	*-yu*	*-yu*	*-wura*
	nasal	*-ku*	*-ku*	*-wura*
Proper name		*-ngu*	*-ngu*	*-ngura*

TABLE 5.2. **Genitive forms of 1sg and 2sg pronouns**

	1sg	2sg	1duinc
NOMinative	*ngayu*	*kartu*	*ngali*
ACCusative	*nganaju*	*kartungu*	*ngali-i*
GENitive	*nganaju*	*kartungu*	*ngali-wu*
SOURCE	*nganajuwura*	*kartungura*	*ngali-ngura*
LOCative	*ngathala*	*kartungka*	*ngali-la*
EFFector	*ngathu*	*kartungku*	*ngali-lu*
stem.GEN.NOM	*nganaju*	*kartungu*	*ngali-wu*
stem.GEN-ACC	*nganaju-u*	*kartungu-u*	*ngali-wu-u*
stem.OBL-GEN-PL.NOM	*nganaju-wu-ngara*	*kartungu-wu-ngara*	*ngali-wu-ngara*

genitive function is often expressed within NPs and the accusative never is. Genitive forms are often followed by a further suffix, such as the accusative. Martuthunira does not allow a sequence of identical suffixes (or sequences of the same morpheme).

Martuthunira pronouns are all vowel-final stems and the regular forms select the nominal genitive suffix, *-wu*. However, the singular pronouns are irregular. The patterns of inflection of the 1sg and 2sg pronouns are shown in Table 5.2, alongside the regular 1duinc. The second part of Table 5.2 shows more complex inflected forms built on the genitive stems.

The accusative and genitive forms of the 1sg and 2sg are identical—a pattern of syncretism that matches that of consonant-final nominals. More complex inflected genitive forms of the 1sg and 2sg include the nominal genitive suffix, -*wu*, following the genitive pronoun stem, which might then be best characterized as a general 'oblique' stem. Note also that the 2sg inflects like the human interrogative/indefinite pronoun, *ngana*. The latter does not, however, select the nominal genitive suffix in complex genitive forms. Further, the 1duinc:SOURCE pronoun patterns like the irregular 2sg:SOURCE. Other pronoun forms are more regular in this respect.

Two further elaborations on the pronominal system need to be mentioned at this point. First, Martuthunira does not have an elaborated third-person pronoun paradigm but relies on the complex demonstrative system to manage anaphoric third-person reference in discourse. However, a particular demonstrative form, *ngurnulangu*—the -*ngu* genitive form of the definite distal demonstrative *ngurnula* (see Dench 1995a: 117)—has effectively been syntacticized as a third-person singular possessive pronoun, and I will gloss it as 3sg:POSS in this discussion. Martuthunira also has a specific 1sg:POSS pronoun, *jurti*, used exclusively for coding close kinship relations. The genitive and source forms of these two pronouns are shown in Table 5.3.

1.1.1 *Pertensive, Proprietive, Privative* There are three nominal suffixes which mark the Pe in a possessive NP, headed by the Pr. The first, and least common of these, is glossed here simply as 'pertensive'. It specifically identifies the possessor as something that is in a controlled possessive relationship and most often codes a kinship relation in which the Pr is the parent of the Pe.[4] There are very few examples of the pertensive suffix on nominals, none on proper names or the interrogative/indefinite pronoun, and none on consonant-final stems. The form on vowel-final stems is consistently -*waya*. The suffix selects oblique stems of the 1sg, 2sg, and a *ngu* stem of the 1duinc. Elicitation testing with kin terms, human terms, and proper names shows that these also select -*ngu*, which for these terms functions as a proper nominal marker rather than as a special oblique stem formative. The proprietive suffix form is consistently -*marta*. The privative has the forms -*wirriwa*/-*wirraa*, in relatively free variation.

TABLE 5.3. Genitive and Source forms of 1sg:POSS and 3sg:POSS pronouns

	GENitive	SOURCE
1sg:POSS	*jurti(ngu)*	*jurtingura*
'3sg:POSS'	*ngurnulangu*	*ngurnulangura*

[4] The suffix identified here as 'pertensive' is glossed as 'owner' in Dench (1995b)—the nominal expressions which incorporate this suffix denote the 'owner' (Pr) of the possessee (Pe) stem.

1.2 *Genitive*

Genitive forms are used to mark ownership of some object or the propositus of a kinship relation (i.e. person chosen as the point of reference from which the relation is calculated). The (Pr) genitive form is most often found preceding the head (Pe), but may also occur in the post-head qualifier slot (see below). In almost all cases, the possessor is human, otherwise it is animate. There is just one example in the corpus in which the understood possessor is inanimate (9) but here the possessor is treated metaphorically as if it were animate.

In 90 per cent of the (approximately 260) examples of NPs involving a genitive expression in the Martuthunira corpus, the genitive marked Pr is a singular pronoun, either 1sg:GEN, 2sg:GEN, 1sg:POSS, or the 3sg:POSS form. The remaining genitive expressions include a few non-singular pronouns and the human interrogative/indefinite pronoun, but the remainder are primarily kin terms and other nominals denoting humans. Some examples are:

(1) kartu wanti-layi wuraal kartungu-la ngurra-ngka, kartungu-lu
2sg:NOM lie-FUT still 2sg:GEN-LOC camp-LOC 2sg:GEN-EFF
nganiyarrangu-lu wantha-rnu. nhiila karri-marri-nguru
family-EFF put-PASS:PERV here stand-RECIP-PRES
kartungu-ngara ngathalwarnti kartungku wantha-rnu-rru.
2sg:GEN-PL cousins 2sg:EFF put-PASS:PERV-NOW
You lie in your place, put there by your family. Here standing together are your cousins, left by you now. [*address to the deceased at a burial*]

(2) nhula walyun kulhawulha-ma-lalha maan-ngara-a
near.you girl heaped.up-CAUS-PAST seed-PL-ACC
ngurnulangu-u ngangka-a wuruma-l.yarra
3sg:POSS-ACC mother-ACC do.for-CTEMP
This girl heaped up seeds (doing it) for her mother.

(3) ngayu nyina-lha ngurriny-tha ngurnu-tharra-wu-la yaanka-wu-la
1sg:NOM sit-PAST swag-LOC that:OBL-DU-GEN-LOC spouse.pair-GEN-LOC
I sat on the swag of those two, husband and wife.

(4) yar.tapalyu kanyara-ngara nhuurarri-wala wantharni-i
others man-PL know-PURP:DS what.like-ACC
ngurnta-a jiwarra-ngara-wu-u
style-ACC white-PL-GEN-ACC
The other (Aboriginal) people will know then what the way of white people is like.

The genitive marked Pr precedes the Pe head in 84 per cent of cases in the corpus, but there is some variation in the relative frequency depending on the Pr. Where the Pr is 1sg or 2sg, it precedes the head in 94 per cent of instances. By contrast, the 3sg:POSS, *ngurnulangu*, precedes the head in 77 per cent of NPs. By contrast, examples in which the Pr is expressed by a nominal show an even distribution of the two patterns. In the few examples in which the Pr is denoted by a non-singular pronoun, this pronoun more often follows the head. The differences in pattern appear to be influenced by at least two factors. First, there is an important difference between the 1sg and 2sg pronouns and the other referring expressions considered here. The speaker and hearer need no introduction and genitive forms identifying them as Pr can function as determiners without further qualification. The referent of the 3sg:POSS needs to be specified, and following such specification the Pr may be introduced as an NP qualifier. In the following example, the 3sg possessor is clearly topicalized (compare it with (2) above).

(5) nhiyu wartirra, pawulu ngurnulangu kangku-nguli-nguru yar.ta-ngku
this woman child 3sg:POSS carry-PASS-PRES other-EFF
This woman, her child is being carried (looked after) by someone else.

Second, there is a tendency for more complex NP possessors to follow rather than precede the head (see (3) above). More complex possessive NPs can include a demonstrative in the determiner slot, with a genitive expression either following (6) or preceding the head (7).

(6) ngunhu pawulu nganaju kamu-nguli-nguru-warntura
that child 1sg:GEN hungry-PSYCH-PRES-EACH
That child of mine keeps getting hungry.

(7) ngayu puni-layi ngulu nganaju-wu-lu wartirra-lu
1sg:NOM go-FUT that:EFF 1sg:OBL-GEN-EFF woman-EFF
yungku-ngu-layi mungka-rninyji
give-PASS-FUT eat-FUT
I'll go and will be given (something) by that wife of mine to eat.

There are just a few examples in which the genitive possessor occurs without a possessee head, and thus in which the genitive expression itself can be regarded as the head of the phrase (8). Example (9) shows that a complex adnominal expression, in this instance a locative form of the 3sg:POSS, can function as the stem from which a verb is derived.

(8) nganaju muyi muya-lalha nganaju-u puni-layi yungku-lu
1sg:GEN dog steal-PAST 1sg:GEN-ACC go-FUT give-PURP:DS
ngurnu-ngura-ngara-a-rru mungka-lwaa
that:OBL-SOURCE-PL-ACC-NOW eat-PURP:SU=OBJ
My dog stole mine to go and give to those (its little ones) now, to eat.

(9) kuliya-l.yu! nhula martamarta muthu-rru puni-nguru kartangkarri-rra
listen-IMP near.you red nose-NOW go-PRES land-CTEMP
thaaput thanturri-lha ngurnulangu-la-ma-lalha
airport go.down-PAST 3sg:POSS-LOC-CAUS-PAST
Listen! This red-nose [airplane] is landing, having descended, [the pilot] having brought it to its [natural place].

Genitive expressions coding the Pr can also stand as predicates in non-verbal predications, including non-verbal clauses making simple ascriptive genitive predications. For example:

(10) mir.ta *yirru* kangku-layi yirna *yirru.* ngunha nganarna-wu-lpurtu *yirru.*
not take-FUT this:ACC that 1plexc-GEN-COMPT
Don't take this one. It's ours!

(11) nhiyu murla mungka-rnu muyi-tharra-lu yirna-ngara-wu
this meat eat-PASS:PERV dog-DU-EFF this:OBL-PL-GEN
kanyara-ngara-wu nyina-marri-nyila-ngara-wu wurrulywa-la
man-PL-GEN sit-RECIP-PRES:REL-PL-GEN leaves-LOC
This meat eaten by the dog belonged to these men sitting together on the leaves.

The Pe head of the NP may denote a range of different things that might be understood to be in the personal possession of the genitive-marked possessor and which typically have some degree of permanence in that relationship. The list includes:

- artefacts typically used as instruments, such as spears, boomerangs, axes, knives, etc.
- articles of clothing, bedding (3), and other personal effects
- home, camp, usual dwelling place (1), (9)
- pets, including dogs (8), chickens, parrots, cats, etc.

The list of relatively permanent possessions extends to more abstract things such as songs, words, or stories (12), dances, or common behaviours.

(12) ngayu yar.ta-wuyu-lpurtu kanyara. mir.ta wiru kuliya-la-ma-rninyji
1sg:NOM other-SIDE-COMPT man not want ear-LOC-CAUS-FUT
nhuwana-wu-u marrari-ngara-a kanparri-marri-nyila-a
2pl-GEN-ACC word-PL-ACC say-RECIP-PRES:REL-ACC
I'm a man of the other side (generation set). I don't want to put in my ears (have to listen to) your words, [you] talking together.

The genitive is also used in identifying kinship relationships, or other connections between people. Examples include (1), (2), (5), (6), and (7).

The genitive can also be used to code less permanent possessions, most obviously food or drink items that are intended for consumption by the possessor.

(13) nhulaa manyarrka wantha-rryu nganaju-wu-la parrka-ngka
near.you sugar put-IMP 1sg:OBL-GEN-LOC tea-LOC
Put sugar in my tea.

There is occasionally some potential ambiguity in the use of the genitive arising from this usage. In (14) the genitive Pr is most easily understood as denoting a beneficiary, though given the marking it is very clearly an adnominal dependent of the object of the verb.

(14) ngayu puni-lha thulharra nhuwa-ru tharnta-a
1sg:NOM go-PAST afternoon spear-PURP:SS euro-ACC
kupiyaji-wu-u pawulu-ngara-wu-u
little:PL-GEN-ACC child-PL-GEN-ACC
I went in the afternoon to spear a euro for the little children.
(*lit.* I went in the afternoon to spear the little children's euro.)

As example (2) illustrates, beneficiaries are more generally coded using a benefactive verb construction. Nevertheless, it is likely that this is a recent innovation and that at an earlier stage beneficiaries were coded with the dative/genitive, *-*ku*, from which both the modern accusative and genitive are descended.

1.3 *Source*

The SOURCE genitive suffix identifies a Pr that can be understood to be the source of the Pe. Thus in the following examples, the Pr is responsible for having built or fashioned the Pe. In (15) the uncle is understood to be the maker of the spears. In (16), the name *Payarrany* was bestowed by Aboriginal people.

(15) ngayu kulaya-lalha nganaju-u mimi-wura-a warrirti-ngara-a
1sg:NOM test-PAST 1sg:GEN-ACC uncle-SOURCE-ACC spear-PL-ACC
I tried out my uncle's spears.

(16) yini wangka-ngu-rra walypala-lu *Sarah*, kanyara-wura yini *Payarrany*
name say-PASS-CTEMP white.man-EFF man-SOURCE name
The name she is called by white people is *Sarah*, her Aboriginal name is *Payarrany*.

The source suffix is most often used to identify offspring and so is used to code specifically consanguinial kinship relations.

(17) a. ngana-ngura ngunhu kuruuru, ngana-ngura ngunhu
who-SOURCE that:NOM round who-SOURCE that:NOM
kuruuru wirtamurtu, parna mirtali?
round middle head big
Whose is that round one? Whose is that round in the middle one, with the big head?

b. nganaju-wura-nu. malhurta-wuyu
1sg:OBL-SOURCE-QUOT middle.child-side
He's mine, my middle child.

(18) ngawu! jankurna-arta puni-lha thathu-rnu, ngayala-tharra ngurnulangu
yes emu-ALL go-PAST send-PASS:PERV nephew-DU 3sg:POSS
ngurnulangu-wura mari-wura pawulu-tharra
3sg:POSS-SOURCE young.sister-SOURCE child-DU
Alright! his two nephews went for emu, having been sent, his younger sister's two children.

Martuthunira allows constructions in which the only constituent of the NP (or all constituents of the NP) are inflected for some adnominal dependency relation within that NP. That is, the adnominal suffix has a limited 'derivational' function. It is common to find the source suffix used in this way, the resulting 'unheaded' NP then denoting the 'belongings' or 'makings' of the identified Pr.

(19) nhartu-npa-lha nhiyu wangka-nguru yimpalaa, kuyil paju,
what-INCH-PAST this:NOM say-PRES like.that bad very
nganaju-wura-ngara-a?
1sg:OBL-SOURCE-PL-ACC
Why is this one speaking like that, in a very bad way, about mine (my boys)?

Example (20) is slightly different from the uses described so far. The underlined expression *muyi-wura*, 'dog-source', denotes something the dog has chewed and has thus effectively ruined for human consumption. The dog is both the Pr and the understood agent of the passive.

(20) ngayu warntitha-rralha-rru murla-a muyi-ngku mungka-rnu.
1sg:NOM throw-PAST-NOW meat-ACC dog-EFF eat-PASS:PERV
ngana-rru kana mungka-lwala ngartil muyi-wura-a mungka-rnu-u.
who-NOW can eat-PURP:DS again dog-SOURCE-ACC eat-PASS:PERV-ACC
I've thrown away the meat the dog chewed.
Who would eat that dog-chewed stuff now?

The source suffix has a secondary function coding an inanimate originating cause of a state or process of the mind or body, for example, see (21).

(21) ngayu punga pangkira-npa-nguru kayulu-wura
1sg:NOM guts swollen-INCH-PRES water-SOURCE
My guts are swelling up from [drinking] water.

1.4 *Pertensive*

The rare pertensive suffix can be described as the obverse of the source suffix. Where the source suffix attaches to the Pr and codes this as the parent of the Pe head, the pertensive attaches to Pe and codes this as the child of the Pr head. In (23), the pertensive-marked pronoun is the head of the NP which then denotes the parents of the children referenced by the pronoun.

(22) wangka-layi ngurnaa piwi-i, ngurnula-waya-a ngangka-a,
say-FUT that:ACC mother-ACC that:DEF-OWNER-ACC mother-ACC
'nhamintha-rru jurrkirta?'
how.many-NOW moon
Say to the mother, the mother of that one, 'How many months [old] now?'

(23) kartu mir.ta yimpala-ma-nmarni-lwa, tharratharra-ma-nmarni
2sg:NOM not like.that-CAUS-COUNTR-ID separate-CAUS-COUNTR
ngaliya-a nganarna-waya-la, ngaliya-waya-la wanka-ngka-l
1duexc-ACC 1plexc-OWNER-LOC 1duexc-OWNER-LOC alive-LOC-THEN
You wouldn't have been able to do that, wouldn't have separated us when our people were alive.

The suffix is not limited in its uses to coding relationships between parent and child. In (24), the Pe denoted by the pertensive expression is inanimate and the Pr head can be seen as the *controlling* owner. In (25), the pertensive-marked expression is the head of the NP which then denotes the owner by their possessions, in this case ownership of a pet dog.

(24) ngunhu puliyanyja panyu paju thurlajinkarri. puni-layi kayulu-u
that:NOM old.man good very poor.fellow go-FUT water-ACC
wii manku-lu pirriyarta-a. mir.ta nyina-layi jina-l.yarra yirla,
maybe get-PURP:SS own.things-ACC not sit-FUT ask-CTEMP only
pirriyarta-waya thurlajinkarri puliyanyja.
own.things-OWNER poor.fellow old.man
That old man is very good, poor fellow. He'll go to get water, for example, his own things. Won't sit just asking (for others to do it). He's in charge of his own things, that poor old man.

(25) ngunhaa muyi, jarraa-rnu-nguru, jaya-lalha-nguru, puni-lha mulurru
that:NOM dog tie-PASS:PERV-ABL escape-PAST-ABL go-PAST straight
waruul-wa-rru kanarri-lu nyina-nyila-a thalu-waya-a. thalu-waya
still-Ø-NOW come-PURP:SS sit-PRES:REL-ACC pet-OWNER-ACC pet-OWNER
panyu-npa-wala-rru wiru ngurnulangu-lu murla-marnu-lu
good-INCH-PURP:DS-NOW feelings 3sg:POSS-EFF meat-ASSOC-EFF
kanarri-yangu
come-PASS:PERV

That dog, having been tied up, having escaped, went straight to his owner sitting there. And so the owner was very pleased having his meat-getter come to him.

1.5 *Proprietive*

The Martuthunira proprietive has a range of semantic functions similar to those described for comitative or 'Having' suffixes in other Australian languages. Nominal expressions bearing the proprietive suffix may denote a characteristic attribute, an object in current possession, an accompanying person or animal, or an object used as an instrument. While proprietive expressions may occur in a qualifying function within an NP (26), this is relatively rare. Proprietive marked nominals typically occur as predicating expressions in non-verbal clauses (28), or as second predications in verbal clauses. Predictably, in untensed constructions (such as NPs or non-verbal clauses) the proprietive expression usually denotes some persistent property. Proprietive-marked nominals can serve as NP heads and the referent of the NP is then understood to be characterized by the presence of the property denoted by the stem (27). Not surprisingly, some such uses have become lexicalized.

(26)	nhiyu	tharnta-nu	nhuwa-rnu	kanyara-lu	kurnangu-marta-lu
	this:NOM	euro-QUOT	spear-PASS:PERV	man-EFF	black-PROP-EFF
	parna-marnu-marta-lu.				
	head-ASSOC-PROP-EFF				

This euro was speared by the man with the black hat.

(27)	murti-i	walarnta-rninyji	waruu	nhuwana	ngurnaa	karnti-marta-a
	fast-ACC	pass.by-FUT	still	2pl	that:ACC	tail-PROP-ACC

You can (will) still overtake the speed of that tail-haver (cat).

(28)	mirntiwul-wa	ngunhu-ngara	marrari	martuthunira,	nhiyu
	all-YK	that:NOM-PL	language	Martuthunira	this:NOM
	ngayal.yu-ngara	*yirru*-marta-lpurtu	marrari-marta		
	devil-PL	*yirru*-PROP-COMPT	word-PROP		

They were all Martuthunira speaking, but these devils had the word *yirru*.

The following examples show the use of the proprietive in indicating an object in current and temporary possession. Example (30) shows that the Pe need not be controlled by the Pr.

(29)	ngaliya,	kampalalha	yaji,	ngaliya	puni-nguru	murla-marta
	1duexc	uncle		uncle	1duexc	go-PRES	meat-PROP
	jankurna-marta.	jankurna	nhawu-ø.	jankurna-marta	ngaliya.	
	emu-PROP	emu	see-IMP	emu-PROP	1duexc	

We two, uncle, we two are coming with game, emu.
See the emu! We have an emu.

(30) parlu-ngka-rru karri-nguru thurlanyarrara pinyjura-marta wangkarr,
top-LOC-NOW stand-PRES poor.fella rope-PROP throat
panyi-l.yarra ngunhaa
kicking-CTEMP that:NOM
Up (in the tree) now, the poor fellow is hanging with a rope round his neck, he's kicking.

The proprietive can be used on kin terms and relationship terms, and typically has a comitative function (31). However, there are examples in which the 'characteristic property' semantics of the suffix are exploited, e.g. *ngayu yaan-marta* 'I'm married/ have a spouse.'

(31) ngayu nhawu-lha ngurnu kanyara-a ngurnulangu-marta-a
1sg:NOM see-PAST that:ACC man-ACC 3sg:POSS-PROP-ACC
kurntal-marta-a.
daughter-PROP-ACC
I saw that man with his daughter.

Proprietives built on body part stems rely on the 'characteristic property' semantics of the suffix. An expression describing someone as 'having ear', 'having legs', having eyes', implies an ability to make productive use of that body part.

(32) minthal warra panyu-ma-rninyji warrirti-i pirri-marta warnu!
self CONTR good-CAUS-FUT spear-ACC fnger-PROP ASSERT
Fix the spear yourself. You've got fingers!

1.6 *Privative*

Australian languages typically add a privative suffix to nominals which is used to indicate the lack of some characteristic, possession, or kin. The privative is often described as providing the mirror to the proprietive, and this is clear in Martuthunira. Privative expressions can describe the lack of possession of some object or of some kin relation, or of a body part. Privative second predications function as adverbs of manner, including specifying that an action has been performed without some instrument.

(33) parla-wirraa nganarna
money-PRIV 1plexc
We've got no money.

(34) ngunhu puni-marri-lha parntuwarnangka-a
that:nom go-COLL-PAST Pannawonica-ACC
yini-wirriwa-a-l warnu muya-ru
name-PRIV-ACC-THEN ASSERT steal-PURP:SS
They went together to steal Pannawonica Hill, when it was still without a name.

The lack of a kinsman, expressed through the use of the privative, can extend from the temporary absence of some usually accompanying relative, to the lack of a kinsman through death or misadventure (divorce).

(35) a. nganangu-ngara pawulu-ngara?
who:GEN-PL child-PL
Whose are those children?

b. ngurnu-ngara yaan-wirriwa-wura.
that:OBL-PL spouse-PRIV-SOURCE
They belong to the one who is without a spouse.

It is reasonably common among Pilbara languages for the privative to be used on kin terms, used as names or heads of NPs to indicate that the particular kinsman is deceased. There are few examples of this in the Martuthunira corpus, however the following naturally occurring example suggests the same pattern may have held more generally in Martuthunira.

(36) ngayu nyina-layi wanka parilha, nyurnti-npa-yaangu.
1sg:NOM sit-FUT alive still dead-INCH-UNREAL
ngayu yirla nhawu-ngu-layi jalya waruul, ngurnta kuyil, thurlajinkarri.
1sg:NOM only see-PASS-FUT bereft still style bad poor.fellow
jurti marryara-ngu-wirriwa-rru ngurangura-a withawitha-ma-lalha
1sg:POSS brother-PNM-PRIV-NOW stylish-ACC cover-CAUS-PAST
I'll still be alive, but I should have died. I'll just be seen as bereft (*lit.* rubbish), in bad shape, poor fellow me. My poor dead brother has buried any good thing in me (by dying).

When suffixed to a body part, or other normally inalienable attribute, the privative indicates the lack of that part. This is clear in (37).

(37) ngayu-lwa wiyaa wuruma-rninyji thurlajinkarri-i,
1sg:NOM-ID maybe do.for-FUT poor.fellow-ACC
yirra-wirraa-a warnu pala.
teeth-PRIV-ACC ASSERT IT
Maybe I'll do it for the poor fellow, he really hasn't got any teeth.

Recall that the proprietive can be used to emphasize the functional use of a body part (32). To code a corresponding loss of function, the privative requires a semblative, as in (38).

(38) yimpala-rru-wa kanarra-lu parnpiingku-yangu wanti-layi.
like.that-NOW-YK wind-EFF throw.down-PASS:PERV lie-FUT
nyingkurlu-lpurtu warnu pirri-wirraa wantharra
first-COMPT ASSERT hand-PRIV like
Just like that she lay, thrown to the ground by the wind. First one must say it's like she had no hands.

1.7 *Interim summary*

The discussion and exemplification presented above describes genitive and pertensive nominal morphology and crosses over the three categories of 'ownership', kinship, and part–whole relations. There is more to say about the latter two types. Table 5.4 summarizes the patterns discussed so far.

2 Kinship relations

In addition to the patterns of genitive and pertensive marking described in preceding sections, there are a number of further morphological systems specifically used for coding kinship possession.[5]

First, a special suppletive form of the first person singular pronoun, *jurti*, '1sg:POSS' is used specifically to code close kinship relations—consanguineal, affinal, and those relations established through male initiation.

(39)	jurti	mirtayi	mir.ta-rru	mungka-lalha	murla-a,	parlura	paju
	1sg:POSS	big	not-NOW	eat-PAST	meat-ACC	full	very

My own elder brother [*lit.* big one] didn't eat any meat, [he was] too full.

Secondly, pronoun stems denoting the Pr can bear one of two suffixes which specify that the referent of the complete expression, the Pe, is the Pr's own mother or own father, or is one of their siblings.

-ngulharn (-PATRI) own father('s sibling)
-wula (-MATRI) own mother('s sibling)

The suffixes select *jurti* and *kartu* stems of 1sg and 2sg respectively. For other pronouns the suffixes are attached to a stem with a lengthened final vowel:

ngalii-ngulharn our (1du) own father
nhuwanaa-wula your (2pl) own mother

The form in (40), based on the distal 'definite' demonstratives *ngurnula*, is perhaps best analysed as a form of the 3sg:POSS pronoun, *ngurnulangu*.

(40)	ngurnula-ngulharn	pirrjilingu
	3sg:POSS-PATRI	name

Pirrjilingu's own father/His own father, Pirrjilingu.

[5] No time will be spent here discussing complex kin terms, other than to note their existence. Like many Australian languages (see Merlan and Heath 1982), Martuthunira has a set of dyadic and group kin terms used to denote pairs or groups of kin who stand in a particular relationship to one another, and to the speaker. Thus dyadic terms incorporate both the Pr and Pe. In Martuthunira (and other Pilbara languages) the same morphology is used to code the relationship between a person and their spirit familiar.

TABLE 5.4. **Summary of 'genitive' and 'pertensive' marking**

Pe	genitive Pr-GEN **Pe**	source Pr-SOURCE **Pe**	pertensive Pr **Pe**-PERT	proprietive Pr **Pe**-PROP	privative Pr **Pe**-PRIV
body part	—	—	—	Pr has functional ability in Pe	Pr is missing part Pe
kin term	kinship relation	child of Pr	Pr is parent of Pe	Pr is with Pe (comitative), Pr has attribute associated with Pe (e.g. 'married')	Pr lacks Pe (due to death, divorce) Pr lacks attribute associated with Pe (e.g. 'unmarried')
human	kinship relation	child of Pr	Pr is parent of Pe	Pr is with Pe (comitative)	Pr lacks, is not with Pe (anti-comitative) Pr lacks attribute associated with Pe (e.g. 'unmarried')
animal	pet, future food item	pet of Pr	Pr is parent of Pe	Pr is with Pe (comitative)	(anti-comitative)
food item	for immediate consumption by Pr	—	?	Pr is with Pe (comitative)	(anti-comitative)
tool, artefact	in possession of Pr	made by Pr	Pr controls Pe	Pr is with/using Pe (comitative/instrumental)	(anti-comitative)
clothing, bedding, place	in possession of Pr	made by Pr	Pr controls Pe	Pr is with/using Pe (comitative/instrumental)	(anti-comitative)
Pr					
animate	[as above]	parent/maker of Pe	Pr is parent of Pe	Pr is with/using Pe (comitative/instrumental) Pr has attribute associated with Pe	Pr lacks, is not accompanied by Pe
inanimate (including part)	—	causer, source	—	Pr has attribute associated with Pe	Pr lacks Pe

(41) jurti-ngulharn wii jurti-wula-thurti. jurti-ngulharn-tharra-a
1sg:POSS-PATRI or 1sg:POSS-MATRI-CONJ 1sg:POSS-PATRI-DU-ACC
yaanka-a jurti-wula-tharra wii panyu wiyaa nhuwala
spouse(pair)-ACC 1sg:POSS-MATRI-DU or good maybe 2du
That's one of your own father's mob together with one of your own mother's mob. Toward those two married people, your father's own people and your mother's own people perhaps, maybe you two should behave properly.

These kin-referring pronoun forms are generally used only between kin in the same alternating generation set. They are generally considered to be too harsh for use within earshot of kin in the opposite generation set (most importantly, those people to whom the term refers). Instead, the source and pertensive suffixes may be used when talking to these kin about members of their own generation.

Third, Martuthunira has three suffixes to kin terms (denoting the Pe) which indicate the person (though not the number) of the possessor. A selection of different forms is shown in Table 5.5.

As this paradigm shows, the second and third person possessive forms involve the simple addition of suffixes *-malyura* and *-nhanu* respectively to the kin term stem. The first person possessive forms, on the other hand, involve three separate processes. First, disyllabic kin terms with a final vowel take a suffix of general form -V_i*ni*, which involves lengthening of the final vowel of the stem. Secondly, trisyllabic kin terms have their penultimate vowel lengthened and thus conform to the pattern of three syllables with penultimate long vowel established by the addition of the -V_i*ni* suffix to disyllabic stems. Finally, kin terms with a final consonant take a suffix *-yu*.

(42) mura-ani! kartu wuraal puni-layi manku-lu ngamari-i?
son-1:POSS 2sg:NOM alright go-FUT get-PURP:SS tobacco-ACC
My son, can you go and get some tobacco?

TABLE 5.5. **Possessed kin terms**

	1POSS	2POSS	3POSS
brother-in-law	*nyinu-uni*	*nyinu-malyura*	*nyinu-nhanu*
son	*mura-ani*	*mura-malyura*	*mura-nhanu*
mother's brother	*mimi-ini*	*mimi-malyura*	*mimi-nhanu*
father's father	*mayiili*	*mayili-malyura*	*mayili-nhanu*
father's mother	*ngapaari*	*ngapari-malyura*	*ngapari-nhanu*
daughter	*kurntal-yu*	*kurntal-malyura*	*kurntal-nhanu*

(43) ngunhaa kanyara mir.ta kanarri-marri-lha mayili-nhanu-ngu
that:NOM man not come-COLL-PAST father's.father-3:POSS-ACC
kulhi-lwarri-lu thungkara-a
bury-COLL-PURP:SS ground-ACC
That man didn't come to bury his grandson in the ground.

Quite complex patterns of kinship possession can be coded through a combination of these different morphological systems. Example (44) illustrates the use of the kin-group suffixes together with the source suffix.

(44) nganarna-wura-wula wurtu pawulu. piyuwa wurtu
1plexc-SOURCE-MATRI HYPTH child nothing HYPTH
yarta-npa-lha paju kampalha paju. pirriyarta-wula wurtu
other-INCH-PAST very kinsman REAL own-MATRI HYPTH
kartu pawulu nganarna-wura-wula wurtu
2sg:NOM child 1plexc-SOURCE-MATRI HYPTH
You're supposedly one of our close kin, one of our 'children' (mother's mob to one of our family), but it seems not, you've gone the other way child. You're supposed to be one of our mob.

(45) ngayu puni-lha ngurnu nhawu-lu, ngunhu-lwa ngurnula-waya
1sg:NOM go-PAST that:ACC see-PURP:SS that:NOM-ID that:DEF-PERT
mayiili-ngu-waya
son's.son:1:POSS-PNM-PERT
I went to see that fellow, that one who is the father of that grandchild of mine.

Example (45) demonstrates a common pattern of referring to kin in the opposite generation set through their children (who are in the same generation set as the speaker). Teknonymic reference of this kind often involves the addition of the pertensive suffix to the name of the oldest child in a family. Direct reference to one's own siblings by name is also considered impolite and similar teknonymic reference is preferred.

Kinship terms and some nominals denoting human relationships can function as non-verbal predicates taking a nominative subject and an accusative complement. In such cases, the subject of the non-verbal clause denotes the Pe, the Pr is the accusative complement.

(46) ngunhu ngurnulangu muyi, ngunhu-lwa pawu ngurnu-ngara-a
that:NOM 3sg:POSS dog that:NOM-ID father that:OBL-PL-ACC
kupiyaji-i
little:PL-ACC
That dog of his, that's the one who is the father of those little ones (puppies).

(47)

nhiyu	puliyanyja	ngaliwa-a	mimi
this	old.man	1plinc-ACC	mother's.brother

This old man is mother's brother to us.

(48)

ngunhu-ngara	winthi	ngurnu-ngara-a-lwa.
that:NOM-PL	enemy	that:OBL-PL-ACC-ID

They are enemies to these fellows.

The construction is preferred over a simple possessive ascriptive clause in making an initial identification (for the addressee) of the relationship between two participants. As the examples show, the pattern is not restricted to use with humans.

Selection of a particular formal device for the marking of the kinship relation depends on the identity of both the possessor and the possessee, though in the case of the Pr this is more a matter of politeness (pragmatic convention) than it is semantics.

3 Part–whole

Part–whole possession is most often coded by simple apposition of the part and the whole. Those relations coded include internal and external body parts, genitalia, bodily fluids (e.g. blood, sweat, and tears), parts of animals and plants, and parts of artefacts. The use of apposition—and hence the 'Martuthunira part–whole relation'—extends to names, to language, to feelings/emotions, and to the traces of an individual or animal, including their tracks or other marks left behind them (50), the shadows of people and the shade of trees.

(49)

ngulangu	karra-ngka	ngayu	jamanu	karta-rnu	kurarra-lu
there	scrub-LOC	1sg:NOMfoot		stab-PASS:PERV	camel.bush-EFF

There in the scrub my foot was pricked by a camel bush.

(50)

nhawu-lha	jamanu-u	muyi-i	nganajumarta	warangarri-la-a
see-PAST	track-ACC	dog-ACC	1du	dingo.trap-LOC-ACC

karri-lha-a	nguritha-l.yarra	nyini-nyila-a	warangarri-i
stand-PAST-ACC	smell-CTEMP	sit-PRES:REL-acc	dingo.trap-ACC

We saw the track of a dog, by the trap, that had been sniffing the trap there.

While nominal suffixes are normally distributed to all subconstituents, this pattern is suspended where the part in a part–whole construction is modified independently of the whole. So compare the following two examples:

(51) a.

ngayu	nhawu-lha	ngurnu	muyi-i	jamanu-u	mirtali-i
1sg:NOM	see-PAST	that:ACC	dog-ACC	track-ACC	big-ACC

I saw the tracks of a big dog.

b.

ngayu	nhawu-lha	ngurnu	muyi-i	jamanu	mirtali-i
1sg:NOM	see-PAST	that:ACC	dog-ACC	track	big-ACC

I saw the big tracks of a dog.

In such constructions, the order of the part and its modifier is fixed; the part precedes the modifier and does not bear inflection. The whole may either precede or follow this construct. While the combination of part and modifier resembles a compound in this fixing of order, that it is not is shown by the selection of length-dependent suffix allomorphs and the intervention of particles between the two words, as in (52). The unusual pattern of coding modification of the part suggests that the whole, rather than the part, heads the part–whole appositional NP.

(52)

kupuyu-tharra	mir.ta-lwa	kalya-rnu	muyi-ngku,	jalya-ngku	waruul,	
little-DU	not-ID	bite-PASS:PERV	dog-EFF	useless-EFF	still	
muyi-ngku	tharta	para-ngku,	parna	yirla	mirtali-lu,	
dog-EFF	crutch	hollow-EFF	head	only	big-EFF	
jalya-ngku	waruul,	ngarnmarr	karta-ngku			
useless-EFF	still	rib.cage	bony-EFF			

The two little fellows weren't bitten by the dog, the useless thing, hollow-crutched dog, only big in the head, useless thing, bony-ribbed thing.

Part and whole are often presented as separate phrases, yet bearing the same inflection. In such cases, the part is treated as a second predication on the whole and typically denotes the 'locus of effect' of some action directed at or by the subject. The use of this 'locus of effect' construction is restricted to entities that exist in a part–whole relation.

(53)

ngunhaa	nhawu-lha	wii	ngali-i	karri-lha-a,
that:NOM	see-PAST	if	1duinc-ACC	stand-PAST-ACC
ngunhaa	warta-a-rru	purra-rninyji	ngali-i	
that:NOM	forehead-ACC-NOW	hit-FUT	1duinc-ACC	

If he had seen us standing there, he would have hit us in the forehead.

However, parts can be treated separately from the whole. This is common for external body parts used as instruments (54), or on which some more direct action is performed by the whole. Example (54) illustrates both patterns. In (55) the 'whole' is the body of the addressee, denoted by *kartu*.

(54)

ngurnaa	thurlwa-rninyji	karla-ngka-nguru-u.	thani-rninyji	juwayu-marta.
that:ACC	pull.out-FUT	fire-LOC-ABL-ACC	hit-FUT	hand-PROP

Then pull it out of the fire. Then hit it with your hand.

(55)

palalyi	kartu	thala	karta-nngulaanu	nhumira-rru	thaatharra-rri-marni	
before	2sg:NOM	chest	stab-PASS:COUNTR	penis-NOW	open-INCH-COUNTR	
payawurtu	wurla	kartu	wartirra-a	paju	nhawu-lha	
savage	MIST	2sg:NOM	woman-ACC	very	see-PAST	
karri-wayara	thurla	karima-lha	nhawu-rra	martura-a	manku-lha	
stand-HAB	eye	jump-PAST	see-CTEMP	middle-ACC	grab-PAST	

nhumira-a pinyjawinyja-ma-l.yarra yalhuru-u kartawura-a kalya-lalha.
penis-ACC shake.about-CAUS-CTEMP tongue-ACC butt-ACC bite-PAST
Before, your chest would have been stabbed and your penis would have opened up like a mouth. You think you're 'deadly' (but) when you've seen a woman, you always stand with your eye's popping out. You grab your penis in the middle and shake it about. You bite the butt of your tongue...

4 Verbal coding of possession

The discussion in the preceding sections has focused on the nominal coding of possession, but without restricting this to the coding of possession within NPs. Thus the discussion has considered the coding of possessive relationships of different kinds through

1. NP internal patterns (inflection of Pr or Pe, apposition of part–whole);
2. non-verbal predication (inflected element is predicate);
3. part as locus of effect secondary predication (part and whole are separate constituents bearing the same case inflection).

Martuthunira lacks specific verbs of possession (although it is interesting that there is a specific 'to do for' verb coding a beneficiary, see (2) and (37)). Verbs used to indicate that something is in the possession of a possessor include: *manku-ø* 'grab, catch, pick up, hold'; *kanyjaL* 'hold, keep'. Martuthunira also has a verb 'steal'. An example, from a traditional mythological text, is (34) above. The following two examples are from the same set of mythological stories.

(56) ngaliwa manku-layi ngurnaa wirra-a,
1plinc grab-FUT that:ACC boomerang-ACC
manku-layi ngurnaa. ngaliwa-rru kanyja-rninyji
grab-FUT that:ACC 1plinc-NOW keep-FUT
We'll grab that boomerang, grab it and then keep it.

(57) wartirra ngunhu jalurra-a manku-lha.
woman that:NOM coroboree-ACC pick.up-PAST
ngana pala ngunhu yini, jalurra-marta....
who IT that:NOM name coroboree-PROP...
nhiyu-nu jalurra-a kanyja-rnuru wartirra
this:NOM-QUOT coroboree-ACC hold-PRES woman
That woman (had) picked up a coroboree (a song with choreography). Who is her name, that one with the coroboree?... so apparently this one is holding a coroboree, a woman.

5 Cultural patterns

The patterns of possession revealed in Martuthunira reflect the importance of kin relationships—and it must be said that the systems described here are not the only grammatical and lexical systems in the language that reference kinship relations.

While Australian kinship systems are recognized as complex classificatory systems that extend kinship to all people who participate in the community, it is clear that distinctions are made between close kin and those more distantly related, and which give some particular importance to parent–child relations. These close kin are typically referred to as 'dear' relatives in the local English vernacular and there is some flexibility in the attribution. Most straightforwardly, 'dear' kin includes one's children, parents, aunts, uncles, and grandparents/grandchildren and may be extended to close affines, to cousins and to those kin most intimately related through male initiation. These dear kin then stand in contrast to the wider network of classificatory kin.

More generally, there are constraints on the use of the genitive—possessors must be (construed to be) animate. Questions—'Whose X is that?'—can only be asked where the possessor is assumed to be animate. The genitive is not used for a wide range of associations between persons, objects, etc. Rather, there is a restricted notion of possession which includes ownership of artefacts, clothing, bedding, campsites and dwelling places, food (to be consumed), and which extends to kinship relations. A gap in the data is any clear discussion of the possession of land, of particular named places, or of people's connections to these. The patterns of personal possession revealed in traditional stories are easily transferred to the possession of modern western artefacts. There is no strong evidence of any change in patterns of possession as a result of contact.

Interestingly, the set of traditional stories in the corpus each have as a central plot conflicts based around contested possession; the introduction and attempted theft of new technology (the returning boomerang) (56), theft of a virtually unscaleable hill (kept by one or another group of 'devils' essentially as an 'artefact' to be used as a fort/sanctuary) (34), food consumed selfishly (where it is expected it should be shared, at the very least with the hunter), and the inappropriate insulting of the 'dear' children of a revered woman who is opening a new coroboree (17). In this last case, the protagonist feigns ignorance of a kin relationship (already an insult), further insults the mother by insulting her children, and thus manages to incite those children to a violent defence of their mother. Certainly the Martuthunira had a very well developed sense of possession.

References

Dench, Alan. 1995a. *Martuthunira: A language of the Pilbara region of Western Australia.* Canberra: Pacific Linguistics.

——. 1995b. 'Suffixaufnahme and apparent ellipsis in Martuthunira', pp. 380–95 of *Double case*, edited by Frans Plank. Oxford: Oxford University Press.

——. 1997. 'Where do complex kinterms come from?', pp. 107–32 of *Boundary rider: Essays in honour of Geoffrey O'Grady*, edited by Darryl Tryon and Michael Walsh. Canberra: Pacific Linguistics.

——. 1998. 'The *Dative split in Martuthunira', *Proceedings of the Australian Linguistics Society Meeting 1998*. http://www.cltr.uq.edu.au/als98/.

Dench, Alan and Evans, Nicholas. 1988. 'Multiple case-marking in Australian languages', *Australian Journal of Linguistics* 8: 1–47.

Merlan, Francesca and Heath, Jeffrey. 1982. 'Dyadic kinship terms', pp. 107–24 of *Languages of kinship in Aboriginal Australia*, edited by Jeffrey Heath, Francesca Merlan and Alan Rumsey. Sydney: Oceania Publications (*Oceania Linguistic Monographs* 24).

6

Possession in Nanti

LEV MICHAEL

1 Introduction

This chapter describes possessive constructions in Nanti, an Arawak language of southeastern Peru. Several features of Nanti possessive constructions are noteworthy from a comparative perspective. Of the languages described in this volume, Nanti possession is among the most semantically restrictive, including only part–whole, kinship, and strict ownership relations. At the same time, Nanti has developed 'non-referential' functions of possessive nominal prefixes, allowing the formal satisfaction of required inalienable possession constructions, while effectively omitting reference to definite possessors.

As the most head-marking and polysynthetic language described in this volume, it is perhaps unsurprising to find the marking of possession within the Nanti noun phrase to be relatively unelaborated. However, the language exhibits several interesting verbal constructions in which possession plays an important role. These include: (1) productive noun incorporation of part terms with possessor ascension; (2) a denominal reversative construction in which the subject of the derived verb denotes the whole (i.e. possessor) from which the original nominal element is detached; and (3) a separative applicative construction in which the applied object is interpreted as the (external) possessor of the demoted former object.

2 Sociolinguistic and typological background

Nanti is a member of the Kampan branch of Arawak, a group of closely related languages spoken from the foothills of the southeastern Peruvian Andes to the adjacent areas of the Peruvian-Brazilian border region. The Kampan branch consists of several dialect continua, which have been divided into anywhere from three to eleven distinct languages by different linguists (Michael 2008: 212–19). Nanti forms a dialect chain with three major Matsigenka varieties: Upper Urubamba Matsigenka,

Lower Urubamba Matsigenka, Manú Matsigenka, and Nanti (position in this list corresponds to position in the dialect chain). Mutual intelligibility between Manú Matsigenka and Nanti is relatively high, but is low between Upper Urubamba Matsigenka and Nanti.

Nanti is spoken by approximately 450 individuals living in some ten settlements located in the headwater regions of the Camisea and Timpia Rivers. Nantis lived in this difficult-to-access region with no sustained contact with non-Nantis until the late 1980s, when they made contact with the Matsigenka, the neighbouring Kampan group. Nantis remain monolingual, except for a few young men who have learned Matsigenka; in more recent years, two young men have learned very basic Spanish.

I first visited the Nanti communities in 1993, and carried out monolingual linguistic fieldwork in the Nanti communities between 1997 and 2005. My data consists almost exclusively of transcribed and translated recordings of naturally occurring Nanti discourse.

Nanti is a head-marking language with extensive, mainly suffixal, verb morphology. Nominal morphology is minimal, and other than the possessive markers and classifiers discussed in the chapter, is limited to plural markers and a single locative suffix. Obligatory verbal inflectional categories include aspect and reality status, and most verbs bear cross-referencing markers (CRMs). CRMs are in complementary distribution with contrastively focused referential NPs. Subject CRMs are verbal proclitics, and object CRMs are verbal enclitics, as in (43). Referential NP subjects tend to be pre-verbal, and objects tend to be post-verbal, suggesting a characterization of Nanti as an SVO language. A pre-verbal contrastive focus position and pre- and post-verbal topicalization positions are responsible for other orders. The locative suffix given in (31) is the sole dependent-marking means of adding an argument to a clause; head-marking means include five morphological causatives and five applicative suffixes. The reader is referred to Michael (2008) for further information.

3 Possession in the noun phrase

3.1 *The structure of basic possessive constructions*

Possession within the Nanti noun phrase is expressed by several constructions that are distinguished by the information-structural status of the possessor and by whether the possessee is alienably or inalienably possessed. The most common type of possessive construction in Nanti discourse is exemplified in (1a, b), where the possessor is indicated solely by a possessive prefix on the possessee. The identity of the possessee in such constructions may be fixed by an antecedent referential NP, or, just as commonly, is fixed by pragmatics.

(1)	a. i-	banko	b. i-	gemari	-te	
	3msg-	house	3msg-	tapir	-ALN.POSS	
	his house		his tapir			

Possessive prefixes are drawn from the paradigm given in Table 6.1. This paradigm exhibits significant gaps for plural possessors, but speakers can make recourse to free possessive pronouns to clarify the plural status of possessors of the relevant cases. If the possessee belongs to the class of inalienably possessed nouns, the possesee further bears an alienable possession prefix, as in (1b).

Possessors can be realized as referential NPs within the possessive phrase, as in the inalienable (2a), and alienable (2b). The possessee continues to bear a possessive prefix, and if the possessor is not contrastively focused, it follows the possessee, as in (2)–(4). The relative order of possessor and possessee is not affected by whether the possessive NP appears in subject or object position, as evident in (3) and (4).

(2)	a. i-	banko	Ihonira	b. i-	gemari	-te	Esekera
	3msg-	house	personal.name	3msg-	tapir	-ALN.POSS	personal.name
	Ihonira's house			Esekera's tapir			

(3)	i=	kent	-ak	-i	=ri	iri-	iri	Santihago
	3msg=	pierce	-PERV	-REAL.I	=3mS	3msg-	father	personal.name
	He shot Santihago's father.							

(4)	i-	banko	Horase	o=	teronk	-an	-ak	-i
	3msg-	house	personal.name	3msg=	collapse	-ABL	-PERV	-REAL.I
	Horase's house collapsed.							

If the possessor is contrastively focused, it appears before the possessee, as in (5a&b).

(5)	a. Ihonira	i-	banko	b. Esekera	i-	gemari	-te
	personal.name	3msg-	house	personal.name	3msg-	tapir	-ALN.POSS
	Ihonira's house			*Esekera's* tapir			

Contrastive possessor focus can also be expressed with a free possessive pronoun, as in (6a, b), where the free possessive pronoun occupies the same position as a focused

TABLE 6.1. **Nanti possessive prefixes**

Possessor	Singular	Plural
1st person	*no-*	*a-* (inclusive)
2nd person	*pi-*	—
3rd person masculine	*i-* ~ *iri-*	—
3rd person feminine	*o-*	—

referential NP. There are no attested cases of the possessive pronoun following the possessee.

(6) a. irashi i- banko
3msg.poss 3msg- house
his house

b. irashi i- gemari -te
3msg.poss 3msg- tapir -ALN.POSS
his tapir

Possessive pronouns are transparently related to possessive prefixes via the addition of the element *ashi*, which is of uncertain origin. In contrast to the possessive prefix paradigm, the possessive pronoun paradigm exhibits a full set of plural forms, constructed by adding the nominal plural suffix -*hegi* to the corresponding singular forms (Table 6.2).

3.2 *Alienably possessed nouns*

Alienably possessed nouns bear the same possessive prefixes as inalienably possessed ones, but additionally bear one of several alienable possession suffixes. The distribution of the two regular alienable possession suffixes, -*ne* and -*te*, is conditioned solely by the size of the nominal root to which they attach. Disyllabic roots take -*ne*, as in (7), and roots that are trisyllabic or larger take -*te*, as in (8). Alienable nouns are minimally disyllabic, in accord with general disyllabic minimum word requirement in Nanti (Crowhurst and Michael 2005).

(7) i- biha -ne
3msg- bow -ALN.POSS
his bow

(8) o- shiropitonki -te
3fsg- needle -ALN.POSS
her needle

In addition to the regular alienable possession suffixes, a third irregular marker -*re*, is found on a small number of forms, as in (9).

(9) i- chago -re
3msg- arrow -ALN.POSS
his arrow

TABLE 6.2. Nanti free possessive pronouns

Possessor	Singular	Plural
1st person	*nashi*	*hashi* (inclusive) *nashihegi* (exclusive)
2nd person	*pashi*	*pashihegi*
3rd person masculine	*irashi*	*irashihegi*
3rd person feminine	*ashi*	*ashihegi*

The irregular alienable possession suffix *-ma* is found on a single form (cf. *tsitsi* 'firewood'), given in (10).

(10) o- tsi -ma
3fsg- firewood -ALN.POSS
her firewood

3.3 *Root allomorphy in possessed forms*

Possessed nouns in Nanti exhibit a form of root allomorphy in which word-initial voiceless stops in unpossessed forms surface as voiced in possessed forms, as in alienable pair (11a, b) and the inalienable pair (12a, b). The forms (13a, b) demonstrate that the allomorphy in question consists of voicing the initial segment of the possessed root, rather than devoicing of the initial segment of the unpossessed form.

(11) a. kemari
tapir
tapir

b. i- gemari -te
3msg- tapir -ALN.POSS
his tapir

(12) a. panko -tsi
house -ALIEN
house

b. no- banko
1sg- house
my house

(13) a. bayana
plantain.variety
bayana (plantain variety)

b. no- bayana -te
1sg- plantain.variety -ALN.POSS
my *bayana*

Voicing in possessed forms occurs only if the voiced counterpart on the initial voiceless consonant is a contrastive segment in the Nanti phonological inventory. This means that only /p/ and /k/ undergo possessive voicing, as in (11) and (12). Other word-initial consonants, such as /t/, are unaffected, as in (14).

(14) a. tabiri
tree.resin
tree resin

b. no- tabiri -te
1sg- tree.resin -ALN.POSS
my tree resin

3.4 *Derivation of alienable nouns*

The Kampan languages exhibit an 'alienator' suffix that derives alienable unpossessed nouns from inalienably possessed ones. The inalienable–alienable pair in (15a, b) illustrate the form and function of this suffix in Nanti. Cognates of this suffix are found in most Arawak languages (Aikhenvald 1999: 82).

(15) a. no- mare
1sg- limb.band
my limb band

b. mare -tsi
limb.band -ALIEN
limb band

In Nanti, the number of pairs like those in (15) is considerably smaller than in other Kampan languages, suggesting that the alienator is no longer productive in the language; there is also evidence that alienators like that in (15b) are becoming lexicalized. With the diminishing productivity of the alienator, other strategies, such as the non-referential use of possessive prefixes, are developing to fill its function.

In Kampan languages such as the closely related Matsigenka, all inalienably possessed nouns may undergo alienation, including part terms, as in (16a, b).

(16) a. no- gito
   1sg- head
   my head

b. gito -tsi
   head -ALIEN
   head

In Nanti, however, no human, animal, or plant part terms (all inalienably possessed) may be alienated. Bodily effluvia are similarly immune to alienation, with a single exception, in (17), representing perhaps the most separable and enduring of effluvia.

(17) a. o- tiga
   3fsg- faeces
   its faeces

b. tiga -tsi
   faeces -ALIEN
   faeces

The small number of nouns that exhibit alienated counterparts include two bodily parasites (*ne-tsi* 'louse', *keni-tsi* 'maggot'), and a small number of personal inalienable possessions (e.g. *maga-tsi* 'traditional garment', *panko-tsi* 'house').

The decrease in the number of inalienable nouns that can take the alienatior *-tsi* suggests a decrease in its morphological productivity. There is also evidence that Nantis no longer recognize *-tsi* as distinct morpheme in the words in which it appears. The relevant evidence involves a pair of recent loans from Matsigenka.

Prior to contact with the Matsigenkas in the late 1980s, Nantis had no canoes, using only rafts (*paroto*). Nantis became familiar with canoes in the early 1990s, and adopted the Matsigenka words, *pito-tsi* (alienated) and *bito* (inalienable). Significantly, there was considerable variation in how Nantis treated these two words, some producing the 'correct' inalienable possessed forms, for example *i-bito* 'his canoe', others producing the 'incorrect' *i-bitotsi-te*, which treated the stem *pito-tsi* as an unanalysable alienable root. Yet others treated *bito* as an *alienable* root: *i-bito-re*. In short, Nantis appeared to have difficulty recognizing the alienator suffix, indicating that it is becoming lexicalized.

With the decline in productivity of the alienator, Nantis have broadened the semantic functions of possessive prefixes to include non-specific or non-referential functions. This broadening allows speakers to satisfy the structural requirement that inalienable roots bear possessive suffixes without necessarily committing to the identifiability of the formally marked possessor.

For inalienable roots with unidentified human possessors, Nantis employ the first person plural inclusive possessive prefix *a-*, as in (18a) and (18b). Both forms can yield either a non-possessed reading or a possessed reading, with the specific meaning determined pragmatically.

(18) a.

a-	gito
1pl.incl-	head

(human) head (*lit.* our head)

b.

a-	tomi	-hegi
1pl.incl-	son	-PL

children (*lit.* our sons)

For unidentified non-human possessors, Nantis employ third-person possessive prefixes, as exemplified in the brief excerpt from a conversation between the author and Bikotoro, a Nanti friend, given in (19). The final conversational turn of this excerpt demonstrates that the possessive prefix in the second line is functioning non-referentially.

(19) LM:

tata	o-	ita?
what	3fsg-	INTER.COP

What is it?

B:

o-	shi.
3fsg-	leaf

(A) leaf (*lit.* its leaf)

LM:

tata	o-	shi?
what	3fsg-	leaf

The leaf of what (plant)?

B:

tera	no=	ogo	-t	-e.
NEG.REAL	1sg=	know	-EPC	-IRR.I

I don't know.

3.5 *Heads of possessive phrases*

Possessees constitute the heads of possessive NPs in Nanti, as demonstrated by verbal cross referencing and animacy agreement. Consider (20), where the possessive NP *iriniro Migero* 'Migero's mother' triggers feminine subject cross-reference marking on the verb. The possessee *iniro* 'mother' is feminine, while the possessor *Migero* is masculine, as indicated by the masculine possessive prefix on the possessee. The cross-reference marking on the verb, however, indicates that the possessive NP is treated as feminine, making the feminine possessee its head.

(20)

iri-	iniro	Migero	o=	sat	-ak	-i	=ro
3msg-	mother	personal.name	3fsg=	pierce	-PERV	-REAL.I	=3fsg

Migero's mother pierced it.

Animacy agreement, which appears on certain underived adjectives and positive polarity existential verbs (Michael 2008: 294), supports the preceding conclusion. Consider (21) and (22), where the possessors are animate in both cases. The existential verb in (22) exhibits agreement with the inanimate possessee, confirming that it is the head of the possessive NP.

(21)	ainyo	Marota	o-	tomi
	EXIST.ANIM	personal.name	3fsg-	son
	Marota has a son.			

(22)	aityo	Ihonira	i-	bito
	EXIST.INAN	personal.name	3fsg-	canoe
	Ihonira has a canoe.			

3.6 *Semantics of possessive constructions*

Nanti possessive constructions express a relatively restricted range of notional relationships between possessors and possessees, compared to the possible range of such relationships attested cross-linguistically (see Chapter 1): part–whole, kinship, and ownership relations.

Part–whole relationships expressed by Nanti possessive constructions include those involving human and animal body parts, plant parts, and subparts of manufactured objects and geographical features. All canonical body parts are inalienably possessed, including relatively easily detachable ones such as hair (*nogishi* 'my hair'), and bodily substances such as blood (*norirana* 'my blood'). Non-canonical body parts, as delimited in Chapter 1, are generally referred to via verbal expressions, as in (23), or nominalizations thereof, as in (24). Perhaps the only non-canonical body part expressed via an inalienable possession construction is *(i-)tsimanki* '(his) shadow'. As discussed in §5, part–whole relations can also be expressed via classifier constructions.

(23)	no=	sompo	-t	-ak	-i
	1sg=	have.a.boil	-EPC	-PERV	-REAL.I
	I have a boil. (= my boil)				

(24)	no=	kahent	-ø	-a	-ra
	1sg=	itch	-IMPERV	-REAL.A	-NOMZ
	where I itch (= my rash)				

Part–whole relationships of manufactured objects are expressed through inalienable possession constructions. There are a small number of object part terms that are not based on metaphorical extensions of body part terms, as in (25), but most constructions that express part–whole relations of manufactured objects are transparent extensions of body part constructions, as in (26). A subpart of a geographical entity is given in (27).

(25)	o-	tenina	pitotsi
	3msg-	interior.surface	canoe
	interior surface of canoe		

(26)	o-	tishita	kobiti
	3fsg-	back	pot
	sides of pot		

(27)	o-	tsapiha	oniroha
	3fsg-	river.bank	main.channel
	bank of main channel		

All kin terms are obligatorily possessed, but the morphological realization of kin term possession varies, with an iconic relationship between the closeness of the kin term to ego and the morphological complexity of the appropriate possessive construction. Kin terms fall into three sets in this respect (Table 6.3).

The closest set of kin (Set 1) consists of parents and siblings and their classificatory extensions. The first-person possessive forms for this set are the structurally simplest of possessed forms, being identical to the vocative form, and exhibiting no possessive morphology whatsoever. Thus, for example, *ina* functions as both the vocative 'mother' and the first person possessive referential form, 'my mother'. Members of this class with second- or third-person possessors exhibit standard inalienable possessive constructions, as evident in Table 6.3. Note the suppletive relation between the vocative/first-person and second-/third-person forms, which holds for all kin terms in this set.

The next closest set of kin (Set 2) consists of spouses and all remaining consanguineal kin. Standard inalienable possession constructions are used for all persons of possessors in this set. One quasi-kin-term *(no-)shaninka* '(my) fellow', used to indicate a fellow Nanti, also belongs to this group.

The most distant set of kin (Set 3), consists of affinal kin. Strikingly, possessed forms of this set require an *alienable* possession construction, as evident in (28), despite otherwise behaving as inalienable nouns. Nanti thus manages to structurally express both the close association of affinal kin (by treating them as obligatorily possessed) and the more transient nature of the kinship ties in question (by requiring

TABLE 6.3. **Possessed kin term constructions**

	Person of possessor	
	1st	2nd or 3rd
Set 1	*ina* 'my mother'	*iri-iniro* 'his mother'
Set 2	*no-shinto* 'my daughter'	*iri-ishinto* 'his daughter'
Set 3	*no-shobaniri-te* 'my brother-in-law'	*i-shobaniri-te* 'his brother-in-law'

an alienable possession construction). Note that the 'son-in-law' form is the one exception with regards to the overlap between Set 3 forms and affinal kin terms, as it is formally identical to the term for 'sister's son' (a reflection of the cross-cousin marriage system), which belongs semantically to Set 2.

(28) no- shobaniri -te
1sg- brother-in-law -ALN.POSS
my brother in law

The final class of possessable items are those which can be owned. With some exceptions arising from recent cultural contacts (see §6), the only entities that are treated as ownable are those things which are created or acquired by human labour, or directly involved in it (e.g. rocks used as tools). This includes manufactured objects, planted cultigens, gathered items, speech, and songs. The vast majority of owned items are alienably possessed. Most things worn directly against the body, such as clothing, women's limb-bands, necklaces, men's headdresses, and climbing cords are inalienably possessed. All other owned entities are alienably possessed, with the exception of houses, bows, and songs. Interestingly, speech (e.g. *no-niha-ne* 'my speech') is obligatorily possessed (Nanti has no conventionalized expression for 'language' as such), but requires an alienable possession construction, much like affinal kin.

Features of the natural world that exist without human intervention and are not parts of larger geographical entities normally do not surface in possessive constructions (e.g. *niha* 'water', *inkenishiku* 'forest', *kenti* 'sun').

4 Possession in the verb phrase

4.1 *Predicative possession*

Nanti employs four major constructions for expressing predicative possession, which are distinguished in terms of the characteristics of the possessive relationship they express: (1) ownership vs. other possession types; (2) definite vs. indefinite owned items; and (3) positive vs. negative clausal polarity.

Nanti employs the verb *ashint* to express ownership of definite referents, as in (29) (Table 6.4). This verb can only express ownership relationships and cannot be used to express either part–whole or kinship possessive relationships.

(29) iryo ashint -ø -a =ro oka saburi.
3msg.FOC own -IMPERV -REAL.A =3fsg this machete
He owns this machete.

TABLE 6.4. Verbs in Nanti possessive expressions

	Ownership		
	Definite possessee	Indefinite possessee	Other types of possession
Positive polarity	*ashint*	*tim*	*ainyo, aityo*
Negative polarity	*tera/ hara... ashint*	*tera/hara... tim/ mameri*	*mameri*

Forms of possession other than ownership of definite entities are expressed with existential constructions. Ownership of indefinite entities by human possessors is typically expressed using the intransitive verb *tim*, as in (30).

(30) o= tim -ø -i i- sapiro
3fsg= EXIST -IMPERV -REAL.I 3msg- clothes
He has (some) clothes. (*lit.* His clothes exist.)

Note that *tim* also serves to express that an individual lives in a particular location, as in (31).

(31) i= tim -ø -i Montetoni -ku
3msg= live -IMPERV -REAL.I Montetoni -LOC
He lives in Montetoni.

The roots *ashint* and *tim* can also be employed to express that a definite or indefinite referent, respectively, is not owned by the subject of the verb, through the use of the clausal negations *tera* or *hara*.

The existential verbs *ainyo* and *aityo*, which are used with animate and inanimate entities respectively, and their negative polarity counterpart *mameri*, are employed to express other possessive relationships. When employed with non-possessed nouns, these existential constructions are typically ambiguous between a simple existential reading and a locative existential reading. When employed with possessed nouns, predicative possession is added to this range of possible meanings, as in (32). Predicative kinship and part–whole possession is exemplified in (32) and (33), respectively.

(32) Ainyo i- koritiri?
EXIST.ANIM 3msg- spouse
Does he have a wife?/Is his wife alive?/Is his wife there?

(33) Aityo i- gesi -ne.
EXIST.INAN 3msg- crest -ALN.POSS
It has a crest (speaking of an eagle).

The negative existential verb *mameri* is used in the negative counterparts to the preceding possessive constructions, as (34) and (35), which express negative kin and part–whole possession, respectively. It also serves as an 'exhaustive' counterpart to the negative possessive construction formed with *tim*, as in (36).

(34)	Mameri	o-	tomi
	NEG.EXIST	3fsg-	son

She doesn't have a son.

(35)	mameri	o-	tsehi
	NEG.EXIST	3fsg-	spur

It doesn't have a spur.

(36)	mameri	i-	sapiro
	NEG.EXIST	3mS-	clothes

He has no clothes at all.

Nanti does not exhibit a counterpart to 'belong', in the sense of having a dedicated lexical verb that denotes possession, whose subject is the possessee. It does, however, exhibit a copular construction that can be employed to focus the identity of a possessor, in which the possessee surfaces as the subject. The possessee is usually not expressed by a referential NP in this construction, and the focused possessor is usually expressed by a free pronoun, which follows a possessive pronoun, as in (37). The free pronoun can be replaced by a referential NP, as in (38).

(37)	o-	nti	nashi	naro
	3fsg-	COP	1sg.POSS	1sg

It is *mine*.

(38)	o-	nti	irashi	Barentin
	3fsg-	COP	3msg.POSS	personal.name

It is *Barentin's*.

A topicalized referential NP may be added to the clause, clarifying either the identity of the possessor, as in (39), or the possesee, as in (40). The latter example also illustrates the negative form of the construction.

(39)	[Reho]$_{TOP}$	o-	nti	irashi	iriro
	personal.name	3fsg-	COP	3msg.POSS	3msg

It is *his*, Reho's.

(40)	[kobiti]$_{TOP}$	iro	-ta	o-	nti	ashi	-hegi	tsinane
	pot	3fsg.FOC	-CNGNT	3fsg-	COP	3f.POSS	-PL	woman
	tera	o-	nti	pashi	-hegi	biro		
	NEG.REAL	3fsg-	COP	2sg.POSS	-PL	2sg		

Pots, *they*, as I was saying, are women's, not yours.

4.2 *Verbal arguments as possessors*

We now consider three constructions in which verbal arguments simultaneously function as possessors of either: (1) nominal elements in the verb stem; or (2) nominal elements external to the verb. The possessive relationships between the verbal arguments and nominal elements is summarized in Table 6.5.

4.2.1 *Noun Incorporation and Possessor Ascension* Nanti exhibits productive noun incorporation (NI) with possessor ascension, which produces constructions in which a verbal argument, marked by a CRM, is also the possessor of the incorporated noun. In Nanti, only inalienably possessed part terms incorporate, and then only when the possessive NPs of which they form a part correspond, in the counterpart sentences without NI, to either: (1) the subjects of intransitive stative verbs, or (2) the objects of transitive verbs. NI into a stative intransitive verb is exemplified in (41b), where comparison with the counterpart sentence without NI in (41a) shows that the root of the erstwhile subject (and possessee of the possessive NP) incorporates immediately after the verb root, and that the possessor of the possessive NP 'ascends' to become the subject of the verb. The verbal subject in (41b) is thus simultaneously the possessor of the incorporated body part.

(41)	a. o=	katsi	-t	-ak	-i	no-	bori
	3fsg=	hurt	-EPC	-PERV	-REAL.I	1sg-	leg
	My leg hurts.						

b. no=	katsi	-pori	-t	-ak	-i
1sg=	hurt	-leg	-EPC	-PERV	-REAL.I
I leg-hurt.					

The intransitive verbs that undergo noun incorporation typically express qualities or attributes, as in (42).

(42)	i=	kuta	-panki	-t	-ak	-i
	3msg=	be.white	-feather	-EPC	-PERV	-REAL.I
	He is white-feathered.					

TABLE 6.5. Possessive relationships in Nanti verbal constructions

Construction type	Transitivity	Possessive relation
noun incorporation	intransitive	[SU]$_{PR}$=V-[N]$_{PE}$-TAM
	transitive	SU=V-[N]$_{PE}$-TAM=[OBJ]$_{PR}$
Reversative	intransitive	[SU]$_{PR}$=[N]$_{PE}$-REV-TAM
	transitive	SU=CAUS-[N]$_{PE}$-REV-TAM=[OBJ]$_{PR}$
Separative	transitive	SU=V-APPLIC-[OBJ]$_{PR}$ [DEMOTED.OBJ]$_{PE}$

Object incorporation into a transitive verb is exemplified in (43a, b), where the possessor of the erstwhile object possessive NP becomes the object of the verb, which is now also the possessor of the incorporated body part.

(43) a.

no=	mapa	-t	-ak	-i	=ro	i-	gito
1sg=	pulverize	-EPC	-PERV	-REAL.I	=3fsg	3msg-	head

I pulverized its head (speaking of a smoked fish).

b.

no=	mapa	-gito	-t	-ak	-i	=ri
1sg=	pulverize	-head	-EPC	-PERV	-REAL.I	=3msg

I head-pulverized it.

The incorporated inalienable root, it should be noted, exhibits slightly different phonological behaviour in transitive and intransitive verbs. In transitive verbs, as in (44b), incorporated roots exhibit initial-consonant voicing, as they do in possessive constructions generally. When incorporated into intransitive verbs, however, the same roots do not exhibit voicing, as is evident in (42).

(44) a.

no=	ag	-ak	-i	=ro	i-	banki
1sg=	get	-PERV	-REAL.I	=3fsg	3msg-	feather

I plucked its feather.

b.

no=	ag	-a	-banki	-t	-ak	-i	=ri
1sg=	get	-EPV	-feather	-EPC	-PERV	-REAL.I	=3msg

I defeathered him.

Examples like the preceding illustrate the communicative motivation for noun incorporation in Nanti: the sentences without NI typically locate the action of the verb relative to a subpart of the affected entity, while the counterpart sentences with NI emphasize the effects on the whole of the affected entity.

The pattern of possessor ascension described above for transitive verbs has one important exception: when the subject of the verb and the possessor of the incorporated noun are coreferential, the possessor does not raise to object, but is instead omitted entirely, as in (45b). The resulting verb is thus syntactically intransitive. In such cases, then, the subject of the verb is also the possessor of the incorporated part, as in the stative intransitive cases discussed above. Interestingly, in cases like these, incorporated nouns appear in their *transitive* incorporated form—that is, with initial consonant voicing—as is evident in comparing (46) with (41a, b), so that these verbs retain indications of their transitive origins.

(45) a.

i=	pote	-t	-ak	-i	=ro	i-	gito.
3msg=	shake	-EPC	-PERV	-REAL.I	=3fsg	3msg-	head

He shook his head.

b.

i=	pote	-gito	-t	-ak	-i.
3msg=	shake	-head	-EPC	-PERV	-REAL.I

He shook his head.

(46)	no= tot	-a	-bori	-t	-ak	-i
	1sg= cut	-EPV	-leg	-EPC	-PERV	-REAL.I

I cut my leg.

4.2.2 *Possession in reversative denominal derivation* Another construction that encodes a part–whole relationship between a verbal argument and a nominal element in the verb stem is the reversative denominal derivation. Nanti exhibits a reversative suffix that attaches to verb stems, as in (47), where the derived stem indicates the reversal of the action denoted by the verb root.

(47)	no=	ashi	-reh	-an	-ak	-i	=ro
	1sg=	cover	-REV	-ABL	-PERV	-REAL.I	=3fsg

I uncovered it.

The reversative can also derive intransitive verb stems from nominal elements such as classifiers and part terms, however, as in (48). When the reversative attaches to a part term, the resulting stem indicates the loss of the part denoted by the nominal root by the possessor of the part, which is expressed as the subject of the derived verb.

(48)	o=	ponkiti	-reh	-an	-ak	-i
	3fsg=	foot	-REV	-ABL	-PERV	-REAL.I

Its foot came off.

When the denominal reversative derivation acts on a classifier, as in (49), the resulting stem denotes the breaking off of a piece of the shape indicated by the classifier from the whole to which it pertains, which surfaces as the subject of the verb.

(49)	o=	kota	-reh	-ak	-i
	3fsg=	CL:PLANK	-REV	-PERV	-REAL.I

A plank-shaped piece broke off of it (a piece of boiled manioc).

Stems formed with the reversative verbal derivation often undergo causativization with the non-agent causative *o*[+voice]-,[1] as in (50). The whole from which the part is broken off by the causer appears, as expected, as the object of the verb.

(50)	i=	o-	gota	-reh	-ak	-i	=ro
	1sg=	CAUS:NAGNT-	CL:PLANK	-REV	-PERV	-REAL.I	=3fsg

He broke a plank-shaped piece off of it (a log, while chopping firewood).

4.2.3 *The separative applicative* Finally, we consider the separative applicative *-apitsa*, which indicates both that the applied object is the erstwhile possessor of

[1] The non-agentive causative morpheme consists of the prefixation of the segment indicated and voicing of the following consonant.

the demoted object, and that the verbal subject is involved in depriving the possessor of the demoted object. Comparing (51a) and (51b), for example, we see that the object of (51a), *kotsiro* 'knife', is demoted when the verb undergoes derivation with the separative applicative in (51b), and that the applied object in (51b) is interpreted as the owner of the knife. The construction in (51b) thus exhibits external possession.

(51) a.

i=	koshi	-t	-ak	-i	=ro	kotsiro
3msg=	steal	-EPC	-PERV	-REAL.I	=3fsg	knife

He stole the knife.

b.

i=	koshi	-t	-apitsa	-ak	-i	=na	kotsiro
3msg=	steal	-EPC	-APPLIC:SEP	-PERV	-REAL.I	=1sg	knife

He stole the knife from me.

The possessive relationship expressed in the separative applicative construction may be an alienable ownership relation, as in (51b), above, or an inalienable relationship involving either kin, as in (52), or inalienably possessed manufactured objects. Deprivation of a part cannot be expressed by this construction, which can, however, be expressed via the reversative derivation (see §4.2.2).

(52)

i=	r-	ag	-apitsa	-t	-ø	-e	=na
3msg=	IRR-	take	-APPLIC:SEP	-EPC	-IMPERV	-IRR.I	=1sg

no-	koritiri
1sg-	spouse

He will take my wife from me.

5 Possession-like constructions: part–whole classifier constructions

One of the common means for expressing part–whole relationships in Nanti involves a possession-like classifier construction. Nanti has a multiple classifier system where classifiers can appear affixed to alienable nouns, incorporated into verbs and adjectives, and infixed into numerals (Michael 2008: 332–9). In the first morphosyntactic context, they often convey part–whole relationships, as in (53), where the alienable noun can be taken to denote the 'whole' and the shape-based classifier the 'part'. Note that while the entire noun-classifier form can be definite, the whole from which it comes cannot be construed as definite, as evident in the gloss for (53), distinguishing it from the part–whole possessive constructions discussed in §3. Moreover, the classifier part–whole relationship grades into a shape-substance relationship, as in (54), demonstrating its indirect association with possession.

(53)

yoga	sega	-shi
that	sega.palm	-CL:slender.leaf

that sega palm leaf, *but not*: a/the leaf of that sega palm

(54)

kuri	-kii
peach.palm	-CL:stick

a stick from a peach palm/a rod of peach palm wood

6 Culture contact and possession

The Nanti possessive system has been affected by recent interactions between Nantis and non-Nantis. Nantis made contact with their Matsigenka neighbours in the late 1980s, and culturally novel concepts and manufactured goods began to filter into the Nanti communities in earnest in the early 1990s (Michael 2008: 28–36).

All introduced items have been treated as alienably possessable, even items such as clothes and machetes, which now number among individuals' most intimate possessions. All associated loanwords have been incorporated seamlessly into the morphosyntax of Nanti alienable possessive constructions, exhibiting both possessive voicing (see §3.3), as in (55a, b) and (56a, b), and alienable possession suffix allomorphy (see §3.2), as evident in comparing (55b) and (56b).

(55) a. kotsiro (< *cuchillo* 'knife', Sp.)
knife
knife

b.

i-	gotsiro	-te
3msg-	knife	-ALN.POSS

his knife

(56) a. pira (< *pila* 'battery', Sp.)
flashlight
flashlight/torch

b.

pi-	bira	-ne
2sg-	flashlight	-ALN.POSS

your flashlight/torch

One aspect of the possessive system that has been affected by contact with outsiders concerns the ownability of land. Nantis previously conceived of ownership as extending solely to manufactured objects, cultigens, and gathered things; land *per se* was not considered ownable, except insofar as someone who had cleared and planted portions of forest had exclusive usufructal rights to it while the cultigens they planted were producing.

Beginning in the mid-1990s however, Nantis began to encounter Western concepts of land ownership through interactions with Matsigenkas, and starting in the early 2000s, with Peruvian government officials. Matsigenkas warned Nantis that unless the government 'gave' the Nantis the land on which they lived, the government could 'take it away' from them, a notion that was clearly both puzzling and worrisome to Nantis. In 2003, officials from the nearby Manu National Park visited the community to explictly forbid them from farming, hunting, and fishing there (despite the fact that the park constituted roughly half of the Nanti hunting range). This interaction was related to me with the *pariki* (park officials) being quoted as saying *oka kipatsi onti nashihegi naro* 'This land is ours'.

As a result of these experiences, Nantis have begun to talk about land being ownable, at least with respect to outside entities such as the government, so that forms such as *no-gipatsi-te* 'my land (alienable)' are now used by Nantis. There is no doubt that Nanti conceptions of ownership are in transition, which is reflected in changes to the possession classes to which formerly unpossessable entities belong.

References

Aikhenvald, Alexandra. 1999. 'The Arawak language family', pp. 65–106 of *The Amazonian languages*, edited by R. M. W. Dixon and Alexandra Aikhenvald. Cambridge: Cambridge University Press.

Crowhurst, Megan and Michael, Lev. 2005. 'Iterative footing and prominence-driven stress in Nanti (Kampa)', *Language* 81(1): 47–95.

Michael, Lev. 2008. 'Nanti evidential practice: Language, knowledge, and social action in an Amazonian society'. PhD dissertation, University of Texas at Austin.

7

Possession and association in Galo language and culture

MARK W. POST

1 Introduction

This chapter primarily discusses the grammar and semantics of possession and related structures in Galo, a Tibeto-Burman language of the Western Tani subgroup spoken in central Arunachal Pradesh state, North East India.[1] Following this introduction, §2 discusses possession in the noun phrase, while predicative possession is discussed in §3. Sections 4 and 5 adopt a cultural-evolutionary perspective, claiming that the robust grammatical expression of possession in Galo is not mirrored by similarly robust cultural concepts of ownership and privacy. It is therefore suggested that a more general concept of ASSOCIATION is more likely to underlie the linguistic expression of 'possession' than is POSSESSION itself—in Galo and, quite likely, in other languages.

2 Possession in the noun phrase: the Genitive

After an overview of Galo noun phrase structure in §2.1, this section discusses structural aspects of Genitive marking in §2.2, core Genitive functions in §2.3, and extended Genitive functions in §2.4.

2.1 *Preliminary on Galo noun phrase structure*

Galo noun phrase (NP) structure is fairly rigid, and consists of well-defined position classes whose constituents are usually grammatical words. In Figure 7.1, PRHD is a

[1] Data are from the *Lare* dialect of Galo (Post 2007). Transcription follows IPA except *c* = tɕ and *z* = dʑ. My primary Galo consultant was *'Ilww Rwbaa* (w = ɨ). I thank him, together with Yankee Modi and Alexandra Aikhenvald, who both read drafts of this chapter and contributed many useful suggestions. I also thank the Workshop participants, and particularly Felix Ameka, Lev Michael, and Zygmunt Frazyngier, for our stimulating discussions and productive disagreements.

PRHD - RELC - NOML - ENUM - QUAL - PSHD

FIGURE 7.1. Galo noun phrase structure; head is underlined

pre-head determiner which may be either a demonstrative or genitive phrase, RELC is a nominalization-based relative clause, NOML is a potentially complex nominal head (i.e. it may be a compound or contain a pre-head nominal modifier), ENUM is either a classifier, a numeral, or both (in that order), QUAL is a referential or relational qualifying expression (including concepts like 'group of' or 'top of'), and PSHD is a post-head referential/relational complex, which may be composed of a demonstrative or article, a postposition, or a single form containing both referential and relational meanings.

Pronominally-headed NPs are more restricted, and for present purposes consist only of a pronoun plus any associated relational material. In what follows, we will primarily be concerned with the PRHD, NOML, QUAL, and PSHD positions in Figure 7.1, as well as with pronominally-headed NPs.

2.2 *Genitive marking: structures*

2.2.1 *Genitive forms and phrases* The basic marker of a possession relation (Prel) in Tani languages reconstructs to Proto-Tani (PT) **kV̀* (*V* is an as-yet-unknown vowel), and ultimately reflects Proto-Tibeto-Burman **ka* or **ki* (DeLancey 1984). This form is labelled 'Genitive' by Post (2007), following the definition in Blake (2001: 149). In modern Galo, PT **kV̀* is reflected in a pronominal case suffix *-kə̀*, and (following an irregular process of regressive lenition) in an NP postposition *gə̀*.[2] The pronominal suffix is frequently reduced to *-k̀* (the tone is spread to an adjacent syllable), which regularly geminates in certain morphophonological contexts.

In addition to these basic Genitive markers, several polyfunctional forms have resulted from fusion of the Genitive with other material. Table 7.1 first provides a summary, showing the fused modern Galo form in the left column, together with a basic gloss and some extended meanings (shown by >). The middle and right columns give the source formatives.

Here, I primarily discuss the basic Genitive markers *gə̀* and *-kə̀*, as most Genitive functions of the forms in Table 7.1 follow from those of the basic markers. Some further discussion of the more complex forms is found in §2.4.

A pronoun or NP terminated by a Genitive marker forms a Genitive phrase (GENP), which may stand in the PRHD position in Figure 7.1 (cf. §2.1). In principle, a GENP is itself an NP; however, as it is the only type of NP which, due to a terminal

[2] Some Tani languages display two markers of possession in the noun phrase, such as Upper Belt Minyong *kə̀* and *kìŋ* (author's field notes) and the potentially relatable Apatani forms *ka* and *kɨ* (Abraham 1985: 48–50). The precise functional distinction between these two markers is unknown; however, only one marker of possession is found in the Galo NP.

TABLE 7.1. **Genitive forms resulting from fusion with other operators**

Modern Form	Source 1	Source 2
lokə̀ 'LOC.GEN > ABL, VIA, MED, PRT.IRR'	**lo* 'LOC'	
hokə̀ 'SPROX/PROXTOP.LOC.GEN > ABL, VIA, MED'	**hò* 'SPROX/PROXTOP.LOC'	
okə̀ 'APROX/ANAPH.LOC.GEN > ABL, VIA, MED'	**o* 'APROX/ANAPH.LOC'	
akə̀ 'DIST.SLEV.LOC.GEN > ABL, VIA, MED'	**à* 'DIST.SLEV'	
tokə̀ 'DIST.UP.LOC.GEN > ABL, VIA, MED'	**tə̀* 'DIST.UP' + **o* 'APROX/ ANAPH.LOC'	**kə̀*
bokə̀ 'DIST.DOWN.LOC.GEN > ABL, VIA, MED'	**bə̀* 'DIST.DOWN' + **o* 'APROX/ ANAPH.LOC'	'GEN'
həkə̀ 'SPROX/PROXTOP.GEN > SEMB'	**hì* 'SPROX/PROXTOP' + VASSIM	
əkə̀ 'APROX/ANAPH.GEN > SEMB, PRT.RLS'	**ə* 'APROX/ANAPH'	
təkə̀ 'DIST.UP.GEN > SEMB'	**tə̀* 'DIST.UP'	
bəkə̀ 'DIST.DOWN.GEN > SEMB'	**bə̀* 'DIST.DOWN'	

Genitive marker, may be embedded within another NP, it is conventionally called a GENP to draw attention to this fact. Since an NP whose PRHD slot is filled by a GENP may in turn be terminated by a Genitive postposition, Genitive phrases may be recursively embedded. However, since a pronominally headed NP has no PRHD slot, only the 'outermost' of a set of recursively embedded GENPs may be headed by a pronoun (1).

(1) ŋó-**kə̀** ˀabó **gə̀** ˀazèn
[[[1sg-**GEN**]$_{\text{GENP}}$ father **GEN**]$_{\text{GENP}}$ friend]$_{\text{NP}}$
my father's friend

2.2.2 *Genitive selectivity* In principle, an NP containing a GENP is headed by a common nominal; thus, Genitive selectivity is in principle limited to common nominals, and excludes forms which cannot stand as NP head. However, since NP head-ellipsis is possible in Galo—given appropriate discourse-contextual conditions, and assuming that sufficiently referential material remains in the NP—this in practice means that GENPs can precede numerals, relator nouns, classifiers, and headless relative clauses; in such cases, the head can always be 're-inserted' to form a semantically-comparable expression (2).

(2) ŋó-kə̀ (ˀikìi) adór go
1sg-GEN (dog) CL:ANIMAL IND
my one (dog); one of my (dogs)

Among common nouns, few restrictions have been found in terms of ability to be modified by a GENP. In addition to nouns denoting material objects, kin terms, etc. (§2.3), GENPS can modify nouns denoting natural objects, spatial locations, and temporal units, in addition to proper human and place names. Certain collocations are considered unlikely by my consultants, such as *ŋó-kə̀ taləə́* 'my sky'. However, such collocations may simply be difficult to conceive and/or absent from ordinary discourse; it may be too strong to attribute such restrictions to a cultural-grammatical prohibition.

Different senses of nouns can be correlated to the presence or absence of GENP modification. For example, as in Tariana (Chapter 1), Galo *doorə́* generally means 'wind; breeze'; but, if modified by an animate Possessor (Pr), the sense as Possessee (Pe) is 'breath'. GENP modification can also correlate with different part-of-speech memberships—usually, when a basic noun has developed a distinct function and class association; for example, the adverb *ˀizì* 'now' reveals its original nominal sense when modified by a GENP (3).[3]

(3) ŋunù-kə̀ ˀizì...
1pl-GEN present
our present (era)...

2.2.3 *Adnominal modification, Genitive marking, and reference* There is a clear difference in Galo between bare ('compound-style') adnominal modification and adnominal modification via a GENP. Since bare nouns have a generic denotation, modification of a bare noun with another bare noun (or two, or three) only restricts the *potential* referential value of the expression by developing a narrower denotation. By contrast, adnominal modification via a GENP restricts *actual* referential value by identifying an individual in the world with whom the NP referent is associated. For example, *taníi ˀagóm* 'people speech' may reference any given instantiation of the speech of human beings (prototypically, that of Tani tribespeople), or else human speech in general; its referential value is not different from the simple noun *ˀagóm* except perhaps to the extent that 'people speech' potentially refers to a smaller set of referents than would 'speech' alone. Addition of a Genitive marker *taníi gə̀ ˀagóm* 'people's speech' restricts reference to the speech of a known individual, named '*taníi*'.[4] Some such formations are infelicitous. For example, *ˀaɲɨ́k talúu* 'eye plank' is a Kamdak Galo expression meaning 'glasses; spectacles'; adding the Genitive */? *ˀaɲɨ́k gə̀ talúu* renders the expression difficult to interpret, seemingly

[3] A nominal source is considered more likely in this case for two reasons: (a) the initial *ˀi-* reflects a Proto-Tani nominal prefix **ˀa-* (harmonized with the root nucleus) (b) the trajectory **nominal > adverbial* is widely-attested in Galo, as in *hiɲɨ̀ɨ* 'this year (adv.)' (< **çì* 'this (dem.)' + **ɲìŋ* 'year (n.)'), while the reverse is not.

[4] In Galo and other Tani tribal folklore, *taníi* is in fact the proper name of the progenitor of humankind.

suggesting either that a particular eye should be understood as somehow having a plank as one of its parts, or that *ʔaɲɨ́k* should be understood as naming an individual who possesses a plank.

2.3 *Core genitive functions*

Core Genitive functions are defined as the semantic aspects of modification of a common nominal head by a GENP.

2.3.1 *'Ownership' relations* One of the core functions of Genitive marking is to mark the relation (Prel) between a human Pr and a usually non-human Pe, when the Pe can be understood to denote an entity which is in some sense 'owned' by the Pr (4). Most such relations can be rephrased in terms of predicative possession (§3). Some further remarks on the semantic content of this type of relation may be found in §4.

(4) bɨɨ̀-kə̀ namə́ lo
3sg-GEN house LOC
'at his house'

2.3.2 *Kinship relations* The relationship between an individual and his kinspeople is marked via the Genitive (5). Such relations can be straightforwardly paraphrased via predicative possession (§3).

(5) nó-kə̀ ʔanə̀
2sg-GEN mother
your mother

2.3.3 *Constituency relations* The relation between an individual and the clan, tribe, or (in modern times) nation-state of which he is a member is also expressed as a possession relation among a (generally plural) human Pr and the network of which he is a constituent (6). While conceptually relatable to kinship relations (which generally go hand-in-hand with clan constituency), such relations are sometimes paraphrasable via predicative possession (§3.6).

(6) ŋunù-kə̀ rɨbáa=ə
1pl-GEN Rwbaa=TOP
our Rwbaa (clan)...

2.3.4 *Part-whole relations* The relation between a human and his/her body parts is coded via the Genitive (7).

(7) nó-kə̀ ʔalák
2sg-GEN arm/hand
your arm/hand

The parts of non-human/inanimate entities are also treated as a possession relation; here, care must be taken to distinguish true possession—marked by the Genitive Prel—and the naming of natural kinds in terms of parent entities (cf. §2.2.3). In (8), note that *pərə́ə* (an unidentified variety of bird) refers to a specific participant in the folktale from which the example derives; the 'hind legs' would therefore normally be understood as attached to *pərə́ə*'s body at the time of reference. In (9), '*pərə́ə* 'hind legs' is named as a natural kind, and does not reference the hind legs of a specific individual; accordingly, the referent would normally be understood as detached from any individual *pərə́ə* at the time of reference.

(8) pərə́ə gə̀ ˀaár=ə̀m
bird.variety GEN hind.legs=ACC
[they snapped] *Pərə́ə's* hind legs

(9) pərə́ə ˀaár=ə̀m
bird.variety hind.legs=ACC
[they snapped some] *pərə́ə* legs

Spatial domains which are either on, in, or otherwise related to a specific entity *may* be linked via Genitive marking. Here, absence of Genitive marking reduces specificity of the Pr, creating a tight, adposition-like bond between 'related' and 'relator' nouns (10)–(11).

(10) pətùp gə̀ ˀagùm lo
container GEN exterior LOC
outside the container [mosquitoes are swarming about] (*lit*. in the container's exterior)

(11) pətùp ˀagùm lo
container exterior LOC
at/in the container-exterior [mosquitoes are swarming about]

2.3.5 *(Other) associative functions* Most other core genitive functions may be roughly understood in terms of a general notion of ASSOCIATION. These include the propensity of an agent or source, or the customs with which a group is associated (12)–(13),

(12) poolò gə̀ loúu
moon GEN radiance
the moon's light

(13) ˀadìi gə̀ nijòm
Adi GEN custom(<Indic)
the customs of the Adi

... the topic or protagonist of a story (14),

(14)	toopó-gonə́	gə̀	doojɨ̀ɨ
	Topo Gona	GEN	story
	the tale of Topo Gona		

... the contents of a container or constituents of a locality (15),

(15)	cɨɨgóo-doogóo	gə̀	horə́=ə	kú=làa	hotə̀=ə	kú
	world	GEN	boar=TOP	COMPL=ADD	elephant=TOP	COMPL
	all the wild animals of the world					

... or a manner or purpose attributed to an entity (16).

(16)	bɨ̀ɨ-kə̀	ləgàa	bə̀
	3sg-GEN	reason	DAT
	for him (*lit.* for his reason; for his benefit)		

2.4 *Extended Genitive functions*

Extended Genitive functions are defined as its semantic and grammatical uses in contexts other than modification of a common NP head.

2.4.1 *Subordinate clause subject marker* The Genitive marks subjects (S/A) of most types of Galo subordinate clause, including subjects of event nominalizations and transitive relative clauses (which are based on nominalizations) (17).

(17)	hɨgɨ̀	nà	ŋunù-kə̀	allòo	nè	lə̀-há=ə
	SPROX.IND	DEC	1pl-GEN	tomorrow	TMP.IRR.PUNC	plant-NOMZ:NSU.IRR=TOP
	This is the [paddy] which we're to plant tomorrow. (*lit.* This is our to-be-planted tomorrow [paddy].)					

Several types of adverbial and other postpositionally subordinated clause types also take a Genitive subject (18). These are not considered to be nominalized by Post (2009, 2011), since they (a) cannot stand in a core argument slot, and (b) take predicate-inflectional affixes rather than nominalizing affixes; furthermore, while it is possible to paraphrase most types of nominalized (including relative) clauses in terms of predicative possession, it is not similarly possible to paraphrase postpositionally subordinated clauses.

(18)	taníi	gə̀	hobə́	pá-dàk	lo
	NAME	GEN	mithun	cut.by.strike-COS	LOC
	at (the time of) Tani's killing of the mithun				

2.4.2 *Comitative construction* The Comitative construction is based on a nominalized clause in *-kò* 'NOMZ:LOC', which is in turn subordinated to a main clause via a

Locative postposition *lo*. The subordinated clause subject, in Genitive case, is understood as initiator of an event whose lead the main clause subject follows. Schematically: *on X's V-ing, Y Vs > Y Vs with X.*

(19) nó jə̀ə-kə̀ ˀín-kò lo=làa ˀín-tà-dùu-kò=ə?
2sg who-GEN go-NOMZ:LOC/OBL LOC=CQ go-INCP-IMPERV-NOMZ:LOC/OBL=TOP
Who are you going to go with? (*lit.* On whose going are you going to go?)

2.4.3 *Oblique marking* The Genitive also marks certain oblique NP types, including Mediative (means) and Viative (path/way). Historically, these constructions may have emerged from Pr–Pe relations, with the Prel marker reanalysed as a case marker to an erstwhile Pr when Pe was contextually ellipsed. However, there is no firm evidence of this; synchronically, these are simply oblique noun phrases.

(20) gaaríi **gə̀** ín-rə́
vehicle(<Indic) **MED(<GEN)** go-IRR
[We'll] go by car.

(21) googàr **gə̀** hilɨ́ɨ mín-áa-làa...
Gogar **VIA(<GEN)** Sili chase-VEN-NF
I chased [the stag] via Gogar (village) here to Sili (village).

2.4.4 *From Locative and Genitive to Ablative* As was shown in Table 7.1, a large number of forms in Galo derive from fusion of Locative postpositions (or related forms) with the Genitive. Such forms can encode Locative+Genitive meanings; for example, a Pr which is a semantic PLACE expresses Prel via a Locative+Genitive postposition (22). Viative functions—which readily apply to a semantic PLACE—are similarly handled by Locative+Genitive forms (cf. (21)).

(22) mookò **hokə̀** ˀamín ə jòo ə?
place **SPROX.LOC.GEN** name TOP what COP
What's the name **of this** place?

Two types of Ablative function are also handled by forms incorporating an earlier Genitive marker; ORIGIN is handled by Locative+Genitive forms as in (22), while SOURCE (of motion) is handled by derivative forms exhibiting a geminate *kk*; the origin of gemination is unknown (23).

(23) **bokkə̀** càa-lèn-làa=zù
DIST.DOWN.ABL ascend-OUT-IMP.SDIR=HORT.INC
Let's go up **from down there**.

In terms of diachronic directionality it would thus appear that Locative+Genitive > Ablative is more likely in the case of Galo than the more widely-attested path Ablative > Genitive described by Noonan and Mihas (2008), following Heine and Kuteva (2002: 35).

3 Predicative possession

We now turn to predicative possession. Following an overview of clause and predicate structures in §3.1, the lack of explicit verbs of possession in Galo is discussed in §3.2. §3.3 then describes clauses headed by *káa-*, a primarily existential verb which handles most types of possession scenarios. Verbs of temporary possession are discussed in §3.4, while §3.5 covers the use of posture verbs in possession-like scenarios. Finally, §3.6 discusses the Tani root **tò* 'entitled in relation to', and §3.7 discusses the semantic and grammatical relationships between propensity predicates and body part nouns, speculating that it could reflect an older external possession construction.

3.1 *Preliminary: clause and predicate structures*

Galo clauses are divided into *predicative* and *appositive* subtypes:

Predicative clauses are headed by an inflecting predicate. Predicates may in turn be headed by an adjective or a verb. The resulting clause hosts one or more NPS, which realize semantic arguments of the predicate. Arguments of transitive and extended transitive verb-headed predicates are labelled A/O and A/O/E, respectively. The single argument of an intransitive predicate is labelled S. Non-argument NPS are labelled 'oblique'.

Appositive clauses prototypically consist of two noun phrases arrayed in the order TOPIC–FOCUS.[5] Only the FOCUS is obligatory. Appositive clauses with a definite (= Identifiable, Specific) FOCUS have become *copula* clauses, with the uninflecting copula deriving from an erstwhile article ə. That this is so is demonstrated by the fact that *only* a copula-headed appositive clause may take *both* adjectival *and* nominal complements (all other appositive clause types permit a nominal FOCUS only; (cf. (44)).

The structures of predicative and appositive clauses are briefly contrasted in (24).

(24) káa-tó-làa, bə̀ə nà
[[look-IMP.ODIR-HORT.POL]$_{\text{PRED}}$]$_{\text{CLAUSE.PRED}}$ [[DIST.DOWN]$_{\text{FOCUS(VCC)}}$ DEC]$_{\text{CLAUSE.APP}}$
Look at that, it's down there.

Certain Galo clauses make use of a 'pre-core topic' slot. By this is meant an NP in sentence-initial position, which is intimately associated with the information

[5] Syntactically, these are realized by a verbless clause subject and verbless clause complement (VCS/VCC) or copula subject and copula complement (CS/CC) respectively. The terms TOPIC and FOCUS provide two pragmatically oriented 'macro-labels' to cover all four categories.

contained in a clause, but which is seemingly not a core argument of that clause. Related discussion and examples are in §3.3.

3.2 *A lexical perspective on possession, ownership, and belonging*

As Aikhenvald (Chapter 1) mentions, many languages have (a) a general and often irregular transitive verb of possession/ownership 'have' and (b) more specific, usually regular transitive verbs of possession, ownership, and acquisition ('H-possession'), in addition to verbs of pertinence such as 'belong (to)' ('B-possession').

None of these verb types are straightforwardly present in Galo. However, there are several verbs which can take on possessive meanings in certain circumstances:

3.3 *Verb of existence, location, and possession* káa- *'be (there); have'*

The Galo verb which best translates English *have*, in the sense of 'possess', is *káa-* 'have/exist'. *káa-* primarily functions as an existential verb 'be (there)', similar to Hindi *he*, Assamese *as-*, Thai *mii*, or Chinese *yǒu*; the majority of *káa-* mentions in my corpus are of this type. In its existential sense, *káa-* is straightforwardly intransitive, with a single core argument S (and often, an optional Locative or Temporal oblique) (25).

(25) ləkɨɨ ogò, omée go **káa**-tó
[time.long.ago TMP.REAL]$_{OBL}$ [child IND]$_{S}$ [**have/exist**-PERV]$_{PRED}$
Once upon a time, **there was** a child.

Second, *káa-* predicates possession; in this case, erstwhile S stands as the Pe and a new entity is introduced as the Pr. There are roughly four ways to do this, all of which are attested in other languages (Chapter 1):

1. NP-internal possession of the Pe (26)
2. oblique NP bearing Genitive-Locative marking (27)
3. 'pre-core topic' NP bearing Genitive marking, plus a Topic marker (28)
4. a subject-like NP, which might be alternatively analysed as a 'second subject', 'pre-core topic', or A argument of a non-prototypical transitive clause (29)

(26) ŋó-kə̀ ʔərə́k go káa-dùu
[1sg-GEN pig IND]$_{S}$ [have/exist-IMPERV]$_{PRED}$
My pig is there (in the group).

(27) ŋó-kə̀ lo ʔərə́k go káa-dùu
[1sg-GEN LOC]$_{OBL}$ [pig IND]$_{S}$ [have/exist-IMPERV]$_{PRED}$
There is a pig with me (among my possessions).

(28) ŋó-kə̀=ə[6] ˀərə́k go káa-dùu
[1sg-GEN=TOP]$_{TOP}$ [pig IND]$_{S}$ [have/exist-IMPERV]$_{PRED}$
≅ Of/for me there is a pig. (*lit.* As for my [part/side], a pig is there.)

(29) ŋó ˀərə́k go káa-dùu
[1sg]$_{A?}$ [pig IND]$_{O?}$ [have/exist-IMPERV]$_{PRED}$
I have a pig.

Type (1) is straightforwardly analysed as an intransitive existential, with the S argument internally-possessed.

Type (2) is structurally fairly straightforward, although the Galo sense is somewhat difficult to translate into English; roughly, it invokes a domain of reference—the set of things which are 'on the side of' or otherwise associated to a Pr—and then asserts that the Pe is or isn't found therein.

Type (3) is challenging from both structural and semantic perspectives. Structurally, it appears that a Genitive phrase is introduced as a pre-core topic, and, as in type (2), invokes a domain of reference pertaining to Pr. Semantically, my consultants consider types (2) and (3) to be similar if not identical. The difference is thus most likely to be found in discourse, though due to the rarity of both types in my corpus it is difficult to know what this might be.

Type (4) is more intriguing. Semantically, it forms the closest Galo equivalent to a transitive possession predication. Structurally, however, it presents a challenge. If it is a transitive construction, it is non-prototypical inasmuch as Pe cannot take Accusative-marking (normally, the primary transitivity test in Galo) (30); accordingly, there is a possibility that 'A' should be analysed not as a subject, but rather as a pre-core topic, and 'O' as in fact S of an existential verb (31).

(30) *ŋó ˀərə́k ə̀m káa-dùu
1sg pig ACC have/exist-IMPERV

(31) ŋó ˀərə́k go káa-dùu
[1sg]$_{TOP}$ [pig IND]$_{S}$ [have/exist-IMPERV]$_{PRED}$
I have a pig. (*lit.* (As for) me, a pig is there.)

However, against such an analysis is the fact that 'S' of a possession construction cannot be definite—(32)—unlike the S of an existential construction (33).

(32) *ŋó ˀərə́k ə káa-dùu
1sg pig TOP have/exist-IMPERV

(33) ˀərə́k ə káa-dùu
[pig TOP]$_{S}$ [have/exist-IMPERV]$_{PRED}$
The pig is there.

6 The surface phonetic realization of this sequence is *ŋokkə̀* (cf. §2.4.4).

Accordingly, it may be that the inability of *káa-* to take an Accusative O is to do with semantic and pragmatic factors rather than grammatical (in)transitivity. Since only specific, identifiable O arguments take Accusative-marking in Galo, the generalization that will best account for the data in (30)–(33) may be that the Pe of a possession construction in *káa-* must be referentially non-specific and/or unidentifiable, but is nonetheless a grammatical O.[7] Support for this view would come from the fact that the Pe of a possession predicate in *káa-* can be referenced using non-subject core nominalizer *-nám* in a relative clause construction, which is typical of O and E arguments (34).

(34) ŋó-kə̀ káa-**nám** ə ˀoròk go
1sg-GEN have/exist-NOMZ:NSU.REAL TOP dao IND
What I have is a dao (machete) [the others may be simply owning knives].

Type (4) uses of *káa-* may be innovative; in elicitation, my consultants often view such sentences as colloquial, claiming that type (2) or (3) sentences are more 'formal' or 'correct' (type (1) being semantically somewhat different). Accordingly, one suspects at least a possibility that 'transitive' uses of *káa-* could owe in part to contact with and calquing of Indo-European languages with transitive possession constructions. If that is so, however, it is a usage which is by now widespread, and is probably not restricted to younger generations or high-Indo-European contact areas; sentences such as (35) are commonly uttered by elder and proficient speakers in my corpus. Here, note that Pe occurs before Pr in the syntax; this would not normally be possible unless Pr were a true subject (and not a pre-core topic or some other type of non-subject NP which is somehow loosely-linked to the clause).

(35) meemó-moláp go bɨ̀ɨ káa-dùu
[inkling IND]$_{O?}$ [3sg]$_{A?}$ [have/exist-IMPERV]$_{PRED}$
He had an inkling [of what he should do next].

I do not take a strong position as to whether *káa-* is best analysed as a transitive verb of possession, or should instead be analysed as an existential verb with a possessive implication when co-occurring with an 'associated' pre-core Pr NP. We will return to this question in §5.

3.4 *Verbs of temporary possession* bə́ə- *'hold; have (with oneself)' and* gə́- *'carry; wear'*

It was noted in §3.3 that temporary possession is not usually handled by the primary verb of possession *káa-*, but is rather handled by two verbs *bə́ə-* 'hold;

[7] Even in English, for example, while it is common to use transitive *have* to denote a case of temporary or time-bound existence or possession, as in *I have the car for two weeks*, permanent possession sounds odd *?I have the car (among my possessions)*.

have (with oneself)' and *gə́-* 'carry; wear (on the body)'. Both regular transitive verbs, *bə́ə-* is primarily used to denote cases in which a subject physically holds or brings an object, as when transporting or using an object as a tool.[8] *gə́-* has a similar meaning, though generally references an entity which is worn on the body.

As a verb of possession, *bə́ə-* indicates possession of usable items, and/or use of items as a cultural practice. In (36), *káa-* would also be possible, but would suggest that the items in question did not previously exist; *bə́ə-* suggests that the items may have existed, but were not used by the speaker's people. Similarly, use of *káa-* in (37) would amount to a query as to whether mithun (a semi-domesticated bovine) happen to be found in a particular area.

(36) ləkɨ̀ɨ ogò bə́ə-máa-tó
time.long.ago TMP.REAL hold/carry-NEG-PERV
We didn't have (these things) in the old times.

(37) nunù hobə́ bə́ə-dóo larèe?
2pl mithun hold/carry-STAT DUB
Do you keep mithun (as a cultural practice, in your area)?

gə́- is extended to denote affections or propensities of the body, such as diseases and possession by spirits; such sentences generally cannot be expressed in *káa-*, and may be only marginally analysable as possession constructions (38).

(38) bɨ̀ɨ hɨgjàa gə́-dùu
3sg rheume carry/wear-IMPERV
He has a cold.

3.5 *Posture verbs*

Posture verbs *dùu-* 'sit', *dóo-* 'lie (down)', and *dàk-* 'stand' fundamentally indicate the position of a human body. They are extended to denote the quality and disposition of a non-human entity: round, bulky, and squat in the case of *dùu-*, sheetlike and prostrate in the case of *dóo-*, and sticklike, with legs and standing in the case of *dàk-* (Post 2008).

Posture verbs also have locative existential and, by extension, possessive functionality: temporary in the case of *dùu-*, permanent in the case of *dòo-*, and contained or attached in the case of *dàk-*. The difference between use of *káa-* and use of a posture verb—which are often grammatically interchangeable—is again that use of *káa-* is biased toward an understanding of the Pe of *káa-* as existing or not existing (in the world or in some other domain). Use of a posture verb is instead biased towards an understanding of the presence or absence of an entity (whose existence is not in

[8] *bə́ə-* is also used to refer to childbirth, i.e. *having a child.*

question) in a particular location; use of *káa-* would also be possible in (39), but would suggest that the speaker is querying whether or not water exists in the place mentioned (as opposed to the present query as to whether it happens to be present or not).

(39) ˀisì dóo-máa larèe?
water lie.down-NEG DUB
Isn't there any water?

Posture verbs take on possessive implications in constructions much like those reviewed in §3.3 with respect to *káa-*; (40) is an example of a 'type (3)' possession construction from my corpus.

(40) nó-kə̀=ə... hobə́-hɨɨpìk dàk-dóo rèe?
2sg-GEN=TOP mithun-mithun.pen stand-STAT PQ
Do you have a mithun pen? (*lit.*, As for you... is a mithun pen standing?)

Type (4) (transitive-like) constructions have also been successfully elicited (41), on the model of (40). However, no such examples occur naturally in my corpus. In this case, there is no possibility of analysing *dàk-* as a transitive predicate (42).

(41) nó hobə́ dàk-dóo rèe?
2sg mithun stand-STAT PQ
Do you have a mithun? (*lit.*, (As for) you, is a mithun standing?)

(42) *ŋó-kə̀ dàk-nám ə hobə́ go
1sg-GEN stand-NOMZ:EV.REAL TOP mithun IND
(putatively, What I have (standing) is a mithun.)

3.6 *Proto-Tani root* *tò- *'author; entitled to'*

The Galo noun *ˀatò* primarily means 'grandfather; father-in-law'. It is also used to denote an individual with a particular entitlement, as to an area of land or a personal item such as a machete. Used together with *ˀatò*, *tò-* can function as a verb root with a related sense (43).

(43) hɨgɨ̀-m̀ kodée hɨgɨ̀-m̀ takár ˀatò
SPROX-ACC land SPROX-ACC NAME entitled.person
tò-dùu
be.associated.to-IMPERV
Takar owns this here land. (*lit.* Takar is associated to this land as an entitled person.)

Verb root *tò-* can be used independently of the noun *ˀatò* when describing a clan relation (44). While sentences like (43) are difficult to translate into English without using words like 'own' or 'possess', examples such as (44) suggest that these English

TABLE 7.2. **Propensity predicates (selection)**

Term	Gloss	Formative 1	Formative 2
dumcì	'aching, of head'	*dúm-* 'head'	*cì-* 'be in pain'
ɲɨgrə́m	'lazy-eyed'	*ɲɨ́k-* 'eye'	*rə́m-* 'look askance'
iikúm	'numb-toothed'	*íi-* 'tooth'	*kúm-* 'drunk; senseless'
gomzùp	'closed-mouthed'	*góm-* 'speech'[a]	*zùp-* 'closed'
pumzàp	'flat-nosed'	*púm-* 'nose'	*zàp-* 'flat'
ləpèe	'cramped, of legs'	*lə̀-* 'leg/foot'	*pèe-* 'tired; cramped'

[a] This is the modern-day Lare Galo sense; the Proto-Galo sense was 'mouth', as in Northwestern Galo *ˀagóm* 'mouth' (Lare 'speech').

concepts do not correspond well to their Galo counterparts. This point is returned to in §4.

(44) bɨɨ ribáa tò-dùu
3sg NAME be.associated.to-IMPERV
He is a member of the Rɨbaa clan.

3.7 *External possession, propensity predicates, and body part nouns*

'Propensity predicates' are a unique predicate type in Galo; structurally, they are disyllabic and composed of two roots: a body part term and a propensity term (Table 7.2).

Diachronically, propensity predicates seem to derive from nominal-predicate incorporation; for example, in the case of *dumcì*, an erstwhile noun **dúm* would have been incorporated into a predicate in **cì-* 'be in pain' (45):

(45) *ŋó dúm-cì-dùu > ŋó dumcì-dùu
1sg head-ache-IMPERV 1sg ache.head-IMPERV
As for me, (my) head aches. I have a headache.

However, that the second analysis in (45) is synchronically the correct one, rather than the first, can be demonstrated via a variety of tests. First, it should be noted that neither *dúm-* nor *cì-* may stand as a grammatical or phonological word in modern Galo, meaning that a synchronic composition *dúm-cì* could only be analysed as root-incorporation rather than word-incorporation; in other words, it would have to be analysed as a case of (morphological) compounding rather than a case of (syntactic) incorporation *per se*. But this analysis is also not tenable, since propensity predicates are also capable of functioning as adjectives, occurring as the CC of a copula construction (cf. §3.1) (46). The propensity root internal to a propensity predicate cannot stand as a CC argument, under any circumstances (47).

(46) ŋó dumcì ə=kú!
[1sg]$_{CS}$ [ache.head]$_{CC}$ [COP=COMPL]$_{COP}$
I've got a headache!

(47) *ŋó cì ə=kú!
[1sg]$_{CS}$ [ache]$_{CC}$ [COP=COMPL]$_{COP}$

The synchronic non-viability of the first analysis in (43) notwithstanding, if we take it as the likely diachronic source it looks very much like an *external possession* construction, as described for Chinese by Chappell (1999): Pr is expressed as the 'second' subject of an 'unaccusative' verb whose primary subject is an inalienably possessed Pr (48).

(48) wǒ xīn hán
1 heart cold
I felt discouraged.

It would not be at all surprising if Galo propensity predicates reflected a fossilized external possession construction of the Chinese type.

Now, however, consider the modern-day Galo external possession construction shown in (49), which appears to have semantic properties similar to those outlined by Chappell (1999) for Chinese; namely, the Pe must be an inalienable possession of the Pr, and is usually a body part term.[9] What is most interesting here is that propensity predicates can also head such constructions—just as in their reconstructed proto-syntax (50).

(49) ŋó ˀakíi ə gòo-káa
1sg belly TOP swell-PER
My belly swelled.

(50) ŋó dumpóo dumcì-dùu
1sg head ache.head-IMPERV
I have a headache (in my head).

4 Possession and ownership in Galo culture

The preceding sections have discussed the linguistic expression of possession. Henceforth, we adopt a cultural perspective.[10]

[9] While space prevents me from discussing the matter in detail, both Pr and body part terms exhibit subject properties in this construction, although not to the same degree.

[10] A qualification: a comprehensive Galo ethnography has not yet been conducted, much less one focusing on possession. It is presumably as impossible to perform an effective armchair anthropological analysis of Galo concepts of possession as it would be to perform such an armchair linguistic analysis.

In Galo culture, we find a salient cultural value against covetousness and the accumulation of personal possessions. When a wild animal is killed, its meat is distributed by the hunter's family to all families in the village; while the hunter himself may gain prestige in the process, he retains few material spoils.

One also notes a general paucity of concepts of personal privacy, ownership, or right of control. There are no lexemes with meanings like 'personal', 'private', 'chief', or 'rule', and there were few traditional means of restricting access to personal property. Galo houses traditionally had no internal room divisions, much less personal room-assignments, and while individuals or families are entitled to agricultural or residential land, such entitlements are mediated by the collective interest; large-scale accumulation of goods was, traditionally, not a practical possibility. There are no native lexemes meaning 'want (to have)', 'need (to get)', or 'desire (as a possession)', and though vocabulary such as *rə́-* 'buy', *pùk-*'sell', and *còo-* 'steal' exist, such terms are mainly associated with an 'outsider interface'; trade and theft were not things which could easily occur among confederates, and no concept of a village shop or intra-Galo trade existed until very recently. Finally, although the Tani root **tò* extends to include modern concepts of ownership, the traditional Tani concept is something closer to 'entitled person in relation to'. This might at first amount to a hair-splitting distinction; however, when we consider that **tò* also denotes 'grandfather' and 'father-in-law', as well as the concept of clan membership (§3.6), it becomes clear that we are dealing here with a very different concept of 'entitlement' than the English word 'owner' would imply.

In short, while it might be too strong to claim that the concept of ownership was completely absent from pre-modern Galo culture, it was almost certainly not as robust as it is in some other cultures, not as widely represented in Galo cultural activities, and not as well-reflected in the Galo lexicon. The concept of ownership has grown more robust in recent years, following political and cultural integration into wider India (where mercantile cultures are abundant). It is increasingly common for Galo houses to be built with private internal rooms, with locks, and for Galo to buy and sell amongst one another. Some Galo seem to lament this as a negative aspect of modernity, while others may regard it as inevitable—nobody, however, can fail to notice the changes.

5 Possession or association? An evolutionary perspective

Accordingly, one might wonder: if it is the case that possession in the sense of ownership is not well-represented in traditional Galo culture, but has rather arrived

What I say here should not be taken as amounting to an assertion either that I have conducted an empirically adequate study of possession and ownership in Galo culture, or that such a study is unnecessary prior to making defensible statements on the matter. It is simply a summary of my personal observations while on linguistic fieldwork in the Galo area, and may be taken for what it is judged to be worth.

(or grown more robust) with the onset of modernity and integration with wider India—how is it that the grammar of 'possession' is nonetheless so richly encoded in Galo language? Similar observations, probably, can be made about many small populations and their languages.

One question to ask, therefore, might be whether POSSESSION in the sense of ownership is indeed the primary concept underlying the grammaticalization of 'possession' structures. As Aikhenvald (Chapter 1) points out, relatively few 'possessive constructions' are actually about semantic POSSESSION (in the sense of ownership). Most 'possessive constructions' are in fact used to describe a semantically more general notion of ASSOCIATION.

Given such facts, we might ask—from an evolutionary perspective—whether it is more likely that a concept of POSSESSION was indeed prior, and gave rise to extensions like 'kin relation', 'part-whole relation', 'topic of a story', etc.... or is it perhaps more likely that a more general concept, say of ASSOCIATION, in fact underlies (and probably pre-dates, in terms of human cultural-linguistic evolution) not only the semantically non-possessive aspects of possessive constructions, but even the concept of POSSESSION itself? This hypothesis would seem to sit better with the relative lack of evidence for a robust concept of POSSESSION in Galo culture and its associated lexicon.[11]

References

Abraham, P. T. 1985. *Apatani grammar.* Mysore: Central Institute of Indian Languages.

Blake, Barry J. 2001. *Case* (2nd edn). Cambridge: Cambridge University Press.

Chappell, Hilary. 1999. 'The double unaccusative construction in Sinitic languages', pp. 195–228 of *External possession*, edited by Doris L. Payne and Immanuel Barshi. Amsterdam: John Benjamins.

DeLancey, Scott. 1984. 'Etymological notes on Tibeto-Burman case particles', *Linguistics of the Tibeto-Burman Area* 8(1): 59–77.

Heine, Bernd and Kuteva, Tania. 2002. *World lexicon of grammaticalization.* Cambridge: Cambridge University Press.

Noonan, Michael and Mihas, Elena. 2008. 'Areal dimensions in case syncretism: Ablatives and genitives', *Electronic Publications of Michael Noonan.* Heidelberg: SafivaDok [Digital Repository South Asian Studies].

Post, Mark W. 2007. 'A grammar of Galo'. Ph.D. dissertation. Melbourne: La Trobe University.

[11] Anticipating that some readers will accuse me of a naïvely utopian view of pre-modern Galo society, in which everything was shared and no one was covetous, and an equally naïvely dystopian view of a modernity which has corrupted this earlier paradise, let me be clear that I mean nothing of the kind. It is just as possible to jealously protect something or someone (such as a wife) which is *associated to* one (by virtue of marriage, e.g.) at the same time as one lacks a concept of *owning* that thing or person.

——. 2008. 'Verbs of posture, existence, location and possession and their grammaticalization pathways in the Tani languages', pp. 127–52 of *North East Indian linguistics*, edited by Stephen Morey and Mark Post. New Delhi: Cambridge University Press India.

——. 2009. 'The semantics of clause linking in Galo', pp. 75–91 of *The semantics of clause linking: A cross-linguistic typology*, edited by R. M. W. Dixon and Alexandra Y. Aikhenvald. Oxford: Oxford University Press.

——. 2011. 'Nominalization and nominalization-based constructions in Galo', pp. 255–87 of *Nominalization in Asian languages: Diachronic and typological perspectives*, edited by Foong-Ha Yap, Karen Grunow-Hårsta, and Janick Wrona. Amsterdam: John Benjamins.

8

Possessive constructions in Mandarin Chinese

YONGXIAN LUO

1 Introduction[1]

A member of the Sino-Tibetan family, Mandarin Chinese[2] is a typical isolating and analytic language with basic AVO and SV constituent order. Some scholars argue that it is drifting to AOV (Li and Thompson 1974; S. Huang 1978; Xu 2006). Modifiers precede the modified items. Other typological features include lexical tone, strong left-headedness in constituent structure, and multi-verb constructions without overt syntactic marking. Chinese has been characterized as 'mono-syllabic' and as 'lacking morphology'. The language has a substantial amount of productive compounding which is clearly not syntactic in nature. The semantics of the whole compound cannot be considered the sum of the meanings of the constituent morphemes. Prosody plays quite an important role in compounding. Bisyllabic compounds and four-syllable elaborate expressions abound. There is also a rich system of derivational reduplication which is clearly a morpho-phonological process with expressive function. A number of items are used as morpho-syntactic markers with restricted syntactic behaviour; these are often derived from full lexical items (mostly verbs).

The 'subject' operates on an S/A pivot. Movement, ellipses, and S = O ambitransitivity are characteristic aspects of Chinese syntax. The movement of core arguments based on their discourse status is common. For example, classifier phrases

[1] I have benefitted greatly from contact with many scholars through reading their works, correspondence, and discussions. The list is too long to include here. Special thanks go to my teachers Bob Dixon, Sasha Aikhenvald, and Tony Diller for their academic education, their encouragements, and most valuable feedback. Randy LaPolla also provides useful comments. I also want to thank the anonymous reviewer for constructive feedback and suggestions. Any errors and inefficiencies are my own responsibility.

[2] Throughout this paper, Mandarin Chinese and Chinese are used interchangeably for Modern Standard Chinese, unless otherwise specified.

may be separated and moved away from the head noun. Virtually any NP may be ellipsed if its referent can be retrieved from the context. A significant number of verbs are ambi-transitive (S = O). About a dozen or so suffixes play an active role in morpho-syntactic operations, some with valency increasing or decreasing functions.

There has been no lack of research on possessive constructions in Chinese, with the enclitic *de* being one of the most elusive and most studied grammatical items. A full review of the literature is not the purpose of this study, but a few remarks on some of the most important works are in order. Chao (1968) approaches the topic from a structural perspective, with many insightful observations, which are expanded in Zhu (1980, 1982). Li and Thompson (1981), and Lu (2007) present a functional analysis. Chappell and Thompson (1992) offer a discourse-based account. James Huang (1998), Sybesma (1999), and Hole (2004) discuss the issue in a generative framework. A substantial amount of recent research by Chinese scholars follows this formalist line of argument (Xu 1999, 2008; Guo 2000; Han 2000; Shi 2000; Wen and Chen 2001; Deng 2004; Pan and Han 2005; Chen and Xiao 2007; Ma 2009). As previous studies deal with the issue from a structural or generative perspective, the aim of this chapter is to offer a typological analysis of possessive constructions in Mandarin Chinese.

2 Possessive constructions and possessive marking in Chinese

2.1 *Defining properties of possessive constructions*

Possession and ownership as a grammatical category in Chinese exhibits a number of interesting typological features. In Classical Chinese, there were declensions in pronouns (Karlgren 1926, 1957; Graham 1973, Pulleyblank 1995), where possessive pronouns used to take different forms. But such declensions are lost in Modern Standard Chinese, where possessive meanings are formed with the enclitic *de*, with the constituent order 'Possessor + *de* + Possessee'.

(1) wǒ *de* shū
1sg POSS book
my book

(2) mǔqin *de* háizi
mother POSS child
the mother's child/the child of the mother

(3) háizi *de* mǔqin
child POSS mother
the child's mother/the mother of the child

Multiple possessives are permissible by stacking the possessive phrases to the left of the head noun.

(4) wáng jiàoshòu *de* xuéshēng *de* xuéshēng *de*
Wang professor POSS student POSS student POSS
xuéshēng *de* xuéshēng
student POSS student
Prof. Wang's student's student's student's student(s)

This possessive enclitic can also be used to express various other semantic relationships between Pr and Pe:

(I) AN INALIENABLE PART OF THE POSSESSOR

(5) tā *de* liǎn / shǒu
3sg POSS face / hand
her face/hand (whole-part)

(II) SOMETHING THAT IS ASSOCIATED WITH THE POSSESSOR

(6) lǎobǎn *de* mìshu / zhùshǒu
boss POSS secretary / assistant
the boss's secretary/assistant (association)

(III) AN ATTRIBUTE OF THE POSSESSOR

(7) tā *de* xìnggé / háoshuǎng
3sg POSS disposition / straightforwardness
his disposition/straightforwardness

(IV) TIME OF THE OCCURRENCE OF POSSESSEE

(8) zǎochén *de* yángguāng
morning POSS sunlight
morning sun(light)

(V) LOCATION OF THE POSSESSEE

(9) tiān shàng *de* xīngxing
sky above POSS star
the stars in the sky

(VI) ORIENTATION OF THE POSSESSEE

(10) qiánmiàn *de* dàolù
ahead/front POSS road
the road ahead (*lit.* front's road)

Not only can locative expressions occur in Pr position, they, too, may occur in Pe position. (11) and (12) illustrate this.

(VII) ORIENTATION OR LOCATION OF THE POSSESSOR

(11) xuéxiào *de* cāochǎng shàng
school POSS playground above/on
on the school playground (*lit.* 'the school's on the ground')

(12) lǚguǎn *de* dàtīng lǐ
hotel POSS lobby inside
inside the lobby of the hotel (*lit.* 'the hotel's inside the lobby')

As can be seen from the above examples, there is no syntactic difference between all these occurrences of *de* in various semantic functions (in contrast to English *of* constructions, as exemplified in Chapter 1 of this volume).

2.2 De *as an attributive marker*

Lyons (1999) makes a distinction between GE (Determiner-Genitive) and AG (Adjectival-Genitive) languages. He classifies Chinese under the AG type. One of the most salient functions of *de* is its use as an attributive marker, marking attributive phrases or attributive clauses.

(13) měilì *de* gūniang
beautiful ATTRIB girl
beautiful girl(s)

(14) lánsè *de* hǎiyáng
blue-colour ATTRIB ocean
the blue ocean

(15) a. nóngmín zhòng *de* shuǐguǒ
farmer grow ATTRIB fruit
The fruit that the farmers grow

Compare (15a) with (15b):

(15) b. nóngmín zhòng shuǐguǒ
farmer grow fruit
Farmers grow fruit.

De can also form nominalizations which look superficially similar to possessive constructions. These can relate to an activity, with the underlying role of the possessor bearing an A, O, or S relation to the verb in question.

(16) [zhè běn shū *de* chūbǎn] shòu dào hǎo píng
this CL book POSS publish receive reach good Comment
The publication of the book has been very well received. (O) (That is, sb. published the book) Pr <underlying O argument>

(17) [tā *de* pīpíng] méi rén Lĭcăi
3sg POSS criticism no person pay attention
His criticisms went to deaf ears (A). (He criticized [sb.]) Pr <underlying A argument>

(18) [tā *de* wúzhī] lìng rén jīngyà
3sg POSS ignorance make people surprised
His ignorance surprised everyone (S). (He was ignorant) Pr <underlying S argument>

2.3 *Obligatory and optional possessive marking*

2.3.1 *Optional possessive marking* It is worth noting that when pronouns appear with kinship terms in the construction 'Pr (Pron) + POSS + Pe (kinship term)', the possessive marker *de* can be left out:

(19) a. tā *de* dìdi b. tā dìdi
3sg POSS y. brother 3sg y. brother
His/her younger brother

This can also extend to entities that are conceptualized as kin:

(20) a. wǒ *de* jiā b. wǒ jiā
1sg POSS home/family 1sg home/family
My home/family

Chao (1956) has pointed out that there is a distinction between *wǒ de fùqin* '1sg-POSS-father' and *wǒ fùqin* '1sg-father', both translatable as 'my father'. The former is a descriptive phrase, while the latter is a designation. From a cognitive point of view, when using expressions like ***wǒ de fùqin***, the speaker is talking about two things, the possessee (*fùqin*) and the possessor (*wǒ [de]* 'I [my/mine]'); by contrast, with the term *wǒ fùqin*, the speaker is talking about only one thing, *fùqin* 'father', which functions like a proper noun. By analogy, this may explain the difference between (19a) and (19b), where the former talks about two entities, *tā de* 'his/her' and *dìdi* 'younger brother' while the latter designates only one thing, *tā dìdi* 'his younger brother'.

2.3.2 *Obligatory possessive marking* While possessive marking is optional for kin possessees, it is obligatory when the possessor pronouns occur with non-kin possessees. Thus, while constructions like (20) are perfectly correct because 'home' and 'family' are conceptualized as kin, those like (21b) and (22b) are not:

(21) a. wǒ *de* fángzi b. *wǒ fángzi
1sg POSS house 1sg house
My house

(22) a. wǒ/nǐ/tā *de* shǒu/liǎn b. *wǒ/nǐ/tā shǒu /liǎn
1sg/2sg/3sg POSS hand/face 1sg/2sg/3sg hand/face
My/your/his hand(s)/face

On this basis, some researchers assumed the existence of a distinction between alienable and inalienable possession in Chinese (Chappell 1996). While this is true in many cases, there are instances where the use of *de* is obligatory as required by semantics; see discussion below.

It is worth pointing out that with kin terms, the use of *de* may denote plurality, while the absence of *de* gives only singular reading. Constructions like (23a) are unacceptable because of the singular reading which is incompatible with the plural meaning given by the quantifier expression.

(23) a. *tā nǚpéngyǒu gè gè dōu piàoliang
3sg girlfriend CL CL all attractive
All of his girlfriends are attractive.

To make sentences like (23a) acceptable, *de* must be used.

(23) b. tā *de* nǚpéngyǒu gè gè dōu piàoliang
3sg POSS girlfriend CL CL all attractive
All of his girlfriends are attractive.

2.4 *No possessive marking*

Not every kind of association and attributive construction takes a possessive marker. Possessive marking is not used in the following circumstances:

(I) A WHOLE–PART RELATION, WHERE THE FIRST NP DENOTES THE SOURCE

(24) a. jī ròu b. *jī *de* ròu
chicken meat
chicken meat

(25) a. yā dàn b. *yā *de* dàn
duck egg
duck egg(s)

(II) WHERE THE NP IN PR POSITION DESIGNATES THE MATERIAL OF WHICH PE IS MADE OR BUILT

(26) a. cǎo/zhuān fáng b. *cǎo/zhuān *de* fáng
thatch/brick house
thatch/brick house/house built of thatch/bricks

(27) a. mián bù b. *mián *de* bù
cotton cloth
cotton cloth

(III) WHERE THE FIRST NP IS THE CONTENT OF THE SECOND NP

(28) a. zhōngguó dìtú b. *zhōngguó *de* dìtú[3]
China map
a map of China

(29) a. shìjiè zhīshí b. *shìjiè *de* zhīshí[4]
world knowledge
knowledge about the world / information on the world

(IV) WHERE THE TWO NPS ARE IN APPOSITIVE RELATION

(30) a. zhuàngzú xiōngdì b. *zhuàngzú *de* xiōngdì
Zhuang brothers
(Our) Zhuang brothers / the Zhuang, (our) brothers

(31) a. táiwān tóngbāo b. *táiwān *de* tóngbāo
Taiwan blood relative
(our) Taiwanese blood relatives / (our) Taiwan compatriots

Constructions like (30a) and (31a) are worth noting. Here possessive marking is not used because the two NPs each specify the other. If a possessive marker were used, (30b) and (31b) would have a different reading; (30b) would then mean 'the brothers of the Zhuang ethnic group' and (31b), 'Taiwan's blood relatives', both of which exhibit a possessive relation.

The semantic types of the *de*-constructions discussed so far can be summed up as follows:

Semantic types	Presence of *de*	Examples
Possessive relationships	yes	(1), (2)
Body part	yes	(5)
Association	yes	(6)
Propensity/property	yes	(7)
Attribution	yes	(13), (14)
Time	yes	(8)
Location and orientation	yes	(9)–(12)
Kinship	optional	(19)–(20)
Part–whole	no	(24a)–(25a)
Material	no	(26a)–(27a)
Content	no	(28a)–(29a)
NPs in apposition	no	(30a)–(31a)

[3] This construction means 'a map/maps that China possesses', or 'a map/maps belonging to China'.
[4] The construction would mean 'knowledge belonging to the world', 'information (gathered and shared) by people over the world', which is not the intended meaning.

3 Possessives, classifiers, demonstratives, and definiteness

3.1 *A question about (in)definiteness*

Possessive phrases in Chinese are correlated with the notion of definiteness. Partee (2006) observes a number of translation 'puzzles' which have to do with possessive phrases in Chinese involving demonstratives and classifiers. The constructions in question occur in the following frames (with some slight modification of gloss from Partee (2006)):

(I) POSSESSOR DE + [BARE NOUN]

(32) Zhāngsān *de* [shū]
Zhangsan POSS book
Zhangsan's book(s)

(II) POSSESSOR DE + [NUMERAL + CL + N]

(33) Zhāngsān *de* [liǎng běn shū]
Zhangsan POSS two CL book
Zhangsan's two books

(III) POSSESSOR DE + [DEM + (NUMERAL) + CL + N]

(34) a. Zhāngsān *de* [nà běn shū]
Zhangsan POSS that CL book
That book of Zhangsan's (*lit.* Zhangsan's that book)

(34) b. Zhāngsān *de* [nà liǎng běn shū]
Zhangsan POSS that two CL book
Those two books of Zhangsan's (*lit.* Zhangsan's that two books)

In English, an NP with a definite pronominal possessor is always definite. In (33), given the translation of the English phrase, there is a presupposition that Zhangsan has exactly two books. But (34) does not carry that presupposition. The issue is more complicated than that, as we will see below.

3.2 *Definite but not unique*

Sentences like (33) pose an interesting question about the notion of definiteness in Chinese. Let us look at some further examples to see how (33) and (34) should be interpreted, and whether they presume definiteness.

Possessives involving classifiers may also have the following constituent order.

(IV) CL + [POSSESSOR DE] + N

(35) zhuō shàng yǒu [běn [Zhāngsān *de* shū]]
desk above exist CL Zhangsan POSS book
On the desk there is a book belonging to Zhangsan.

(V) NUMERAL + CL + [POSSESSOR DE] + N

(36) zhuō shàng yǒu [liǎng běn [Zhāngsān *de* shū]]
desk above exist two CL Zhangsan POSS book
On the desk there are two books belonging to Zhangsan.

(VI) DEM + CL + [POSSESSOR DE] + N

(37) [nà běn [Zhāngsān *de* shū]] bù jiàn le
that CL Zhangsan POSS book not see PART
That book of Zhangsan's is missing.

(VII) DEM + NUMERAL + CL + [POSSESSOR DE] + N

(38) [nà liǎng běn [Zhāngsān *de* shū]] bù jiàn le
that two CL Zhangsan POSS book not see PART
Those two books of Zhangsan's are missing.

Note that when a Possessor intervenes between a CL and a noun as in (37)–(38), we get a partitive reading, that is, the examples imply that Zhangsan has more than one, and more than two, books. The following minimal pair of examples, partly repeated from (33), further illustrates this.

(39) a. Zhāngsān *de* liǎng běn shū
Zhangsan POSS two CL book
Zhangsan's two books

(39) b. liǎng běn Zhāngsān *de* shū
two CL Zhangsan POSS book
Two of Zhangsan's books

Example (39b) implies that Zhangsan has more than two books; (39a) does not. It may mean Zhangsan has only two books. (39a) behaves like a referential or specific nominal phrase while (39b) behaves like an indefinite noun phrase. This can be seen from the fact that (39a) can occur at sentential subject position and may not appear in the existential construction, as in (40), and that (39b) behaves in the opposite way, as shown in (41), both taken from Huang (1998: 47) with a slight modification of gloss.

(40) a. Zhāngsān *de* liǎng běn shū zài nàr
Zhangsan POSS that CL book at there
Zhangsan's two books are over there.

(40) b. ??yǒu Zhāngsān *de* liǎng běn shū zài nàr
exist Zhangsan POSS two CL book at there
There are Zhangsan's two books over there.

(41)	a.	??liǎng	běn	Zhāngsān	*de*	shū	zài	nàr
		two	CL	Zhangsan	POSS	book	at	there

(41)	b.	yǒu	liǎng	běn	Zhāngsān	*de*	shū	zài	nàr
		exist	two	CL	Zhangsan	POSS	book	at	there

There are two of Zhangsan's books over there.

The interesting thing about (39a) and (40a) is that we have a definite NP in Chinese and a definite NP in English which appear to have the same parts in the same arrangement but they turn out to be not semantically identical. This seems to suggest that we are dealing with different strategies in different languages to express different notions of definiteness. In the Chinese case, definiteness does not subsume uniqueness.

4 Possession within the clause

4.1 *Verbs of ownership*

Chinese has two canonical verbs of ownership, *yǒu* 'have, possess, own' (H-possession), and *shǔ(yú)* 'belong (to)' (B-possession).

(42)	xiànzài	hěn	duō	rén	**yǒu**	fáng	**yǒu**	chē
	now	very	many	people	own	house	own	car

Nowadays a lot of people own houses and cars.

(43)	zhèxiē	zīyuán	**shǔyú**	yánhǎi	guójiā	suǒyǒu
	these	resources	belong	coastal	country	possession

These (natural) resources belong to the coastal countries.

In addition, Chinese also uses a copula clause to express ownership, where the possessor noun or pronoun takes the possessive marker as in (44):

(44)	fáng	shì	tā	*de*;	chē	shì	wǒ	*de*
	house	be	3SG	POSS	car	be	1SG	POSS

The house(s) is (are) his/hers; the car(s) is (are) mine.

There are quite a number of verbs in Chinese that can be used to express possession and ownership. Each of these verbs has selection preference over the possessed object. They each exhibit stylistic features of their own.

(45)	Xiǎowáng	dé	cái	jiān	**bèi**
	Xiaowang	virtue	talent	concurrently	have in stock

Xiaowang has both virtue and talent.

(46) zhè liǎng zhǒng chǎnpǐn gè **jù** tèsè
this two type product each possess feature
Each of these two products has its own features.

(47) quánjùdé kǎo-yā jiǔ **fù** shèngmíng
Quanjude roast:duck long possess fine-name
Quanjude Peking Roast Duck has long enjoyed a fine reputation.

(48) zhè gè **guī** wǒ, nà gè **guī** nǐ
this CL belong 1sg that CL belong 2sg
This one belongs to me, and that one belongs to you.

4.2 *The 'double subject' construction, and sentences with 'possessor-subjects' and 'possessee-object'*

4.2.1 *The 'double subject' construction* No discussion of Chinese possessives would be complete without talking about the so-called 'double subject' construction, where there is a possessive relation between the two NPs.

(49) nà gè gūniang yǎnjīng dà, biànzi cháng
that CL girl eye big braid long
That girl has big eyes and long braids. (*lit.* that girl eyes big braids long)
That girl's eyes are big, and her braids are long.

(50) wáng lǎobǎn qīnqi péngyǒu hěn duō
Wang boss relative friend very many
Mr Wang has got many relatives and friends.
Mr Wang's relatives and friends are plentiful.

(51) zhōngguó fúyuán liáokuò, rénkǒu zhòngduō
China area vast population plentiful
(The situation is that) China has a vast area and a large population.

In (49)–(51), we have two NPs which can be analysed as subjects of the sentence. The first NP functions as the possessor, and the second, the possesee. An inalienable whole–part relation exists in (49). In (50), the possessive relationship is one of association and in (51) one of attribute.

4.2.2 *Sentences with 'possessor-subjects and possessee-object'* Possessive relationship can also be observed in another type of construction where the relation can be established between the two core NPs, as given below.

(52) lǎowáng xiā le yī zhí yǎnjing
Laowang blind ASP one CL eye
Laowang lost one eye. (*lit.* Laowang blind one eye)

(53) wángmiǎn sǐ le fùqin
Wangmian die ASP father
Wangmian has lost his father. (*lit.* Wangmian died father)

It is worth noting that in (52) and (53) the possessor is not the subject of the main verb which is prototypically intransitive. Rather, it is the possessee that is the subject of the intransitive verb. Here we have a possessor who is an experiencer affected by the event described by the verb in question, and a possessee who is the intransitive subject. Sentences like (52)–(53) have been dubbed as '*lingzhu shubin ju*' ('sentences with possessor-subject and possessee-object') by Chinese scholars (Xu 1956; Guo 1990; Shen 2006) due to the apparent semantic relations between the possessor and the possessee.

The possessive meaning of sentences like (53) can be seen in (53′), which is a paraphrase of (53):

(53′) wángmiǎn *de* fùqin sǐ le
Wangmian POSS father die ASP
Wangmian's father died.

Not only can animate subjects occur in the possessor position, inanimate subjects can also occur in that position.

(54) xuéxiào zǒu le hǎo jǐ gè xuésheng
school go ASP good several CL student
Several students have left the school. (*lit.* the school has gone several students) (the students are associated with the school)

(55) jiānyù táo le liǎng míng qiúfàn
prison escape ASP two CL prisoner
Two prisoners escaped from the prison. (*lit.* the prison has escaped two prisoners) (the prison houses the prisoners)

The possessive relation can easily be seen through the association between the two NPs, although the possessors in both sentences can be analysed as the source. Cognitively, the possessor in both sentences is deemed as being adversely affected by the event described by the act that was undertaken by the possessee. In order for sentences like (53′) to be acceptable, this condition must be satisfied.

While sentences like (54) and (55) are not sentences with possessor-subject and possessee-object, there are constructions in Chinese that can be considered as such.

(56) xiányífàn bèi kǔn le shuāng shǒu
suspect PASS tie up ASP two hand
Both the suspect's hands were/have been tied up. / The suspect had both his hands tied up. (*lit.* the suspect is tied up two hands)

(57) tā jiā bèi wā le zǔ fén
3sg family PASS dig ASP ancestor:grave
His family's ancestral graves were/have been dug. / His family had their ancestral graves dug. (*lit.* His family was dug ancestor graves.)

In (56)–(57) the possessee is the object of the verb. Thus, in (56), it is the hands of the suspect that are tied up, not other parts of the body. Likewise, in (57), it was the grave that was dug, not the family. The possessor and possessee are separated by the verb.

4.3 *Possessive raising, topicalization, and relativization*

4.3.1 *Movement, and split possessive NPs* It could be seen in the previous section that sentences like (56) seem to involve some sort of NP movement, with the possessive NP split into two parts. The possessor occurs in subject position and the possessed in object position separated by the verb. The status of such split NPs is a topic of heated discussion. A number of scholars are arguing for possessive raising as a grammatical operation in Chinese syntax (Xu 1999, 2008; Han 2000; Chen and Xiao 2007) while others are against the idea of raising or NP movement (Zhu 2005; Shen 2006), believing that such split possessive NPs are the basic structure, not the result of NP movement. To see to what extent each of the arguments will hold, let us look at some examples.

Recall that, in (53) and (54), we have a possessive relationship between the two NPs which are separated by the verb in each sentence, which can be rephrased as (58) and (59) respectively:

(58) wángmiǎn *de* fùqin sǐ le
Wangmian POSS father die ASP
Wangmian's father died.

(59) xiányífàn *de* shuāng shǒu bèi kǔn le
suspect POSS two hand PASS tied up ASP
Both hands of the suspect were/have been tied up. / The suspect had both his hands tied up.

However, the possessee in (58) or (59) cannot occur in subject position. It cannot occur before the possessor, either.

(58′) a. *fùqin wángmiǎn sǐ le
father Wangmian die ASP
Wangmian's father died on him. (*lit.* Father died Wangmian.)

(58′) b. *fùqin sǐ le wángmiǎn
father die ASP Wangmian
Wangmian's father died on him. (*lit.* Father died Wangmian)

(59′) a. *shuāng shǒu xiányífàn bèi kǔn le
two hand suspect PASS tie up ASP
Both hands of the suspect were/have been tied up.

(59′) b. *shuāng shǒu bèi kǔn le xiányífàn
two hand PASS tie up ASP suspect
Both hands of the suspect were/have been tied up.

The ungrammaticality of (58′) and (59′) indicates that we are dealing with a grammatical rule in Chinese whereby split possessive NPs have quite a fixed word order whereby the possessor must precede the possessee.

4.3.2 *Topicalization and relativization involving possessive meaning* Previous sections deal with possession in the NP within a clause. This section discusses possession as manifested in topicalization and relativization.

In Chinese, a wide range of constituents can occur in topic position. These include:

(I) POSSESSOR AS TOPIC, POSSESSEE AS A OR S

(60) wángxiānsheng, érzi kǎo shàng le dàxué
Mr Wang son exam succeed ASP university
(Talking about) Mr Wang, his son has passed the entrance examination for university.

(61) zhè zhǒng diànshì, bǎoxiū qī hěn cháng
This kind TV warranty:term very long
This kind of television, its term of warranty is long.

(II) POSSESSOR AS TOPIC, POSSESSEE AS OBJECT

(62) (wǒ) wàipó, wǒ zhǐ jiàn guò zhàopiān
(1sg) grandma 1sg only see ASP photo
My grandma, I have only seen photos (of her).

(63) xīn fángzi, gōngchéngshī gāng huà hǎo túzǐ
new house engineer just draw up plan
The new house, the engineer has just drawn up a plan (of it).

It is worth noting that in (60)–(61), we have the possessor in topic position without a possessive marker. No referring expression is used in sentences of this kind.

When another element can intervene between the topic and the subject, zero possessive becomes less acceptable.

(64) a. nà gè xuésheng, bàba hěn yǒu qián
that CL student father very have money
That student, (his) father is very wealthy.

(64) b. *nà gè xuésheng, yǐqián bàba hěn yǒu qián
that CL student before father very have money
That student, previously (his) father used to be very wealthy.

The unacceptability of (64b) is due to the fact that the element *yǐqián* 'before, previously' is inserted between the possessor and the possessee, creating a barrier for the accessibility of the possessee. To make (64b) acceptable, a referring expression is to be used, as (64c):

(64) c. nà gè xuésheng, yǐqián **tā** bàba hěn yǒu qián
that CL student before 3SG father very have money
That student, previously his father used to be very wealthy.

5 Possession in morpho-syntax, lexicon, and society

The two canonical verbs of ownership, *yǒu* and *shǔ*, can each form a set of compounds describing different types of possession, association, and affiliation. Syntactically, compounds taking *yǒu* as head are mostly verbs; those taking *shǔ* are predominantly nouns. Each of these compounds displays their own semantic functions and syntactic behaviours depending on the types of relationship between the possessor and possessee.

5.1 *Compounds with* yǒu

The *yǒu*-compounds can be subcategorized in terms of the nature of relationships between the possessor and the possessee: whether the possessor is animate or inanimate; or whether the possessee is a concrete object, or an abstract entity. Each of these compounds points to different contents of the possessed, and different orientation. They exhibit different semantic functions and syntactic behaviours. Some of the compounds can be used interchangeably; others cannot be.

Table 8.1 captures some of the differences in meaning with the *yǒu*-compounds and their restrictions in taking certain types of possessions.

Of the items in Table 8.1, *zhànyǒu* 'take control of', *suǒyǒu* 'possess', and *zhuānyǒu* 'own exclusively' may occur in passive constructions. Others do not have this property.

5.2 *Possessor-oriented vs. possessee-oriented: compounds with* shǔ *and* zhǔ

Chinese also has a number of noun and verb compounds with *shǔ*, which is related to B-possession. There is yet a third-type of compounds with *zhǔ* 'lord, master; take control, be in charge', which is associated with H-possession. Both types of compounds exhibit different morpho-syntactic functions and semantic orientations

TABLE 8.1. **Different meanings of ownership with *yǒu*-compounds**

Possess, own (wealth, properties)		Entitled to; entrusted with (rights)		Exhibit (features)	
*jùyǒu		*jùyǒu		*xiǎngyǒu	
*xiǎngyǒu		*zhànyǒu		*zhànyǒu	
yōngyǒu		**xiǎngyǒu**		**jùyǒu**	tèzhēng, tiáojiàn
zhànyǒu 'take control'	Cáichǎn (properties, wealth)	**yōngyǒu**	quánlì (rights)	*yōngyǒu	(features, conditions)
suǒyǒu		**suǒyǒu**		*suǒyǒu	
zhuānyǒu		**zhuānyǒu**		*fùyǒu	
*fùyǒu		*fùyǒu		*hányǒu	
*hányǒu		*hányǒu			
Have, enjoy (reputation)		Have (responsibility)		Have (as elements), contain	
*jùyǒu		*jùyǒu		*xiǎngyǒu	
*zhànyǒu		*zhànyǒu		*zhànyǒu	
xiǎngyǒu	shēngyù/quánlì	*xiǎngyǒu		*jùyǒu	
*yōngyǒu	(reputation/ rights)	**fùyǒu**	zérèn (duty, responsibility)	**hányǒu**	chéngfèn (elements, ingredient)
*suǒyǒu		*suǒyǒu		*suǒyǒu	
*fùyǒu		*yōngyǒu		*fùyǒu	
*hányǒu		*hányǒu		*yōngyǒu	

which are complementary. Compounds taking *shǔ* are possessee-oriented while those taking *zhǔ* are possessor oriented.

Table 8.2 lists the meanings of *shǔ*-compounds and Table 8.3 gives the meanings of *zhǔ*-compounds.

To sum up, we have in Chinese a two-way split in expressing possessor-oriented and possessee-oriented possession in the lexicon. This is done by way of forming compounds with *shǔ* ('belong to'), which focuses on possessee, and *zhǔ* ('take control'), which focuses on possessor.

5.3 *Pseudo possessives*

There are a number of constructions in Chinese which contain possessive phrases but which in fact do not convey possessive meaning.

Table 8.2. The meanings of possessee-oriented *shǔ*-compounds in Chinese

A. Possessive, belong to	B. Attached to, be affiliated with, affiliation	C. Member of a family, or a relative of a certain group of people
lǐng-shǔ **(lead + shǔ)** 'possess, possessive'	***fù-shǔ*** **(attached + shǔ)** 'attached to, affiliation'	***jiā-shǔ*** **(family + shǔ)** 'family member'
guī-shǔ **(return + shǔ)** 'belong to, come under the control of'	***zhí-shǔ*** **(direct, straight + shǔ)** 'affiliated to, directly under the administration of'	***juàn-shǔ*** **(relative + shǔ)** 'spouse, husband and wife'
*lì-**shǔ*** (slave + shǔ) 'be under the administration of'	***xià-shǔ*** **(below/under + shǔ)** 'subordination, subordinator, subordinating'	***jūn-shǔ*** **(military + shǔ)** 'spouse or other family member of a serviceman'
	shàng-shǔ **(above + shǔ)** 'superior' (to which one is subordinated or attached)	***liè-shǔ*** **(martyr + shǔ)** 'family member of a martyr'
	*jiù-**shǔ*** (old + **shǔ**)'former associate; formerly affiliated with'	*qiáo-**shǔ*** **(alien+ shǔ)** 'family member of the aliens'
	*bù-**shǔ*** **(department + shǔ)** 'affiliated to the central department'	*qīn-**shǔ*** **(blood-related + shǔ)** 'relatives, blood relations'

(65) lánlan *de* gāngqín tán dé hǎo
Lanlan POSS piano play COM well
Lanlan plays the piano very well. (*lit.* Lanlan's piano plays well)

(66) bù yào kāi tā *de* wánxiào
not want make 3sg POSS joke
Don't make jokes about him. (*lit.* Don't make his joke)

(67) tā yǒu gè jiāngjūn *de* fùqin
3sg have CL general POSS 1sg
He has a father who is an army general. (*lit.* He has an army general's father.)

Although each of the above sentences appears to contain a possessive phrase, none expresses possessive relationship.

5.4 *Other grammatical functions of possessive marker and possessive verb*

Chinese possessive marker and possessive verb have a number of non-possessive functions other than the 'pseudo-possessives' discussed above. Like English 'have', which can be used in 'previous aspect' (Dixon 2005: 211), Chinese *de* can convey similar temporal-aspectual meaning:

TABLE 8.3. **The meanings of possessor-oriented *zhǔ*-compounds**

Owner		Head, chief		Be in charge, control	
diàn-zhǔ **(shop + *zhǔ*)**	'shop owner'	*hù-zhǔ* **(household + zhǔ)**	'head of the household'	*zhǔ-chí* (*zhǔ* **+ hold, command)**	'be in charge, to chair (a meeting)'
dì-zhǔ **(land+ zhǔ)**	'landlord, land owner'	*jūn-zhǔ* **(lord+ zhǔ)**	'Monarch'	*zhǔ-dǎo* (*zhǔ* **+ lead)**	'lead, leading'
fáng/wū-zhǔ **(house + zhǔ)**	'house owner'	*zhǔ-rén* (*zhǔ* + **person)**	'host, master'	*zhǔ-guǎn* (*zhǔ* **+ be in charge)**	'in charge, person in charge'
yè-zhǔ **(property + zhǔ)**	'property owner'	*zhǔ -xí* (*zhǔ* **+ chair)**	'chairman, president'	*zhǔ-jiàn* (*zhǔ* **+ view)**	'personal view'
núlì-zhǔ **(slave + zhǔ)**	'slave owner'	*mín-zhǔ*	'master of the people (Pr as O); people who are masters (Pr as A)'	*zhǔ-quán* (*zhǔ* **+ right /power)**	'sovereign-ty'
				zhǔ-yì (*zhǔ* **+ opinion)**	'idea, opinion'
				zhǔ-zhāng (*zhǔ* + **spread)**	'advocate'

(68) a. tā shénme shíhòu dào?
3sg what time arrive
When is he/she arriving/When will he/she be arriving/When did he/she arrive?

(68) b. tā shénme shíhòu dào *de*?
3sg what time arrive ASP
When did he/she arrive?

Without any temporal-aspectual marking, (68a) is ambiguous. It may refer to an event in the past, or in the future. By contrast, (68b) unambiguously refers to an event that has occurred. Likewise, the canonical possessive verb *yǒu* can express a perfective meaning, very much like English 'have + V-ed.' This typically occurs in negative perfective as (69):

(69) wǒ hái méi*yǒu* chī fàn
1sg still not:have eat meal
I haven't had my meal yet.

5.5 *Possession and authority: the case of* wǒ *'I'*

A very notable feature in Chinese discourse is the use of first person singular pronoun *wǒ* 'I' without a possessive marker to express the meaning of a possessive in the plural form, as in (70):

(70)	a. **wǒ** dǎng	b. **wǒ** guó	c. **wǒ** jūn
	1sg party	1sg country	1sg army
	a. 'our party'	b. 'our country'	c. 'our army'

An utterance of this kind will carry an authoritative tone. Such expressions are generally reserved for high-level officials, very much like an American president would say '*my* government' or '*my* administration'. This is reminiscent of similar patterns with first person possession having a special status in other languages, including Moskona (Chapter 3), and Nanti (Chapter 6) (also see §2.3.1 of Chapter 1).

Besides the authoritative tones, prosody also seems to play a significant role. While it is perfectly alright to say *wǒ guó* 'our country' and *wǒ jūn* 'our army', it is odd, if not totally unacceptable, to say **wǒ de guó* or **wǒ de jūn*. This is because a noun phrase in Chinese favours prosody and symmetry in bisyllabicity. The examples are unacceptable because they violate this rule.

6 Summary

Possessive constructions in Chinese exhibit a number of features that are found cross-linguistically. On the other hand, Chinese has quite a significant number of possessive constructions that are language-specific, and only some of which have possessive meanings. Chinese possessive expressions have many manifestations in the noun phrase, typically represented in the double-nominative constructions and the 'possessor-subject' and 'possessee-object' sentences. The notion of definiteness interacts with possession; however, definiteness does not subsume uniqueness. Movement, topicalization, and relativization are a feature of possessive phrases. Topicalization and relativization are sensitive to both syntactic and semantic considerations. Movement and possessive raising often give rise to discontinuous possessives, which need to obey certain syntactic rules. Different orientations in the lexicon are expressed through different compounding strategies.

References

Anderson, John M. and Charles Jones (eds). 1974. *Historical linguistics*. Amsterdam: North Holland.

Chao, Yuen Ren. 1956. 'Chinese terms of address', *Language* 32: 217–41.

——. 1968. *A grammar of spoken Chinese*. Berkeley: University of California Press.

Chappell, H. 1996. 'Inalienability and the personal domain in Mandarin Chinese discourse', pp. 465–527 of Chappell and McGregor 1996.
Chappell, H. and William McGregor (eds). 1996. *The grammar of inalienability: A typological perspective on body part terms and the part–whole relation*. Berlin: Mouton de Gruyter.
Chappell, H. and S. A. Thompson. 1992. 'The semantics and pragmatics of Associative DE in Mandarin discourse', *Cahiers Linguistiques Asie Orientale* XXI: 199–229.
Chen, Zongli and Defa Xiao. 2007. '"Lingzhu shubinju" de shengcheng jufa fenxi' [A generative account of 'possessive-subject and possessee-object' sentences], *Waiyu yu waiyu jiaoxue* [*Foreign Languages and Teaching*] 8: 9–12.
Cheng, Jie. 2007. 'Lun fenlie feli shi lingyou mingci yu lishu mingci zhijian de jufa he yuyi guanxi' [On split possessive phrases], *Xiandai Waiyu* [*Modern Foreign Languages*] 1: 19–28.
Deng, Siyin. 2004. 'Zuogehua yu hanyu beidongju' [Ergativization and Chinese passives], *Zhongguo Yuwen* 4: 291-301.
Dixon, R. M. W. 2005. *A semantic approach to English grammar*. Oxford: Oxford University Press.
Feng, Shengli 2008. 'Yunlu yufa lilun yu hanyu cifa he jufa yanjiu' [Prosodic syntactic theory and the study of Chinese morphosyntax], pp. 83–96 of Shen and Feng 2008.
Graham, A. G. 1973. 'The terminations of Archaic Chinese pronouns', *Bulletin of the School of Oriental and African Studies* 36(2): 293–98.
Guo, Jimao. 1990.'Ling zhu shu bin ju' [Sentences with possessor-subjects and possessee-objects], *Zhongguo Yuwen* 1: 24–9.
Guo, Rui. 2000. 'The shift of descriptive function and the role of DE', *Dangdai Yuyanxue* [*Contemporary Linguistics*] 1: 37–52.
Han, Jingquan. 2000. 'Possessive raising and the case theory', *Xiandai Waiyu* [*Modern Foreign Languages*] 3: 261–72.
Heine, B. 1997. *Possession*. Cambridge: Cambridge University Press.
Hole, Daniel. 2004. 'Extra argumentality—A binding account of "possessor raising" in German, English and Mandarin', pp. 365–83 of Ji-Yung Kim, Yury A. Lander, and Barbara H. Partee 2004.
Huang, C.-T. James. 1997. 'On the lexical structure and semantic projection', *Chinese Languages and Linguistics* 3: 45–69.
——. 1998. *Logical relations in Chinese and the theory of grammar*. New York/London: Garland Publishing, Inc.
Huang, Guoying. 1982. '"De" zi de yongfa he yuyi gongneng' [Syntactic property and semantic function of "de"], *Yuyan Yanjiu* [*Studies in Language and Linguistics*] 1: 101–29.
Huang, Shuanfan 1978. 'Historical change of prepositions and the emergence of SOV word order', *Journal of Chinese Linguistics* 6: 212–42.
Karlgren, Bernhard. 1926. *On the authenticity and nature of the Tso Chuan*. Göteborg: Göteborgs Högskolas Årsskrift XXXII.
——. 1957. *Grammata Serica Recensa*. Stockholm: Museum of Far Eastern Antiquities.
Kim, Ji-Yung, Yury A. Lander, and Barbara H. Partee (eds). 2004. *Possessives and beyond: Semantics and syntax*. Amherst, MA: GLSA Publications.

Li, Charles and Sandra Thompson. 1974. 'Historical change of word order: A case study in Chinese and its implications', pp. 199–217 of John M. Anderson and Charles Jones 1974.

—— and ——. 1981. *Mandarin Chinese: A functional reference grammar.* Berkeley: University of California Press.

Lu, Bingfu. 2007. '"De" de fenbu jiqi jiben gongneng he paisheng gongneng' [The basic function and derived function of DE as viewed from its distribution], pp. 294–329 of Xu and Zhong 2007.

Lyons, Christopher. 1999. *Definiteness.* Cambridge: Cambridge University Press.

Ma, Zhigang. 2009. 'Tiyuan zhunze, feibinge jiashe yu lingzhu shubin ju' [Counter-arguments, theta-criterion, unaccusative hypothesis and the possessor-subject and possessee-object construction in Chinese]', *Hanyu Xuebao* [*Chinese Linguistics*] 25: 74–82.

Pan, Haihua and Jingquan Han. 2005. 'Xianxing feibinge dongci jiegou de jufa yanjiu' [The syntax of surface unaccusative constructions], *Yuyan Yanjiu* [*Studies in Language and Linguistics*] 25(3): 1–13.

Partee, Barbara H. 2006. 'A note on Mandarin possessives, demonstratives, and definiteness', pp. 263–80 of *Drawing the boundaries of meaning: Neo-Gricean studies in pragmatics and semantics in honor of Laurence R. Horn*, edited by Gregory L. Ward and Betty J. Birner, Amsterdam; Philadelphia: John Benjamins. (Also available at: http://people.umass.edu/partee/docs/HornFestPartee.pdf, accessed 6 March 2012)

Pulleyblank, Edwin. 1995. *Outlines of Classical Chinese grammar.* Vancouver: UBC Press.

Shen, Jiaxuan. 2006. '"Wangmian si le fuqin" ji qi shengcheng fangshi' [On the generative mechanism of "Wang Mian's father died on him"], *Zhongguo Yuwen* 4: 291–300.

Shen, Yang. 1995. 'Lingshu fanchou ji lingshuxing mingci duanyu de jufa zuoyong' [Syntactic function of possessives and possessive construction], *Journal of Peking University* 5: 85–92.

Shen, Yang, and Feng Shengli (eds). 2008. *Dangdai yuyanxue lilun he hanyu yanjiu* [*Contemporary linguistic theories and related studies on Chinese*]. Beijing: The Commercial Press.

Shi, Yuzhi. 2000. 'Lun "de" de yufa gongneng de tongyixing' [On the homogeneity of the syntactic function of 'de'], *Shijie hanyu jiaoxue* [*Chinese Teaching in the World*] 1: 16–27.

Shou Yongming, and Zhu Shaoqin. 2002. 'Lingshu guanxi zhuwei weiyuju fenxi' [An analysis of Subject-Verb constructions], *Journal of Zhejiang University* 32(2): 112–16.

Sybesma, Rint. 1999. *The Mandarin VP.* Dordrecht: Kluwer Academic Publishers.

Teng, Shou-hsin. 1974. 'Double nominatives in Chinese', *Language* 50(3): 455–73.

Wen, Binli and Zongli Chen. 2001. 'Lingyou mingci yiwei: jiyu MP de fenxi' [Movement of possessive noun: an MP analysis], *Xiandai Waiyu* [*Modern Foreign Languages*] 4: 412–16.

Xu, Dan. 2006. *Typological change in Chinese syntax.* New York: Oxford University Press.

Xu, Jie. 1999. 'Liangzhong baoliu binyu jushi ji xiangguan jufa lilun wenti' [Two types of verb–object constructions and related theoretical issues in syntax], *Dangdai Yuyanxue* [*Contemporary Linguistics*] 1: 16–29.

——. 2008. 'Yuanze benwei yufa lilun yu hanyu lingyou mingci tisheng yiwei yanjiu' [Principles and parameters and possessive noun raising in Chinese], pp. 444–56 of Shen and Feng, 2008.

Xu, Jie and Zhong Qi (eds). 2007. *Hanyu cihui, jufa he yuyin de xianghu guanlian* [*Interface in Chinese: Morphology, syntax and phonetics*]. Beijing: Beijing Language and Culture University Press.

Xu, Liejiong and Danqing Liu. 2003. *Huati yu jiaodian lilun* [*Topic and focus: A new perspective*]. Shanghai: Shanghai Educational Press.

—— and ——. 2007. *Huati jiegou yu gongneng* [*Topicalization: Structure and function*]. Shanghai: Shanghai Educational Press.

Xu, Zhongren. 1956. 'Wangmian si le fuqin' [On the sentence 'Wangmian died father']. *Yuwen Zhishi* 9: 34–8.

Yang, Henrietta Shu-Fen. 2005. 'Plurality and modification in Mandarin nominal phrases'. Ph.D. dissertation, University of Texas at Austin. (ch. 5 deals specifically with Possessive Phrases).

Zhu, Dexi. 1980. 'Zizhi he zhuanzi: hanyu mingcihua biaoji "de, zhe, suo, zhi" de yufa gongneng he yuyi gongneng' [On the syntactic and semantic function of the nominalizers 'de', 'zhe', 'suo', and 'zhi'], *Fangyan* 1: 16–31.

——. 1982. *Yufa Jiangyi* [*Lectures on Chinese grammar*]. Beijing: The Commercial Press.

Zhu, Xingfan. 2005. 'Qingdongci he hanyu bujiwu dongci dai binyu xianxiang' [Light verb syntax and intransitive verbs taking objects], *Xiandai Waiyu* [*Modern Foreign Languages*] 28(3): 221–31.

9

Possession in Hone[1]

ANNE STORCH

1 Introduction

Like every speech community, the Hone are not a homogenous nor a uniform group. They constitute a multilingual society with various ideologies of identity and religion. Their language underwent significant structural transformations due to contact and socio-political changes. This is important for the following analysis of possession; in its grammar of possession, the language combines features of an ancient, now largely dysfunctional, noun class system with properties characteristic of languages in contact with Hone. While the mechanisms for expressing possession resemble those of the contact languages, the meanings of the possessor and possessee clearly bear a resemblance to the original grammatical and functional categories of Hone.

This chapter explores the grammar of possession within and beyond the NP, and also concentrates on the semantics of possessors and possessees. We look at three different NP constructions in detail—involving possessive pronouns, juxtaposition, and genitives. We also show how a formerly conventionalized social hierarchy and world view continue to play a role in the expression of possessive relations in the modern language. The grammatical formatives which express possessive relations are diverse in their origin. The idea of possession in Hone is linked to the conceptualization of the 'self' and its control over the environment.

1.1 *Classification and setting*

Hone is a Jukunoid (East Benue-Congo) language and represents the group's northernmost surviving expansion. Most of the Jukun languages are spoken in

[1] My thanks are due to Sascha Aikhenvald, Bob Dixon, Doris Richter genannt Kemmermann, and Brigitta Flick for their many helpful and constructive comments. This contribution is based on research that has been generously funded by the German Research Society (DFG), to whom I am grateful for their support.

northeastern Nigeria, but there are also speakers of several lects and languages in Cameroon. Hone is spoken by about 6,000 people. However, many villages in the area were originally inhabited by Hone-speaking communities and have now undergone language shift towards Hausa, the dominant Chadic (Afroasiatic) lingua franca of northern Nigeria.

Both linguistic and historical evidence suggest that the decline of the linguistic identity of the Hone began with the Jihad movements and demographic changes due to the slave raids in the first half of the nineteenth century (Harnischfeger 2004; Adelberger and Storch 2008). The Hone finally became Muslims around 1930, after relocation from their old settlements and massive political pressure from both local Islamic powers and the colonial administration. This led to the abandonment of their original religion, and the matrilineal kinship system, which had regulated inheritance of power and possessions through the mother's line.

1.2 *Typological profile*

Hone is a weakly agglutinating language with little nominal and verbal inflection. The constituent order in intransitive clause is SV=V-NOMZ. In explicitly transitive clauses, the order varies between AVO and AAuxOV (note that objecthood in Hone is somewhat problematic, due to pervasive conversion and fluid transitivity: Storch 2009). Roots are generally monosyllabic (CV, CVC), and are the domain of tone, which may be high, mid, low, or any combination.[2] The NP consists of a noun, which may be followed (in this order) by a possessive pronoun, an adjective, a numeral, a demonstrative, and a relative clause. Verbs take subject pronouns and TAM markers as prefixes. The verbal root may be extended by the following enclitics (in this order): voice marker, stem-forming morpheme, derivational morpheme, modality marker. There is no agreement on verbs or nouns in number, gender, case, register, etc., with the exception of a few nouns denoting human beings, which may have a plural form and trigger plural agreement.

The marking and expression of possession include the use of a special set of possessive pronouns, a genitive marker, and also juxtaposition of two nouns. The genitive derives from a grammaticalized locative verb. Apart from this example, grammaticalization processes do not play a salient role in the marking of possession in Hone.

Originally, noun phrases in Hone had a developed system of prefixed noun classes (Welmers 1968; Shimizu 1980; Storch 1997). This has largely been lost. As a consequence, noun classes do not play any role in the grammar of possession. However, the pronoun system preserves a few forms reminiscent of the lost noun classes, which are of relevance in possessive constructions.

[2] Tone is noted in all examples as [á] = high, [a] = mid, [à] = low; nasal vowels are represented as [ã] Hausa loans and examples are written in italics.

2 Nominal possession

Nominal possession in Hone differs from predicative possession (which basically expresses acquisition and location) in so far as it mostly expresses ownership and identity, association and part–whole relations. The word order in the possessive NP is always possessee–possessor (unless a deverbal noun is involved: see §2.2.2). The possessee is the head of the phrase. This order is maintained in constructions with a pronominalized possessor (1a) and with a nominal possessor (1b):

(1) a. [gyű̃ű̯ű̃-wuu] páná
year-POSS.3sg INTER
How old are you? (*lit.* your age how much?)

(1) b. ɔ-saa-náŋ bə́ [[wii dìrì-wuu]?
2sg-do-feel COP meat body-POSS.2sg
How do you feel? (after convalescence; *lit.* you do feel with your body's flesh?)

Both types of nominal possession differ in degrees of multi-functionality and polysemy. The following sections show that possessive pronouns occur in a relatively wide range of construction types, and that grammatical markers involved in noun–noun compounds express various concepts besides possession (see (1b)).

2.1 *Possessive pronouns*

Hone has an elaborate pronoun system which consists of several sets of pronominal forms. Subject pronouns fall into four sets, and always precede the verb. They cannot express the possessee or a possession relationship directly, but they may refer to the possessee in a clause. Object pronouns fall into three sets: affirmative and negative direct object pronouns and indirect object pronouns. They are always postposed to the predicate. While indirect object pronouns may express concepts related to possession and ownership in clauses, direct object pronouns do not.

Table 9.1 shows that all sets exhibit two forms for the third-person singular: one with a human referent, and the other with a non-human referent. The former is a reflex of the old concord marker of the Proto-Benue-Congo (PBC) class 1 (reconstructed as **gwu*, **ɣa*; Meinhof 1948), which refers to human beings in the singular. The latter goes back to the pronominal concord for class 3 (**gu*; Meinhof 1948), which originally covered body parts, plants, and animals. The third-person plural pronoun goes back to the old concord marker of Proto-Benue-Congo class 2 (plural of human beings). There are no other concord markers or productive class markers in Hone.

The table also shows that there is no indirect object pronoun referring to inanimate referents in the third-person singular. This reflects a principle based on animacy: the indirect object is introduced by a grammaticalized verb *yí* 'give', which cannot be used in conjunction with an inanimate third-person marker, as

TABLE 9.1. **Subject, object, and possessive pronouns in the 3rd person (sg)**

subject				object			possessive	PBC
absolute		verbal prefixes		direct		indirect		
non-emphatic	emphatic	neutral	subjunctive	aff.	neg.			
kùù	ákùù	ku-	kú-	-kù	-kó	yáà	-a(a)	*gwu (cl. 1)
kə̀ə̀	ákə̀ə̀	kə̀-	kə̀	-kə̀	-ké	ø	-ka(a)	*gu (cl. 3)

non-human and inanimate objects are conceptualized as referents which cannot be given anything.

Inanimate and non-human referents can be possessors, as the third-person singular possessive pronouns distinguish between human and non-human referents. Possessive pronouns are suffixes, and they are more closely bound to the noun than subject and object pronouns when affixed to verbs. For example, possessive pronouns assimilate to the vowel quality and tone pattern of the possessed noun, thus forming an inseparable entity. Some examples for the use of possessive pronouns are given in (2) and (3). These morphemes express ownership in (2) and association in (3).

(2) bá-kánò máá-bìy bə́ [dar-bee] bə́-bì mə̀-hun
PL-Kano COND-come COP wealth-POSS.3pl 3pl-come CONS-buy
When the Kano-people come with their wealth, they come and buy.

(3) n-ní nə́m bú àyí bə̀ə̀ [àkwù-yii] saa
1sg-say DEM thing REL AUG.3pl forefathers-POSS.1pl do
I say this is what our forefathers did.

In the third-person singular, a possessor is marked for animacy and can have inanimate or non-human referent. This is the case in (4) where the possessive pronoun expresses location and association:

(4) dɔ̀k í-yak [pínpínù-kaa]
get_up.IMP SUBJ.1pl-go road-POSS.INAN.3sg
Get up, let's walk its [= the town's] road!

Headless forms of the possessive pronoun are based on the same principle. An inanimate possessee—namely the pertensive form *bú* of *ábu* 'thing'—takes the possessive suffix which refers to the possessor. The resulting forms are as follows:

(5) *bú-míí* 'mine'
bú-wáá 'his/hers'
bú-káá 'its', etc.

We have already mentioned that there are no inanimate indirect object pronouns, and that possessive phrases bear no traces of noun categorization. The possessee is typically low in animacy, while the possessor is usually high. Thus, the two have a different status in the animacy hierarchy. Constructions with headless possessive pronouns can be considered instances of topicalization. Subject properties are then transferred to the possessor. This is illustrated by constructions such as *bú-wáá kə́-kə́n* his/her own: it is finished', or *bú-míí kə́-ŕ-saa àsaa* 'mine: it can be done'. Here the possessor is topicalized, and occurs sentence-initially. In such constructions, the sentence-initial head needs to be followed by the pronominal prefix *kə́-*, which is not needed in sentences without topicalization (e.g. (2)). Comrie (1989: 219–25) demonstrated that the correlation between animacy, topicalization, and subjecthood plays an important role in the shift of subject properties from the possessed NP to the possessor NP. In Hone, a similar process is taking place. One aspect of this development is the grammaticalization of 'thing' as the base of headless possessive pronouns (which can be used as nominal subjects in sentence-initial position).

2.1.1 *Referents that are always possessed* Hone makes no formal morphological differentiation between alienable and inalienable possession. However, other strategies play a role in making this distinction. Some nouns are always possessed. This applies to just one specific type of kinship nouns: terms describing consanguineous female ascending kin such as *zàà-* 'mother', *àyá-* 'mum', *shíhòw àyá-* 'maternal aunt', *yààkú-* 'female ancestor'. These always take possessive suffixes in natural speech (but may be artificially elicited without suffixes), as in the following examples:

(6) zàà-mɪy miá-ták yírzáà nə̀n-bán bíʒùù
mother-POSS.1SG COND-plant guinea-corn 2pl-get food
When (my) mother plants guinea-corn you will get food.

(7) yààkú-yíí nə́m-wàà shɛ̃́ɛ̃́
female_ancestor-POSS.3PL HAB-drink beer
(Our) female ancestors used to drink beer.

Kinship terms referring to male kin, descending kin, or to affinal relations are not affected by this constraint; they do not have to always be possessed. In addition, obligatorily possessed kinship nouns may be used as the base of a generic plural, as in *bá-zàà* 'mother's folks'. Note that in this construction, the kinship term *zàà* 'mother' is not marked for possession.

Why is this so? Before Islamization, the Jukun were a matrilineal society, in which all titles and rights over land and spiritual resources were passed on from the mother to one of her sons (Meek 1931). In this system, the mother of the divine king of the Jukun was the one who represented the royal clan's ability to create a succession of kings (with their spiritual powers) over the generations.

As a consequence of colonization and the advent of Islam, this has drastically changed. Women were deprived of their former privileges after the society became patrilineal. This experience of marginalization had a traumatizing effect on women in a number of Jukun-speaking societies and this was expressed in folktales and stories (Harnischfeger 2004). The treatment of kinship terms in the grammar of possession still reflects social history before the emergence of contemporary society, when elder and reproductively active women in one's family were conceptualized as an inseparable part of a larger whole, a source of common power and spiritual resources.

Obligatory possessive marking also reflects an older kinship system, which would have been a descriptive or Sudanese one. Such systems typically have separate terms for almost every relation, based on distance and gender. In such descriptive kinship systems, possessive marking of the specific kinship terms renders them classificatory (this is the case in many Western Nilotic languages; Storch forthcoming). This strategy is reflected by possessive marking in the classificatory kinship system of present-day Hone.

2.1.2 *Non-possessible referents* There are also a number of nominal referents that cannot be possessed by humans. Nouns which are hardly ever used with a possessive suffix include taboo words such as 'sperm', 'urine', 'penis', and 'testicles', and also all expressions of the body effluvia of adult men. That is, form such as **ʒùr-mii* 'my penis' or **sùm-mii* 'my (masc.) urine' are not acceptable.

The context of this 'avoidance' strategy is the same as that of the examples given in §2.1.1. That men have genitals and body effluvia is a secret and taboo in many Jukun-speaking societies. This directly relates to the idea of potentially dangerous women. Women were largely excluded (and often still are) from religious practices and the religious knowledge of the men, and they were forced to 'believe' that men have non-secreting bodies (Dinslage et al. 2000). Consequently, men are claimed to have no genitals and produce no body effluvia such as sperm and faeces, so that the male body can be kept as a delicate and protected entity, with all its secretions and traces. In this sense, it is the vulnerable male body in transformation that is not to be possessed verbally.

Another group of nouns that cannot be possessed are personal names. Neither Jukun, nor Hausa, nor Western names can occur with a possessive suffix. This is a purely grammatical restriction.

Nouns were originally marked for class and number. The contemporary nominal lexicon of Hone preserves nouns with petrified class prefixes and a few nouns denoting human beings that exhibit productive number-marking prefixes (e.g. *m̀-hɔ̃ne*, pl. *bá-hɔ̃ne* 'Hone person'). Personal names bear no noun class markers, especially if they come from contact languages. Furthermore, names do not inflect for number in Northern Jukun. Consequently, names cannot occur with possessive pronouns because they lack specific prototypical properties of nouns (and not because there is any common sense behind this constraint). Of course, there is no reason why one shouldn't be able to refer to 'my Sophie' or exclaim something like 'oh my Lord'. Such constructions—as in (8a)—were always rejected by Hone speakers, who suggested replacing them by an additive construction with the copula *bə̀* (as in 8.2):

(8) a. *Màhámàŋ-mii
Muhammad-POSS.1.sg
my Muhammad

(8) b. mìì bə̀ Màhámàŋ
AUG.1sg with Muhammad
I and Muhammad.

The names of gods also cannot be possessed. An exclamation meaning 'oh my Lord' can only be expressed by an associative construction, as in the following example:

(9) wòò [mìì [ŋwù zàànkàr]]
INTERJ AUG.1sg child Zankar
Oh my Lord! (cry of despair; *lit.* 'oh me, son of Zankar')

2.1.3 *Multi-functionality of possessive pronouns* Apart from expressing possession, possessive pronouns also express reflexive, reciprocal, and mirative meanings.

The first two grammatical categories employ the possessed form of *dìrì* 'body'. Reflexive constructions use the copula *bə̀* 'with' (10):

(10) ku-yak [bə̀ dìr-aa]
3sg-go with body-POSS.3sg
She went herself.

The copula is not used in reciprocal constructions:

(11) i-shán [dìr-yìy]
1pl-cry body-POSS.1pl
We wailed at each other.

Mirative pronouns are constructed with the copula *bə̀* plus a pronominal element that expresses person. They literally translate as 'I with me', 'you with you', 'he with him', etc., but actually express meanings such as 'I nevertheless, I unexpectedly' (Storch 2009), as in (12) and (13):

(12) [ku-làk bɔ́à]
3sg-fly MIR.3sg
He flew off unexpectedly.

(13) n-tì-ɲi-é kyèr-u [n-kyèr bə́mìì]
1sg-NEG.PERV-know-NEG cook-NOMZ 1sg-cook MIR.1sg
I didn't know yet how to cook, but cooked nevertheless.

2.2 *Compounding*

To express possessive relations, Hone uses two compounding strategies: juxtaposition and genitive constructions. Both strategies are simple in their morphological and syntactic structures, but have complex semantic patterns. They play an important role as nominalization strategies in word formation.

2.2.1 *Juxtaposition* In noun–noun compounds a free noun is used as an attributive modifier. The modifying element is usually a noun. The second, 'modified' component of the construction may be a noun, an adjective, or a numeral. Nouns that do not belong to a semantically prototypical class, that is, do not denote discrete, concrete, three-dimensional entities (Dixon 2010: 39), often cannot feature as possessors. For example, *fúnì àʒǐ́wu* 'thief's belly' is readily acceptable, but *fúnì nkúú* ?'forfeiture's belly' is problematic.

Most of Hone's compound nouns are formed by juxtaposition of two nouns. Not all of them encode possessive relations (as in Likpe: see Ameka, Chapter 10 of this volume). The range of relations expressed includes:

A. Ownership

(14) [zən [zàà-mɪy]] àkánì ní
name mother-POSS.1sg Akani EMPH
Mother's name is Akani.

(15) bə-shɔ́rhùk [bɔ́ní zɔ̀mdǎ́w]
3pl-confiscate granary hare
They confiscated the hare's granary.

B. Part–whole relations

(16) ákùù-tər [[núú ŋáán] kí] ku-zə̀k-wɔ̀b-zə̀
EMPH.3sg-push mouth excrement ghost 3sg-take-move_quickly-COMPL
dìr-aa
body-POSS.3sg
He there, he pushed the anus of the ghost and quickly took its body firmly.

C. Kinship relations

(17)

[no	yá-yíí]	ɔ-báyì	ngɔ̀m-mii
husband	mother-POSS.1sg	2sg-be_ugly	capacity-POSS.1sg

Husband of my [our] mother, you are ugly beyond my comprehension.

D. Association, origin, and group-membership

(18)

[*bàtúúrèè*	mìstàkálàyì]	bìy
colonialist.PL	Mr_Carlisle	come

The colonialists' Mr Carlisle came.

E. Location and time

(19)

àrí	[núú	bàr]	[núú	bàr]
DEM	mouth	fate	mouth	fate

This is close to fate, close to fate.

(20)

bə́-rì-hwóy-é	mə̀ŋ	hár	kə́-kȁŋ	[záámàníʔ	násààráʔ]
3pl-NEG.PERV-be_big-NEG	NEG	until	INAN.3sg-become	time	white_man

They were not influential before colonial times.

F. Attribute

(21)

bə́-zək	[yírzáà	kɔ̀ndóʔ-kɔndóʔ]	mə̀-ń	sɔ́n-yí-yáà
3pl-take	guinea-corn	basket-REP	CONS-say	take-give-OBJ.3sg

They took many guinea-corn baskets and said: take them to him!

(22)

[záà	bɔ́ní	zȕŋ]	zɔ̀mdа̋w	ŋaŋ	[shìján	bɔ́ní	zȕŋ
guinea-corn	granary	one	hare	refuse	groundnut	granary	one
zɔ̀mdа̋w	ŋaŋ	mə̀-ŕ-zə̀m			káá		
hare	refuse	CONS-IMPERV-love			INTER		

One granary of guinea-corn the hare refused, one granary of groundnuts the hare refused, loving what?

These associative constructions involve free nouns. The second type consists of a nominal base no longer used as an independent noun. The modifying noun in these regular noun–noun compounds cannot itself be modified, and has lost the ability to occur with affixes (such as possessive markers). The resulting constructions resemble noun class-marked nominals, and are semantically similar. They resemble noun classes which are still productive in Benue-Congo languages south of the Hone area, covering 'liquids', 'collectives', 'diminutives', 'things', 'locations', and 'animals'. Table 9.2 provides some examples (showing fully bound nouns and nouns that may also occur as free forms).

Pseudo-noun class constructions and modifying compounding constructions may be marked as a whole for possession. In this case, the possessive pronoun is suffixed to the second part of the compound. The first part of the construction cannot be modified independently. The entire construction is a single unit.

TABLE 9.2. **Modifying compounding and pseudo-classes**

Compound	Gloss	Source	Pseudo-class
zaa-pərè	'water'	zaa 'water'	liquids
zaa-àmáán-bîì	'fruit juice'		
ʒee-pìŋgé	'Jukun, villagers'	ʒee 'people'	plural of persons
ʒee-kánò	'Hausa, city dwellers'		
ʒán-nay	'calf'	ʒán 'offspring'	diminutives
ʒán-kùnì	'chick'		
bú-hwɔ̃̀y	'necklace'	ábu 'thing'	inanimate objects
bú-hwãy	'clothes'		
bɛr-gìní	'land'	bɛr 'place'	locatives
bɛr-nə́ŋì	'Benue river'		
wii-gírí	'buffalo'	wii 'animal'	animals, animate objects
wii-pɔ̀wù	'wild animal, ghost'		

2.2.2 *Genitive* Genitive constructions involve a suffix marking the second part of the construction, which is a noun. The first noun, which denotes the possessee, undergoes apocope if it ends with a vowel, while the second noun (expressing the possessor) suffixes *-ì/-ì* unless it ends with a long vowel. In the latter case, the suffix does not appear. The tone of the elided final vowel of the head noun may cause tonal changes on the following syllable.

The suffix is affected by vowel harmony and assimilates to the vowel quality of the preceding syllable. Its source is the now largely defective positional verb *ri* 'to be at', which underwent several, and possibly independent, grammaticalization processes. (Note that this form is less grammaticalized in closely-related Wapha: *nú ǹkər-rí* 'palace, king's house'.) Besides its function as a genitive morpheme, it also occurs as a focus marker and tense-aspect marker. Its original meaning, indicating location or space and not time, is preserved in genitive constructions. It also occurs in clauses expressing ownership and possession in the sense of 'being/existing with'. According to Heine (1997: 205 f.), this construction is an almost prototypical example of locative attributive possession.

Juxtaposition tends to express arbitrary relationships conceptualized as separable. Genitive constructions express a closer link between the referents. Here, both components are conceptualized as being inseparable and closely linked. There are also strong overtones of inherent inalienabilty: most of the genitive constructions attested in texts and non-elicited data express inalienable possession (while juxtaposition does not). Consider the expression 'house of the chief':

(23) a. ŋwùno [tánù kùrù] ánéé
Man house chief INTER
Sir, where is the house of the chief?

(23) b. bə̀-máá-bìy nərí [tán kùr-ì] bə̀-ŕ-shíí
3pl-COND-come formerly house.PERT king-GEN 3pl-IMPERV-sit
mə̀-ŕ-gáp kìm rí
CONS-IMPERV-divide heap FOC
When they formerly came to the palace they sat and divided the lot.

Example (23a) is taken from a dialogue, in which a speaker inquired after the chief's house (not necessarily his palace). A house in this context is alienable, and may be one of several houses of a person or family. In contrast, (23b) stems from a text in which the chief's palace is a specified place within the village. Here, possessor and possessee form one inseparable entity, as the palace is a defined and singular unit. This is almost like an instance of lexicalization. However, genitives also exhibit other prominent semantic features. Number – or rather singularity – as well as proximity and inseparability are important semantic properties of the following genitive-marked constructions:

(24) ku-ń m̀pər bə́ [ʒín kínì] ɔ-do-ŕ-saa-kù nánéé
3sg-say person COP hair.PERT head.GEN 2sg-do-IMPERV-do-O.3sg how
He said: man with hairy head, what are you doing to him?

(25) bú ke [shár záapə̀r-ì] ku-ŕ-kǎŋ sə̀m
thing DEF hole.PERT water-GEN 3sg-IMPERV-return back
It's the water hole [from which] she returns.

(26) bə̀-hun [zȗn wuńyìì]
3pl-buy tooth.PERT elephant.GEN
They bought ivory.

Summarizing our observations so far: the analysis suggests that Hone has an incipient morphological distinction between alienable and inalienable possession based on two different compound types. Other techniques, such as specialized pronominal forms and grammatical morphemes, are absent. There are no nouns that are always inalienably possessed. Heine (1997: 172 ff.) observes that inalienability does not emerge as a semantically defined category (which it is in Hone), but as a morpho-syntactic or morpho-phonological entity, which develops through the exclusion of certain nouns when 'a new pattern for marking attributive possession arose' (Heine 1997: 182).

Another aspect of genitive-marked constructions needs to be mentioned here: the loss of part–whole (and therefore alienability) semantics. If the possessee is represented by a deverbal noun, the word order of the construction changes, since a verb may not act as head. Here, the syntactic SV=V-NOMZ constraint is at work, which does not permit a verb to stand in clause-final position. This constraint also affects non-clausal constructions such as compounds, like in *kyèru* 'cook (N)' + *zàà-mìy* another → *zàà-mìy kyèr-ì* 'mother's cooking' (this refers to culturally preferred possessions; a woman's culinary knowledge and cuisine are considered her intellectual property). In such constructions, possession is expressed only indirectly and related meanings are emphasized instead. Benefaction, purpose and 'specialization' seem to be the more salient meanings when verbal nouns are involved.

3 Predicative possession

Predicative possession may occur in two different guises, involving either a verb of acquisition, or a copula. Both types of possessive clauses are based on a limited number of formatives. This is partly due to the lack of a certain group of verbs in Hone (which may have existed before). Hone has no fully productive positional verbs that denote 'be (with)', and no verbs expressing ownership in the sense of 'own, possess'.[3]

3.1 *Verbs*

As a consequence of the absence of 'have' and 'own' verbs, there seem to exist two different conceptualizations of possession in Hone. One emphasizes the inchoative semantics of possession—acquiring, seizing, and gaining. The other expresses the continuing or stative aspect of possession, in the sense of 'be/exist with'. This is paralleled by the occurrence of two nouns which express these two different concepts of ownership: *sɔ́n* 'property, luggage', i.e. property acquired, and *bɛr-yìy* 'our land' or *bɛr-shíu* 'settling place' (or just *bɛr* 'land'), which refers to a permanently owned property.

Ownership in the sense of temporal ownership or acquisition is much more commonly expressed than permanent ownership. Verbs used in this context are:

(27)	shɔ́n	'acquire'
	zə̀k	'take'
	bàn	'get'
	pàn	'catch, seize'
	shɔ́rhùk	'confiscate'

[3] This does not imply that there was not a verb 'have' originally. Westermann (1927: 244) mentions a fairly common root for 'have', which seems to be etymologically related to 'hand'. A similar relationship is attested for other languages world-wide, for example Mandarin Chinese (see Chapter 8, this volume).

These verbs do not classify the possessee or possessor, as in languages with two or more 'have' verbs (see §3.1.4 of Chapter 1). They simply refer to the way in which an object can be possessed.[4] Examples are:

(28) i-máá-tí-bàn *local government* i-tí-bàn pínpínù
1pl-COND-FUT-get local government 1pl-FUT-get road
If we get the Local Government we will get a (non-permanent) road.

(29) ɔ-rí-pànpàn hwóy-u
3sg-FUT.DEF-receive be_great-NOMZ
You will have greatness.

(30) bə̀ə̀-bə́ àddíínii bə́-bìy-nù-bə̀ bə̀ kánú mə̀-shɔ́rhùk kpát
AUG.3pl-COP religion 3pl-come-wage-O.3pl COP war CONS-confiscate all
Those with religion came and waged war with them and confiscated everything.

Verbs expressing control over property are action verbs referring to various concepts of acquisition. Completed acquisition, that is possession, is expressed by a completive form of any of these verbs. The completive derivation is formed by suffixing a grammaticalized form of *zə̀k* 'take'. An example is:

(31) bə́-shɔ́n-zə̀ tán-yíí
3pl-acquire-COMPL house-POSS.1pl
They acquired our house (and now own it).

More permanent ownership is expressed by the largely defective positional verb *rí*. Most verbs in Hone inflect for aspect and can occur with the marker of the perfective or imperfective aspect. In contrast, the positional verb *rí* is always suffixed to an imperfective marker when it encodes possession, but never to a perfective morpheme. This may be due to the original semantics of *rí* 'be, exist'. That is, if the clause is in imperfective aspect, the state of 'being with' the possessee can be viewed as continuing. However, *rí* cannot form an imperative or a verbal noun. It cannot take a pronominal subject. This is an argument in favour of this restriction as an acquired one, rather than an original constraint.

In the following examples, the possessed NP has subject properties and takes the syntactic role of the subject. As a light verb, *rí* occurs clause-finally in (32).

(32) bɛr-shíí-u tí-rí
place-sit-NOMZ IMPERV-be
There is a settling place.

[4] However, classificatory verbs occur as an areal feature in some neighbouring Chadic languages (Hellwig 2011).

(33) bǎ̀yì tí-rí m-mùŋ
money IMPERV-be 1sg-at
I have money. (*lit.* Money is present at me)

The unusual features of these examples closely resemble expressions of possession in the area's dominant contact language Hausa. Here, a form unmarked for person, aspect, and tense is used to express ownership. Compare the following example from Hausa:

(34) àkwái kúɗíi
there_is money
There is money.

It is very likely that Hone uses calques from Hausa, in a form of grammaticalization of positional verbs. This is also the case in the copula constructions expressing concepts of possession and ownership.

3.2 *Copula constructions*

Copula constructions express similar concepts of ownership to clauses with verbs. The focus is not necessarily on the possessee (as in the verb phrase); it may also be on the possessor. The following forms illustrate that the order of possessor and possessee may change without any semantic consequences:

(35) a. bǎ̀yì bə̀ mìì
money COP AUG.1sg
I have money.

(35) b. m-bə̀ bǎ̀yì
1sg-COP money
I have money.

Both forms express the same meaning, but differ pragmatically. The first example emphasizes the possessee ('I have *money*'), and may originally be based on a focus construction. Example (35a) is in line with possessive constructions used with nouns that cannot take a suffixed possessive pronoun. The form given in (35b) is more unusual. Here, the copula *bə́* 'with, and' is the predicate, with a prefixed subject pronoun expressing the possessor. The possessor NP has the most subject properties, while the possessed NP has no subject properties. The ultimate cause for this development is likely to be the incipient loss of word class distinctions in Hone. However, language contact could have played a role in the emergence of the construction. Like the forms with *rí* discussed above, this construction is most likely a calque from Hausa, where possession and ownership can be expressed by a partly defective locative verb *nàa* (Heine 1997: 201). This verb forms an inseparable unit with the subject marker and is mostly used as a progressive marker. In a possessive clause, this form, together with the copula *dà*, expresses the meaning 'have' as in the following example:

(36) ínàa dà kúδíi
1sg.PROG with money
I have money.

In a very general way, copula constructions and idiomatic constructions based on verbs are more part of pragmatically marked, high-frequency discourse than possessive NPs. While the latter retain characteristic Jukunoid features, verbs and copulas are used in a way that closely resembles construction types found in neighbouring and dominant Chadic contact languages. In Chadic, locative and possessive constructions are much closer to one another than in Jukun, where constituent order is more fixed so that more distinctive formatives for both domains have to be used. It is only through the loss of a critical group of verbs that Hone became prone to borrowings from Hausa.

4 Summary

The grammar of possession and ownership has lost its former morphological complexity in present-day Hone. That language contact and linguistic convergence played an important role in grammatical accommodation processes—loss of noun classes and gender, grammaticalization of specific functional types of verbs, etc.—becomes more obvious in predicative than in nominal possession.

Contact-induced change is also observed in the conceptualization of ownership and of what may be possessed. In Jukun-speaking societies, permanent possession is linked to the land someone cleared for farming. Most stories on the founding of villages emphasize bush-clearing as the actual founding event. With colonial and post-colonial law, this idea became disputable. The land formerly farmed by the Jukuns was forcibly given to migrants from the north. Concepts of land ownership changed significantly, as did concepts of the ownership of soul and shadow, name and language. These are all part of complex linguistic taboo in other Jukun languages, but no longer in Hone. However, the former concept of ownership is still visible in constructions such as *nám hɔ̄ne* 'language of the Hone' (marking identity) vs. *nám hɛnɛ* 'language of priests' (being reserved for someone).

The complex polysemies and multi-functional organization of possession-marking devices and possessive constructions suggest a process of transformations, from expressing location and association to denoting possessive relations. While animacy plays into nominal possession, predicative possession is more shaped by acquisition as a characteristic feature of how possessions are obtained. These semantic characteristics have emerged through frequency in culture-specific discourse as well as through contact and language-internal processes of grammatical restructuring.

References

Adelberger, Jörg and Anne Storch. 2008. 'The Jukun of Kona, the Emir of Muri and the French adventurer: An oral tradition recounting Louis Mizon's attack on Kona in 1892', *Afrikanistik Online*. http://www.afrikanistik-online.de/archiv/2008/1573/. Last visited 03 March 2010.

Comrie, Bernard 1989. *Language universals and linguistic typology*. Chicago: University of Chicago Press.

Dinslage, Sabine, Rudolf Leger, and Anne Storch. 2000. 'Space and gender', *Anthropos* 95: 121–7.

Dixon, R. M. W. 2010. *Basic linguistic theory*. Vol. 2, *Grammatical topics*. Oxford: Oxford University Press.

Harnischfeger, Johannes. 2004. 'Rivalität unter Frauen. Häusliche Gewalt und Hexerei in einer Erzählung der Jukun, Nigeria', *Fabula* 45(1/20: 33–54.

Heine, Bernd. 1997. *Possession: Sources, forces and grammaticalization*. Cambridge: Cambridge University Press.

Hellwig, Birgit. 2011. *A grammar of Goemai*. Berlin: Mouton.

Meek, C. K. 1931. *A Sudanese kingdom*. London: Kegan Paul.

Meinhof, Carl. 1948. *Grundzüge einer vergleichenden Grammatik der Bantusprachen*. Berlin: Reimer.

Shimizu, Kiyoshi. 1980. *Comparative Jukunoid*. Vienna: Afro-Pub.

Storch, Anne. 1997. 'Where have all the noun classes gone? A case study of Jukun', *Journal of African Languages and Linguistics* 18: 157–70.

——. 2009. 'Hone (Jukun)', pp. 123–40 of *Coding participant marking. Construction types in twelve African languages*, edited by Gerrit Dimmendaal. Amsterdam: Benjamins.

——. Forthcoming. A grammar of Luwo.

Welmers, William. 1968. *Jukun of Wukari and Jukun of Takum*. Ibadan: University Press.

Westermann, Diedrich. 1927. *Die westlichen Sudansprachen und ihre Beziehungen zum Bantu*. Berlin: de Gruyter.

10

Possessive constructions in Likpe (Sɛkpɛlé)

FELIX K. AMEKA

1 Introduction

Many linguists would agree with Taylor (1989: 679) that '[P]ossession is a difficult concept.' Its difficulty arises, in my view, from the dominant assumption in nearly all frameworks of linguistics of linking possession to 'ownership'. 'Ownership' has been assumed to be a central semantic relationship (Dixon 2010: 263) and the prototype meaning of NP internal possessive constructions. This assumption has been entrenched by suggestions from the anthropological literature that 'property rights', 'inheritance patterns', 'exchange', and 'trade' might be cultural or human universals (Murdoch 1945; Hockett 1973; Brown 1991). At best these are etic and classificatory universals (see Evans and Levinson 2009; Levinson and Evans 2010) and their content varies widely across languages and cultures. 'Ownership' is not a central relationship coded in the Likpe possessive construction, nor in many other languages. Hence I do not assume 'ownership' to be central nor prototypical for possessive constructions. I will argue below that from a co-evolutionary perspective of language and culture, the primary meaning coded by possessive constructions is that of kinship and other socio-cultural relationships. As Lyons (1977: 473–4) points out, NP internal possessive constructions in many languages, that is a phrase like X's Y, 'means no more than 'the Y that is associated with X'. In fact in some African grammatical traditions, such phrases are called 'associative' phrases (Welmers 1973). For Akan, a Kwa language like Likpe, Boadi (2010: 30) expanding on Christaller's (1881) analysis of possessive noun phrases insists that the common meaning relation underlying all the relations identified by Christaller is that of 'associated with' and hence labels all such phrases in Akan the Associative Phrase.

I assume that nominal structures of the form [X POSSESSIVE Y] signal conceptual relations between the entities so linked. The canonical relation is one of a person and their relationship to kin. This feature is assumed to be a universal of world views (Kearney 1984). Apart from this canonical relationship two other features of world view are relevant: the distinction between self and other as well as classification. As the conceptual relations are bio-cultural by nature, such structures also code a relation between a person and their parts (see Chapter 1 and Dixon 2010; Seiler 1983; Chappell and McGregor 1996). Such phrases are an important site for the exploration of the reflexive relation between language, culture, and modes of thinking and in particular of the ways in which culture and cognition are encoded in grammar (see Chapter 1 and also Wierzbicka 1988; Ameka 1996, 2004; Enfield 2002; Evans 2003).

This chapter provides a survey of attributive, predicative, and external possessive constructions used in Likpe (autonym Sɛkpɛlé), a Na-Togo, Kwa (Niger-Congo) language (Blench 2009). In Likpe, nominal possessive structures do not signal 'possession' or 'ownership' per se, they rather indicate that one entity is associated with another. There is no robust differentiation between alienable and inalienable structures, unlike in Ewe or Nanti (Arawak), for example (Chapter 6). The syntactic nature of the possessor in a nominal structure determines whether a linking strategy or a juxtaposition structure is used. Pronominal possessors are juxtaposed to the possessee, while lexical nominal possessors are linked to the possessee by a possessive linker. Likpe is thus a split possessor language (Chapter 1; Güldemann 1999). Inalienability becomes relevant in the clausal constructions where body part terms enter into various external possessor constructions. An alienable–inalienable grammar seems to be emerging at the phrasal level also, probably under influence from Ewe.

Likpe uses various locative verbs to predicate possession. It is thus like many other languages in which there is a relation between location, existence, and possession (e.g. Clark 1978; Heine 1997; Stassen 2009). However, it raises questions concerning the relationship between these domains. I argue below that Likpe provides evidence that the cognitive connection between possession and location might be via existence (Payne 2009). Even though Likpe has several verbs for predicative possession, the alternations in their use does not relate to alienability as is the case in some languages (Chapter 1).

The Likpe language is introduced in §2. Section 3 discusses nominal possessive structures: the linked, the juxtaposed, and constructions involving possessor and possessee formatives. Section 4 presents the clausal possessive constructions: the predicative and the external possessor constructions. Section 5 explores the traces of contact in the Likpe possessive structures. Section 6 concludes the chapter.

2 Likpe: the language and its speakers

Sɛkpɛlé is the auto-denomination of the language spoken in twelve villages in the Likpe area, east and northeast of Hohoe (the district capital and an Ewe (Gbe) speaking town) as far as the Togo border in the northern Volta Region of Ghana.

Sɛkpɛlé or Likpe (lip) has two major dialect divisions: Sɛkpɛlé and Sekwa.[1] It is a tone language with three level tones High, Mid, and Low as well as Falling and Rising. Each syllable is a tone bearing unit. Contour and high tones are marked throughout. Likpe has an eight vowel system with both oral and nasalized counterparts: /i ĩ e ẽ ɛ ɛ̃ ə ə̃ a ã ɔ ɔ̃ o õ u ũ/. It has a root-controlled Advanced Tongue Root (ATR) vowel harmony system, with height assimilation involving stepwise rise in height triggered by /i, u, ə/ where the first syllable of the stem determines the ATR value of the prefixes. For instance, the two syllables of *-kɔbé* 'calabash' have opposite ATR values, but it is the ATR value of the first syllable that determines the ATR value of prefixes: *lɛ-kɔbé* 'calabash (sg)' and *a-kɔbé* 'calabashes'. When this root is compounded with *n-tə́* 'alcoholic drink' and the verb *nə* 'drink' and functions as the head, and therefore determines the class of the resulting word, the prefix has ATR value because the vowel of the first syllable in the stem is +ATR. Thus we have the compounds *di-tə́-nə-kɔ́be* [CM-alcohol-drink-calabash] 'alcohol drinking calabash' and *ə-tə́-nə-kɔ́be* [CMPL-alcohol-drink-calabash] 'alcohol drinking calabashes'. The value of the vowels in the verb root also determines the value of the verbal prefixes but not of the verbal suffixes (see Tornu 2007; Delalorm 2008 on the phonology and morphology).

Likpe is an SV/AVO language. Grammatical relations are determined by constituent order supported by cross-referencing of the Subject (S/A) on the verb and the forms of pronominal arguments in the clause. Objects are not cross-referenced on the verb. The Subject cross-reference markers do not signal agreement. They are distinct from the Subject pronominal clitics and other pronominal forms. Independent pronominal subjects are cross-referenced on the verb like lexical nominals. Pronominal subjects are not cross-referenced on the verb.

The cross-referencing of Subjects is a covert characterization of clause types with two sets of markers distinguished: one set, glossed Subject Cross-Reference (SCR), occurs in pragmatically unmarked main clauses and another set, glossed Dependent

[1] I am greatly indebted to my Likpe language consultants over the years, especially the late Mr A. K. Avadu, Mr E. K. Okyerefo, Mr Cyprian Somevi, Madam Ekudi Atsyor, Madam Georgina Dzata, Ms Justina Owusu, and Mr Tevor and his daughter, Betty, for helping me to understand this and other aspects of their language. I am very grateful to Sasha Aikhenvald and Bob Dixon for inviting me to their 10th international workshop and for comments on an earlier version. I appreciate their patience, understanding, and support. Thanks are also due to the participants for their thoughts about reversing the status quo. I dedicate this chapter to the the memory of my sister, Lucy Ameka, who passed away on 23 September, 2010, around the same time I was arriving in Cairns for the Workshop on 'Possession and Ownership'.

(DEP), occurs in dependent as well as pragmatically marked clause types such as relative clauses, term focus, and content question constructions where the lexical Subject is in the scope of focus.

The SCR has two forms—a central or a mid-front vowel /a/ (1a) or /ə/ (1c) or /e/ (1b) whose choice depends on the cross height of the stem verb vowel, and ∅ (1d)—which are used in 'action' and 'stative' clauses respectively, as illustrated in (1).

(1) a. ḿbé a-bokó ń-tu n-tsyuə́
mother SCR-bring CM-water AGR-some
Mother brought some water.

(1) b. akɔ́nɔfí bá-mə́ e-tsyətsyí bé-lu.fə́ lə́ ɔ-púnú kálɔ
cat AGR-DEF SCR-run 3pl-enter LOC CM-table under
The cats ran under the table.

(1) c. u-sióbí ə́-mə́ ə́-bə́ dí-yó
CM-girl AGR-def SCR-come CM-house
The girl came home.

(1) d. li-kplíbí nə́-mə́ tə́kə́ lə́ ɔ-púnú əsúə́
CM-pot AGR-DEF be.on LOC CM-table surface
The pot is on the table.

The dependent cross-reference markers (DEP) are *n-* and *lV-* where the V harmonizes with the vowel in the verb stem. The former is used with general present time hence used in present stative constructions (2b, c). The latter tends to be associated with non-present situations and hence more active situations. The focus counterpart of (1a) with a dependent cross-reference marker on the verb, signalling that the Subject is in focus is (2a). In (2b) the relativized Subject is cross-referenced by the dependent marker on the verb. A where-question involving the subject also takes the dependent cross reference marker, as in (2c).

(2) a. ḿbé lé-bokó ń-tu n-tsyuə́
mother DEP-bring CM-water AGR-some
MOTHER brought some water.

(2) b. o-saní ə́ n-kpé kɔ-nɔ́
CM-man AGR DEP-be.in CM-goodness
the man who is good, i.e., who has goodness

(2) c. sé fə ke-yifo-kɔ́ n-kpê?
where 2sg CM-work-place DEP-be.in
Where is your work place?

There are three double complement constructions. In one type expressing TRANSFER the DATIVE argument precedes the THEME. For the PLACEMENT type, the THEME precedes the LOCATIVE but the Figure–Ground alignment can be reversed where the LOCATIVE precedes the THEME. In a third type, the second complement is a situational argument, and typically coded as a nominalized verb. This structure is used to characterize various circumstantial aspects of states of affairs such as modality, attitudinal meanings and aspect (Ameka 2002, 2009a). Likpe also makes use of serial verb constructions (SVCs) in which the verbs must share the same Subject. The Subject is expressed on subsequent verbs by a Subject pronominal concord. Example (1b) above is an instantiation of an SVC where the Subject 'cats' is cross-referenced on the first verb *tsyətsyí* 'run' by the SCR *e-*. It is, however, marked on the second verb by the pronominal *bé* '3pl'.

Negation is marked on the verb by a nasal prefix which occurs immediately before the verb root, except when there is a future marker, and after Subject proclitics. It undergoes homorganic nasal assimilation depending on the root consonant in the verb, for example, *m-bə́* 'not come'; *n-tá* 'not throw'.

Modifiers follow the head in a noun phrase and, except for the qualifiers and intensifiers, agree with the noun head in number and class. The possessor precedes the possessed in a possessive nominal phrase. Pronominal possessors are juxtaposed to the possessed while nominal possessors are linked by a marker *(e)to* 'POSS' (§3).

Likpe has two classes of adpositions. The preposition class has two members: a locative *lə́/lí* and a comitative/instrumental *kú*. Both prepositions are deployed in marking possessive relations. The locative marks the oblique possessee in external possessive constructions (§4) while the comitative links a temporal part possessee to its dependent whole (§3.3). The dozen or so members of the postposition class denote spatial regions. They have grammaticalized from body parts and environment terms (Ameka 2007b).

Likpe has retained a number of verb derivational suffixes. These include the productive causative *-sə́* and the associative *-ko* and a semi-productive 'contactive' extension *-fə́* (Ameka 2009b).

The structure of a mono-verbal predicate is shown in (3), and that of a simple noun phrase is displayed in Table 10.1, with illustrations in (4) and (5).

(3) Subject Pronoun/ cross-reference—TAM-NEG-FUT-Verb root-suffix-suffix

TABLE 10.1. **Simple NP structure**

Head	Qualifier	Quantifier	Determiner	Intensifier
Noun	simple	numbers	definiteness	
Pronoun	ideophonic		indefinite	
	de-verbal words		demonstratives	
	− CONCORD	+ CONCORD	+ CONCORD	?

(4) a. [se-bo la-la siə́-mə́]
CM-towel REDUP-cut AGR-DEF
the torn towel

(4) b. [be-bo la-la bi-núə] kpé mɛ
CMPL-towel REDUP-cut AGR-two be.in 1SG
I have two torn towels.

(5) a. [ku-yi kplɛ̂ kɔ-ni]
CMPL-tree big AGR-one
one big tree

(5) b. [e-yi kplɛ̂ ə-núə ə-tsyúə]
CMPL-tree big AGR-two AGR-some
some two big trees

The difference between the pairs of phrases in (4) and (5) is in number. The (a) expressions are singular while the ones in (b) are plural with quantifiers marked for agreement added. Two or more of such simple noun phrases can be linked to form complex NPs. Thus a pronoun such as *bo* '1pl' and the noun *bakpɛlé* can be combined in an appositive complex NP to express 'we the Likpe people'. Similarly, any two or more NPs can be linked in a complex NP with an associative (or possessive) relation between them.

3 Nominal possessive constructions

As noted in §2 two major patterns are used for linking a possessor to a possessee within a complex nominal phrase: (i) the linker *eto* 'POSS' (§3.1) and (ii) juxtaposition (§3.2). The choice depends on the nature of the possessor. If the possessor is expressed as a lexical NP then it is linked to the possessee by the linker strategy; if it is a pronoun then it is juxtaposed. Likpe is therefore a split possessor language. There is a minor prepositional linking strategy for marking temporal parts (§3.3). There are two nominal formatives, a personalizing suffix used to designate a possessor (§3.4.1) and a possessee pronominal (§3.4.2). The motivations for variation with some categories of nouns in the use of the strategies are discussed in §3.5.

3.1 *The possessive linker construction: NP* (e)to *NP*

Any two lexical NPs that are conceptually associated with each other in terms of relationship, classification, or part–whole relation can be represented by a complex [NP *(e)to* NP] structure. The form of the linker varies between *eto* and *to* within individuals and across speakers. The variation may be linked to the difference between a dependent NP cross-reference marking on the linker and one without. The *e-* is like the SCR but it is in the process of disappearing, hence its fluidity. In the examples that follow the optionality of the *e-* form is indicated where relevant.

The range of conceptual relations between the entities covered by this construction is rather wide. A mere association between entities can be expressed using this construction, see (6).

(6) [dí-yɔ́ eto be-tídi] kpé a-le?
CM-house POSS CMPL-person be.in CM-strength
Are the people of the house well?

Example (6) is a how-are-you inquiry about the people associated with the house. Such questions are an areal feature. Interestingly, in Ewe 'the people of the house' idea is expressed by a noun involving a personalizing (possessor) suffix, as in (7).

(7) Ewe:
afé-me-tɔ́-wó ɖé?
house-containing.region-PRSUF-pl UFP
How are the people at home?

Similarly, entities that pertain to one another are linked by *eto* 'POSS', see (8).

(8) sé buu-yifɔ́ be-tidi ba la-n-la [le-ma eto
as 1pl:HAB-do CMPL-person AGR DEP-NEG-want CM-war POSS
a-sa] ...
CMPL-thing
Since we are people who don't like war affairs...

Entities related by kin (§3.5) or socially (9), or by group membership (10) may be linked by *eto*. The linked structure may also signal that the possessee originates from a place (10).

(9) lɔ́ i-bə bɔ́ə [u-tsyúə eto u-tídi] ə-kpə́ ...
LOC 3sg-come COMP CM-someone POSS CM-person SCR-die...
If it happens that a relative of someone dies...

(10) ... [basel eto ba-bloní] lee ba-sɔ́fo be-tsywə́ ə́-bə́
Basel POSS CMPL-European DISJ CMPL-priest AGR-some SCR-come
... Europeans or priests came from Basel.

Spatial relation terms (11a) and locations can also be linked to reference objects with *eto*. Some spatial relation terms can only be juxtaposed to their dependent NPs as in (1b, d) above (see §3.5 for the difference between these strategies).

(11) nya tsyidɔn káma-káma bəə-tsyé wə n-si lɔ́
and backwing.chief after-after 3pl-put 3sg DEP-sit LOC
[omahene eto ká-ma]
paramount.chief POSS behind
And the back-wing chief was installed much later who sits behind the paramount chief.

A conceptual relation that is expressed with the linked construction is part–whole, as in:

(12) i-tə́ bə́ [Tunkpa eto kú-tsyuə] ə-lu bə́-bá-lá
3sg-give COMP Name POSS CM-part SCR-leave 3pl-VENT:POT-cut
u-mé
CM-town
It made it so that a part of Tunkpa left and they came to found a town.

A nominalized event can function as possessee in the *eto* structures (13). In some cases the relation between the linked entities is one of modification. Example (14) is a case of temporal modification.

(13) [sikuu eto bu-bə́] kú [ananto-tiki bu-bə́] ka-kpɛlé-sɔ́ lá ...
school POSS CM-come COMIT God-word CM-come CM-Likpe-land TOP
the coming of schools and God's word (churches) to Likpe land...

(14) sé [ke-kú eto di-yi nə́-mə́] lé-yo-o ...
when CM-funeral POSS CM-day AGR-DEF DEP-reach-TOP
When the day of the funeral arrived...

Ownership can be the relation between the entities linked, as in (15).

(15) [[u-sió ə́-mə́ (e)to [ká-mɔ́ (e)to ɔ-kuɛ́]] á-mɔ
CM-woman AGR-DEF POSS CM-rice POSS CM-farm SCR-become.big
The woman's rice farm is big

In the complex possessive phrase in (15) the referent of the first NP 'the woman' owns the referent of the second complex NP 'the farm of rice' (*lit.*). The second NP illustrates a 'kind of' relation conveyed by *eto* phrases. This classification relation is expressed in several languages by classificatory compounds but is realized as a linked possessive phrase in Likpe. For instance in Ewe, an 'envelope' is labelled with a classificatory compound *agablẽ-kotokú* 'paper-pocket/bag'. In Likpe it is *ku-kúɔ́ eto o-tôbé* 'paper of bag'.

Possessors in an *eto* phrase can be questioned as in (16).

(16) [we (e)to awui] ni
who POSS garment COP
Whose garment is it?

In sum, two or more lexical NPs linked by *eto* can be related conceptually in a number of ways. These relations are listed in Table 10.2. Some of the *eto* constructions can be paraphrased as predicative possessive constructions. However, those involving nominalized possessees or expressing temporal modification and abstract possessions do not have predicative paraphrases (see Table 10.2).

TABLE 10.2. Conceptual relations between *eto* linked phrases

Relation	Illustrated in example	Predicate possession paraphrase?
(General) association	6	no
Kinship	9	yes
Social relations	9	yes
Pertaining	8	no
Group membership	10	no
Origin	10	no
Spatial relations	11	some
Location	11	no
Part–whole	12	some
Ownership	15	yes
Classification	14	no
Abstract	13	no

3.2 *Pronominal possessive constructions: juxtaposition strategy*

The same range of conceptual relations between entities covered by the linked construction is covered by the juxtaposed construction. The difference between the two constructions is in the syntactic expression of the possessor. For the juxtaposed construction, the possessor is realized as a pronoun. Thus kin (17) and social (18) relations can be expressed with this construction.

(17) [bo bá-ná] li-siə́ mfo
1pl CMPL-grand.parent DEP-sit there
Our ancestors lived there.

(18) ba-tɛyi [mə́ bə́-tsyuə́] bə́.ŋkə bɔ-lɛ́ a-ba bu-luə́
3pl-tell 3pl CMPL-neighbour COMP 3pl-hold CMPL-stone CM-sharpen
They told their neighbours that they were sharpening stones.

Abstract human attributes can also be linked to their pronominal possessors by juxtaposition.

(19) [wə se-tá àbi-kɛ sía-mə́] eso woa-n-ka-yɛ́
3sg CM-money-get AGR-DEF therefore 3sg:HAB-NEG-IMPERV-walk
sɛ-yɛ-tsyú ə
CM-walk-someone
Because of his wealth, he used not to move with any social group.

The derived nominal *se-tááàbi-kɛ* 'riches/wealth' is formed by the permutation of the V + NP phrase kɛ 'get' and *atáàbí* 'money' plus the prefixation of an appropriate class marker.

The word *se-le* 'language' can occur as possessee in this construction, reflecting an artefactual ideology of language, see (20). Such a structure reflects the view that the language belongs to us and we can manipulate and appropriate it. We can do things with it the way we want.

(20) [bo se-lé] si-n-ní sɛ-kɔbɔ́ si-n-ní si-n-kpé tsyá
1pl CM-language AGR-NEG-COP CM-Akan AGR-NEG-COP CM-LIG-Ewe also
Our language is neither Akan nor Ewe.

A decade ago, 'Bosele' was suggested as the name for the Likpe language. However, this was rejected after intense deliberations.

3.3 *Comitative linking strategy*

The comitative preposition *kú* is used to link a temporal part nominal to its whole as in (21).

(21) [di-yi lɔ-ní kú o-lesiə tú]
CM-day AGR-one COMIT CM-morning early
In the early morning of one day,...

As this construction expresses a semantic relation of part–whole I consider it functionally related to the *eto* linked and juxtaposed constructions. This usage of the comitative preposition is doubtless related to its use to introduce temporal adjuncts, as exemplified in (22).

(22) ə́-bə́ [kú o-lesiə tú]
3sg-come COMIT CM-morning early
He came at dawn.

A plausible interpretation of the temporal adjunct phrases like (22) is that the possessor is elided as it is recoverable from the context.

3.4 *Possessive formatives*

Like other languages in the area, Likpe uses a personalizing suffix to represent a possessor (§3.4.1). It also has a possessee pronoun (§3.4.2). These are discussed in turn.

3.4.1 *Possessor suffix* -nyə There is a personalizing suffix *-nyə* used to form nominals interpreted as 'a person associated with the N stem'. On an ethnic or place nominal, the construction signals a person originating from a place or is a member of the group. Thus *ɔ-kpɛlé-nyə* [CM-Likpe-PRSUF] is 'a Likpe person', and a *tunkpá-nyə* is 'a person from Tunkpa (one of the Likpe villages)'. If the N stem is a concrete noun, the understood relationship between the person and the referent of the stem is that of ownership and the construction gets interpreted as 'owner of N', (23). (Example (7) contains the Ewe equivalent of this suffix, see Ameka 1991 for its semantics and Claudi and Heine 1986 on the metaphorical motivation.)

(23) i-bə bə́ə ke-ní e-yifo [a-tá àbí-nyə] wə di-sí-ə
3sg-come COMP CM-skunk SCR-do CM-money-PRSUF 3sg DEP-sit-SUF
It happened that skunk was a rich person who lived (there).

The plural of such nouns comes in two forms: If the form is based on an ethnonym such as *ɔ-kpɛlé* then the plural is formed by the use of the plural class of animates. Thus *ba-kpɛlé* [CMPL-Likpe] 'Likpe people' is the plural of *ɔ-kpɛlé-nyə* 'Likpe person'. However, if it is based on a toponym such as *tunkpá* then it is pluralized by the suffixation of *-fuɔ* 'people' an Akan loan, hence *tunkpa-fuɔ* 'Tunkpa people', and not **ba-tunkpá*.

3.4.2 *Possessee pronoun* -lé Likpe has a pro-form for the possessee. It has various functions. First it has a pronominal function substantivized by a class marker, as in the *eto* phrase in (24).

(24) sé ɔ́-lɛ [kasɔ-kasɔ eto o-lé] o-lo-sə́-ə...
when 3sg-pluck ground-ground POSS CM-PEPRO 3sg-finish-CAUS-TOP
When he finished plucking the ones at the bottom...

It is also used in forming substantives from qualifiers. It combines with *kpɛ* 'big' in the stem *kpɛlé* 'big one' of the autonym for Likpe.

Possessive pronouns are derived by suffixing the possessed pro-form to independent person markers, as in (25).

(25) mua-lé ní
1sg-PEPRO COP
It is mine.

Other forms in the paradigm include *fa-lé* 'yours'; *bo-lé* 'ours'.

The possessee pro-form is also used to add a comparative reading to nominals. Compare, *ninə* 'elder' with *ninə-lé* 'eldest' and 'elder one'. The possessee pronoun is similarly used in the formation of ordinals of some cardinal numbers. Compare (26a) and (26b):

(26) a. e-yi a-na
CMPL-tree AGR-four
four trees

(26) b. na-lé
four-PEPRO
'fourth'

Languages in the area, including Ewe, have similar forms with similar functions (Ameka 1991).

3.5 *Variation in the linking of some categories of possessees*

3.5.1 *Kin terms* Two kin terms *(a)mbe* 'mother' and *(a)nto* 'father' can be linked to their possessors by *eto* or by juxtaposition.

(27) be-kpefi (eto) anto / ambe / * ɔ-nyimi
CMPL-child POSS father / mother / CM-sibling
The father/mother/*sibling of the children

Perhaps a direct linking of 'father' and 'mother' to their lexical possessors expresses a close relationship. If so then Likpe is extending the juxtaposition structure to lexical possessors to establish another sub-construction.

Another word which can be juxtaposed to a lexical possessor is *ká-fo* 'family'. The word *ká-fo* is heterosemous: as a noun it has the senses of 'stomach' (body part) and 'family' (kinship); as a postposition it has a spatial relation sense of 'inside' (Table 10.3).[2] As a spatial relation term, *ká-fo* 'inside' can be linked to its reference object by *eto* or by juxtaposition. In example (28), the title-plus-name reference term is suffixed with the group plural marker (Ameka 2006) and functions as the possessor of *ká-fo* 'family'.

(28) ... muu-nyə n-tɛyi ní [Mr Kafe-mə́ ká-fó]
1sg:POT-see 1sg-tell COP Title Name-PL family
... that I see to say is the family of Mr Kafe.

Incidentally, Ewe would use the alienable structure to express such a relation: *Mr Kafe-wó fé fomɛ* [Title Name-pl POSS family]. It would appear that there is a change in progress leading to the creation of split marking based on the nature of the possessee. The words involved in the change are the foundations of bio-socio-cultural kin relations which are being given special treatment in the grammar of possession.

3.5.2 *Spatial relation terms* Table 10.3 displays different members of the postposition class. Those in column one are the most grammaticalized and they are only

[2] The Ewe word *fome* has the same nominal polysemy of stomach > family. Could the Likpe pattern be contact-induced?

Table 10.3. **Spatial relation terms and their linking strategies**

Linked to dependent NP by juxtaposition	Linked to dependent NP by juxtaposition or possessive linker *eto*	Linked to dependent NP by possessive linker *eto*
ə-súə́ 'surface' <BODY	**ka-tó** 'up, above' < SKY,HEAVEN	**á-kɔ** 'vicinity' 'place' <?LIVER
é-flɔ 'near, place'	**lí-si** 'peak, summit' <HEAD	**ko-tosi** 'edge'
ká-lɔ 'under'	**sɛ-tɔ́** 'front'	
kə-míə 'INSIDE'	**ká-ma** 'back, behind' <BACK	
kə-nyə̃ 'opening'<MOUTH	**ká-fo** 'inside' < STOMACH	
	n-tí 'middle, among, between'	
	kə-siə́ 'entrance	

juxtaposed to their dependent nominal phrases. Those in column three are at the beginning stages of grammaticalization and are linked by *eto*. The items in column two show variation: they can be connected to their possessors by *eto* or by juxtaposition.

Consider the term *ká-ma* 'behind' where the interpretation in both phrases refers to space behind the reference object.

(29) a. omahene eto ká-ma
paramount.chief POSS behind
behind the chief

(29) b. bo dí-yó ká-ma
1pl CM-house behind
behind our house

There is no obvious semantic difference between the two expressions that should lead to the use of two different constructions. It seems to be a matter of grammaticalization in progress where an NP *eto* N[spatial nominal] is being grammaticalized into an [NP Postposition] structure.

It seems that Likpe is now developing a distinction involving possessees where some kin and spatial relation terms mark a difference between conceptual closeness and conceptual distance which is mirrored by the distance between the linguistic expressions in the complex nominal phrases. Interestingly, body part terms also exhibit a separate clausal syntax suggesting the relevance of inalienability in that area of the grammar of possession.

4 Predicative possessive constructions

In Likpe, bivalent locative verbs *kpé* 'be.in', *tə́* 'be.at' and *tə́kə́* 'be.on' are used in expressing predicative possession meanings. These verbs are discussed in Ameka (2007b, 2009a). Although they are involved in the predication of existence, location, and possession, each of the constructions are formally and semantically distinct. The existential is a one-place construction. The locative is also a one-place construction with an obligatory locative adjunct. The possessive, by contrast, is a two-place construction with no overt subject cross-reference.[3] The possessive constructions are not only used for predicating the possession of material and concrete things (30 a, b), they are also used for abstract qualities, as in (2b) above, and for kin (31).

(30) a. a-táàbí kpé o-saní ə́-mə́
CMPL-money be.in CM-man AGR-DEF
The man has money.

(30) b. kɔ́pu ə́-mə́ tə́kə́ ku-tsyə́
cup AGR-DET be.on CM-crack
The cup has a crack.

There are two options for mapping the Possessor and Possessee to the functions of Subject (A) and Object. Sentence (31a) is about the establishment of chiefs; (31b) is from another text on yam-planting, authored by the same speaker (Ring 2008: 60).

(31) a. bo-kpé ko-dia-ni eto o-ka
1pl-be.in CM-right-hand POSS CM-chief
We have a right wing chief.

(31) b. di-siɛkpɛ kpé bo ...
CM-fortune be.in 1pl
We have luck...

In both clauses the possessor is *bo* '1pl', but in (31a) functions as Subject and in (31b) as Object. There is Figure–Ground reversal. It has been noted that the Possessor-as-Subject predicative constructions are like HAVE-constructions while the Possessee-as-Subject are BELONG-constructions (Heine 1997; Stassen 2009). In Likpe this is a matter of the same predicates with the information packaged differently.

Recall that some of the attributive constructions involving different conceptual relations can be paraphrased as predicative constructions (Table 10.2). Thus kin and

[3] The existential can be thought of as an intransitive clause; the locative as an extended intransitive, and the possessive as a transitive clause.

affinal relations can be presented predicatively, as in (32 a, b). The two sentences talk about a woman having a husband.

(32) a. o-kpé ku-sə́
3sg-be.in CM-husband
She has a husband.

(32) b. u-si ku-sə́
3sg-sit CM-husband
She has a husband, i.e. she stays with a husband.

While *kpé* 'be.in' is used in a predication about a man having a wife, *si* 'sit' cannot be used thus. 'A man does not settle in a woman's house' is the explanation offered.

Another verb that predicates a possessive relation is *nyə* 'see':

(33) Sáka ə́-nyə a-táàbí
Name SCR-see CM-money
Saka has money.

Some languages, including Ewe, use a 'see' verb in predicative possessive constructions. It reflects the idea that what is in one's perceptual domain belongs to them. The Likpe construction is not treated as stative as the Subject-Possessor is overtly cross-referenced on the verb as in (33). There is no reversal of alignment possible. The question is whether this Likpe construction is induced by contact with Ewe (see §5).

4.1 *Expressing 'lack'*

There are two strategies for expressing 'lack': the predicate can be negated by the clause negator (34b), or a negative existential verb *mbə́* is used, as in (34a). The existential use of the three locative verbs is negated by *mbə́* 'not.exist' while the two strategies are available for their locative and possessive uses.

(34) a. a-táàbí ə́-mbə́ mɛ
CM-money SCR-not.exist 1sg
I don't have money.

(34) b. a-táàbí ə́-n-tə́ mɛ
CM-money SCR-NEG-be.at 1sg
I don't have money, i.e. I don't have much money.

This supports the distinctions between the constructions and suggests that existence is the cognitive bridge between location and possession. A similar link has been demonstrated for Maa (Nilo-Saharan) (Payne 2009).

4.2 *External possessor constructions*

There are various sub-constructions in which the possessor and the possessee do not belong to the same constituent in the clause. All these external possessor (EP) constructions have body parts as possessees.

In one sub-construction, the body part is the locus of effect of the action in the clause and is coded as an oblique locative prepositional object.

(35) baa-kpɔ́ wə n-tu lɔ́ dí-si
3pl-pour 3sg CM-water LOC CM-head
He was baptized. *lit.* they poured him water at head

Clothing and ornaments on specific parts of the body are also presented in different constituents.

(36) le-súkpɛ kpé wə li lɛ́-nimí
CM-ring be.in 3sg LOC CM-finger
lit: a ring is on him/her at a finger
She/He has a ring on the finger.

The two EP constructions mentioned so far code the Possessor as a direct argument of the verb while the body part is an oblique. In some experiential constructions, however, the body part as locus of effect is presented as a direct argument as in (37) where it occurs as a second object.

(37) i-fi ba-kpɛlé ka-fo tíntín
3sg-pain CMPL-Likpe CM-stomach very.much
It angered the Likpe very much.

In some EP constructions, because of co-reference between the possessor of the body part and another expressed participant in the clause, the possessor of the body part involved in the situation is not expressed.

(38) məə-flɔ́ ə-nəmí ʊ-lésiə sáá
1sg.HAB-wash CMPL-eye CM-morning every
I wash my face every morning.

Unpossessed body parts of the kind in (38) are interpreted on pragmatic grounds as being possessed by another participant in the clause, in this case, the Subject argument.

5 Contact and areal dimensions

Likpe is in an asymmetrical contact relation with Ewe. Consequently, several areas of Likpe grammar are influenced by Ewe: aspect and use of 3pl pronoun as plural suffix. Areal semantic patterns are also manifest in collocations: 'get hear' for 'believe' or 'see road' for 'hope' (Ameka 2006, 2007a). As mentioned all along, some areas of the Likpe grammar of possession seem to be contact-induced, these are explored further here.

(i) While the extension of a juxtaposition strategy to certain kin terms (§3.4) can be an internal development it could have been promoted by the occurrence of Ewe kin terms in a juxtaposed inalienable construction (Ameka 1991, 1996). This is even more plausible as Ewe has a 'peculiar' alienable grammar: body parts occur in the alienable construction while kin terms occur in the inalienable structure. The extension of juxtaposition to three kin terms so far could thus have been modelled on Ewe.

(ii) In Likpe, a possessive relation of 'coming to have something' can be expressed with the verb *nyə* 'see' (§4). Ewe has a similar construction involving the verb *kpɔ́* 'see' (Ameka 1991: 230–5). The parallels between the Ewe and Likpe constructions are striking: the possessee must have a non-definite interpretation for a possessive reading of the structure.

Furthermore, some calques of Ewe experiential collocations involving 'see' have been adapted into Likpe, for example, 'see happiness', 'see anger'. It is plausible that along with such expressions, the 'see' possessive expression is also copied to augment the possessive constructions. One effect is that a possessor in Likpe can also be viewed as an experiencer in addition to a theme or location.

(iii) We have illustrated the linking reversal possible with the locative verbs *kpé* 'be.in', *tə́* 'be.at', and *tə́kə́* 'be.on'. It is plausible that the development of the sub-construction [Subject=Possessee]–Verb–[Object=Possessor] is contact-induced. In the Ewe locative verb-based possessive construction, the possessee always occurs as Subject and the Possessor is coded as a dependent NP of the postpositional phrase headed by *sí* 'hand'. This may have provided the model for the alignment reversal in Likpe.

6 Concluding remarks

In the foregoing, I have examined the structures that are used to code a conceptual relation of association between two or more NPs in Likpe. The *eto*-linked and the juxtaposed constructions are chosen depending grosso modo on the nature of the possessor. The former for lexical NPs and the latter for pronominal NPs. Likpe is thus a split possessor language. A split possessee distinction is emerging where three kin relation terms as well as some spatial relational terms can be linked to their possessors by juxtaposition reflecting variation and grammaticalization in progress. Three locative verbs are deployed in the expression of predicative possession in two place constructions. Body part terms partake in predicative external possession constructions. Contact-induced effects in the Likpe grammar of possession were also noted. For instance, it is argued that the emergence of a split possessee marking could be due to influence from Ewe.

The Likpe possessive constructions surveyed suggest a re-examination of received assumptions in the linguistic analysis of possession: possession and ownership should be delinked. A canonical typological approach based on low-level features of possessive relations of the kind involved in the *eto* constructions is needed. The organizational principles of adnominal and predicative possessives are also different. Moreover, location, existence, and possession are distinct yet connected domains.

References

Ameka, Felix K. 1991. 'Ewe: Its grammatical constructions and illocutionary devices', Ph.D. thesis. Canberra: Australian National University.

——. 1996. 'Body parts in Ewe grammar', pp. 783–840 of *The grammar of inalienability. A typological perspective on body part terms and the part–whole relation*, edited by Hilary Chappell and William McGregor. Berlin: Mouton.

——. 2002. 'Progressive aspect in Likpe: Its implications for aspect and word order in Kwa', pp. 85–111 of *New directions in Ghanaian linguistics*, edited by Felix K. Ameka and E. Kweku Osam. Accra: Black Mask.

——. 2004. 'Grammar and cultural practices: The grammaticalisation of triadic communication in West African languages', *Journal of West African Languages* 30(2): 5–28.

——. 2006. 'Grammars in contact in the Volta Basin (West Africa): On contact induced grammatical change in Likpe', pp. 114–42 of *Grammars in contact: A cross-linguistic typology*, edited by Alexandra Y. Aikhenvald and R. M. W. Dixon. Oxford: Oxford University Press.

——. 2007a. 'Grammatical borrowing in Likpe (Sɛkpɛle)', pp. 107–22 of *Grammatical borrowing in cross-linguistic perspective*, edited by Yaron Matras and Jeanette Sakel. Berlin: Mouton.

——. 2007b. 'The coding of topological relations in verbs: the case of Likpe', *Linguistics* 45: 1065–104.

——. 2009a. 'Likpe', pp. 239–80 of *Coding participant marking: Construction types in twelve African languages*, edited by Gerrit J. Dimmendaal. Amsterdam: John Benjamins.

——. 2009b. 'Verb extensions in Likpe (Sɛkpɛle)', *Journal of West African Languages* 36(1–2): 139–57.

Blench, Roger M. 2009. 'Do the Ghana-Togo-Mountain languages constitute a genetic group?' *Journal of West African Languages* 36(1–2): 19–35.

Boadi, Lawrence A. 2010. *The Akan Noun Phrase: Its structure and meaning*. Accra: Black Mask.

Brown, Donald E. 1991. *Human universals*. New York: McGraw-Hill, Inc.

Chappell, Hilary and William McGregor (eds). 1996. *The grammar of inalienability. A typological perspective on body part terms and the part–whole relation*. Berlin: Mouton.

Christaller, J. G. 1881. *A grammar of the Fante and Twi language called Tshi (Chwee, Twi) based on the Akuapem language*. Basel: Basel Evangelical Missionary Society.

Clark, Eve V. 1978. 'Locationals: Existential, locative and possessive constructions', pp. 85–126 of *Universals of human language. Vol. 4 Syntax*, edited by Joseph H. Greenberg. Stanford CA: Stanford University Press.

Claudi, Ulrike and Bernd Heine. 1986. 'On the metaphorical base of grammar', *Studies in Language* 10(2): 297–335.

Delalorm, Cephas 2008. 'A description of some morphological and allomorphic issues in Sekpele', M.Phil. thesis, Norwegian University of Science and Technology (NTNU), Trondheim.

Dixon, R. M. W. 2010. *Basic linguistic theory. Volume 2: Grammatical topics.* Oxford: Oxford University Press.

Enfield, Nicholas J. (ed.) 2002. *Ethnosyntax.* Oxford: Oxford University Press.

Evans, Nicholas 2003. 'Context, culture and structuration in the languages of Australia', *Annual Review of Anthropology* 32: 13–40.

—— and Stephen C. Levinson 2009. 'The myth of language universals: language diversity and its importance for cognitive science', *Behavioral and Brain Sciences* 32(5): 429–92.

Güldemann, Tom. 1999. Toward a grammaticalisation and typological account of the -ka possessive in southern Nguni. *Journal of African Languages and Linguistics* 20(2): 157–84.

Heine, Bernd 1997. *Possession. Cognitive forces, sources and grammaticalisation.* Cambridge: Cambridge University Press.

Hockett, C. F. 1973. *Man's place in nature.* New York: McGraw-Hill, Inc.

Kearney, Michael. 1984. *Worldview.* California: Chandler & Sharp.

Levinson, Stephen C. and Nicholas Evans. 2010. 'Time for a sea-change in linguistics: Response to comments on 'The Myth of Language Universals'', *Lingua* 120: 2733–58.

Lyons, John. 1977. *Semantics* (2 vols). Cambridge: Cambridge University Press.

Murdoch, George P. 1945. 'The common denominator of cultures', pp. 123–42 of *The science of man in the world crisis*, edited by Ralph Linton. New York: Columbia University Press.

Payne, Doris L. 2009. 'Is possession mere location? Contrary evidence from Maa', pp. 107–42 of *The expression of possession*, edited by William McGregor. Berlin: Mouton.

Ring, Andrew J. (ed.) 2008. *Language structures of Sɛkpɛle (Likpe).* Tamale: GILLBT.

Seiler, Hansjakob. 1983. *Possession as an operational dimension of language.* Tübingen: Gunter Narr.

Stassen, Leon. 2009. *Predicative possession.* Oxford: Oxford University Press.

Taylor, John R. 1989. 'Possessive genitives in English', *Linguistics* 27: 663–86.

Tornu, Cecilia E. 2007. 'Aspects of Sɛkpɛle (Likpe) phonology'. M.Phil. Thesis, University of Ghana, Legon.

Welmers, William E. 1973. *African language structures.* Berkeley: University of California Press.

Wierzbicka, Anna. 1988. *The semantics of grammar.* Amsterdam: Benjamins.

11

Possession in Wandala

ZYGMUNT FRAJZYNGIER

1 Introduction

1.1 *The goal of the chapter*

In the domain of modification by nouns or pronouns, Wandala (Central Chadic) makes a distinction between two subdomains: the modification of inherently relational nouns and the modification of all other lexical categories, including all other nouns.[1] Although modifying constructions in either subdomain may imply some of the semantic relations listed under the label 'Possessive constructions' in Dixon (2010) and in Chapter 1 of the present volume, neither subdomain codes possessive modification as it is understood in traditional linguistic terminology (Matthews 1997). Wandala does, however, have a domain of possessive predication that is distinct from all other predications in the language. Although the possessive predication has the form '[be] with X', it is distinct from the predication of co-existence. Possessive predication can also be inferred from affirmative and negative existential predications.

Within the theoretical model adopted in the present work, the meaning of a grammatical form is determined by the place of the form within its functional domain (Frajzyngier and Mycielski 1998; Frajzyngier and Shay 2003; Frajzyngier to appear). The relationship of this meaning to any inferences about the surrounding world including the cognitive system of speakers depends on the categoriality of lexical items chosen for the coding of the domain and often on individual lexical items.

[1] The work on Wandala was supported by the NSF grant 'Grammars of Wandala and Giziga'. All data for this study come from speakers of Wandala. I would like in particular thank Ramadan Abba, who was an enthusiastic, patient, and critical language assistant. The bulk of this study was written at the University of Nantes where I held the Chaire Régionale de Chercheur Étranger de la Région Pays de la Loire. The work on this study benefited from the critical comments of Erin Shay, who read several versions of this study, pointed out a number of weaknesses in argumentation and suggested a number of improvements in organization. I am most grateful to Sasha Aikhenvald for constructive comments regarding the content and organization of the study. For any errors of fact and interpretation I alone am responsible.

1.2 *Basic information about Wandala*

Wandala [Mandara] is a Central Chadic language spoken by some 23,500 speakers in Northern Cameroon and 20,000 speakers in Nigeria (www.ethnologue.com). The Mandara (Wandala) Sultanate, an important political entity in Northern Cameroon in the sixteenth to nineteenth centuries has contributed to the sense of ethnic identity among Wandala.

Lexical categories in Wandala include: verbs; nouns; adjectives; adverbs; prepositions; a locative predicator; an affirmative existential predicator; a negative existential predicator; and ideophones. Within the category 'noun' there exists a distinction between inherently relational nouns and all other nouns. The language has two numbers: singular (unmarked) and plural (marked on pronouns, verbs, and some nouns). All lexical categories and grammatical morphemes, whether free or bound, can undergo inflectional changes consisting of the phonological reduction of the stem, addition of the suffix *a*, and retention of stem final vowel. The inflectional markers code clausal boundary (vowel retention), and the role of the ensuing constituent in the predication (vowel reduction and the addition of the vowel *a*). These inflectional changes are the fundamental coding means in Wandala, as they indicate how the elements of the utterance should be parsed (Frajzyngier 2012).

The pragmatically neutral clause has the form (Pro) Verb (NP) (PP) (PP). The clause may have two noun phrases only if one of the arguments is topicalized. The clause then has the structure NP V NP, and the roles of the noun phrases are computed from the inherent properties of verbs and the inflectional marking on the verb.

Existential affirmative predication has the form *áŋkwà* NP, where *áŋkwà* is the existential predicator. Existential negative predication has the form NP *ɓákà* or *ɓákà NP*, where *ɓákà* is the negative existential predicator.

The inflectional and derivational markers on the verb include: verbal extensions; several types of reduplication, coding aspect and plurality; *a* insertion, coding plurality; tonal changes, coding tense; and pronominal markers of subject and object (there is no distinction between direct and indirect object). All lexical categories, that is nouns, verbs, adjectives, and adverbs, can have a suffix *á* ('pertensive') added to indicate that the lexical item is modified by the ensuing pronoun or noun.

The following are the allowed structures of the noun phrase. The gloss N[root] refers to the form without the final vowel. The gloss X + *a* refers to the root form of any lexical category augmented by the suffix *a*. Use of the suffix *a* indicates that what follows is a constituent of the same predication, even though the lexical properties and or linear order of the constituents involved would indicate otherwise:

N[root]-PRO
N-PERT-PRO N
N[root]-PRO g NP
N[root] ADJ

ADJ+a N
N[root] NUM
N PRED N (PRED is the locative predicator á)
N[root] DET
NP PREP NP

While Wandala has the noun *ɬìɗé* 'property, place that one has', it has no nouns corresponding to 'ownership', 'owner'. This does not appear to have cultural correlation. The reader should be aware that many Wandala are merchants and have a long tradition of commerce, trading a variety of goods, including salt, across the wide areas of West and Central Africa. The Wandala culture knows very well the concepts of ownership, property, and trade. The exchange of goods in the transaction of marriage requires a very precise method of keeping a record of what is being offered. None of these elements of the culture appear to be reflected in the grammatical system of the language. Below I describe the functional domains from which 'possession' as a nominal relation, as defined in Chapter 1 of this volume, can be inferred. This is followed by a description of the possessive predication in Wandala.

2 Relational modification

Relational modification narrows the scope of a constituent by adding another noun or a pronoun. This is distinct from modification by determiners, adjectives, relative clauses, and other categories that a language might have.

Hypothesis: The morphological system of Wandala distinguishes between the modification of inherently relational nouns and modification of other nouns and other lexical categories.

An inherently relational noun is one 'whose meaning involves a relationship between one entity and another' (Matthews 1997: 316). Such nouns cannot be interpreted without a modifier. For example, the terms corresponding to 'father', 'wife', and 'husband' in English cannot be interpreted in Wandala without a complement such as 'father/wife/husband of X' or 'X's father/wife/husband'. Non-relational lexical items, in contrast, do not require anything else for full interpretation. The term 'dog' belongs to this class, as 'dog' can be fully interpreted without a complement. The relational modification in Wandala subsumes most of the functions that Dixon (2010) and Chapter 1 include under 'Possessive constructions' but it also subsumes other types of modification not included in 'possessive constructions'. These are illustrated later in the study. For related issues in other languages represented in this volume, see the chapters by Ameka, Luo, and Post.

The forms coding the two subdomains in Wandala are as illustrated in Figure 11.1:

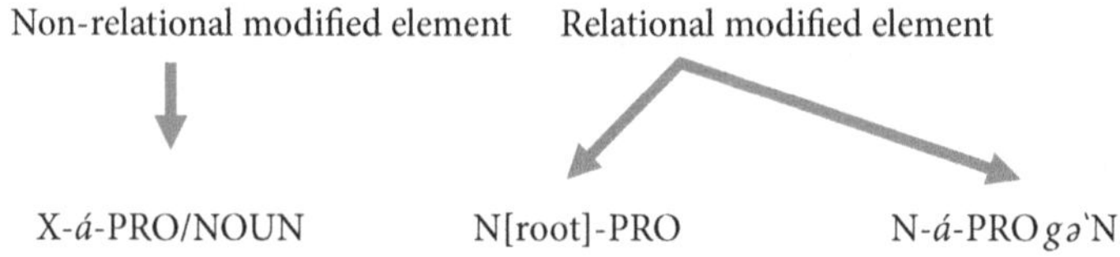

FIGURE 11.1. Relational modification

The pronouns shown in Table 11.1 are used in both constructions:

TABLE 11.1. **Modifying pronouns (phrase-final forms)**

Person	Singular	Plural
1	*r(ú)wà*	*ŋrè*
		myà
2	*ŋà*	*kùrè*
3	*rà* (*nè*; Pulka dialect)	*tàrè*
	ŋàrà (for constituents identifiable from preceding discourse)	

3 Modification of non-relational constituents

3.1 *The form*

The modification of a non-relational constituent has the form X-*á*$_{[\text{PERT}]}$-PRO for pronominal modifiers and X-*á*$_{[\text{PERT}]}$ N for nominal modifiers. The term X represents the modified constituent, and PRO and N represent pronominal and nominal modifiers. The modified constituent (X) can be a noun, a numeral, an adjective, an adverb, or a verb. The pertensive marker replaces the final vowel of the modified element (illustrated on nominal constituents):

ìrè	'head'	*írè*	'iron'
ìr-á-rà	'his head'	*ír-á-rà*	'his iron'
ìr-á-tàrè	'their head'	*ír-á-tàrè*	'their iron'
bàrámà	'road'	*bàràm-á-rwà*	'my road'
kwánjàr	'hook' (Kanuri)	*kwánjàr-á-rwà*	'my hook'
dzàkwà	'hat'	*dzàkw-á-rwà*	'my hat'

3.2 *The function of modification with pertensive marker*

The construction with the pertensive marker codes a single, fairly abstract function, namely the modification of any non-relational lexical category by a noun or pronoun. The nature of the modification is not specified any further. The evidence follows.

The linguistic tradition (including writings by this author) overwhelmingly labels pronouns attached to nouns as 'possessive', reflecting an axiomatic approach to the meaning of the construction. But is this axiom really justified? I demonstrate below that pronouns in Wandala can be added to all lexical categories and that the resulting inference may be possessive only when the modified constituent is a noun. The pronouns suffixed to lexical categories in Wandala narrow the scope of the category without specifying what kind of relationship is involved between the lexical category and the pronoun.

The evidence that pronouns do not code the possessive function is provided by natural discourse examples in which possession and ownership are ruled out. These include constructions in which the modified element is a lexical category other than a noun. Dixon's (2010) test is a useful tool for determining whether the construction is possessive or not.

The modified element can be the numeral *pállè* 'one', whose referent is not an object; consequently, the modifier cannot be a possessor:

(1)	á	bà	**páll-á-tàr,**	wá	nó	kínà	dìgíyà
	3sg	say	one-PERT-3pl	COM	PRES	now	COMP

One among them says, thus.

The expression 'they have one' does not yield 'one of them'.

Pronouns can be added to adverbial expressions. In this construction, no possessive interpretation is possible. The following example contains the adverbial phrase *án əngy* 'in the morning' modified by the first-person singular pronoun:

(2)	yá	záɗáfàánəngyárwà	ánìcìvàcíyà				
	yá	zá	ɗáfà	án	**əngy-á-rwà**	án	yəcìvàcíyà
	1sg	eat	food	ASSC	morning-PERT-1sg	ASSC	evening

I eat my food morning and evening. (*I have a morning)

A verb can have a modifying pronoun suffixed. Such a construction codes the point of view of the subject rather than a possessive function (Frajzyngier 1977, 2011):

(3)	mádàddàm	ŋánjáŋrè	ányàlàhárwà		
	má	dàddàm	ŋá	**nj-á-ŋrè**	án
	HYP	meantime	EXCL	remain-PERT-1EXCL	ASSC
	yàl-àh-á-rwà				
	family-PL-PERT-1sg				

In the meantime, we remain with my family.

Hence, pronouns in combination with other lexical categories do not carry a possessive function in Wandala, although some instantiations of modification of nouns may result in a possessive interpretation.

Modification by a noun provides further evidence that the construction with the suffix *á* codes unspecified modification. The head of the modifying construction can be a quantifier, ruling out any possessive interpretation:

(4) a. xàl-əf-xàl kyàlmá ƴír nà
gather-AP:PL-gather half:PERT beans DEM
Gather half of the beans!

(4) b. xàl-əf-xàl úmlá ƴír nà
gather-AP:PL-gather another:PERT beans DEM
Gather some of the beans!

The expression **ƴír án kyàlmá* '*beans have half' and **ƴír án úmlá* '*beans have another' are as nonsensical in Wandala as they are in English. English has two modifying constructions with quantifiers, one genitive and the other prepositional: 'his half' and 'half of him'. The first is interpreted as possessive while the second is not (cf. Chapter 1). The construction X-*á* PRO/NP in Wandala subsumes both of these domains and several others, depending on the categoriality of the component X.

When the modified noun refers to time and the modifier refers to an inanimate noun, the possessive interpretation is ruled out:

(5) yó ásò hárá làrúskùmàɮàrà
yó á sà-w **hár-á** **làrús**
well 3sg come-VENT day-PERT betrothal
kwà màɮàrà
RQ now
Well, there finally comes the day of the betrothal. (*betrothal has a day)

(6) yò, ádəsò hàránìkà ŋánnà
yò, á də sà-w **hár-á** **nìkà** ŋánnà
well 3sg FUT come-VENT day-PERT marriage DEF
Well, then the very day of the marriage will come. (*marriage has a day)

Similarly, when the modifier is an abstract noun, the possessive interpretation is ruled out:

(7) ánɓákìrá kwárà
án ɓák **ìr-á** **kwárà**
ASSC NEG.EX head-PERT order
without any orders (*order has a head)

(8) **əlv-á** ndzà
word-PERT past
the old speech, old words

Even when the modifier of the noun *lvà* 'story' has the feature [+human], the construction means 'a story about X' rather than the 'story that X told', hence it does not have a possessive interpretation:

(9) yò tàsálvàmdə kíɗyé
yò tà s-á **lv-á** mdə kíɗyé
well 3pl come-GO story-PERT people three
They brought a story of three people.

Similarly, the modifying construction cannot be interpreted as possessive when the modified constituent is the noun 'type':

(10) yò jìbámdəná tànjámbá žílnà
yò **jìb-á** **mdə** ná tá njà
well type-PERT people DEM 3pl stay
á mb-á žíl nà
PRED home-PERT man DEM
Well, the type of people who remain at the husband's,...

Body part terms are grammaticalized in Wandala, as in many other Chadic languages (Frajzyngier with Shay 2002), as spatial specifiers can precede other nouns in pertensive modification. They cannot have a possessive interpretation in this function:

(11) máfàtərm skùw ámhùɗávwà
má fà-tər-m skù w á-m **hùɗ-á-vwà**
HYP put-3pl-IN like what PRED-IN belly-PERT-body
What should one put into their bodies? (i.e., what should one tell them?)

3.3 *Possessive interpretations*

Some instantiations of the pertensive construction with a noun as the modified element can have a possessive interpretation in the traditional sense (Matthews 1997), and their elements can be used in the possessive predication of the type X *án* Y, corresponding to 'X has Y'. A large variety of possessive inferences can be drawn from such constructions.

(I) SOCIAL RELATIONSHIPS

(12) tájàhámmà wálúàhà bwà
tá jàh-á-mm-à wálw-a bwà
3pl unite-GO-TOG-CN representative-PL two
wàlwá žílé ántàr wàlwá mùksè
wàlw-á **žílé** ántàr **wàlw-á** **mùksè**
representative-PERT man ASSC representative-PERT woman
They get together the two representatives, a representative of the man with a representative of the woman.

(13) ŋán tàràpàtróŋárwà
ŋà ántàrà **pàtróŋ-á-rwà**
1EXCL ASSC:PL boss-PERT-1sg
We are together with my boss.

(II) KINSHIP RELATIONSHIP

(14) tàrdádámámá ántàrgdzá tàržílé
tàr dádá mámá ántàr **gdz-á-tàr** žílé
3pl father mother ASSC:PL child-PERT-3pl male
They are a father, a mother, and their son.

(III) BODY PARTS AND VOICES

(15) yáwwà átù ánìcá wáyà tásəksàgyálè ƫʒàbádàlyè
yáwwà á tù án **ìc-á** **wáyà** tá sə
well PRED before ASSC eye-PERT night 3pl come
ksà gyálè ƫʒàb á dàlyè
take girl yet PRED more
Well, before the night, they come to take the girl as well.

(16) májàrà mmùjìyá tàrè
má jà-rà-n-mmə-j **yà-á-tàrè**
HYP unite-3pl-3sg-TOG-unite voice-PERT-3pl
If they agree,... [if they unite their voices]

(IV) PROPERTIES

(18) á ɗàbà yìyékní yètàpántàp kárárà cìkwángùɗì
á ɗàbà ìyá kní yè tàpá-n-tàp **kár-á-rà**
because 1sg C.FOC 1sg taste-3sg-taste fire-PERT-3sg
cìkwángùɗì
a little bit
What I am telling you, is because I myself tasted its fire a little bit.

A content question about the pertensive modifier has the form: NP-PERT *wàr*, where *wàr* is the unspecified human 'who':

(18) əgdzá wàrónà
əgdz-á wàr-à únà
child-PERT who-CN that
Whose child is this?

(19) á njà **mb-á** **wàrè**
3sg stay house-PERT who
At whose house is he staying?

The discussion above has demonstrated that pertensive modification can be used to modify any lexical category, that is a verb, an adjective, an adverb, or a noun, by a noun or pronoun without specifying the nature of modification. It is only when the modified constituent is a noun that the pertensive modification may yield the possessive inference. Wandala also has another modifying construction with a narrower function, as described below.

4 Modification of relational nouns

Relational nouns include what anthropologists label 'kinship terms' and 'non-kinship terms'. The defining characteristic of a relational noun is that it implies a relationship to a noun from another set. Thus, the term 'husband' is a husband of somebody, 'friend' is a friend of somebody. There are two constructions for modifying relational nouns, one with a pronominal modifier and the other with a nominal modifier. Since the modified constituent is always a noun, relational modification often implies possession.

4.1 *Pronominal modifiers of relational nouns*

The pronominal modifier is added to the root form of the noun without the pertensive marker *á*:

(20) *gí-rwà* my grandchild
xàm-rúwà my sibling-in-law

The noun *ɬàkàté* 'buddy' has the root form with first-person singular and plural pronouns, second-person singular and plural pronouns, and the third-person singular pronoun:

(21) a. ɬàkàtə̀ ŋàrà/ŋà
fellow 3sg/2sg
his/your buddy

(21) b. ɬàkàtə̀ myà/ŋrè/kùrè
fellow 1INCL/1EXCL/2pl
our (INCL/EXCL) your buddy

With the third-person plural pronoun, this noun must have the pertensive marker *á*:

(22) ɬàkàt-á-trè
fellow-PERT-3pl
their buddy

4.2 *Forms of kinship nouns*

The inherent relational nouns *dàdà* 'father' and *màmà* 'mother', and the non-relational noun *ə̀gdzrè* 'child', all classified as 'kinship terms' in the anthropological literature, constitute a lexical class of their own, as evidenced by the formal alternations in their stems. These nouns have the forms as listed above when not followed by a pronominal modifier. When these nouns have pronominal modifiers, with or without the pertensive suffix, they are reduced to *(d)d* 'father', *m* 'mother' and *gdz* 'child'. Epenthetic vowels are added as required by syllabification rules. The tone on the epenthetic vowel is polar to the ensuing tone:

(23) *ə̀d-rùwà* my father
ə̀ddə̀-ŋà your father
ə̀ddə̀-ŋàrà his father
ə̀ddə̀-myà our (incl) father
ə̀ddə̀-ŋrè our (excl) father
ə̀ddə̀-kùrè your (pl) father
ə̀ddə̀-tàrè their father

The epenthetic vowel following the labial consonant *m* is *u*:

(24) mágyávgyè mágàyáŋrè
má gyá-v-gyè mágày-á-ŋrè
HYP cook-APpl-cook hungry rice-PERT-1EXCL
ŋázàn bàŋrántàrmrùwà
ŋà zà-n bà ŋr ántàr **mù-rwà**
1EXCL eat-3sg FOC 1EXCL ASSC:PL mother-1sg
When our hungry rice is cooked, we will eat it, me and my mother.

4.3 *Intimate kinship terms*

The terms for 'mother' and 'father' have intimate variants that are used without modifying pronouns (see also Bril, this volume, for a similar situation in Nêlêmwa). The term *máyè* 'our mother' is used only among siblings. Instead of the form *ddərwà* 'my father', a daughter uses the term *ddà* 'daddy':

(25) àhá'á **ddà** há dónə nàní ìyèkənì wènwéyà
àhá'á ddà há dó-nə nà ní
ah father ah man-DEM DEM INTENS
ìyè kənì wàyà-n-wàyà
1sg C.FOC like-1sg-like
Ah, daddy, the man whom I like...

4.4 *Functions of relational modification*

Any relational noun may occur in relational and pertensive modification. Non-relational nouns may be modified only by pertensive modification. The nouns *žílé* 'man', *mùksè* 'woman', *ə̀gdzrè* 'young one' (i.e. child) are not relational and are modified through the pertensive construction:

(26) žíl-á-rà
man-PERT-3sg
her husband

(27) mùks-á-rà
woman-PERT-3sg
his wife

(28) ʃòl-á-rù žílé
in-law-PERT-1sg male
'my father-in-law' or 'my son-in-law' (either wife's or husband's)

(29) gdz-á-rà
child-PERT-3sg
his/her child

For inherently relational nouns, relational modification indicates kinship relations, while pertensive modification indicates social relations. Consider the noun *màlé* 'older male relative'. In the relational modification it means 'older brother'. In the pertensive modification it means 'superior, boss': *mál-rùwà* 'my oldest brother', *mál-á-rwà* 'my superior'. The following natural discourse sentence contains a telling error by the narrator:

(30)

yó ə̀lv	wándàl	ŋánnà	à	fyàrà	málrùwà [error]
yó	ə̀lv	wándàl	ŋánnà	à	f-y-àr-à
well	speech	Wandala	DEF	3sg	put-1sg-ON-CN

mál-rùwà
older brother-1sg
This Wandala speech is requested from me by my older brother.

The error consists in using the form *mál* 'older' without the pertensive marker, which suggests a kinship relation, for example 'older brother'. In the next sentence, the speaker corrects himself and uses the form *mál* with the pertensive marker *á* to mean 'boss':

(31)

málárù	ŋán	nùmú	wàré
mál-á-rùwà	ŋánn-mú	wàré	
superior-PERT-1sg	DEF-FOC	who	

Who is this boss of mine?

Here is an example of the use of the noun *ədd* 'father' in the two constructions:

(32) *əd-rùwà* my father (kinship)
ədd-á-rwà my boss, my superior (the same as *màl-á-mí-nà*) (social)

The terms for 'father' and 'mother', when modified by the third-person plural rather than singular pronoun, refer to positions within the household that may include kinship relations. The third-person plural pronoun in the expression *ddə-tàr*, *lit.* 'their father', in the following example refers to the son and the wife of the man, a combination of the kinship and social meaning:

(33) ée, bàddətàrŋánnà kín tàxɗám

ée,	á	bá	**ddə-tàr**	ŋánnà	kín	tà	hɗà
well	3sg	say	father-3pl	DEF	now	3pl	bury

fátàrŋánnə kínì wá

á-m	f-á-tàr	ŋánnə	kínì	wá
PRED-IN	field-PERT-3pl	DEF	C.FOC	COM

And now, their father, who was buried in the field,...

The noun *màmà* 'mother' can occur in the pertensive rather than the relational construction, but in that case it serves as a modifier of a noun rather than the head:

(34)

ùsów	əgdzàrà	màm-á-rwá
ùsáawà	əgdzàr-a	màm-á-rwá
greeting (F)	child-PL	mother-PERT-1sg

Greetings, my brothers and sisters!
[The high tone on the last syllable of *màmárwá* indicates that the speaker is keeping the floor while searching for the next thing to say.]

5 Nominal modification of relational nouns

Nominal modification of relational nouns has the structure $N_{[head]}$-*á*-Pro *gə* $N_{[mod]}$, where the pronoun (PRO) encodes the number of the modifier and *gə* is the preposition 'to'.

(35) dárgə gdzàrà béetàrè séí dóolè

d-á-r	**gə**	**gdzàr-a**	à	bà-ítáré
father-PERT-3sg	TO	child-PL	3sg	say-3pl

séí dóolè
then necessary (H, F)

tádágdzàrá tàrè dəmbá žílé

tá	d-á	gdzàr-á-tàrè	d-əm	mb-á	žílé
3pl	go-GO	child-PL-PERT-3pl	go-IN	house-PERT	man

Parents say that it is necessary for them to marry off their daughters. [*lit.* 'take their daughters to a husband']

(36)

é	ttàrkín	əgdzàrà	wáz-wàhà			
é	ttàr	kínà	əgdzàrà	wázù-a		
eh	how	now	small	exhortation-PL (Fula: *waazu*, Noye 1989)		
kínì	mávàtərtə	gəmárgəgdzàràhà				
kínì	má	và-tər-tə	gə	**m-á-r**	gə	**gdzàr-àhà**
C.FOC	HYP	give-3pl-T	TO	mother-PERT-3sg	TO	child-PL

And how to give some advice to the mothers of those children?

Questions about modifiers of relational nouns have the form NP 3sg:PRO *g wàr-à* NP, where *wàr* is the unspecified human 'who':

(37)

ddəŋàr	gwárónà			
ddə	ŋàr	g	wàr-à	únà
father	3sg	TO	who-CN	DEM

Whose father is he?

6 Definiteness of the head with the third-person pronoun

The purpose of this section is to explain the function of two third-person singular modifying pronouns, *rà* and *ŋàrà*. Although the distinction they represent is not central to the topic of the study, it points to a subdomain seldom marked by modifying pronouns.

A noun preceding the form *ŋàrà* has the root form:

(38)

átsé	áɮàlà	mánùrárà			
ná	wá	á	tsé	á	ɮàlà
DEM	COM	3sg	get up	3sg	go
m-án	**ùr-á-rà**				
HYP-ASSC	man-PERT-3sg				
máɬà	kàtəŋàrómlè				
má	**ɬàkàtə**	**ŋàrà**	úmlè		
HYP	fellow	3sg	another		

He gets up and goes either with his man or with another fellow.

The third-person pronoun *ŋàrà* indicates that the identity of the noun should be recovered from the previous discourse. The third-person pronoun *rà* is used to modify the first mention of the noun. The evidence for this hypothesis comes from natural discourse. Compare the noun *láh* 'song' in the following fragments from the same discourse by the same speaker:

(39)

ámhərɗə	ŋánnà	əgdzər	bàmáɮàɮálà	dəm	fátàrwá
á-m	hərɗə	ŋánnà	əgdzrè	bà	má
PRED-IN	farm	DEF	child	FOC	HYP

ʄà-ʄálà	d-ə̀m	f-á-tàr	wá
go-go	go-IN	field-PERT-3pl	COM

áɓlà làhárà

á	ɓlà	**làh-á-rà**
3sg	send	song-PERT-3sg

While farming, when the child goes to their field, he sings his song.

In the subsequent discourse, seven sentences later, the speaker uses the form *ŋàrà* with the same head noun:

(40) àdəɓlàláxŋàrà ʄàbàdàlyé

à	də̀	ɓlà	**láh**	**ŋàrà**	ʄàb	á	dàlyé
3sg	SEQ	sing	song	3sg	yet	PRED	again

And he sang his song again.

7 Possessive predication

Though Wandala has not lexicalized the verbs 'have', 'possess', or 'own', it has grammaticalized a possessive predication that is distinct from all other predications in the language.

The possessive predication has the form NP1 *án* NP2, where NP1 is the pronominal or nominal subject, interpreted as the possessor; *án* is the associative preposition; and NP2 is the complement of the preposition, the possessum. Subject pronouns in possessive clauses have low tone. The third-person subject pronoun *à* fuses with the associative marker and acquires high tone. All instantiations of NP1 *án* NP2 have possessive meaning:

(41) a. án ʃúŋgù

3sg:ASSC	money

she/he has money

(41) b. y-án ʃúŋgù

1sg:ASSC	money

I have money

(42)

má	bàní	bàɗə̀	mírámyà	**mándìyámyà**
má-á	bàní	bàɗə̀	ìr-á-myà	**mà**
HYP-PRED	concern	all	head-PERT-1INCL	1INCL
án	**dìy-á-myà**			
ASSC	knowledge-PERT-1INCL			
wá	ʃágrónà			
wá	ʃágrà	úna		
COM	well	DEM		

Because we have all of this knowledge, it is good.

All members of the sequence NP1 *án* NP2 must be within the same syntactic group; that is, there cannot be a prosodic or another boundary within the group. If there is a boundary, the sequence NP ASSC NP is not a possessive predication. The boundary is marked by the vowel *e* on the lexical item preceding the associative preposition:

(43) kálkálè ŋázàɗàfáŋgrè

kálkálè	ŋá	zà	ɗàf-á-ŋgrè
properly (F)	1EXCL	eat	food-PERT-1EXCL
án	ə̀ngy-á	**án**	yə̀cìvàcíyà
ASSC	morning-PERT	ASSC	evening

We eat our own food in the morning and in the evening.

The nominal object of possessive predication may have a modifying pronoun coding the number of the subject, regardless of whether the subject is in predicate-initial or predicate-final position. The modifying pronoun occurs in the pertensive construction. It appears that the use of the modifying pronoun with the object of possessive predication indicates permanent as opposed to temporary possession. This hypothesis needs further confirmation. In addition to example (40) above, consider the following:

(44) é, vàcíylàrús ŋánnə̀má ámtàtómlè ə̀dármándòksárà

é,	vàcíy	làrús	ŋánnə̀	má	á-m	
well,	day	marriage	DEF	HYP	PRED-IN	
tàtà	úmlè	**ə̀ddá**	**rà**	**má**	**án**	**dùks-á-rà**
place	some	man	Q	HYP	ASSC	thing-PERT-3sg

Well, the very day of the marriage, if there is a rich person,…

(45) a.

án	dìy-á-rà	ɬə̀ksè
3sg:ASSC	knowledge-PERT-3sg	chief

The chief has his knowledge.

(45) b.

tán	dìy-á-tàrà	ɬə̀ks-àhà
3pl:ASSC	knowledge-PERT-3pl	chief-PL

The chiefs have their knowledge.

The evidence that the form *án* is indeed the associative preposition is provided by adverbial complements of time and associative complements of the verb, all marked by *án*:

(46) **án** **wùdr-á-rà** tápyàntámbà

án	wùdr-á-rà	tá	pyà-n	t-ámbà
ASSC	situation-PERT-3sg	3pl	forbid-3sg	T-house

In her situation, they confine her to home.

(47) žílé	ádá	názù	ádəndàvànánŋàné			
žílé	á	d-á	názù	á	də̀	ndàvà-ŋ
man	3sg	go-GO	that	3sg	FUT	ask-3sg
án	ŋànè					
ASSC	3sg					

The man brings that with which he is going to ask for [the girl].

The evidence that the construction NP1 ASSC NP2 indeed codes possessive predication is provided by the contrast with the construction NP1 ASSC:PL NP2, which codes the predication of co-existence:

(I) POSSESSIVE PREDICATION

(48) án mùksè
3sg:ASSC wife
He has a wife.

(II) CO-EXISTENTIAL PREDICATION

(49) ántàrà mùks-á-rà
3sg:ASSC:PL wife-PERT-3sg
He is with his wife.

(50) ŋán tàrà pàtróŋárwà
ŋà ántárà pàtróŋ-á-rwà
1INCL ASSC:PL boss-PERT-1sg
We are together with my boss. (not *we have my boss)

8 Possessive interpretations of existential predications

In addition to the dedicated possessive predication construction, Wandala can express possessive predication through existential affirmative, negative, and interrogative constructions. For the negative and interrogative modalities, the existential construction is the main means to express possession.

The existential predicator *áŋkwà* is not a verb, as it does not take subject pronouns and cannot occur with tense, mood, or aspect markers. It always occurs in clause-initial position, followed by a single nominal or pronominal argument. The existential predication can have a possessive interpretation when the nominal argument has a modifying pronoun in the pertensive construction. The relevant structure has the form *áŋkwà* N-Pro:

(51) áŋkwà dìyárwà dìgìyá
áŋkwà **dìy-á-rwà** dìgìyá
exist knowledge-PERT-1sg behold
I have my knowledge, behold.

Without the modifying pronoun, the possessive interpretation is ruled out:

(52)

ám	hùɗá	hàyè[pause]	dìyàkùrdíyáŋkwà	yàwè	
ám	hùɗ-á	hàyè	dìyà-kùr-díyà	**áŋkwà**	**yàwè**
IN	belly-PERT	river	know-2pl-know	exist	water

In the river, you know, there is water.

But even with a modifying pronoun, the construction does not have to be interpreted as possessive:

(53)

áŋkwà	dàd-á-myà
exist	father-PERT-1INCL

God exists. (not 'we have a father' or 'our father exists', the latter excluded by the pertensive modification)

The existential predication of the form *áŋkwà* N-Pro, followed by the question marker *hè*, is the main means to code polar questions about possession:

(54) a.

áŋkwà	gdz-á-**rá**	hè
exist	child-PERT-3sg	Q

Does he have a child? (the interrogative clause has high tone preceding the interrogative marker)

(54) b.

áŋkwà	bə̀ls-á-rá	hè
exist	horse-PERT-3sg	Q

Does he have a horse?

The negative existential construction is used to code the absence of the possessum. The possessum is followed by a pronoun. The negative existential predicator is *ɓákà*. It can follow or precede the subject:

(55)

áyáwə̀lvá	rùɓákà		
á	yà-wà	ə̀lvà-á-rwà	ɓákà
well	1sg-DET	word-PERT-1sg	NEG.EX

Well, I have no words.

(56)

ŋánkínì	sé	àhàyà	bà	dónə̀	ŋánnà			
ŋán	kínì	sé	à	hàyà	bà	dó	nə̀	ŋánnà
3sg	C.FOC	only	3sg	like	FOC	man	DEM	DEF
ɓákà	péɗárnàkà							
ákà	**péɗà-á-r**			nà	kà			
NEG.EX	means-PERT-3sg			DEM	NEG			

She, she likes only the man that does not have any means.

Without a modifying pronoun, the negative existential predication cannot have a possessive interpretation:

(57) ùrà fáɬìmɓákà
ùrà fá ɬìmà ɓákà
person put ears NEG.EX
There is nobody who minds.

9 Conclusions

Within the domain of modification, Wandala makes a distinction between the modification of relational nouns and the modification of all other categories, viz. verbs, nouns, adjectives, and adverbs. The latter type of modification uses the pertensive marker *á*, which is suffixed to the head. Modification of relational nouns has two constructions, one used for modification by pronouns and the other for modification by nouns. When the head of the pertensive modification is a noun, such a construction may receive a possessive interpretation.

Though Wandala does not have a grammaticalized form coding possessive modification, it has grammaticalized a possessive predication that is distinct from all other predications in the language. The possessive predication is marked by the structure NP1 ASSC NP2, where NP1 is the possessor and NP2 is the possessum. This construction is in contrast with the co-existential predication marked by the form NP1 ASSC:PL NP2.

References

Dixon, R. M. W. 2010. *Basic linguistic theory.* Vol 2. *Grammatical topics.* Oxford: Oxford University Press.

Frajzyngier, Zygmunt. 1977. 'On the intransitive copy pronouns in Chadic', *Studies in African Linguistics* Supplement 7: 73–84.

——.2011. 'Possessive subject pronouns in Wandala: Point of view of the subject', pp. 47–64 of *Copy pronouns. Case studies from African languages*, edited by Anne Storch, Gratien G. Atindogbé, and Roger M. Blench Cologne: Rüdiger Köppe.

——.2012. *A grammar of Wandala.* Berlin and New York: Mouton de Gruyter.

——.to appear. 'Non-aprioristic typology as a discovery tool', in *Functional-historical approaches to explanation: In honor of Scott DeLancey*, edited by Tim Thornes, Erik Andvik, Gwen Hyslop, and Joana Jansen. Amsterdam: Benjamins.

——and Jan Mycielski. 1998. 'On some fundamental problems of mathematical linguistics', pp. 295–310 of *Mathematical and computational analysis of natural language*, edited by Carlos Martin-Vide. Amsterdam/Philadelphia: Benjamins.

——, with Erin Shay. 2002. *A grammar of Hdi.* Berlin: Mouton de Gruyter.

——and Erin Shay. 2003. *Explaining language structure through systems interaction.* Amsterdam/Philadelphia: Benjamins.

Matthews, Peter. 1997. *The concise Oxford dictionary of linguistics.* Oxford: Oxford University Press.

Noye, Dominique. 1989. *Dictionnaire foulfouldé-français: dialecte peul du Diamaré, Nord-Cameroun; illustrations de Christian Seignobos.* Paris: P. Geuthner, Librairie orientaliste.

12

Spirits of the forest, the wind, and new wealth: defining some of the possibilities, and limits, of Kamula possession

MICHAEL WOOD

1 Some mainly Melanesian arguments about possession

In discussions at our workshop we at times struggled to come up with a definition of possession that would cover all our concerns. Some participants suggested that possession in its ur-form involved a 'relationship' or 'association' between a person and another entity. In this chapter I highlight some recent contributions from within anthropology to property talk that qualify this point. Following Robbins (2006) and Stasch (2009) I argue that the relational view of possession can rest on an 'over-social' model of property and offer, as an anti-social supplement, an emphasis on possession and ownership as exclusion, as exemplifying control by others.

In our workshop relational notions of possession were contrasted with Western property notions that were, perhaps, understood as intrinsically anti-social and antithetical to local non-Western concepts. In this kind of rhetoric the Western concept of ownership entails absolute and exclusive individual rights to use, alienate, and exclude, with these rights entrenched in norms of commodification and commensurability through price-based market exchanges (Carpenter, Katyal, and Riley 2009: 1045–6). More relational, and sometimes collective, notions of possession are typically contrasted to this globally hegemonic understanding. And it is often argued that understanding possession as relationship contains greater capacity for registering cultural and linguistic specificities that may be incommensurable with Western accounts of value and property.

But I argue that the relational concept of possession can itself risk excluding forms of otherness and difference that may be crucial to local understandings of possession and property (Stasch 2009). This happens because relational, or 'social', accounts of possession can replicate certain standard Anglo-American understandings of the relationship between identification and sociality where difference is often external to such sociality. Relational accounts can replicate understandings of property, found for example, in some strands of Anglo-American legal theory that have defined property in purely social terms as a 'bundle of rights' people hold against other people (Robbins 2006: 179). This shift to property as a social relation is an amendment to earlier, more individualistic, notions of property as a relationship between a person and a thing. In the relational accounts, some linked to Hegel (1967), the core of property refers us to possession defined as the 'intersubjectively recognizable identification of a characteristic (object) to a specific person (subject)' (Schroeder 1998: 38). This kind of possession by forms of identification can be presented as logically fundamental to the existence of other property relations—such as alienation and use (Robbins 2006: 180). My concern here is that identification or identity, rather than difference, becomes the key to understanding possession.

Recently Strathern (1988, 1999) has attempted to avoid some of these difficulties by trying to think about Melanesian material without deploying the categories of 'individual' and 'society'. She tries to use Melanesian concepts to re-think Western concepts. In her account persons and things are not taken to be naturally distinct. Subjects and objects are analysed less as pre-defined entities and more as outcomes of social relationships, exchange activities, and talk. Things insofar as they exist tend to be discussed as attributes of a person such that persons take the form of partible entities. All 'objects' are extensions of a person (understood as a human, spirit, ancestral figure, totem, etc.). Things and individuals simply do not exist in the way often implied by some Western property theory. Through this understanding of a person, the argument can incorporate others, but does so in a way that typically highlights their relational equivalence rather than radical difference. Finally, Strathern's destabilization of distinctions between person and things can also be understood as an extension of those strands of Western property thinking, and ideas about the 'gift', that are primarily based on forms of identification (Schroeder 1998). Such accounts often rest on a relational notion of an underlying 'sociality' that allows difference, and others, little role in the constitution of that sociality (Stasch 2009).

In this chapter I tend to counter-emphasize the role of difference by highlighting features of exclusion and degrees of dispossession in Kamula property talk. What emerges is a social field of multiple claims to control and possess that involve both Kamula and spirits. From the Kamula's perspective this often involves relationships of estrangement, and limits on possession, as much as identification and full control of resources and valuables.

2 Possession, spirits, and sources

In addition, emphasizing local relational understandings of property does not always allow much of a role for the western property concepts that now permeate the Papua New Guinea (PNG) state and all forms of locally relevant capital. Recent work in PNG has indicated the role of the state and resource extractors in eliciting specific kinds of property owning groups, persons, and relationships (Weiner and Glaskin 2007). The literature documenting such processes emphasizes the co-creation of new property claiming groups (such as incorporated land groups, landowner companies and other corporations) and associated 'traditional' customs, especially concerning land ownership. It might also appear that the recent history of property in PNG involves a tension between declining relational understandings and the expansion of private property claims, such as state and corporate claims to monopolies on gas, oil, and timber rights. But as I show below, in parts of PNG these new claims to property have also involved the extension of ownership and possessive claims over the same resources by bush spirits (*masalai* in Tok Pisin) or other kinds of spirits.

Robbins has recently argued that in parts of PNG 'possession is foregrounded in accounts of the way spirits own property' (2006: 180). For Urapmin speakers the bush spirits' 'grasping possession' of places and resources is the fundamental fact about them (Robbins 2006: 180). Equally among the Kamula there are a diversity of spirits who possess many things—cliffs, large bodies of water, large trees, domestic pigs that can manifest in this world as wild pigs, certain swamps, and some mountains. Some of these spirits played a crucial productive role in Kamula life—they participated in raiding, in ritual, and helped cure Kamula ailments. *Dali patale* were, and still are, responsible for some men becoming superb hunters. These spirits would sometimes actively participate in a hunt as an unseen double to the hunter—when he shot at game a spirit would also do so ensuring that the game was killed. While spirits helped the Kamula to create significant value (meat, health, and ritual effects), these spirits were also dangerous and could sanction the Kamula with illness and/or death for breaches of taboos or perceived lack of reciprocity.

Given this understanding of spirits two points, further developed below, can be made. First, following on from Robbins spirits play a role in Kamula property thinking in ways that supplement more relational understandings of possession, things, and people. While some Kamula understanding of possession and ownership involves processes of identification, we also need to think about the possession of places and valuable things by human-like, and non-human, others. Second, the Kamula's spirits, in varying degrees now often control, sometimes embody, own, or are the origin of, virtually all forms of new wealth now being produced in the Kamula's world. Spirits now own and run their own logging concessions (Wood 1998), others are the origin of oil and another kind controls valuables such as money, guns, knives, and steel axes. The spirits were, and still are, crucial to the Kamula's mode of hunting and social production, but they have now become spirits of commodity capitalism.

The texts I use to support these points emerged from recorded conversations between myself, and typically one Kamula speaker, often with supporting input from those gathered at the recording session. Some of the Kamula texts about land were, in 1999 and 2000, transcribed, and then intensively analysed with Kamula co-researchers, and the linguist David Wilkins. In 2009 I also had Hawo Kulu, an SIL trained research assistant, translate from English into Kamula about 20 pages of text explaining carbon trade from the perspective of the developers—who in early 2009 were Carbon Planet and Nupan. We also worked on material developed by those opposed to the carbon trade. The most important of these documents were the written opinions of a lawyer working for the logging company Rimbunan Hijau. The material reflects many of the concerns and debates ongoing among the Kamula about the emerging carbon market and the often highly speculative claims made by carbon brokers to have secured ownership of the relevant resources. I am interested in showing how this recently, and only partially, developed resource was linked, by some Kamula, to bush spirits, albeit implicitly and tentatively. But first readers may like to learn a little more about the Kamula and their language. I then provide some brief examples of the Kamula's more 'relational' talk of property interests in land, before moving on to emphasize the way spirits both facilitate, and limit, Kamula claims to valuable resources.

3 The Kamula and their language

The word 'Kamula' can refer to a language, speakers with rights to that language and non-speakers with primarily patrilineal links to those speakers. Kamula is spoken mainly at Wawoi Falls, in the Western Province of the PNG, where some seven hundred speakers reside. It is also spoken in a number of other villages such as Somokopa, and, in the south towards Gogodala land, Makapa, Kamiyame, Pikiwa, and Bamustu. The total number of Kamula speakers may be around 1,400. However, in the southern villages Kamula is being replaced with other languages such as Dipiyaso and Doso. The ancestors of Kamula now living in the southern villages moved down from Kamula country to be closer to schools, goods, and education mainly during the 1950s and 1960s. The last major population shift occurred in the 1970s when a large group of people living in the south returned north to Somokopa. Population movements have been a feature of Kamula history over the last 90 years or so. And as a result the Kamula are now saturated with capacities to speak other languages and create forms of identification with non-Kamula groups. And there are relatively few Kamula kin-groups that have origins within Kamula territory linked to creator figures like Kaiyalo and Hadlipi. In a sense most of the time when

I worked with Kamula it was actually relatively difficult to be in the presence of 'true' Kamula people.

The Kamula language is a family level isolate adjacent to the Bosavi family group of languages (Ross 2005). Final verbs take a maximum of 3 affixes—one prefix and two suffixes (Routamaa 1994: 18). Tense, mood, and a switch reference system are conveyed by these suffixes. Noun words do not generally distinguish number, gender, or case. And, apart from some kin terms, that do not evoke an easily analysable pattern, and a few other nouns, there is no division between alienably and inalienably possessed nouns. Body parts are generally possessed, but such possessive forms are not obligatory. Other nouns 'including possessions, household / clothing articles are optionally preceded by a possessive pronoun' (Routamaa 1994: 12–13). Subject, object, and possessive pronouns have the same form (Routamaa 1994: 45), but Kamula has a set of inalienably possessed possessive nouns, equivalent to mine, yours, ours (Routamaa 1994: 14–15).

4 Person, place, and possession

These possessive nouns are routinely applied to personal possessions, land, and other entities such as totems. Such possessions are also represented as materializations of social relationships and forms of identification. And the Kamula often make subtle adjudications on the extent of the identification between person and thing possessed. The following texts shows how Kamula talk of person–place relationships can be saturated with reference to concepts like 'equivalence', 'likeness', 'replacement', and 'appearance'. The result is a particular form of identification that falls just short of the full ontological unity of person and place. Person and place both actively enter into transactions with each other, but in these texts, the emphasis is on similarity rather than fused identity:

Text 1

When Sam goes to Musipi the men say that 'Now you take on your father's appearance (and likeness)'. And so you are enhanced and equivalent. Why? Because you stay at Musipi, Musipi becomes equivalent by taking on your appearance or transforms into your father's appearance. Because Sam stays at Musipi, he is appropriately matched, and is strong and has spirit (Wood 2004: 247).

The text outlines how person and place are mutually implicated in their co-constitution. In these kinds of accounts place becomes like a person just as a person becomes like that place. Each are agents in the other's coming to 'equivalence' via transactions in 'appearance' and name. As a result of these transactions person and place also become 'powerful', 'enhanced', and enlivened (Wood 2004). When fully engaged, person and land each gain attributes such that they are more human and more like a place. These attributes are attached to them and like clothes these attributes can be 'detached' or 'taken off' when the relationship ends. The end of the relationship is that place and person become lifeless and without vigour and spirit (*nesama*). In addition, the person–place relation enacts a power to intensify the historical associations of both land and person—the relationship brings past time to the present so that dead family members become a more intimate part of both the place and the person (Weiner 1992: 210).

Such accounts also emphasize that attachment to the land derives from action—such as being on the land, using it and other activities that inscribe your memory into it. In reference to land the Kamula, like the Korowai (Stasch 2009), are Lockeans. Converting belonging into something like ownership is achieved by working on the land to make a house or a garden. But this emphasis on action serves to highlight the contingency of the attachments which can be lost as soon as the interaction ceases.

These kind of transactions in similarity can also be used to assert notions of more exclusive ownership that are more like claims enacted by radically powerful others such as the spirits and to an extent by developers. This possibility is conveyed by the following text. In contrast to the emphasis on a relational interaction between person and place presented in Text 1, some Kamula emphasize that these relationships between person and place are based on possession, and that a possessive relationship is prior to the formation of the person–place relation, rather than vice versa:

Text 2

And so the presence of where Sam's father lived is there. When Sam is living there (Sam's father's memory and Sam) are equal and made equivalent, Sam gets his father's appearance. When Sam's father dies, Sam replaces him. Sam gained his father's appearance, the land and the place Musipi and the lake. Why? Because all these land related things are mine.

Sam's inheritance is presented here as deriving from his ownership of 'the things of the land' rather than from relational interactions between person, place, and father. This is highlighted by the final, and dramatic, switching back to the first person position, and the claim that ownership can be distinguished from, and made causally foundational to, the kind of similarities between person and place evident in Text 1. Given this, Kamula accounts of place–person relationships are best understood as involving differences about the salience of relational and more exclusive possessory claims.

5 Fathers

In the context of new resource developments, the Kamula have intensified claims to exclusive possession. One indication of this trend is the use of the Kamula word for father (*a*) to translate the recently introduced terms 'landowner' (*taena y'a* 'the land's father') and the Melanesian Pidgin *papa bilong graun*. To be a father or a mother of a thing is now presented as equivalent to owning that entity, especially land, in a way that is potentially subject to compensation. While these areas of compensation to individuals and landowner groups have expanded in the new natural resource economy, the use of the term father and mother to related kinds of ownership, also points us to kinship relations, especially parenting, as a dominant Kamula way of thinking about belonging and possession. It is also worth noting here that, in the past, Kamula fathers and mothers did not have autonomous control over their children. Crucial here were certain affines and matrilateral kin who were able to control whether a wife had children and whether these children would survive till they were adolescents. If they became angry they could curse a man's wife, or children, with the effect that either the wife would not have children or the children would become sick or die. This power was conventionally understood to be a property of the child's mother's younger brother who some Kamula described as being their 'real mother'. This man also had the capacity to take and use at will any desirable property of his elder sister's husband. As a result key components of fathering and mothering were distributed between multiple agents such that the health of any child and the capacity to control personal property were not actually controlled by the parents. These ideas and practices associated with the mother's brother have been largely abandoned which has lead to the rise of a more autonomously controlling sense of a father's capacities. This change supplements talk of a father being the individual controller, or owner, of a thing or land.

Reference to being 'the father of the land', or a sago swamp, commonly occurs in talk of control. Such a 'father' can exert considerable power. When Hadlipi, as 'father' of the sago swamps close to Sutuma, was reported by a neighbouring resident of an unrelated kin group to have spoken about the possibility that the sago in these swamps would soon be exhausted, the response of some of Hadlipi's neighbours was to immediately start talking about leaving Sutuma and establishing a new village on land not controlled by Hadlipi. His reported talk was taken as a threat to prevent the Sutuma residents from using the sago swamps in the land he controlled. His capacity to enforce such a threat was not questioned. But his authority on this issue was not just based on his status as senior landowner, it also rested on the widely held belief that he had within him an evil spirit (*aiyalma*) that could devour people. Prior to this incident Hadlipi had demanded that no one, except himself, would be allowed to build stores that were separate from their houses on his land. This has meant that he, and his immediate family, operated the only free standing store in the entire community. For other traders his ruling was more inconvenient than fully disabling—some of Hadlipi's competitors developed innovative extensions to their houses that continue to function as stores. These stories highlight how many long-term residents of Sutuma often experience home as belonging to, and subject to degrees of control by, someone else who many think has the attributes of an *aiyalma*.

6 *Aiyalma* and edging toward exclusive possession

I now want to further consider elements of exclusion in Kamula talk of ownership and possession in places associated with powerful spirits. What I focus on in this section are beings or powers called *aiyalma*. *Aiyalma* is something powerful and has a number of senses such as 'prohibited' or to be avoided, 'law', 'rule', and 'dangerous beings' including 'evil spirits' that cannibalize people. As place-based spirits *aiyalma* do not easily enter into social relations with the Kamula. Typically they are known less by their capacity to support Kamula and more by their power to kill or make ill any person who transgresses rules governing a place. They can exclude humans from fully utilizing the site or even visiting it. The *aiyalma*, and some ancestral figures, can exert claims that verge on ownership by exercising something like Blackstone's understanding of possession as exclusive dominion (Rose 1998: 601, Robbins 2006). The Kamula are interested in merging some of this kind of possessive power, and otherness, into their social relations with place and in their property claims.

The *aiyalma*'s powers do vary from place to place and over time. Some can become quiet and less angry, leave the place, or die. Where the power is diminished people start to intrude more freely onto the domain previously occupied by the spirit. One older man explained such developments at Diliki situated on the Wawoi River:

Text 3

The *aiyalma* is not there. It disappeared. The water is cool and lifeless. When the *nesama* ('spirit' or 'likeness') is there, the *aiyalma* thing is there.... Before the *nesama* was angry. Now it is quiet and satisfied. It is quiet and cool. Before Diliki was really angry. But the father died. The children are staying there quietly.

This text is saturated with complex references to Kamula understandings of place, but what I would emphasize is the way *aiyalma* are bound to place by taking on the proper name of that place (Diliki) and by being continuously, and 'inalienably' (Weiner 1992) linked to that place through reproduction and inter-generational transmission in a manner somewhat similar to processes outlined for ordinary humans in Texts 1 and 2.

Another powerful place, Magela, a swamp with blood red water, can cause people to bleed to death and also assist Kamula in their hunting. Pouring Magela's water on a bow can make pigs and cassowaries easily bleed to death when shot. Magela also contains other possibilities:

Text 4

There is an *aiyalma* and the water is red.... Inside the swamp you sometimes hear a noise like the buzzing drone of hornets. Sometimes you hear it and then it disappears and then it comes back. What is there we don't know gas, oil or gold? (fieldnotes of talk with Nathan Dekopowe 29/11/05).

Places and associated *aiyalma* have a capacity to become, and contain, what the colonial periphery values and creates. A few place-based *aiyalma* appropriate these new things into themselves. One monster is known for being made up of knives and steel axe heads that are used to flay any intruders. This figure embodies an equation of *aiyalma*, Europeans and their uniquely valuable things: during the early phases of contacts between the Kamula and the colonial order steel axes were initially referred to in Kamula as *aiyalma peya* (prohibited axes) and Europeans themselves were *aiyalma opa* (prohibited/powerful men). This kind of conjunction of *aiyalma* and the colonial persist in other bush spirits who exhibit an equivalent capacity to replicate and own things of value associated with current forms of natural resource extraction (such as oil and logging operations).

Another relationship between landscape and *aiyalma* is made evident in Kamula accounts of being in the forest hunting. Sometimes a hunter is threatened by 'evil spirits' (*aiyalma*), that often take the form of pigs. If this happens the hunter immediately seeks refuge on the buttresses, and roots, of trees. The evil spirits have no capacity to injure the hunter when he is so positioned off the ground. In this very specific context the ground itself facilitates the flow of dangerous powers that have the capacity to temporarily alienate Kamula from their land.

Some *aiyalma*, and other bush spirits, have had their residences damaged by recent logging and have become angry at this dispossession. Damage to one well-known place resulted in a number of accidents involving vehicles. In another site a bush spirit (*banakaka*), whose house (a tree) was destroyed by road construction, now threatens any vehicle that drives by without acknowledging the spirit's presence by tooting the horn. In these contexts the landscape is experienced as risky, volatile, and transgressive (Stasch 2009: 32). It is not under the effective control of the Kamula.

7 Climate change, clean wind, and oil as theft

I now want to look at how the Kamula talk about their recent entanglements with carbon trading and climate change. The most recent form of development to emerge as relevant to the Kamula, it is also the most unstable and provisional. No one yet really knows if such a market can be established in PNG and nor is it clear if the proposal now before the Kamula is anything more than a speculative scam. In the new carbon economy polluters would pay the Kamula to preserve their timber resource as a carbon sink that would off-set their pollution. But it is not clear to the Kamula, nor anyone else, what these benefits might amount to. Since PNG lacks specific legislation covering carbon trade, the proposed Kamula Doso carbon project may well be illegal. But the amounts of money that may be involved are dazzling even if they are impossible to work out accurately. Using figures from a Macquarie Capital Advisors (2007) proposal—at a market price of $US4 per tonne, total revenue might be $US15.7 million per year, at $US10 it might be $56 million. Or it could be some other amount.

Like the carbon brokers, Kamula understandings of their property claims in carbon are imaginative and provisional. They are partly based on 'awareness' information provided by various carbon brokers who have visited the region and on material circulated by logging companies opposed to any carbon credit scheme that would stop logging in the area. Some Kamula think that a carbon market involves Europeans acquiring the 'good wind' produced by Kamula forests and reciprocating by sending their bad or polluted wind to the Kamula. While the Kamula may get paid for the transaction the result is that Kamula trees and plants will not grow well.

Bakadiye, a man of around 60 with limited understanding of English, provided the following highly improvised example of how the Kamula might talk about threats to their access to good air. In this account he attempts to link what he has heard about climate change and deforestation to changes in air quality. While readers may think his merging of logging and carbon trading is mistaken, it is worth noting that some developers have proposed this conjunction for Kamula forests and it is a serious possibility under proposed carbon trading schemes being discussed under the auspices of the UN (McKinsey 2009).

Bakadiye conveys a sense of how the new property regime of carbon leads to a sense of threat and disruption very different to the kinds of equivalences the Kamula make between person and place outlined at the beginning of this chapter. What he is interested in is the possible equivalence between outright theft and the resulting negative effects of climate change manifesting in Kamula country. He outlines a theory of climate change that is derived from the effects of logging. He is worried by the possibility that resources are simply being appropriated ('stolen') without the Kamula's knowledge. He also explores some conjectures about how the Kamula can make property claims to unpolluted air or what are now called 'ecological services'. In the process he implicitly links bush spirits (in this case *dali patale*) to these property claims:

Text 5

And so yes we are living in the forest. Our forest, our trees, our weeds, our vine, our *soso* rope. Our *woli* rope. Our *tototi*.... The leaves of these that are living there make it cold there and we are good and our lives are good. If that diminishes the heat will make us sick. When we get sick what will we eat?... And the wind is really powerful. Its name is wind. What makes the wind come?... The wind comes with a really loud roaring noise.... From the fig tree's (*bakati*) big leaves the big wind comes bringing thick cloud. And that *to* tree will bring the wind. That *bolipi* will bring the wind. That *mipi* will bring the wind. That *kopola* brings the wind. *Hoholapi* brings the wind. *Aliama* brings the wind. And so given that what is the real issue that you come and cut down trees? Here inside our place the good life will disappear. The company...we don't want it to come. What is the real cause of making our country bad? You are a company man. We are ground people, forest people, place people living here and we are happy and good.

And so you cut the trees that will bring the wind's power to us. Us forest people, our wind. It is not good that you steal our wind. The origin is not yours, the origin is mine. Our trees, forest people, are ours. Our wind is ours.

Bakadiye presents the Kamula experience of carbon related environmental change in 'otherness-charged terms' (Stasch 2009: 47). There is a continuity with equally other saturated experiences of place outlined earlier. In this case the other is the company that may cause massive environmental change. He is also offering a provisional theory of the Kamula's ownership of unpolluted air via claims about the link between the wind, trees, the Kamula, and, to an extent, tree dwelling spirits who inhabit four out of the six trees he mentions. Bakadiye is stressing this connection in his naming of the trees since bush spirits live in less than 10 per cent of the total number of trees (around 300) on which I have collected reasonable data. In some accounts the spirit (*nesama*) of the tree (*dali*) is said to be the bush spirit (*dali patale*—with *patale* not analysable). So most of the trees Bakadiye mentions are *dali patale* and/or their dwelling places.

Bakadiye's analysis was offered in a context where any Kamula control of carbon, and the air, was possibly being alienated and diminished by carbon-brokers who were making up their own innovative property claims while Kamula were attempting to do the same. Bakadiye's account of a carbon market as appropriation, and environmental depletion, is reiterated in other accounts of the effects of natural resource projects. In one account of the development of oil fields, one Kamula argued that the origin of the oil was the blood of a two headed dragon (an *aiyalma*) that lived underground. When developers take this blood, or oil, out of the ground, the result is the drying up of the ground in such a way that plants and trees will no longer grow. The lack of blood in the ground means that the environment will change into something like a desert. Both oil and gas projects may also involve outright theft—with the developers able to drill under ground into numerous oil or gas fields without locals being aware that this was happening. Some Kamula think they will only have a chance of monitoring what the developer takes out if the gas or oil is transported above the ground. And some Kamula, such as Bakadiye, see carbon trading in similar terms arguing that the Europeans are stealing the air the Kamula own.

8 Conclusion

I have argued that Kamula property thinking needs to be considered as permeated by notions not just of belonging, attachment, and detachment, but also by degrees of estrangement and exclusion. I have relied on the assumption that exclusion is central to any notion of property, ownership, and possession (Penalver and Katyal 2007: 103). Developing arguments made by Robbins (2006) I made the point that spirits, who can exert exclusive control, and occupancy, in parts of the landscape, mediate

Kamula understandings of possession and ownership of many valuables. Showing how the Kamula's control of resources and land were often limited by bush spirits highlighted exclusion as a key element of the Kamula's understanding of property. But as we saw with claims to the wind, spirits also facilitate Kamula claims to an interest in new valuable resources. These claims to resources are structured by the constraints of the spirits, who more effectively identify with, control, and possess the new resources than do the Kamula. This asymmetry derives from a fundamental feature of Kamula cosmology where potentially every feature in the manifest world has an unseen double or spirit (*nesama*) that is often a more determinant part of that entity than what we might call its expression in this world. Kamula property claims to new valuables (logs, oil, pollution) negotiate this distinction by reference to the bush spirits' often more powerful claims to possess those resources.

Kamula property talk thus indicates a fascination with the imaginative possibilities of spirits in various ways controlling, and possessing, natural resources valued by capital. This fusion of spirits and commodified natural resources—unstable, revocable, but generative of often astounding possibilities concerning the creation, and loss, of wealth for the Kamula—defines some of the contexts, and content, of current Kamula talk about what they do, and do not, possess. In the new era of natural resource appropriation, and commodified protective conservation of nature, spirits continue to partly structure the way value is produced, possessed, and alienated. As a result Kamula property claims are not just social relationships defined by forms of identification, but are also crucially defined by exclusionary relations with powerful, often radically different, others. Our own understandings of possession and property may need to take more account of this possibility.

References

Carpenter, Kristen, Sonia Katyal, and Angela Riley. 2009. 'In defence of property', *The Yale Law Journal* 118: 1022–125.

Hegel, Georg. 1967. *Philosophy of right*. Translated with notes by T. M. Knox. Oxford: Oxford University Press.

McKinsey & Co. 2009. Supporting the development of PNG's national REDD and climate change plans. Available at http://pngexposed.wordpress.com/2010/09 27/mckinseys-paid-us2-2-for-4-months-work-on-redd/.

Macquarie Capital Advisors Limited 2007(?). Avoided deforestation: Kamula Doso and Western Province. Unpublished manuscript.

Penalver, Eduardo and Sonia Katyal. 2007. 'Property outlaws', *University of Pennsylvania Law Review* 1095: 101–87.

Robbins, Joel. 2006. 'Properties of nature, properties of culture: ownership, recognition, and the politics of nature in a Papua New Guinea society', pp. 171–94 of *Reimagining political ecology*, edited by Aletta Biersack and James Greenberg. Durham: Duke University Press.

Rose, Carol. 1998. 'Canons of property talk, or, Blackstone's Anxiety', *The Yale Law Journal* 108 (3): 601–32.

Ross, Malcolm. 2005. 'Pronouns as a preliminary diagnostic for grouping Papuan languages', pp. 15–66 of *Papuan pasts: Cultural, linguistic and biological histories of Papuan-speaking peoples*, edited by Andrew Pawley, Robert Attenborough, Robin Hide, and Jack Golson. Canberra: Pacific Linguistics.

Routamaa, Judy. 1994. *Kamula grammar essentials.* Ukarumpa: Summer Institute of Linguistics.

Schroeder, Jeanne. 1998. *The Vestal and Fasces: Hegel, Lacan, property and the feminine.* Berkeley: University of California Press.

Stasch, Rupert. 2009. *Society of others: Kinship and mourning in a West Papuan place.* Berkeley: University of California Press.

Strathern, Marilyn. 1988. *The gender of the gift.* Berkeley: University of California Press.

——. 1999. *Property, Substance and effect: Anthropological essays on persons and things.* London: The Athlone Press.

Weiner, Annette. 1992. *Inalienable possessions: The paradox of keeping-while-giving.* Berkeley: University of California Press.

Weiner, James and Katie Glaskin (eds). 2007. *Customary land tenure and registration and Papua New Guinea: Anthropological perspectives.* Canberra: ANU E Press.

Wood, Michael. 1998. 'Logging, women and submarines—some changes in Kamula men's access to transformative power', *Oceania* 68(4): 228–48.

——. 2004. 'Places, loss and logging among the Kamula', *The Asia Pacific Journal of Anthropology* 5(3): 245–56.

13

Being and belonging: exchange, value, and land ownership in the Western Highlands of Papua New Guinea

ROSITA HENRY

1 Introduction

Since colonial times there has been a division of land in Papua New Guinea (PNG) between 'customary' land and 'alienated land'. In line with colonial government policy that indigenous land interests should be protected, land could not be bought directly from customary landowners by outside individuals or companies, but could only be leased after prior acquisition by the state. Today, all over PNG, so called 'alienated land' (that is, land that has been acquired by the state) is held uneasily by the state and/or its current lessees in the face of the customary landowners for whom land is not something that is conceptually alienable. As Gregory (1982: 163) notes, 'Land is the ultimate inalienable gift and . . . it is not easily converted into the simple private property right of an individual' (see also Weiner 1992 on 'inalienable possession').

In this chapter I explore changing concepts of land ownership among speakers of Temboka (Tembagla) in the Western Highlands of Papua New Guinea, in the circumstances of state intervention in transactions concerning land. I pay particular attention to anthropological debates on property, theories of value and the role of land in how value continues to be measured and realized in the Western Highlands. My exploration is via a case study on the relationship between the Temboka speaking Ganiga people and their neighbour Joe Leahy, who established a coffee plantation on their land (the subject of the well-known documentary films *Joe Leahy's Neighbours* and *Black Harvest*). I analyse the complexities of the relationship between the Ganiga and Joe Leahy and provide an update on the fortunes of the coffee plantation today. The Ganiga are part of a large 'tribe', Ulka, numbering about 7,000 people who live in the Nebilyer Valley of the Western Highlands province. Ulka has six levels of named subdivision. The two higher level segments are Ulka Kundulge and Ulka Pinga. The Ganiga are on the Ulka Kundulge side along with the Gaimelka, with whom they were about to engage in a 'tribal fight' in the film *Joe Leahy's Neighbours*. But, when it comes to conflict with others, the Gaimelka are the Ganiga's closest allies. A central feature of social organization in the Nebilyer Valley and other parts of the Western Highlands is the pairing of tribes and tribal segments. This tendency towards pairing occurs not only in relation to the segmentary tribal structure but also in many other aspects of social life.

In relation to land, Ganiga and other Temboka speaking people use the term *ma(i)* (*graun* in Tok Pisin, which is a local lingua franca, and one of three official languages of PNG) or *kolya* (*ples* in Tok Pisin). But both *mai* and *kolya* and their Tok Pisin translations (*graun* and *ples*) are more than mere ground or soil. They carry value through association with human sociality, activity, practice, lived experience, and memory. In other words, they stand for social relations. For example, *as ples* (*lit.* base place) refers to 'original place, hometown, and birthplace' but can also be used to refer to the original *people* of that place, the customary landowners themselves. These are referred to as *kolya pul* (*lit.* 'place base/root'); also used is the phrase *pul yab* (*lit.* 'base people'). *Pul* can also translate as ancestor, god, and foundational essence. Thus, the core of what it means to be human is to be planted in some place and to be sustained by its *kopong* ('grease' or 'fat'; *gris* in Tok Pisin), the substance that is constitutive of life itself and a fundamental resource in the cycles of reciprocity and exchange that define social life.

David Graeber (2005: 451–2) defines value: 'as a way people's own actions become meaningful to them, how they take on importance by becoming incorporated into some larger system of meaning'. Graeber links value to the creative energy that people put into creating social persons. In the Western Highlands, in order to effect the reproduction and growth of social persons, much creative energy is focused on the transformation of land, as mere ground or soil, the material source of exchange relations, into place (*kolya*, *ples*), valued as an articulation of human sociality.

Land is not alienable for the very reason that it is the *source* of the *kopong* ('grease') that forms and sustains the human body. According to the indigenous model of human life in the Western Highlands, a fetus is produced from *kopong* created out of a combination of female blood and male semen. After being born, a child grows through ingesting the *kopong* in breast milk and food, the produce or 'fat' of the land. The *kopong* of the land is transformed through human reproductive and productive labour into human corporeal and social life, especially via the ceremonial exchange of pigs fed on the produce of the land. The value of pigs in the system of gift exchange lies in the fact that they represent *kopong* in its most concentrated form. Thus land is fundamental to human sociality in that it is 'transformed into exchange' (Strathern and Stewart 1998: 220). In this context, just as land is valued as inalienable so also is the labour that harnesses and transforms the 'fat' of the land since the products of human labour accrue social value through their conversion into inalienable gifts (Feil in Strathern 1988: 154). As Marilyn Strathern (1988: 167) puts it, gift exchange 'involves a process in which human value is made apparent'.

2 Temboka

Most of the people in the Western Highlands province of Papua New Guinea 'speak dialects belonging to a single language continuum which ranges east at least as far as Kujip, north to Ruti, West to the Kaugel Valley, and south to Ialibu in the Southern Highlands Province' (Merlan and Rumsey 1991: 322). The language continuum is classified as Papuan, of East New Guinea Highlands Stock and of the Chimbu-Wahgi family.

Anthropologists are probably most familiar with the name of the dialect spoken in the Mount Hagen area, Melpa, mainly through the work of Andrew and Marilyn Strathern. According to Andrew Strathern (1971: 6) Hageners divide themselves into speakers of Melpa, Temboka, and Kowul. 'Temboka talk' is said to be spoken in the Nebilyer Valley (and into the Kuta Range above the town of Mt Hagen) and by groups who have migrated from this area.

Nebilyer people themselves do not use the name Temboka. Each dialect group calls their way of speaking *bo ung* (*lit.* seedling/cutting/human talk/language). The metaphor of planting, growth and fertility is a key theme in the cosmology of peoples of the Western Highlands and people themselves are referred to as *bo*, as planted beings, seedlings, cuttings, or offshoots. This is crucial for understanding concepts and principles of land tenure.

There does not appear to have been any linguistic work published on the dialects of the Nebilyer Valley, apart from a grammatical sketch of Ku Waru (meaning 'steep stone' or 'cliff') by Merlan and Rumsey (1991) and some rich material by Rumsey[1] on this dialect in several journal articles and book chapters (e.g. 2000, 2002). Ku Waru is spoken by people who have grown up at Kailge, near the stone cliffs. These people refer to peoples and dialects of the Valley floor, such as the Ganiga, as Meam. The *bo ung* of Ganiga people is evidently only slightly different to Ku Waru, and Melpa and people say they have no problems understanding one another.

[1] I owe a deep debt of gratitude to Alan Rumsey for his help and advice on Ku Waru, particularly in relation to helping me understand the way 'classificatory verbs' of being are constituted in the language. Without Alan's outstanding linguistic scholarship and his generous assistance this chapter would not have been possible. I also acknowledge Alexandra Aikhenvald and Robert Dixon for inviting me to participate in their workshop on 'Possession and Ownership' at the Cairns Institute. I am thankful for their trust in me, their encouragement, and the invaluable advice that resulted in the development of my presentation at the workshop into this chapter. A very special thankyou is owed to Joe Leahy and his son Jim Leahy for the gift of their time and their willingness to share their experiences and insights with me.

3 Principles of social organization and land tenure in the Nebilyer Valley

Ganiga people of the Nebiyer Valley have a system of social organization very similar to the patrilineal segmentary lineage system which has been extensively described for the Melpa. Nebilyer people use the generic term *talapi (taglaip)* to refer to the segmentary lineages within a tribe (this term tends to be used for clan; there is no generic name for tribe). Within clans there are sub-groupings that are referred to as *lku tapa* ('men's house') or *haus man* (Tok Pisin). The system is not a segmentary lineage system in the classic anthropological sense derived from African ethnography, such as Evans-Pritchard's description of the Nuer. On the contrary, according to Merlan and Rumsey (1991: 36) 'notions of descent and apical ancestor are of little or no relevance in the Nebilyer area... Nebilyer *talapi* are segmentary in the simple sense that, within a single *talapi*, distinctions are made among multiple, homologous, named sub-groupings, each of which is further subdivided in the same way, etc'. While *talapi* can be translated as 'something like "line", "row", or "column"' (Merlan and Rumsey 1991: 36), this does not refer to a line of descent from an apical ancestor. 'What is locally relevant is not a vertical, genealogical line, but a horizontal, tactical one: the line of men who form a single flank on the battlefield and dance as a single row at ceremonial exchange events' (Merlan and Rumsey 1991: 36). As Merlan and Rumsey have documented for Ku Waru speakers, and I have also documented for the Temboka-speaking Penambi Wia clan living in the Kuta range, the known genealogical ancestry of groupings is relatively shallow (only about three generations).

All land 'except for the deepest forest hinterlands and certain interstitial or contested no-man's lands', is divided into the *kolya* ('place', 'region') of one *talapi* or another. Any place or piece of land that is identified with a lower level grouping such as a *haus man* (*lku tapa*) 'is also identified with all higher level segments that subsume it' (Merlan and Rumsey 1991: 41). For example, the land of the Ulkamp *haus man* (patriline) which is a segment of the Penambi Wia clan, is identified at a higher level as Penambi Wia land, which is in turn subsumed within the higher level segment, Penambi. Similarly, the territories of each of the different Ganiga *haus man* are identified as Ganiga and Ganiga territory in turn is subsumed by even higher levels of the tribal category Ulka. While men of each *haus man* tend to live and work the land identified with their particular segment, *haus man* that are routed in war, or have to move for some other reason, can be given refuge by other groups and provided with land to use. If they stay on, their descendants become like siblings and their group is eventually incorporated as a segment of the clan. This is the case, for example, with the Kwel Melka who are in the process of becoming a segment of the Penambi Wia clan. I shall show below how and why this happens below in my interpretive account of the relationship between Joe Leahy and the Ganiga. Their relationship demonstrates that even in the face of dramatic social change, state intervention, and the introduction of very different principles of land tenure and ownership, there is cultural continuity in terms of how the connection between people and place is conceptualized and realized, or practised. But first I will discuss some linguistic dimensions of possession and ownership in Temboka in order to enable exploration of the associations between language and culture with regard to principles of land tenure.

4 Linguistic dimensions of possession and ownership

Temboka has a three-term person system in the singular and a two-term system in the non-singular categories (Merlan and Rumsey 1991: 325). With regard to mechanisms for expressing 'possession' in Ku Waru, Merlan and Rumsey (1991; Rumsey 2002) note that 'instead of word-level case suffixes as in Latin or German (or prepositions as in English), Ku Waru has case *postpositions*, which occur only on the last word within a noun phrase which they modify' (1991: 335). The Genitive *-nga* marks the possessor. The relations between Possessor and Possessee vary from possession in a narrow sense as in (2) to association as in (3). All the examples below are from Merlan and Rumsey (1991: 328–42).

(1)

ul	olto-nga-yl
affair	we two-GEN-DEF

It's our (du) affair.

(2)

abayl-n	mol	kangabola	kanyiyl-nga
woman-DEF:ERG	no	child	man-GEN
kangyiyl-n	kangabola	na-nga	mol
man-ERG	child	I-GEN	no

The woman says 'no, the child is the man's; the young man says 'the child is not mine'.

(3)

olyo-nga	uj	lu-n	sulymulu
we-GEN	wood	ax-INST	split:HAB:1pl

We split our wood with axes.

(4)

olyo-nga	langi-ma	onlyo-nga	tara-ma-n	bo
we-GEN	food-COLL	we-GEN	ancestor-COLL-ERG	plant

tok	tiring	tep	molymolu
strike/do:NF:2/3pl	do:REM.PAST:2/3pl	do:NF:1	stay:HAB:1pl

In the same way as our ancestors planted foods, so we still do.

(5)

ab	keyn-nga	*kot*	kongun	*tuned*	tingi
Woman	Keyn-GEN	court	day	Tuesday	do:FUT:2/3pl

They are going to hold Keyn's court case on Tuesday.

(6) don-nga lku si nyim
Don-GEN house crowdedness be/say:PERV:3sg
Don's house is crowded.

(7) na-nga mai Sprali tek lying-lum na tena pab
I-GEN land Seize do:NF:2/3pl take-PERV:2/3pl.if I where go:OPT:1sg
If they take my land, where am I supposed to go? [i.e. where do you suppose that I go?].

The Genitive *-nga* has a number of other functions, including 'for the benefit of' or 'affecting' (dative sense) in (8) and 'about' in (10).

(8) calunsab na-nga po kani makunsun-lum
Cook:BEN:OPT:1sg I-GEN sugar cane that tie up-BEN:PERV:2sg:if
I'll cook for you if you tie up my sugar cane for me.

(9) na *leda*-ti yab-ma-nga tonsikir
I letter-sg/INDEF person-COLL-GEN strike/do:BEN:PRES. PROG:3sg
I am writing a letter for some people.

(10) i tepa pelym peba-nga
thus do:NF:3sg remain:HAB:3sg remain-FUT:3sg:GEN
mol nyik telymeli
no say:NF:2/3pl do:HAB:3sg
Concerning the fact that it has always been that way and will remain so, they say no [i.e. they deny it].

Example (11) shows that possession of any item appears to be marked in the same way; that is, there is no grammatical difference based on what can be possessed.

(11) *na-nga kola* 'my place' [hand, pig, land, etc.]
nu-nga kung 'your pig' [hand, land, place]
olto nga our (dual) [true friend, men's house]
olyo-nga our [uncles, mourning house, skins, friend]
kolya-ma-nga my ancestor (place-pl-GEN)

On the other hand, there is a difference in the way the possession of items is marked in possessive clauses constructed on the basis of existential verbs.

4.1 *The possessive use of existential verbs (classificatory verbs of being)*

According to Merlan and Rumsey (1991: 339) Ku Waru has no verb for 'to have'. They note that 'instead of predicating possession by placing the "possessor" NP in the transitive subject position, in Ku Waru it is done by making the "possessed" NP the subject of an intransitive verb of "being"'. Merlan and Rumsey (1991: 338; see also Merlan et al. 1997) identified four classificatory verbs of being for Ku Waru but have more recently added a fifth (Rumsey 2002: 188, 192). These five existential verbs are:

pe- 'lie, sleep'—used with internal body parts, abstract nouns referring to sources of trouble, e.g. *kapo el* 'property dispute', and 'of almost any kind of animate or inanimate object, generally only if it is lying flat' (Merlan and Rumsey 1991: 338);

mol- 'live', 'be' (animate)—used of liquids, certain other inanimate objects (e.g. shoes when wearing them) and all living things (including plants);

angaly- 'stand', 'protrude'—used mainly for certain body parts, mainly but not exclusively the appendages) and certain kinds of human artifact, e.g. *lku* 'house';

le- 'lie, be prostrate, be'—generally of an inanimate entity, but if of an animate, implying prostration or impairment; used of nouns referring to wealth objects;

o- like *ipa-* in Enga occurs with subject NP 'whose typical referents are to be judged to be intermittent, capable of growth, liquid or gas; e.g. 'river', 'rain', 'hair', 'blood', and 'vine' used for rope (Rumsey 2002: 180).

There are resonances here with Moskona (Gravelle, Chapter 3) which also has classificatory verbs. Like the Ku Waru verb *le-*, the verb associated with 'lie, prostrate' in Moskona is used as a possessive verb. Existential clauses in Ku Waru can be expanded into a corresponding possessive by making the possessed NP the subject of an intransitive verb of 'being' as follows (from Rumsey 2002: 188–91 and reviewed by Rumsey, pers. com. 20 October 2011):

(12) *pe-* 'lie', 'sleep'

a. ung mari pelym
words some *pe*+HAB:3sg
Words remain ('...to be said' i.e. 'We haven't heard the last of this').

b. olto ung mari pelym
we (du) words some *pe*+HAB:3sg
We two still have some words (to say).

As the subject *ung mari* is not grammatically plural, the interlinear gloss of *ung* could also be 'verbiage' or 'talk' (Rumsey, pers.com. 20 October 2011).

(13) *mol-* 'live', 'be' (animate, liquid)

a. no bia naa molym
liquid beer not *mol*+HAB:3sg
There's no beer.

b. Na no bia naa molym
I liquid beer not *mol*+HAB:3sg
I have no beer.

(14) *angaly-* 'stand', 'protrude'
a. kub-ki angure angalyilym
leg-arm four *angaly*+HAB:3sg
There are four limbs.

b. yabu-ma kub-ki angure angalyilym
people-COLL leg-arm four *angaly*+HAB:3sg
People have four limbs.

(15) *le-* 'lie', 'be prostrate', 'be'
a. ku moni ya naa lelym
stone money here not *le*+HAB:3sg
There's no money here.

b. olyo ku moni naa lelym
we Stone money not *le*+HAB:3sg
We have no money.

(16) *o-* 'capable of growth', 'intermittent'
a. kidipidi olym
beard/whiskers *o*+HAB:3sg
There's a beard/whiskers.

b. yi ada-ma kidipidi olym
man old-COLL beard/whiskers *o*+HAB:3sg
Old men have beards.

In terms of the semantics of Ku Waru existential verbs, Rumsey (2002: 195) argues that there are 'two cross-cutting axes of contrast that figure centrally in the meanings of four of them'.

> One involves a difference between things that are openly visible or manifest vs those that are concealed or latent, and the other a difference between things that are or may be 'in place' through a process that is beyond their control, vs others for which this is not necessarily so. With respect to the first of these axes, *pe-* and *le-* are on the LATENT side of the opposition and *mol-*, *o-*, and *angaly-* on the MANIFEST. With respect to the second, *le-* and *angayl-* are on the PLACED side of the opposition and *pe-* and *mol-* on the other (Rumsey 2002: 195–6).

There are no linguistic markers to distinguish alienable and inalienable possession in Temboka and there do not seem to be any obligatorily possessed nouns that might be interpreted as a form of linguistic coding of an emic concept of inalienable possession with regard to land. However, while he is not currently able to give specific examples, Rumsey (pers com. 28 September 2010) suggests that in the case of a possessive clause with land (*mai*) as the possessed NP, the existential verb *le-* might be used, which is associated with being 'placed' and 'latent' or 'concealed' rather than 'manifest'. While further field research is required to confirm that *le-* is indeed used with land, this would correlate, I suggest, with the idea of people as planted beings, in or under the ground, and thus a principle of inalienability with regard to land. Perhaps the use of the 'segmentary person' (Merlan and Rumsey 1991; Rumsey 2000) among Temboka speakers can provide further insight into the relationship between people and land.

5 The 'Segmentary Person'

In their public speeches, it is quite common to hear big-men of the Western Highlands using the first-person singular in reference to their whole *haus man*, their clan, or even their entire tribe, and the second-person and third-person singular when referring to a segmentary group different from their own. Segmentary groups can also be referred to as 'the man' or 'the boy' without the collective postposition *-ma*. Merlan and Rumsey (1991) and Rumsey (2000) argue that this phenomenon is common in oratory used at inter-group events, but I have found this also in ordinary conversation and not only when the speaker is talking in *bo ung* but also in Tok Pisin and in English. During an interview I conducted with a Ganiga man, he used the first-person singular in English to refer not to himself as an individual, and not even to the Ganiga as a group, but to the whole tribe of which Ganiga form a segment, the Ulka. In their use of these forms, men (and on occasion today also some women) do not just speak on behalf of the segmentary group but actually project themselves as the group; they personify the segmentary group as a total social entity. A big-man will claim recognition for his own deeds at the same time as representing his segmentary group as a homogeneous entity with its own agency. I have also recorded a Ganiga man using the segmentary person in relation to land ownership. He said, 'I gave my land to Joe Leahy', referring to land associated with his *haus man*. The use of the 'segmentary person' sheds light on the relationship between concepts of being and belonging, personhood and segmentary social organization, the idea of humans as planted beings belonging to segmentary groups that are related offshoots of one another, growing in and of the land. Perhaps it also conceals tensions and contradictions between the autonomous agency asserted by big-men and the collective agency of segmentary groups in relation to one another (Merlan and Rumsey 1991: 95).

6 The Ganiga and their neighbour, Joe Leahy

I will now explore the relationship between the Ganiga and Joe Leahy, in order to provide some interpretive leads for a better understanding of changing concepts of possession and ownership in post-independence PNG. There has been increasing conflict over land ownership due to tensions between customary land tenure principles and Western legal concepts favouring individual title deeds. The case study of Joe Leahy is important because it reveals that even in the face of great change, there is also continuity with regard to notions of ownership and of how land value is measured and realized.

Joe Leahy was born in the late 1930s, the biological son of a Western Highlands woman (of the Jiga tribe, not Ganiga). His father was Michael Leahy, the eldest of the Australian gold prospecting brothers who were among the first Europeans to make contact with the peoples of the Western Highlands. Michael Leahy had two other sons with Highland women, Clem and John. Like his two brothers, Joe was never recognized by Mick Leahy, and when his biological mother died he was adopted and reared by another Highland woman and her husband, who worked for Daniel Leahy, Mick's brother, at his alluvial gold mine at Kuta. Joe grew up as a Highlander. It was not until he was in his teens that his uncle, Daniel Leahy, recognized him, gave him the Leahy name, sent him briefly to school and then employed him on his coffee plantation in the Nebilyer Valley (Korgua Plantation).

6.1 *Becoming a plantation owner*

Joe worked his way up the ladder at Korgua, learning the coffee business. Eventually he decided he wanted to start his own plantation and acquired Kilima, the plantation featured in the films. In fact, there are two plantations featured in the films—Kilima and Kaugum. Kilima plantation is held by Joe Leahy under a 99 year lease from the government. Kaugum, on the other hand, was established as a joint venture between Joe Leahy and the Ganiga on a 60/40 share basis, with the Ganiga contributing the land and Joe Leahy contributing his expertise and his security as guarantee for a bank loan to develop the plantation. *Joe Leahy's Neighbours* documents the dissatisfaction among the Ganiga at this 60/40 arrangement.

The relationship between Joe Leahy and the Ganiga began in the early 1970s when Joe Leahy was working for Dan Leahy at Korgua Plantation. One of his best friends and work mates was Ganiga Korowa Tuga. Joe had made an arrangement with customary landowners near his Uncle's plantation (Korgua) to obtain some land to start his own plantation. He convinced them to sell their land to the State with the idea that he would bid for the lease when it came up for open tender. Uncertain of his chances, Joe asked his uncle, Dan Leahy, to bid on his behalf. However,

Dan instead submitted the bid in the name of his own company (Korgua Farming and Trading Co. Pty Ltd). Joe was devastated. I interviewed Ganiga Korowa Tuga about what happened after Joe discovered he had been betrayed by his uncle. The following is a rough paraphrase in English of his account (spoken in Temboka):

> I cried with Joe and felt sorry for Joe so I went back to my people to see if they might give land to him. I found out that there was some 'fight land' at Kilima, land over which we had fought and which no-one was using. Part of this land belonged to my father Ganiga Aipatul and to Tumul's father, Ganiga Pui. They had recently won it in battle with neighbouring tribes. I approached Tumul and also took five tins of fish to the old men to open negotiations. I told Tumul to come and work at Korgua to meet and get to know Joe. I suggested to Tumul that he and I give the land at Kilima to Joe since it was half mine and half his. I persuaded Tumul by saying that Joe was not a white man like Dan, but one of us, that he could speak our language. Before the fortnight was over, Tumul and I went back and informed the four Ganiga house lines that we wanted to give the land to Joe. I talked to all the influential Ganiga leaders. Some were reluctant. Dubai Yok objected because he said that Joe was a white man and would not look after us, but Tumul was determined and they had an argument. Tumul went and 'cooked' his own house [burnt it down to show how strongly he felt]. They had a fight on the ceremonial ground and Dubai was cut with an ax. He gave up his protestations after that.

In saying that the land belonged to his father and to Tumul's father, Korowa meant that the land belonged to the pair of Ganiga segmentary groups (*haus man*) which the old men represented. He used the third-person dual ('They had recently won it in battle') to refer not to the men as individuals but as a pair of Ganiga segmentary units (*haus man*).

Some of the Kilima land also belonged to the neighbouring Ulka Kundulge. Korowa and Tumul went to see Ulka Kundulge Manda, who was a big-man with his own coffee trees. According to Korowa Manda said 'What's new? I don't want to sell my land. I've already got a car and coffee'. He taunted Korowa and Tumul but this made them all the more determined. They went to see the *kiaps* (government officials) to arrange to sell the land to the state, knowing that by law they could not sell the land directly to Joe. However, they told the *kiaps* that they wanted to sell the land only on the condition that it would be leased to Joe Leahy only and not advertised for open tender. They sought support from a few Hagen big-men on the provincial government land-board and then went with them, the *kiaps*, and the police to negotiate the deal and survey the land. According to Korowa, Manda eventually gave in and agreed to sell the Ulka Kundulge part of the land because 'in those days people were scared of the *kiaps* and the police'. Korowa concluded: 'Yes, it was disputed land, and we fought over it even up to the day it was sold to the *kiaps*'.

Some of the younger generation Ganiga I talked to in January 2000 said they had not been aware until recently of the process that had led to Joe's acquisition of the land. They did not realize that the land had actually been alienated to the State. As one man noted (in English):

> Actually we were not selling the land to him, but we asked him to come across and *stay* with us, but Joe being a businessman organised to buy the lease through the government. In fact none of us knew that that was the deal until recently.

I suggest that even for those Ganiga who were aware of the State purchase of the land (such as Korowa), the transaction was simply a necessary means to affect their purpose of making the land available to Joe for coffee. They did not see the transaction as an act of alienation, but just as a necessary initial payment in an intended continuing relationship with Joe, by which they would be able to enhance the wealth and status of their clan.

According to Joe (January 2000) the Kilima land was a source of conflict which Ganiga were glad to get rid of: 'because they know it belongs to everybody so they wanted to get rid of this land...' However, by placing Joe there, in effect, the Ganiga were also taking the opportunity to secure for themselves rights over the land that were otherwise tenuous.

6.2 *Tribal war*

Joe Leahy is one of the few large plantation owners still operating in the Nebilyer Valley. Tribal fighting, which broke out during the filming of *Black Harvest* in 1990, escalated and continued for the next six years with many deaths on both sides, until the signing of a peace treaty in January 1996. However, sporadic fighting has continued throughout this first decade of the twenty-first century. According to Joe's son, Jim Leahy (September 2009):

> There have been so many peace ceremonies.... It is not going to end when some Lutheran pastor or some Catholic priest or anyone in the religious society comes down and makes a ceremony.... All they are doing is just making temporary peace.... It will never end because it's in those systems. Is it ended? No. The last spurt was 2–3 years ago. It's sporadic; it pops up for a couple of months and then it dies down again...

The film *Black Harvest* filmed during the late 1980s concludes with Joe Leahy leaving the plantation because of the tribal war and applying for Australian residency. However, Joe returned to his plantation a few months later, sat out the war between the Ulka and the Kulka, and lives there to this day. Although his coffee factory and other buildings on the plantation were destroyed, his house remained untouched.

6.3 *Becoming Ganiga*

Why has Joe managed to maintain Kilima plantation while other plantations in the Nebilyer Valley, and other parts of the Highlands, have been destroyed and/or divided into small holdings by the customary landowners? For example, Kuk Station, a government owned Agricultural Research Station and tea plantation originally bought from the Kawelka, was 'reclaimed' by them and divided into small holdings for cash-cropping (Strathern and Stewart 1998). Joe's brother, Clem Leahy, also owned a plantation (Malda Plantation) in the Nebilyer Valley. He had bought the lease on this plantation directly from an Australian planter just before PNG independence. During the period of tribal fighting, Clem found it increasingly impossible to run his plantation. The plantation was eventually repossessed by the bank, which placed its own manager there in a vain attempt to recover costs. The manager lasted less than a fortnight. He was attacked and barely escaped with his life. According to Clem, the *as ples* (Kulka) over-ran the plantation, breaking it into small plots, and he could never safely return.

Joe, on the other hand, remains under the protection of the Ganiga. During my field trip in January 2000, a section of Kilima plantation was 'pegged' (claimed by marking it with stakes) one night (19 January 2000) by some Ulka Kundulge tribesmen (according to Joe, the part of the land that they had considered theirs before the sale to the State). Ganiga were up in arms, wanting to take action against the Ulka Kundulge on behalf of Joe. As Joe (20 January 2000) put it:

> They want to go and fight. They want to go and kill. But I said I don't want anybody to die over the plantation. Because, traditional way, they reckon, these Ganigas, they reckon it's mine now [the plantation].

The marking of the land was one of the main topics of the speeches at a funeral a couple of days later. Significantly, Ganiga speakers at the funeral said they considered Joe to be a Ganiga and listed Joe's lineage among their *haus man*: Yamaga-amp, Ulka–amp, Kundul-amp, Kundulge, Joe-amp (*amp* means woman). Actually, this was not the first time I had heard Joe's line listed as a Ganiga line. A few days earlier, I had asked an old man, named Simeon Dubi, to name the Ganiga house lines and was astounded when he listed Joe-amp as a fifth line. More recently, Jim Leahy (September 2009) confirmed:

> In English they are calling it 'Group 5'. There's four groups that make up the Ganiga and since Joe has been adopted into the tribe they have adopted a new *haus man*.... But for me, and my brothers and sisters, if they stayed, we are more part of the Ganiga than Dad will ever be, because we're the second generation. We were born there with them. We have grown up with them.

A fundamental principle which enables an individual or group to claim customary rights in land in the Western Highlands is their active participation in the creative transformation of land as mere ground or soil into place, that is, into human sociality grounded in exchange relations. Significantly, this principle, I argue, continues to operate even in the context of introduced individual title deeds such as that held by Joe Leahy over Kilima Plantation. Legitimacy of land tenure is linked to the significance of place in human procreation and reproduction, and is tied to concepts of personhood and individual and group identity. Descent is conceived of in terms of the contribution of procreative maternal and paternal substance ('grease' or *gris* in Tok Pisin) to a child. The contribution of 'grease' (*gris*) is a key to kinship. The essential matter of all living things is thought of as 'grease', or 'fat', and the ultimate source of all 'grease' is thought to be the soil. As Merlan and Rumsey (1991: 43) point out 'there is in this view no essential difference between pre-natal and post-natal influences in their power to make us what we are'. According to Weiner (1979: 88), most Highland societies 'equate the sharing of food with the sharing of biogenetic substance. In such societies one finds an emphasis on locality or co-residence as a determining factor in the creation of kinship ties, as has been amply documented... people who eat food grown on the same land are considered kinsmen...'. As Jim Leahy (September 2009) put it:

> All the young fellows here, they are all the trouble makers. I grew up with them so I have no problem.... I don't feel that I have to fear them because they are part of me and I am part of them.... For me, I don't doubt that land is mine. It's mine. I grew up on it.

What I wish to stress here is the significance of 'the cycle of circulation of life principles' (Lemonnier 1991: 14) in the relationship between Joe Leahy and the Ganiga. Joe and his children become part of the Ganiga through partaking in the products of Ganiga land and through being nurtured of its *gris*. In time, much like an incoming wife, Joe becomes planted. As Marilyn Strathern (1988: 256) writes: 'The term that signifies a human being, a planted being (*mbo*), is also the term for a new shoot, a point of growth. Incoming wives give their own clan names to the growing subclans as they differentiate themselves like so many shoots from the homogenous body'.

Chris Gregory (1997: 23) in his book *Savage Money* proposes the term 'reciprocal recognition' (that is, 'reciprocally recognised relations of consanguinity, affinity and contiguity') for the form of consciousness that underlies the values at stake here. Tension between Joe Leahy and the Ganiga erupts, I suggest, because of a Ganiga quest for reciprocal recognition and their evaluation of Joe's actions as inadequate in meeting their expectations. Joe Leahy is a Highlander deeply involved in networks of exchange. Admittedly, he is ambivalent about his obligations to the Ganiga and resists them. However, explanation for this ambivalence should not be reduced to his identity as the son of a white man, but must be understood as part of his identity as a Highlander. Like other Highlanders, Joe is enmeshed in a total web of connections from which he strives to free himself. Like other Highlanders he strives, as Weiner (1992: 3) puts it, 'to pre-empt the duties of debt and obligation'. An appeal to Western values is a means that many Highlanders today use to attempt to resolve tensions and contradictions between relatedness and individual autonomy.

Conflict between Joe Leahy and Ganiga people erupts over the land because of tensions about the perceived inadequacy of operation of practices of exchange. Joe has to constantly work at maintaining his position and legitimacy in relation to the land, through exchange transactions. Like other Ganiga *haus man* he is expected to contribute to bridewealth payments, to funerary gifts, and compensation payments as well as to 'help' Ganiga in their ventures in the coffee industry.

By stressing the significance of exchange, I do not mean to argue that there is some kind of traditional cultural logic, or an abstract, a-historic principle at work behind all land tenure conflict in the Highlands. What I wish to emphasize is that these principles, or values, are in fact constituted in/through the contemporary politicking of place, or practices of place, such as occur in the case of the Ganiga and Joe Leahy as they negotiate relationships of relatedness and difference, being and belonging.

The relationship between Ganiga and Joe Leahy needs to be understood as a relationship between Highlanders. By this, I do not mean to imply that there has been no impact from global economic forces or the introduction and expansion of cash-cropping, but simply that it is inadequate to reduce the analysis to one in terms of binary opposition between modernity and tradition. Although Joe himself stresses that he is 'mixed race' and that he has 'one foot in each camp', he is still a Highlander. As his son Jim puts it:

> We are not strangers that are going to leave this land. We are part of this land; we were born here. Like they say, people are *underneath* the ground; we are *under* the ground. We are part of it. To be part of it, you have to be here. You cannot just pack up and move to town and not expect someone to come and squat on it. I was shooting birds and catching fish in the river and running around with all these young blokes that now have guns in their hands.... Like dad, I never left, you know... Dad has always seen himself as a Western Highlander, a Papua New Guinean *and* a Ganiga.... And Dad, the only reason he hasn't left is because in his heart and his mind, he's settled there and he's part of the people.

7 Conclusion

The tensions between Ganiga people and Joe Leahy could be explained in terms of contradictions between state-based legal concepts of land ownership and customary law. Even though Joe holds legal title deeds to Kilima Plantation, under customary law his rights are based on usufruct, where usufruct is not simply the right to use the land but the right to use it based on working relationships of exchange, by which he grows as a Ganiga kinsman, and becomes consubstantial with them. He is made a Ganiga through sharing in the 'fat' (*gris*) of their land, and his continued legitimacy as a landholder is founded on that connection, and on his continuing engagement with Ganiga in terms of gift exchange and a sociality based on nurturance. Joe's rights in land are established, not by being able to trace decent from a Ganiga, but by transforming the land they have provided him with into a means for engaging in social exchanges by which he eventually effects his own transformation.

The relationship between Joe Leahy and the Ganiga reveals contradictions between exclusive and inclusive conceptions of property. Carrier (1998: 86) defines an inclusive notion of property as one 'wherein an object is embedded in and reflects durable relationships between those people implicated in its past' and an exclusive notion of property as one wherein the object is 'under the sole control of and associated only with the person who happens to own it at the moment'. Joe claims the land on which he established his plantation as his exclusive property. Yet, in *practice*, his (and his children's) continuing engagement in exchange transactions with the respective customary landowners reinforces the identity of the land as *inclusive* property 'embedded in and expressive of a social relationship' (Carrier 1998: 99). While Joe might hold official title deeds to the land, in practice the land remains inalienable as, through gift transactions, land value is continuously transformed into place value, the value of place as a form of sociality, imbued with social relations.

References

Carrier, James C. 1998. 'Property and social relations in Melanesian anthropology', pp. 85–103 of *Property relations: Renewing the anthropological tradition*, edited by C. M. Hann. Cambridge: Cambridge University Press.

Graeber, David. 2005. 'Value: Anthropological theories of value', pp. 439–54 of *A handbook of economic anthropology*, edited by James C. Carrier. Cheltenham UK: Edward Elgar.

Gregory, Chris. 1997. *Savage money*. London: Routledge.

Gregory, C. A. 1982. *Gifts and commodities*. London: Academic Press.

Lemonnier, Pierre. 1991. 'From great men to big men: Peace, substitution and competition in the Highlands of New Guinea', pp. 7–27 of *Big men and great men: Personifications of power in Melanesia*, edited by M. Godelier and M. Strathern. Cambridge: Cambridge University Press.

Merlan, Francesca and Alan Rumsey. 1991. *Ku Waru: Language and segmentary politics in the Western Nebilyer Valley, Papua New Guinea*. Cambridge: Cambridge University Press.

Merlan, Francesca, Steven Powell Roberts, and Alan Rumsey. 1997. 'New Guinea "classificatory verbs" and Australian noun classification: A typological comparison', pp. 63–103 of *Nominal classification in Aboriginal Australia*, edited by M. Harvey and N. Reid. Amsterdam: Benjamins.

Rumsey, Alan 2000. 'Agency, personhood and the "I" of discourse in the Pacific and beyond', *The Journal of the Royal Anthropological Institute* 6(1):101–115.

——. 2002. 'Men stand, women sit: On the grammaticalization of posture verbs in Papuan languages, its bodily basis and cultural correlates', pp. 179–211 of *The linguistics of sitting, standing, and lying*, edited by John Newman. Amsterdam/Philadelphia: John Benjamins Publishing Company.

Strathern, Andrew. 1971. *The rope of Moka: Big men and ceremonial exchange in Mt Hagen, New Guinea*. Cambridge: Cambridge University Press.

—— and Pamela J. Stewart. 1998. 'Shifting places, contested spaces: Land and identity politics in the Pacific', *The Australian Journal of Anthropology* 9(2): 209–24.

Strathern, Marilyn. 1988. *The gender of the gift: Problems with women and problems with society in Melanesia*. Berkeley: University of California Press.

Weiner, Annette. 1992. *Inalienable possessions: The paradox of keeping-while-giving*. Berkeley: University of California Press.

Weiner, James. 1979. 'Restricted exchange in the New Guinea Highlands', *Canberra Anthropology* 2(2): 75–93.

14

Possession and also ownership—vignettes

R. M. W. DIXON

Further remarks are here offered on a couple of topics mentioned—but not explored in detail—in earlier chapters. These comments are based on my extensive fieldwork (extending over forty years) on Dyirbal, from north-east Australia, and (over twelve years) on Jarawara, belonging to the small Arawá family from southern Amazonia, Brazil. They concern using comitative and privative derivations for predicative possession (in §1) and having an inalienable possessor as the head of a possessive NP (in §2). To round out the volume, §3 considers the semantic range, in English, of the verb *own* and various forms of *possess*. It then briefly reflects on the extent to which 'name', 'language', and 'land' may be regarded as being either possessed or owned within various types of culture.

1 Comitative and privative used for predicative possession

Many Australian languages are like Dyirbal in lacking any verb 'have' (or 'own' or 'possess' or 'lack') or 'belong to', which could show predicative possession. Some Australian languages do have a copula construction (Dixon 2002) which can be employed for predicative possession ('John has a black dog' being rendered by something like 'A black dog is to John').

But a fair few languages lack a copula. Instead, they employ a verbless clause construction to indicate a property, as the Dyirbal sentence:

(1) [balan]$_{VCS}$ [muygam]$_{VCC}$
SHE pregnant
She's pregnant.

This involves the apposition of two NPs, a verbless clause subject (VCS), and a verbless clause complement (VCC). Both VCS and VCC are in absolutive case (which has zero realization), as are NPs in S or O function. An NP in A function takes ergative case.

Dyirbal is like many other Australian languages in having comitative ('with') and privative ('without') derivational suffixes which may be added to a noun, to an adjective, to a 'noun marker', such as *balan* in (1), or indeed to all the words in an NP. These derive an adjectival expression, which can modify the head noun within an NP, or function as a VCC.

In §§1.5–6 of Chapter 5, Dench describes, for Martuthunira, something which is typical of Australian languages—derivational affixes 'privative' and 'proprietive' (the latter being essentially an alternative name for 'comitative'). In Dyirbal we have the following derivational suffixes:

- Comitative *-bila* (in southern dialects) ~ *-ba* (in northern dialects) 'with'
- Privative *-ŋaŋgay* 'without'

Each of these may be added to a noun; for example, *wuju-ŋangay* 'food-WITHOUT'. Or they may be added to noun plus modifying adjective, as *yara [guda-bila jugi-bila]* 'man dog-WITH big-WITH' for 'man with a big dog'. Textual examples include:

(2)	[ŋaja	baŋgay-bila]$_S$	jana-ñu
	1sg	spear-WITH	stand-NON.FUTURE

I stood with (holding) a spear.

(3)	[bayi	midi	yibi-ŋaŋgay]$_S$	yalŋgay-ja	ñina-ñu
	HE	small	wife-WITHOUT	single.man-LOCATIVE	sit-NON.FUTURE

The small man (i.e. younger brother) without a wife sat with the single men.

If an NP is in ergative case, then an ergative suffix (which has a number of allomorphs) must be used on every word within the NP. If one said 'the small man without a wife saw me' then *bayi midi yibi-ŋaŋgay*, which is in absolutive case in (1), would become *baŋgul yara-ŋgu yibi-ŋaŋgay-ju* ('HE:ERGATIVE small-ERGATIVE wife-WITHOUT-ERGATIVE').

There are two ways of expressing predicative-type possession in Dyirbal, both involving a verbless clause construction. The first is to use a possessive pronoun or noun as (or in) the VCS. For example:

(4)	[ŋaygu	baŋgay]$_{VCS}$	bulayi$_{VCC}$
	1sg:POSSESSOR	Spear	two

I have two spears (*lit.* my spears are two).

The second method does not employ a possessive noun or pronoun but instead has a comitative or privative expression as VCC. For instance:

(5) [giñan bangay]$_{VCS}$ jambun-ba$_{VCC}$
THIS:FEMININE spear grub-WITH
This spear has a grub impaled on its end (*lit.* is with grub).

(6) [jigal-bara balan]$_{VCS}$ [bigay-bila]$_{VCC}$
good-better IT handle-WITH
The (basket) is better (than the other one), (in) having a handle (*lit.* (being) with handle).

(7) wirru-ŋaŋgay$_{VCC}$ ŋaja$_{VCS}$
husband-WITHOUT 1sg
I have no husband.(*lit.* I (am) without husband).

A privative *-ŋaŋgay* form may be used in predicative possession with any type of possessor, for example, human in (7) and (8). However, it appears that a *-bila* form tends to be restricted to use when the possessor is inanimate, as in (5) and (6).

These principles were borne out when I indulged in elicitation on this topic with Bessie Jerry, asking her how to say the following:

(8) I haven't got a dog. ŋaja$_{VCS}$ guda-ŋaŋgay$_{VCC}$
1sg dog-WITHOUT
(*lit.* I am without a dog)

(9) I have a horse. ŋaygu$_{VCS}$ yarraman-bu$_{VCC}$
1sg:POSSESSOR horse-ONLY
(*lit.* mine is only a horse)

(10) I have two cats. [ŋaygu buligan]$_{VCS}$ bulayi$_{VCC}$
1sg:POSSESSOR cat two
(*lit.* my cats (are) two)

In all of these sentences, the possessor has human reference. Bessie used a privative construction for negative predicative possession in (8), but for positive predicative possession, in (9) and (10), she eschewed the construction with a comitative NP as VCC, preferring a possessor-as-VCS construction, similar to (4).

Note that Dyirbal has free ordering for words within a sentence and also a great deal of ellipsis. An NP can consist of just an adjective with no head noun stated—as *midi* 'small' in (3)—or just a possessor with no possessee stated within the NP—as *ŋaygu* 'my, mine' in (9). In fact, sentence (10) could alternatively be parsed as *ŋaygu*$_{VCS}$ [*buligan bulayi*]$_{VCC}$, literally 'mine are two cats', with no difference in meaning.

Then I enquired of Bessie how she would say 'I have two daughters and one son', and received the response:

(11)	[bulayi	gajin]$_{VCC}$	ŋaygu$_{VCS}$	[yuŋgul	yara]$_{VCC}$
	two	girl	1sg:POSSESSOR	one	man

Literally: mine are two girls and one man.

Sentence (11) involves apposition of two verbless clause constructions, which share the same subject, *ŋaygu* 'my'. This follows the VCC of the first clause—as the VCS does in (7)—and precedes the VCC of the second clause—as the VCS does in most of the other examples quoted above.

In summary, predicative possession in Dyirbal is shown through a verbless clause construction. There are two alternatives. Either (a) the possessor, marked in possessive form, is VCS and the possessee is stated, in plain form, as VCC; this is illustrated by (4) and (9–11). Or (b) the possessor is stated in plain form as VCS and the possessee, with comitative or privative suffix, makes up the VCC, as in (5–8).

Clausal negation is shown by including the negative particle, *gulu*, anywhere before the verb. For example, the negative version of (3) would be *bayi midi yibi-ŋaŋgay yalŋgay-ja gulu ñina-ñu* 'The small man without a wife did not sit with the single men'. The corpus does not include any instance of a predicative possessive clause with *gulu* (but I see no reason why this should not be possible).

For a human possessor, it appears that positive predicative possession is shown by construction type (a), and the negative variety by type (b), with privative suffix *-ŋaŋgay* on the possessee. For an inanimate possessor, construction (b) may be used for both positive and negative predicative possession.

2 Possessor as head of an inalienable construction

As pointed out in Chapter 1—and exemplified for Nêlêmwa, Chinese, and Likpe in Chapters 2, 8, and 10—some languages do not really have a possessive construction per se. What they have is a general modificational technique, with the marking of possession being one of its several functions. When this occurs, it is always the modified element which is head of the construction; when it relates to possession, it is the possessee which is head.[1]

English is typical of languages which have one possessive construction used for all of ownership (*my notebook*), kinship (*the boss's wife*), and whole–part (*Mary's foot*). In the case of a single possessive construction, it is always the (alienably or

[1] I use the term 'head (of an NP)' in its traditional sense (Dixon 2010a: 229). Generally, the head is the only obligatory component and may make up a complete phrase on its own. It is the head which dictates agreement on other items in the NP, and it is the head which determines the properties of the NP as a whole (for instance, its gender, for gender agreement on the predicate).

inalienably) possessed item which is head of the construction—here *notebook*, *wife*, and *foot*. When a speaker of English hears *Mary's foot*, they view this as a type of foot.

Many languages have a number of possessive constructions—perhaps one for ownership, one for kin relationships, one for whole-part. Each of them will be marked in a distinctive way. Generally, it is still the case that the possessee is head.

Ownership almost always involves explicit marking on either the possessor (genitive) or the possessee (pertensive); the possessee is the head of the construction. In contrast, inalienable possession—for whole-part relationships and sometimes much more as well—may be shown simply by apposition. And for some languages with this, it is the possessor (not the possessee) which is the head of the possessive construction. This applies for Jarawara, and for Dyirbal.

2.1 *Jarawara*

Nouns in Jarawara divide into two sets—'free' and 'possessed'. A free noun may make up an NP by itself. Each free noun has an inherent gender—either feminine (the functionally unmarked term in the system) or masculine. This is not shown in the form of the noun itself, but by gender agreement (i) on possessed nouns, adjectives, and demonstratives which modify the free noun within its NP, and (ii) on gender-determined suffixes in the predicate of the clause.

An alienable possessive phrasal construction involves possessive marker *kaa* coming between the possessor (which can be any kind of free noun, or a full NP) and the possessee (which will be a free noun): Pr *kaa* Pe. This construction relates to ownership; a slightly modified form of it is used for kin relationships.

The Pe is head of an 'Pr *kaa* Pe' construction. For instance:

(12) Okomobi kaa taokana
name(m) POSS gun(f)
Okomobi's gun (f)

The Pr is a man's name, *Okomobi*, which is masculine; the Pe is *taokana* 'gun', which is feminine. The possessive NP, *Okomobi kaa taokana*, is feminine, taking the gender of the Pe. For instance the adjective 'small' could be added and this must be in feminine form, *bite* (masculine is *biti*)—*Okomobi kaa taokana bite* 'Okomobi's small gun'.

Like other languages from the small Arawá family, Jarawara has a sizeable set of 'possessed nouns' (PNs). In proto-Arawá, each PN had distinct feminine and masculine forms (shown by suffixes *-ni* and *-ne* respectively) to an invariable root. A number of phonological changes have applied in the development from proto-Arawá to Jarawara; as a result, only slightly less than half of the PNs have distinct gender forms (see Dixon 1995, 2004: 316–25).

In fact, my corpus features about 175 PNs, covering a wide semantic range. This includes parts of human and animal bodies and of plants, physical attributes such as 'smell', orientation terms such as 'top surface of', 'inside of'; plus 'name', 'noise', 'voice, sound, talking, language', 'dream', 'companion of', 'container of', 'path', 'grave', and 'home'.

Those PNs which are marked for gender show this in a variety of ways (all of which can be explained in terms of diachronic changes). Quoting feminine (the unmarked gender) / masculine:

'foot' is *tame/teme*, gender being shown by the first vowel;
'home' is *tabori/taboro*, gender being shown by the final vowel

The other type of phrasal possessive construction in Jarawara involves apposition between Pr and Pr (in that order) with no special marker of the relationship.

(13) Okomobi teme
name(m) foot:m
Okomobi's foot (m)

The important point is that in this construction type, it is the inalienable possessor, here *Okomobi*, which is the head of the NP. *Okomobi* is masculine; it selects the masculine form of PN *tame/teme* 'foot'. And if *Okomobi teme* were modified by the adjective 'small', the masculine form *biti* would be used, giving *Okomobi teme biti* 'Okomobi's small foot'.

As stated above, in English *Mary's foot* is looked upon as a type of foot. In Jarawara, *Okomobi teme* is not regarded as a type of foot but rather as an aspect of Okomobi, a further specification of Okomobi within the discourse. Justification for this interpretation in terms of discourse organization in Jarawara is in Dixon (2004: 291). Exactly the same interpretation is appropriate for Dyirbal, and discourse justification for it is provided in §2.2.

The declarative mood suffix on a verb has the form *-ke/-ka*. When the alienable possessor NP in (12) is in S function for intransitive verb *bisa* 'be dirty', the alienable possessee, *taokana* 'gun', which is feminine, is head of the NP and selects the feminine form, *-ke*, of the declarative suffix:

(12′) [Okomobi kaa taokana]$_S$ bisa-ke
name(m) POSS gun(f) be.dirty-DECLARATIVE:FEMININE
Okomobi's gun (f) is dirty.

When the inalienable possession NP in (13) is in S function for *bisa*, the inalienable possessor, Okomobi, which is masculine, is head of the NP and selects the masculine form, *-ka*, of the declarative suffix:

(13′) [Okomobi teme]$_S$ bisa-ka
name(m) foot:m be.dirty-DECLARATIVE:MASCULINE
Okomobi's foot (m) is dirty.

The structure of an NP in Jarawara, has three components:

A Alienable possessor—an embedded NP
plus alienable possession marker *kaa*

B Head—generally a common or proper noun
plus optional modifiers (modifying noun, adjective(s), augment marker, etc.)

C Possessed noun(s)
plus optional modifiers (adjective(s), etc.)

The head, B, is usually obligatory and parts A and C optional. It is always the (stated or understood) head that determines the gender of the NP. An NP can have all three components, as in (14a), or just parts A and B, as in (14b) or just parts B and C, as in (14c, d):

(14) a. mati kaa jomee teme
mother(f) POSS dog(m) foot:m
A B C
mother's dog's foot (m)

(14) b. mati kaa jomee
mother(f) POSS dog(m)
A B
mother's dog (m)

(14) c. jomee teme
dog(m) foot:m
B C
the dog's foot (m)

(14) d. mati tame
mother(f) foot:f
B C
mother's foot (f)

In each case it is the head, part B, which determines gender. This is the alienable possessee element if there is a part A but inalienable possessor if there is a part C, or both at once if both parts A and C are present.

2.2 *Dyirbal*

Dyirbal is unlike Jarawara in that all nouns are free, and can make up an NP on their own. Each noun belongs to one of four genders (or noun classes); these can roughly be characterized as 'masculine', 'feminine', 'edible vegetable', and 'neuter'. Gender is shown not on the noun itself but by the form of a 'noun marker' which may accompany it. These are (in absolutive case form): *bayi* for masculine, *balan* ~ *ban* for feminine, *balam* ~ *bam* for edible vegetable, and *bala* for neuter. A sample of nouns with their gender-specifying noun markers is:

bayi wirru	'husband'	*bayi gugar*	'black goanna'
balan gajin	'girl'	*balan baŋgay*	'spear'
balam wuju	'non-flesh food'	*balam mirrañ*	'black bean'
bala diban	'stone'	*bala jiba*	'liver'

A noun may occur in an NP with or without a noun marker. And a noun marker may make up an NP by itself—as in (1)—rather like the anaphoric use of third-person pronouns in other languages.

Dyirbal is like Jarawara in having two possessive constructions:

(I) ALIENABLE POSSESSIVE CONSTRUCTION Ownership and kin relationships are shown by:

- Possessor marked as genitive. This involves a special genitive form for pronouns—for example, 1sg *ŋaygu* 'my' in (4) and (9–11)—and a genitive suffix *-ŋu* on a common or proper noun—for example *Jarrmay-ŋu wirru* 'Jarrmay's husband'.
- Possessee in plain form.

The two components may occur in either order. One would hear both *Jarrmay-ŋu wirru* and *wirru Jarrmay-ŋu*, and both *ŋaygu baŋgay*—as in (4)—and *baŋgay ŋaygu* for 'my spear'.

(II) INALIENABLE POSSESSIVE CONSTRUCTION A whole–part relationship does not have any formal marking but simply involves apposition of the noun referring to the whole (the Pr) and the noun referring to the part (the Pe) within an NP; they may occur in either order. For example:

gajin jina	(or *jina gajin*)	'girl's foot'
gugar jina	(or *jina gugar*)	'goanna's foot'

The Pr can be anything which has parts—person, animal, plant, artefact, etc.—and the Pe can be any name for a part. This is all rather straightforward, except that—for a human—'name' is regarded as a part, in the same way that 'eye' and 'foot' and 'liver' are. Thus, one would say *wirru dirra* for 'husband's name', and not (with genitive suffix for alienable possession) **wirru-ŋu dirra*.

Exactly as in Jarawara, in an alienable possessive construction the Pe is the head, but in an inalienable possessive construction it is the Pr which is head. This can be shown by the gender of the noun marker.

(a) *Alienable construction*:

	Pr	Pe
bayi	Jarrmay-ŋu	wirru
MASCULINE	name(f)-GENITIVE	husband(m)
Jarrmay's husband		

The overall NP is masculine, and takes noun marker *bayi*, from the gender of the possessee, *wirru* 'husband'.[2]

(b) *Inalienable construction*:

	Pr	Pe
bayi	gugar	jiba
MASCULINE	goanna(m)	liver(neuter)
the goanna's liver		

If *jiba* 'liver' were the sole noun in an NP and thus its head (for instance, if you visited a butcher's shop to purchase some liver to cook for dinner) it would take the neuter noun marker *bala*. But in the NP here the gender of the Pe is of no account. This inalienable possession construction takes the noun marker *bayi*, from the gender of the Pr, *gugar* 'goanna'.

As in Jarawara, alienable and inalienable possession may be combined within one NP. For example: *bayi Jarrmay-ŋu wirru jiba* 'Jarrmay's husband's liver. The head of the NP is *wirru* 'husband', selecting the masculine noun marker, *bayi*. *Wirru* is both Pe of alienable possession (with proper name *Jarrmay* being the Pr) and Pr for inalienable possession (with *jiba* 'liver' being the Pe).

It was pointed out that while in English *Mary's foot* is looked upon as a type of foot, in Jarawara *Okomobi teme* is regarded as a further specification of Okomobi. The same principle applies in Dyirbal. An NP such as *(bayi) gugar jiba* does not describe a type of liver; rather it refers to a goanna in relation to its liver. This can be illustrated by examination of a text segment.

First note that Dyirbal operates in terms of an S/O pivot (what is called 'ergative syntax'). A pivot argument (grammaticalized topic) will run through a number of clauses. The pivot must be stated (or understood to be) in one of the pivot functions in each clause of the chain—either an intransitive subject (S) or a transitive object (O).

The following is an excerpt from the story, told by the late Ida Henry, of how a black goanna (*Varanus varius*), *gugar*, changed into a crocodile. The goanna was supposedly killed by two women, his guts extracted, and then turned over and his stomach opened up in preparation for heated stones to be inserted so that he could be cooked in an earth oven. The two women went out to gather leaves with which to

2 The alienable possessor is an NP, which can include its own noun marker, in possessive form. Thus [*baŋun Jarrmay-ŋu*] *bayi wirru* ('[FEMININE:POSSESSOR Jarrmay] MASCULINE husband'), literally 'her Jarrmay's he husband'.

cover the earth oven. However, they had omitted to extract the liver, which holds life-force. Since the goanna still had his liver, he was able to recover, turned himself over, ran to the water to escape from the women and—since a goanna cannot live in water—transformed himself into a crocodile.

The pivot argument is *(bayi) gugar* 'black goanna'. This is in O function in lines (a–d) and (f), and in S function in lines (e) and (g–j). The goanna had been introduced into the discourse earlier on, during the account of his detection and capture. Where *gugar* 'goanna' is understood to be head of an NP but is not actually stated, it is enclosed in square brackets in the pivot column, [gugar].

The point of interest is that the pivot NP begins as just 'goanna', is elaborated in line (a) to 'goanna's guts', reverts to being just 'goanna' in line (b), is again elaborated to 'goanna's liver' in lines (c) and (d), once more reverts to being just 'goanna' in lines (e–g), is again elaborated, this time to 'goanna's front' in line (h), and reverts to 'goanna' in (j), the final line from this extract. (Masculine noun marker *bayi* is included in the pivot NP in lines (a), (h), and (j).) There are inalienable possession constructions in lines (a), (c), (d), and (h); in each instance the Pr, *gugar* 'goanna' is head of the construction and determines that each NP is masculine (whereas each of *guna* 'guts', *jiba* 'liver', and *mirra* 'front', used by itself, is of neuter gender).

		PIVOT	FUNCTION
(a)	guna$_O$ bundi-n bayi$_O$ guts take.out-NON.FUTURE HE The [goanna's] guts were taken out (by the two women)	[gugar] guna +bayi	O
(b)	yanda galga-n gugar$_O$ TRY leave-NON.FUTURE goanna The goanna was left (there by the two women while they went out to get leaves to cook the goanna in an earth oven)	gugar	O
(c)	gulu jiba$_O$ bundi-n NOT liver take.out-NON.FUTURE [His] liver was not taken out	[gugar] jiba	O
(d)	jiba$_O$ galga-n liver leave-NON.FUTURE [His] liver was left	[gugar] jiba	O
(e)	balay-jilu bungi-li THERE:LOCATIVE-EMPHATIC lie-PURPOSIVE [For him] to lie there (dead, as the women thought, ready to be cooked)	[gugar]	S

					PIVOT	FUNCTION
(f)	yuba-n	bayi$_O$			[gugar]	O
	put.down-NON.FUTURE	HE				
	gana-gala-mba-n					
	belly-UP-TRANSITIVISER-NON.FUTURE					
	He was put down belly-up					
(g)	bungi-li . . .				[gugar]	S
	lie-PURPOSIVE					
	To lie (there)					
(h)	bayi$_S$	gugar$_S$	mirra$_S$	waymbarra-ñu	gugar mirra	S
	HE	goanna	front	turn.over-NON.FUTURE	+ bayi	
	The goanna turned over (*lit.* the goanna's front turned over)					
(j)	bayi$_S$	bana-gu	birba-ñu		[gugar]	S
	HE	water-TO	jump-NON.FUTURE		+ bayi	
	He jumped into the water (and became a crocodile)					

There is a further example of topic elaboration and reversion for Dyirbal in Dixon (1972: 72), and a similar example for Jarawara in Dixon (2004: 291).

In compiling a thesaurus/dictionary for Dyirbal, a number of words with highly culture-specific meanings were encountered. They include the intransitive verb *wurrali-*. At first sight, *wurrali-* seems to have two, rather different meanings.

(I) 'BOAST, SHOW OFF' Examples of this use include:

(15) ŋaja$_S$ wurrali-ñu gubi$_S$
1sg boast-NON.FUTURE shaman
I consider myself a shaman (although others might not think so).

(16) ban gajin ñalŋgirrgan wurrali-ñu
SHE girl very.good.looking boast-NON.FUTURE
The girl considers herself very good looking (she is showing off).

In each of these sentences, the NP in S function has as head a pronoun (*ŋaja* 'I') or noun (*gadjin* 'girl') plus a modifier. This is adjective *ñalŋgirrgan* 'very good looking' in (16) and noun *gubi* 'shaman' in (15). (Since word order is free, the words making up one NP can be separated from each other within the clause, as in (15), (17), and line (a) of the text fragment just quoted.)

(II) 'TAKE ON IDENTITY OF ONE'S TOTEM (AND ASSUME TOTEM POWER)' Each member of the Dyirbal-ngan tribe is identified with an animal or plant as their totem. Before an important occasion (such as a fighting corroboree), a man or woman would stretch their body, and by mental power take on the identity of their totem, saying, for instance:

(17)	ŋaja$_S$	wurrali-ñu	gañarra$_S$
	1sg	identify-NON.FUTURE	crocodile

I am now a crocodile (my totem, and no crocodile can touch me).

(18)	ŋaja$_S$	miyabur$_S$	wurrali-ñu
	1sg	red.silky.oak	identify-NON.FUTURE

I am now a red silky oak tree (*Carnavionia araliifolia*) (and will have the status of an oak tree in the forthcoming fight).

I discussed the verb *wurrrali-* with half-a-dozen consultants and each provided an example sentence featuring their own totem. Note that these were not by any means all powerful things; they included kangaroo, white cockatoo, eel, and wood-grub. It appears that it is *identification* with a totem which engenders unusual powers, irrespective of the status of the totem in the real world.

Consultants insisted that what I had identified as two senses of *wurrali-* are 'the same word'. It seems that the general meaning is: 'identify, assume for oneself some special attribute'. Particular senses of the general meaning of this are:

(i) a worldly sense 'boast, or fancy oneself'
(ii) a mystical sense 'take on the identity of one's totem'.

From a grammatical point of view, the point of special interest is that sentences (15), (17), and (18) each have an NP (in S function) which consists of two words in apposition—either two nouns or pronoun and noun. This is similar to what we earlier described as an inalienable possessive construction. In each instance, the underlying idea is one of identification. Thus:

gajin jina ('girl foot')	A girl identified in terms of her foot
gugar jiba ('goanna liver')	a goanna identified in terms of its liver, as in (c–d)
ŋaja gubi ('I shaman')	me identified as a shaman, as in (15)
ŋaja gañarra ('I crocodile')	me identified as a crocodile, as in (17)

In summary, it is inappropriate to describe the appositional construction as some kind of 'possession' (in Dyirbal and also in Jarawara). Rather, it should be recognized as a type of 'identification'.

3 What can be possessed, and owned

In English, there are two ways of marking possession within an NP. The suffix with orthographic form *'s* may be attached to Pr, giving 'Pr's Pe', as *the table's leg*

/ðə=teibl-z leg/. Or the preposition with orthographic form *of* may be placed between Pe and Pr, giving 'Pe of Pr', In fact, *of* is generally realized as proclitic ə*v*= to Pr; thus, *the leg of the table* is /ðə=leg əv=ðə=teibl/ (where '-' is an affix boundary and '=' indicates a clitic boundary). It can be seen that, for each alternative, it is Pr which is marked, by suffix or by proclitic.[3]

Recapitulating from Chapter 1, the semantic range of the nominal possessive construction in English covers the following:

A. Ownership. Pr is recognized to have control over Pe and can do things with it:

(19) [John's bicycle] is a racing model.

B. Whole-part relationship, whether a body part of a human or animal, a part of a plant, of an artefact, of a geographical feature, or of something else:

(20) [Jane's leg] is broken.

C. Kinship relationship, whether blood relations or relations through marriage, as in:

(21) [Tom's mother-in-law] lives in Oodnadatta.

D. An attribute of a person, animal, or thing:

(22) [John's anger] was beyond belief.

E. A statement of orientation or location:

(23) [The side of that truck] is dented.

F. Association, involving a conventional link between Pr and Pe:

(24) [Kate's accountant] plays the trumpet.

(25) [Tamsin's name] is of Cornish origin.

(26) [My language] has five vowels.

(27) [Our home] is in the valley.

There are a number of ways of telling what is and what is not a possessive construction. General criteria listed by Aikhenvald, in §2.2 of Chapter 1, include being able to be rephrased as predicative possession. Applying this test to English, all of A–F may be rephrased with *have*; for example, *Tamsin has a name which is of Cornish origin*. A *have* construction is used most often when some fairly significant property is attributed to the possessee, as in *Tom has a dragon of a mother-*

[3] For discussion of the conditions of use for 's and *of* see Dixon (2005: 317–30; 2010b: 295–6), and further references therein.

in-law who lives in Oodnadatta and *That truck has a multicoloured side which is dented.*

There are other functions for *'s* and *of* which do not relate to possession. For example, *a glass of whisky*, *a woman of eighty*, *north of the city*, and nominalizations such as *John's decision to marry Mary*. All of these fail the *have*—and other—tests.

'Possession' is a technical term in linguistics, referring to a certain construction type. Quite apart from this, it is interesting to look at English lexemes *own* and *possess* and variant forms such as *possession* and *possessions*, to see what semantic range each has.

(a) **The verb *own* relates just to possession type A.** If John is recognized by the community in which he lives to own X, then he has control over what happens to it. It is accepted that John can sell X, or give it away, or even deface or destroy it.

The adjective *own*, which is far more common than the verb, has a far wider range of significance. It may be used for all of A–F, but is generally restricted to a human referent: *my own leg/mother-in-law/acountant/name/language/home*. And I can opine *My own anger, strong as it might have been, was surpassed by Tom's.*

(b) **The verb *possess* has a wider range than *own*,** but tends to be used to draw attention to some noteworthy property. This can be within sense A, as *He possesses great wealth*; *The Duchess possesses four hundred thousand acres of prime farmland.* Referring to a catcher in a ball game, one could say *He possesses a safe pair of hands*, which falls under sense B (but one would be unlikely to hear *After the accident, he only possesses one hand*; instead, *has* would be used). *Possess* may also be used for sense D, as in *He possesses an insatiable appetite for gossip*, and *She possesses the power to bankrupt our company.*

One can own a property (have legal deeds to it, and be able to sell it) without necessarily have possession of it (in the sense of being able to live there), if there is a current tenant who cannot be dislodged. If a property is advertised as *with vacant possession*, this means that it has no current tenant and a buyer would be able to both own and possess it. If X *takes possession of* Y, this means that Y is now in the custody of X, but is does not necessarily imply that X is the owner.

Further, rather tangential, senses of *possess* include: *A raging fever/an evil spirit possessed her* (typically used in the passive), the rather archaic *He possessed her* (sexually), also *She possessed the audience with her graphic tale*, and the idiomatic *What possessed you to do that?*

(c) **The noun *possession* has a rather different significance from verb *possess*.** Basically, anything which is owned by Pr is Pr's possession. That is, it relates to sense A, and the Pe need not have any unusual features. For example, *my private possessions* and *their household possessions*. Note also *The manuscript came into her* *possession through a bequest* and *He took possession of a derelict cottage which no one else wanted and lived there happily for twenty years.*

Colonial holdings are typically referred to as possessions: *The Falklands Islands is a possession of Great Britain*, and *Her North American possessions were lost at the end of the eighteenth century.*

(d) ***In possession of*** **has a meaning all of its own**, stating that the Pe was apparently in the custody of Pr (irrespective of whether Pr owned it). A typical context of use is: *The police arrested John for being in possession of a gun / of five kilos of heroin.* Note that, in place of *in possession of*, one could say *possessing*, with little difference in meaning.

There is also the adjective *possessive*, which has a different meaning again, referring to a Pr who tries to dominate or unnecessarily control a Pe—*A man with a possessive mother is less likely to get married than one without*, and *He was highly possessive over the library his father had left him even though he never reads a book.*

3.1 *Name, language and land*

(a) Name. To many people, their name is essentially a part of them, like chin and chest, and like their hopes and fears. Indeed, for a high proportion of languages which make a distinction between alienable and inalienable possession, 'name' counts as inalienable (see Dixon 2010b: 279–86). This can be illustrated from three languages on which I have done extensive field work, and know well.

In Fijian, nouns divide into 'free' and 'bound' sets (Dixon 1988: 127–8). A bound noun must bear a suffix showing the inalienable possessor; thus *liga-qu* 'my hand', *liga-mu* 'your (sg) hand', *liga-na* 'his/her hand'. A free noun may be used alone; for instance *isele* 'knife'. If an alienable possessor is stated, this is shown by a separate word: *qou isele*. Bound nouns cover reference kin terms (*tama-qu* 'my father'), most body part terms, and just a handful of further items: 'piece of', 'cause of', 'use of', 'shape of'. And also *yaca-* 'name'; 'my name' is *yaca-qu*, similar to *liga-qu* 'my hand'. (Interestingly, there is also a free noun *yaca* meaning 'namesake'. We get *qou yaca* 'my namesake', parallel to *qou isele* 'my knife'.)

It was pointed out in §2.1 that Jarawara shows a similar division between 'free' and 'possessed' (that is, 'bound') nouns. The large set of possessed nouns includes *ini* (f) / *ino* (m) 'name'. Within an NP, this follows a free noun (which is NP head) and agrees with it in gender. Thus *mati ini* 'mother's name' and *bati ino* 'father's name (parallel to *mati tame* 'mother's foot' and *bati teme* 'father's foot').

As described in §2.2, Dyirbal shows alienable possession by the suffix *-ŋu* on the Pr noun (or by the possessive form of a pronoun) and it also has an inalienable possession construction, in which whole and part nouns are simply apposed. One says *ŋuma-ŋu waŋal* 'father's boomerang' but just *ŋuma jina* 'father's foot'. Lexemes entering into the appositional construction are those referring to parts (of human and animal bodies, plants, artefacts, mountains) and also *dirra* 'name'. That is, one says *ŋuma dirra* for 'father's name' (never **ŋuma-ŋu dirra*).

In these and many other societies, a name could not be said to be owned. It is rather an intrinsic attribute of its bearer. In Chapter 4, Aikhenvald explains how a Manambu identifies with a set of names, and with the totems and territories they are associated with. Person and name are simply linked together. Similarly in English and many other languages—some people possess/have a long list of names but they could never be said to 'own' them.

(b) **Language.** How does language fit into schemes of possession? Well, it is seldom or never considered to be something that can be owned.

In Jarawara there is an alienably possessed noun *ati/ati* (one of those possessed nouns for which feminine and masculine forms coincide, through diachronic change), meaning 'voice', 'sound', 'talking; what is said' and also 'language'. Thus 'my language (has many words)' uses the same appositional NP construction as 'my foot (hurts)'.

In Fijian, lexeme *vosa* functions both as an intransitive verb 'speak, talk' and as a noun meaning 'word' or 'speech' or 'language'. For example *na vosa vaka-Viti* 'the Fijian language', where adverbalizing prefix *vaka-* is added to *Viti* ('Fiji'). A popular radio programme is called *Na noda vosa* 'Our language', with the first-person inclusive possessive pronoun *noda* 'our'. But no one would ever talk of 'owning' a language.

The tribe called Dyirbal-ngan speaks the Dyirbal language in two varieties—Guwal, the everyday register used in unmarked circumstances, and Jalnguy, the 'avoidance' (or 'mother-in-law') register, used in the presence of a taboo relative. People say 'I am Dyirbal-ngan' or 'I speak Dyirbal', but I have never heard anything like 'My/our language is Dyirbal' (indeed, there is no generic term 'language'). The language just *is*—it is part of you, certainly not something which could be regarded as possessed or owned.

Like 'name', 'language' could never be included under 'ownership', type A of possessive construction from the beginning of §3. These notions are either a matter of association, sense F, or they are treated like a part of a person, sense B.

(c) **Land.** In many languages 'home' is treated in a similar way to 'name' and 'language'; the noun 'home' is inalienably possessed in Nanti (see Chapter 6) and in Jarawara. But what about 'land'?

Typically, in small-scale tribal societies, land is somewhere to live on, to hunt and gather in, to grow crops on, to look after and nurture. 'Land' is not even something which is inalienably possessed. It is a part of the pattern of life, of the scheme of things, relating to a whole social group. In Galo (Chapter 7) and in Temboka (Chapter 13), one may say 'our land' but never 'my land'. In Australia, Aboriginal people say that they belong to the land, rather than that the land belongs to them. Their spirits come at birth from conception sites and they return to them at death. Such sites are sacred, and must be tended and protected.

This is all in stark contrast to the perception of 'land' in societies with a different economic basis. A large or small tract of land can be owned. In fact, *all* land is owned, either by individuals or by the national government. If you want to build a house, a block of land must be bought or leased. Land is indisputably owned, in the same way that a knife or a hat or a motor car is. The owner of a piece of land can do whatsoever they want—build on it, mine under it, sell it or give it away, desecrate it, as they will.

And this is where cultures may collide. In §5 of Chapter 7, Lev Michael states that the Nanti had 'conceived of ownership as extending solely to manufactured objects, cultigens, and gathered things; land per se was not considered ownable, except insofar as someone who had cleared and planted portions of forest land had exclusive usufructal rights to it while the cultigens they planted were producing'. Then mainstream Peruvian society intruded and the Nanti realized that in order to continue to farm, hunt, fish, and live on their traditional lands, they would have to get the government to 'give' them their own land, then they would 'own' it. Thus does a minority group now situated within a European-type society have to modify its mental perceptions in order to continue with some vestige of traditional life.

Chapters 12 and 13 discuss societies in a very different milieu. The indigenous people of Papua New Guinea are in charge of their own country, rather than being subservient to foreign invaders. But some European ideas have been taken over, at least in part. Rosita Henry (Chapter 13) explains that 'today, all over Papua New Guinea, so called "alienated land" (that is, land that has been acquired by the state) is held uneasily by the state and/or its current lessees in the face of the customary landowners for whom land is not something that is conceptually alienable'. (Here 'landowner' does not imply 'ownership' in my sense A.) Henry provides a fascinating account of the balancing of ideas concerning property in modern day Temboka-speaking society. This is more-or-less understandable in terms of extensions from western ideas. A quite different dimension is opened up by Michael Wood in Chapter 12. The Kamula believe that 'there are a diversity of spirits who possess many things'—from geographical features to such enterprises as modern logging concessions. In the merging of cultures, ownership rights should surely be assigned not to Kamula people but to the spirits to whom they are beholden.

Aboriginal people in Australia are in a similar situation to the Nanti in Peru, but much worse placed. There are many times more Aborigines than non-Aborigines in prisons, education and health standards are appallingly poor, life expectancy is low, and employment levels are deplorable. Occasionally, the government indulges in tokenism. After several years of debate 'should we or shouldn't we', in February 2008 the then Prime Minister said 'sorry' to all Aboriginal people for the wrongs that had been done to them. However, it is not apparent that anything much changed. (Maybe a second apology will in time be promulgated, for further wrongs done to them.)

Some pieces of land—most of them tracts that are of little economic interest to society at large—have been given up into the 'ownership' of Aboriginal groups. And there has arisen a new form of tokenism. In many big and small cities, it is customary to open any meeting (even of five or six people around a table) by 'acknowledging the traditional X of this place'. The noun that is used as X varies. At the opening of parliament in September 2010, the new Prime Minister used 'inhabitants'. But it is much more usual to hear 'owners'. This is, in effect, adding insult to injury, imposing on original inhabitants the idea of ownership of land, which is alien to them. The most appropriate formula (of which my Aboriginal friends approve) is to refer to 'traditional custodians' or 'traditional guardians' of the land. This is not possession, but it corresponds to ownership and possession in other cultures and their languages.

References

Dixon, R. M. W. 1972. *The Dyirbal language of North Queensland.* Cambridge: Cambridge University Press.

——. 1988. *A grammar of Boumaa Fijian.* Chicago: University of Chicago Press.

——. 1995. 'Fusional development of possessed nouns in Jarawara', *International Journal of American Linguistics* 61: 263–94.

——. 2002. 'Copula clauses in Australian languages: a typological perspective', *Anthropological Linguistics* 44: 1–36.

——. 2004. *The Jarawara language of southern Amazonia.* Oxford: Oxford University Press.

——. 2005. *A semantic approach to English grammar.* Oxford: Oxford University Press.

——. 2010a. *Basic linguistic theory*, Volume 1—*Methodology.* Oxford: Oxford University Press.

——. 2010b. *Basic linguistic theory*, Volume 2—*Grammatical topics.* Oxford: Oxford University Press.

Index of authors

Index of languages, language families, linguistic areas, and ethnic groups

Index of subjects